10 September 11

KU-798-477

A HISTORY OF THE IRISH NOVEL

Derek Hand's *A History of the Irish Novel* is a major work of criticism on some of the greatest and most globally recognisable writers of the novel form. Writers such as Laurence Sterne, James Joyce, Elizabeth Bowen, Samuel Beckett and John McGahern have demonstrated the extraordinary intellectual range, thematic complexity and stylistic innovation of Irish fiction. Derek Hand provides a remarkably detailed picture of the Irish novel's emergence in the seventeenth and eighteenth centuries. He shows the story of the genre is the story of Ireland's troubled relationship to modernisation. The first critical synthesis of the Irish novel from the seventeenth century to the present day, this is a major book for the field, and the first to thematically, theoretically and contextually chart its development. It is an essential, entertaining and highly original guide to the history of the Irish novel.

DEREK HAND is a lecturer in English at St Patrick's College, Drumcondra.

A HISTORY OF
THE IRISH NOVEL

DEREK HAND

CAMBRIDGE
UNIVERSITY PRESS

CAMBRIDGE UNIVERSITY PRESS
Cambridge, New York, Melbourne, Madrid, Cape Town,
Singapore, São Paulo, Delhi, Tokyo, Mexico City

Cambridge University Press
The Edinburgh Building, Cambridge CB2 8RU, UK

Published in the United States of America by Cambridge University Press, New York

www.cambridge.org
Information on this title: www.cambridge.org/9780521855402

© Derek Hand 2011

This publication is in copyright. Subject to statutory exception
and to the provisions of relevant collective licensing agreements,
no reproduction of any part may take place without the written
permission of Cambridge University Press.

First published 2011

Printed in the United Kingdom at the University Press, Cambridge

A catalogue record for this publication is available from the British Library

Library of Congress Cataloguing-in-Publication Data
Hand, Derek.
A history of the Irish novel / by Derek Hand.
p.   cm.
Includes bibliographical references and index.
ISBN 978-0-521-85540-2
1. English fiction – Irish authors – History and criticism.
2. Literature and society – Ireland – History.
3. Literature and history – Ireland – History.   4. National characteristics, Irish, in literature.
5. Ireland – in literature.   I. Title.
PR8797.H36   2011
823.009′9415–dc22
2010032792

ISBN 978-0-521-85540-2 Hardback

Cambridge University Press has no responsibility for the persistence or
accuracy of URLs for external or third-party internet websites referred to
in this publication, and does not guarantee that any content on such
websites is, or will remain, accurate or appropriate.

For Paula

Contents

vii

viii   *Contents*

Acknowledgements

I would like to thank my editor Ray Ryan of the Cambridge University Press for encouraging me to take up this project: a casual conversation many years ago has led to this book coming into being. He has been a great help throughout, and his patience and understanding have been very much appreciated. Maartje Scheltens has also been of great assistance as the project came to a conclusion.

I would like to thank the Irish Research Council for the Humanities and Social Sciences for a Research Fellowship Award 2008–2009, St Patrick's College for a Research Fellowship 2005–2006, and An Foras Feasa for research leave in 2008. I would also like to thank the staff of the National Library of Ireland, Trinity College Library, and St Patrick's College Library.

Declan Kiberd – as a teacher and friend – is one of the reasons that this book exists at all. I thank him for many years of encouragement, as I thank P. J. Mathews for being a great friend and a true inspiration. I would also like to thank Noreen Doody and Anne Fogarty who read the first draft of the manuscript. They offered many insights but all errors are now my own. I would like to acknowledge my departmental colleagues in St Patrick's College, Drumcondra: Brenna Clarke, Tom Halpin, Celia Keenan, Eugene McNulty, Pat Burke and Julie Anne Stevens. I would also like to thank for many years of friendship and sustaining conversation on a variety of topics Tony Roche. Other friends and colleagues who have been a source of ideas and debate are Frank McGuinness, Brian Donnelly, Eamon Maher, Alan Roughly, Eibhear Walshe, Pauric Travers, Malcolm Sen, Katherine O'Callaghan, Stanley Van Der Ziel, Dermot O'Brien, John Kenny, Keith Hopper, Eugene O'Brien, John McDonagh, Laura Izarra, Caroline Walsh, Hedwig Schwall, Elke d'Hoker, Enrico Terrinoni, Jefferson Holdridge, Wanda Balzano, Ian Campbell Ross, Edwina McKeon, Sharon Murphy, Jim Shanahan, Margaret Kelleher and the late John Devitt with whom I shared many a canter. I would also like to thank the numerous members of the committees I have the pleasure to have served on, the Literatures in

English Committee of the Royal Irish Academy and the European Federation of Associations and Centres of Irish Studies (EFACIS). Some of the ideas here have been rehearsed at symposia and I would like to thank Patrick O'Donnell and Jim Rogers in St Paul, Minneapolis, Hedda Freiberg in Sweden, Rui Carvalho Homem in Portugal, and Neil Murphy in Singapore. Over the years I have had the opportunity to discuss writing with a number of contemporary Irish writers: the late John McGahern, John Banville, Joseph O'Connor, Claire Keegan and Éilís Ni Dhuibhne, and I would like to acknowledge their insights into the form of the novel in Ireland.

My family of course are the real sustaining energy in a project such as this and I would like to thank my mother Mary and brother Brian, Mick and Bridie Hastings, Noreen and Paul, Alan and Caroline, Emma, Alex, Jared and Luke, Mary, Peter, Grace and Conor and all the Mainers, and Ruth and Michael. Of course, this book would not have been possible without the constant support and belief of my wife Paula and last, but not least, Sophie Dang who reminds me every day how extraordinary the world actually is.

Introduction: A history of the Irish novel, 1665–2010

Countless are the novels of the world.

(Franco Moretti)[1]

While some literary critics have traced the origins of the novel back to ancient Greece,[2] the modern novel as an access to the narratives of bourgeois modernity emerged into Western culture in the late seventeenth century. The struggle of the bourgeois towards definition and the striving to articulate its character is central to the novel and the stories it tells. Its novelty is found in a formlessness that nonetheless aspires to some idea of order and unity. Indeed, the energies of the early modern novel form can be discerned in its constant assertion of narratives that enact that search for completeness while also allowing for a kind of mourning for the security that older, traditional forms and stories allowed. Thus, novelists, then as now, revel in the possibilities that formal innovation permits, while their characters find themselves forced to acknowledge the newness of their world and their experiences in that world. The novel's link to news, as something immediate and pertinent, is obvious as it self-consciously craves to be the chronicler of the here and now, each novel trying to encapsulate the urgency of being indispensably relevant. And yet, as Franco Moretti argues, while traditionally tied to the codification of bourgeois values, the novel is actually a means for the pre-modern imagination to continue to inhabit the modern capitalist world.[3] In other words, while the novel encapsulates Enlightenment thinking in its exposure of the inner machinations of the individual consciousness, and of laying bare all that had been until this moment hidden, it also harbours within it that which opposes such revelatory actions, suggesting realms beyond positivist knowledge, hinting at mysteries outside accepted epistemological structures. Thus, the destructive elements of the pre-modern picaro – the character that would dismantle the codes of polite society even as he or she apes them and who would, in their blatantly self-centred individuality, simply ignore communal values – are never quite abandoned by the novel. Nor is the adventurous possibility of the romance and the fantastic quite subdued in the modern moment, with the potential of magic always lingering just over the next rainbow. Thus, while the modern world is a place of the mundane and mediocrity, characters still harbour a desire to be adventurous heroes.

Randall Jarrell defines the novel as 'a prose narrative of some length that has something wrong with it',[4] capturing perfectly this sense of profound confusion and contradiction surrounding the form. It is, in many ways, a devastating remark because it blatantly challenges some of the more stereotypical notions about a literary form that have been most associated with the idea of stability. The novel is basically awash with contradictions and, perhaps, beyond any final definition[5] as it wilfully plunders various forms and genres for its own ends. Indeed, it could be argued that it is these contradictions which energise the novel – its rage for order straining against a shapeless form endlessly and necessarily redefining itself, its desire to map the emerging middle-class individual contrasting dynamically with the novel's ability to focus on society. The novel undoubtedly celebrates the flourishing of the individual as the new measure of all things, and yet it also suggests the peculiar condition of modernity as one of 'transcendental homelessness':[6] the ability to be anywhere and anything means that one is finally nowhere and a nobody. What is being questioned, too, is the notion that the novel's evolution is linked only to certain places and certain cultures, and that it perfectly reflects the developments of those particular places and cultures. No longer need the novel be thought of as singularly attached to modern metropolitan life;[7] rather, it becomes a vehicle for investigating the periphery, those neglected spaces where, perhaps, contradictions abound. What is clear from much recent criticism is that any history of the novel must be pluralist and open to the reality that many more people were writing novels other than those that are integral to the traditional canon.

The potential for uncertainty that this characterisation of the novel affords resonates profoundly alongside the idiosyncrasies of the Irish experience, meaning that it is writ large in works of fiction that emerge on the geographic, political and cultural margins of Europe. Thus, writing and reading the Irish novel are acts fraught with the confusion and contradiction that underpins the novel form itself. This is so because of the numerous circulating misconceptions about the form generally and in Ireland particularly. The major misconception is that there is no such thing as an Irish novel. Or if there is, it is but a pale imitation of what a real novel ought to be. Until very recently, one result of this mistaken belief was that the novel inhabited a peculiarly tangential position in Irish writing when compared to the more evolved theorisation of drama and poetry. The reasons for this marginal position are many and varied, as are the consequences of it. The flawed mirror through which literary critics, especially, have usually approached the novel in Ireland is an invention of the 1940s and 1950s. Frank O'Connor and Sean O'Faolain, in keeping with the notion that the novel was a harbinger of order and stability and mesmerised by the thought of a 'grand tradition', argued that the novel form was best suited to 'made' societies and cultures. Therefore, the argument goes, the prose form best suited to articulating the Irish experience of becoming, along with the provisional nature of modern Irish culture, is the short story.[8] The short story's obvious links to orality also suggests its distinct receptiveness to rendering an Irish reality. What might be overlooked is that neither O'Faolain nor O'Connor were particularly adept in the art of the novel and it suited both to champion a rationale for their inability to express themselves expertly within the form. More importantly, though, is how both wed their aesthetic theories to a wider critique of Irish society and the lack of development in Ireland when compared to the modernity of, seemingly, everywhere else; or everywhere else that mattered to them, which was Britain and America especially. Their quarrel is not with any aesthetic notion of what the novel can or cannot do, or with their own and other writers' inadequacies as would-be novelists; rather, their quarrel is with Ireland itself and its lack of societal depth and normality. This manoeuvre of connecting Irish society's progress with art, and also inferring a need to constantly compare Irish efforts with what is going elsewhere, suggests artists, and literary critics, need not expose themselves or their own art and their own pronouncements to any serious critique. It is society's failing, not theirs. They link the novel to a notion of cultural and communal stability with the form at once reflecting and, in many ways perhaps, creating a sense of coherence and stability for its readers. Such thinking can lead to an interpretation which charts Ireland's cultural progress towards a moment of well-adjusted and acceptable conventionality so that, as a recent work of contemporary history suggests, Irish short stories eventually, and belatedly, have become novels.[9] The implication, of course, is that there is some accepted level of normality going on elsewhere which ought to be aspired to and emulated. Applying this kind of thinking to the novel in Ireland means that any true appreciation of it is doomed from the outset as its various expressions are already condemned to be pallid imitations of a flourishing form existing elsewhere.

Much of this type of critique is a dangerously simple misreading of the novel form itself which, while certainly attuned to worlds where shared ideas and commonly held beliefs exist, actually has always revelled in and amplified anxiety and uncertainty rather than merely reflecting mundane constancy. Indeed, O'Connor's and O'Faolain's theories are born out of their immediate past, looking narrowly to the realisms of the nineteenth-century novel as the ideal to be copied, forgetting that the form's original power emanated from the vulgar chaos of the picaresque and the whimsy of romance. Their opinions are coloured, too, by the outstanding transformative success of the literary and cultural revivalists of the late nineteenth and early twentieth centuries who celebrated especially the Gaelic possibilities of poetry, as well as by the immediacy of impact offered by theatre. The novel being the uncouth reflector of rude modernity seemed, perhaps, too wedded to popular concerns and sentiment, thus running counter to the hoped-for presentation of elevated and serious Irish character and emotion beyond the merely comic and stereotypical. Another influencing factor is that, despite O'Faolain's and O'Connor's desire for an Irish novel, they secretly abhor its utterly disposable nature with its obvious link to the mediocrity of the present moment, and how it runs counter to the prevailing revivalist desire to raise literary efforts into the realm of immutable art.

Recent scholarship has begun to reassess the novel in Ireland, to excavate and engage with the myriad novels that have been produced from the seventeenth century to the present day.[10] What is clear from the varying perspectives through which the Irish novel is being currently viewed is that such confusion about the form is not exclusively an Irish phenomenon. What the novel is and where it might occur are questions increasingly being raised, even concerning what has been viewed as the traditional canon.[11] This whole-sale re-evaluation of what the novel might be is important because the stranglehold of supposed traditional traits has severely restricted the conception of the form and where it might flourish. Indeed, beginning to read the Irish novel as a part of this general reappraisal breaks down the idea of universalities, of single movements such as romanticism or modernism, opening up the possibility of romanticisms and modernisms. Different cultures and different societies bring indigenous issues and concerns to bear upon literary and philosophical fashions and movements. Irish writing, therefore, is both a part of these wider mainstream currents and simultaneously apart from, and at an angle to, those various flows and eddies, meaning that the Irish novel consciously occupies a space that challenges easy assumptions about the form.

For many Irish prose writers, for those who would actually aspire to writing a novel as opposed to those who critique its alleged absence, a consequence has been the presentation of themselves in the brilliantly modernist move of being utterly self-created. Maria Edgeworth, for instance, initiated her own tradition with *Castle Rackrent*, consciously ignoring the reality that there were many novelists before her and, in doing so, staking a claim for the total originality and innovation of her own work. James Joyce would do the same over one hundred years later. While such a contrivance is perhaps *de rigueur* for any author, surprisingly for many years the majority of literary critics, with very few exceptions, took Edgeworth and Joyce and others at their word and constructed a very narrow Irish novelistic canon from 1800 onwards. And yet paradoxically, in the face of this seeming critical disregard, Ireland has produced some of *the* globally recognised great examples of the novel form: writers such as Laurence Sterne, James Joyce, Elizabeth Bowen, Samuel Beckett and John McGahern have demonstrated how wide-ranging Irish prose fiction has been, and can be. But even this obsession with the singular achievements of certain writers has itself been part of the problem when approaching the form, skewing the literary landscape by suggesting that when Irish writers bothered at all it was only to write great novels. Such a limited focus obscures the work of those minor contributors to the form. Indeed, this is a problem in the study of Irish writing in general. That many of these writers (such as Joyce and Edgeworth) produced works that seem to test, stretch and break the boundaries of what a novel is thought to be – in fact, might be thought as not being novels at all – means the impression still lingers that the novel is singularly unsuited to the task of rendering the Irish world and Irish experience.

Within this context, this history of the Irish novel is a history of the struggle towards articulation, of making the novel form express Irish stories and Irish concerns. It is also a history of developing Irish identities, of misrepresentations and the effort by writers to offer something genuinely authentic and complicatedly real. The novel – its sheer size – allows for the bringing together of difference in terms of native and visitor, Gaelic and Anglo-Irish, Catholic and Protestant, aristocrat and peasant. Thus the pages of the Irish novel are where issues concerning identity are played out repeatedly. Ireland's colonial relationship to Britain is obviously figured in this confrontation between differing identities and differing loyalties. It will be possible, in addition, to reflect on Irish culture's developing relationship not only to Britain but also to Europe, America and the wider world in the contemporary moment of globalisation. A history of the Irish novel is a history of power and authority, a history of questions concerning colonial and native narratives, and of questions surrounding who speaks and writes and who is spoken and written about. A gradual movement from exclusively Anglo-Irish authors up to the nineteenth century, to the emergence of Irish authors in the nineteenth and twentieth centuries registers that shift in power and its consequences for a culture imagining and reimagining itself. The novel in the nineteenth century, for instance, becomes a medium through which the nascent middle-class Catholic population can aspire to power and political position – the relative straightforwardness of the novels being written is a literary manifestation of that desire. On the other hand, for the Protestant novelist the form has been, from its inception, something to be approached with apprehension – for a class that increasingly imagines itself in aloof aristocratic terms, the novel's vulgarity and its access to the privacies of the inner world of the consciousness signal a loss of power rather than its realisation. For some, then, the novel is not a means for revealing truth; rather it allows truths to be concealed. Indeed, this is something quite peculiar to Irish culture where, since the enactment of the Penal Laws in the seventeenth century, there has been the incongruous situation where the hidden world is always in full view. This is evident most obviously with regard to political, economic and religious scandals, though the notion that that which is hidden actually exists in plain view permeates all aspects and levels of society. The difficulty for the novelist is to negotiate between this reversal of the public and private spheres, to make the novel's thirst for exposé relevant in a culture where, at some level, there is nothing to uncover.

A history of the Irish novel is furthermore a history of a changing landscape. This transition can be observed, obviously, at the level of content and story: stories that recreate Ireland as a rural space on the margins, to stories that subvert that often stereotypical representation, to narratives centred on the urban and city space. But novels also interrogate the idea of landscape, showing how notions of Irish space have been manufactured and how the meaning of the Irish landscape has altered over the years, as changing ideologies and circumstances project their peculiar meanings onto it. The move of the Irish novel's location of action from the south-west of Ireland, those midland spaces of Munster which in the seventeenth, eighteenth and early nineteenth centuries were where English and Irish culture coexisted and intermingled on a daily basis, to the wilds of the west coast, and Connaught especially, displays this altering conception of where stories can be told from and what they might signify. Ireland as a space is at times teeming with life and then suddenly depopulated and devoid of human activity. This is true, too, of how the city operates in the Irish novel.

Novels tell stories and this study is a history of the stories that have been told. Different types of stories emerge, from different perspectives, and different genres impose themselves on the Irish frame. The prevalence of certain types of novel at particular points in time offers an insight into underlining concerns and attitudes of authors at any given moment. Throughout the eighteenth and nineteenth centuries, novels dealt with the notion of Ireland as an ongoing project, a place to be improved and modernised, mirroring the underlying desire of the colonial vision. The Irish

Gothic novel in the mid-nineteenth century becomes more comprehensible when it is thought of as an expression of the increasing unease and fear of an Anglo-Irish population whose position of power and authority is being challenged and eroded. The Gothic focus on inheritance and continuity perfectly brings to the fore the anxieties of a class which comes to realise that the colonial project of improvement has all but failed. Thus, the Gothic novel maps a nightmare move inwards, away from outward concerns, concentrating on the guilt and failings of the Anglo-Irish themselves. It is also a manifestation of the darker, denied, aspects of the romantic revolution in the imagination; a recognition of all that Enlightenment knowledge cannot shine a rational light upon. The popularity of the Big House novel, too, especially in the twentieth century, can also be seen as a reflection of the concerns of an Anglo-Irish community feeling increasingly under threat. Other genres that operate quirkily within an Irish context are, for instance, the *Bildungsroman*, where the expected emphasis on the development of a bourgeois individuality shifts between the personal and public spheres, never escaping the concerns of national identity. The influence of the Catholic Church is witnessed in how an emerging sexuality becomes central to these novels of development in the twentieth century especially, as if the sexual act were the only indicator of authentic maturity. The history novel, from the nineteenth century onwards, has possessed a certain weighty, if not oppressive, significance in Irish fiction: history being obviously a major field of contention in Irish cultural discourse. A feature of many Irish novels from the early nineteenth century on is the presence of a potted history of Ireland, as if each new reader must first be acquainted with Ireland's entire story before engaging with any one particular story. Consequently, the facts of who did what and when and, of course, how history is written remain a continuing fascination for both the reader and the writer. The novel also allows for alternative histories to be told, acknowledging the human realities of great events beyond the realm of deadening fact. This enthralment to history is linked to the prevalence of realism and naturalism in the Irish novel. It is peculiar that for a people who are said to be truly imaginative, in the realm of the novel at least, that kind of creativity appears mostly absent. Many novelists in Ireland are not concerned with fiction-making, but with reality and disguised biography. Perhaps colonisation encourages an anthropological approach to art: each writer laboriously detailing the nuances of their own time and place in an effort to overcome endless caricatures and distortions of Ireland and Irishness. The real act of rebellion, then, is to be found in the power of rendering one's own story in one's own inimitable style. At times, it seems, the imposition of story itself – with beginnings, middles and, particularly, endings – is far too harsh an obligation on the delicate nature of this act of reproduction. Thus, and here the novel does borrow from the short story, some of the best Irish novels seem formless and without direction: mood pieces rather than strict narratives.

There is a sense in which the present moment or the recent past is the most difficult to capture in art: critical distance and perspective being absent. Yet, it is the modern novel which as an artistic medium is seen mostly to concern itself with the immediate moment: with the here and now. Though, of course, it is not simply the immediacy of capturing the moment that is of significance for the novel or its readers; rather, it is making the novel and its themes relevant to the moment which is pertinent. This is one of the major difficulties with the novel being judged in its own time of production: what might appear innovative and new in any given moment will seem stale and uninspired viewed from the perspective that only hindsight can offer. The novel form's tendency towards the present moment is destabilised and disrupted in an Irish context usually figured as overly concerned with the past and tradition. But Ireland is a place and an idea constantly reinventing itself. Despite the stereotype of the alleged 'backward look' in Irish writing and Irish culture, Ireland has in fact been a place of almost constant transition. Perhaps the Irish novel looks both backwards and forwards simultaneously, and increasingly so in the contemporary period as writers attempt to be faithful to tradition while also wanting to engage with the possibilities of the unknown. This peculiar 'doubleness' of modern Irish consciousness is manifested in the Irish novel. While conflict and difference underpin the Irish experience, it would be a mistake to view the Irish novel as simply reflecting oppositional positions. Its ambiguity in terms of content and form registers the fluid nature of an Irishness that oscillates between the poles of tradition and modernity, Gaelic culture and English culture, between the Irish and the English languages. What can be observed, then, is a negotiation between opposites and the acceptance of difference.

A history of the Irish novel is, above all else, a history of Ireland's modernity. The Irish novel's emergence in the seventeenth century and thus its association with modernity, being indeed a herald of modernity, allow for a mapping of Ireland's relationship to modernisation. But, rather than the reductive assumption previously mentioned which imposes a kind of seamless move towards perfection, what is clear is how the novel form – with all its inherent contradictions and tensions – chronicles the complexities of that movement into modernity. In an Irish context this means that the novel can be thought of as *the* ideal literary form through which to chart the numerous tensions, divisions and diversity within Irish life and culture over the last four hundred years. The novel form, oscillating between containment and chaos, between the simplicity of narrative progress and the complexity of expression, seems best suited to capturing the energies of an Irish culture which also moves between the poles of stability and social coherence and the ever-present realities of division and conflict.

If it is accepted that Irish culture is in a state of constant transition, then it follows it is always in a state of beginning and ending – a new Ireland is continually being born or is about to be born while an old Ireland is forever passing or about to pass away. From the earliest novels that deal partly or wholly with Ireland, Richard Head's *The English Rogue* (1665) and the anonymously written *Virtue Rewarded; or, the Irish Princess* (1693), this responsiveness to transitional moments is to the forefront, with both of these novels telling stories of new beginnings and possibilities while simultaneously registering the necessary abandonment of an old world and an old culture. Indeed, this emphasis on transitional points in time has allowed for numerous false origins for the Irish novel: does it begin with *The English Rogue* or *Virtue Rewarded; or, the Irish Princess*, or perhaps with Sarah Butler's *Irish Tales, or Instructive Histories for the Happy Conduct of Life* (1716)? Maria Edgeworth and William Carleton in the nineteenth century certainly inaugurate new modes for the Irish novel, and, of course, James Joyce in the twentieth century opens up the Irish novel, as he does the novel form generally, to radically new possibilities. Literary critics search for the first proper representations of, for instance, the Catholic middle classes and many candidates have been put forward: Kate O'Brien's writing from the 1920s, or perhaps Gerald Griffin in the early nineteenth century? Or they search for the first realistic rendering of urban life: is it to be found, not in James Joyce, but in the work of May Laffan Hartley from the 1870s onwards, or in John Banim's *The Nowlans* (1826)? More worthwhile, though, in beginning to talk of a history of the Irish novel – and beginning to come to some knowledge of its particularities and peculiarities – is to consider some particular endings of the Irish novel. In the late eighteenth and early nineteenth centuries, for instance, Irish novels ended in a marriage between characters from Anglo-Ireland and Gaelic Ireland or Britain and Gaelic Ireland. This individual union between old and new Ireland offered an image of hope for the wider political union between Great Britain and Ireland, reflecting a need for reconciliation between the various parties that make up Irish society. From one of the earliest Irish novels, *The Irish Princess* (1693), to a novel such as George Moore's *A Drama in Muslin* (1884), many concluded with a departure from Ireland. The repercussions of such a leave-taking are obvious, signalling an abandonment of Ireland as a site of impossibility and the opportunity of a fresh start elsewhere. But there is another way of considering endings which highlight the centrality of the double perspective of content and form in understanding and appreciating the nature of the Irish novel. Looking briefly at the endings of James Joyce's *A Portrait of the Artist as a Young Man* (1916), Elizabeth Bowen's *The Last September* (1929), Seamus Deane's *Reading in the Dark* (1996) and Éilís Ní Dhuibhne's *The Dancers Dancing* (1999), it can be seen how the close of each of these novels upsets the trajectory of each novel in terms of both its content and its form: in terms of the story being told and how that story is being told. *Portrait* ends with Stephen Dedalus's diary entries: a formal precursor to the stream of consciousness employed in the subsequent *Ulysses* (1922). Dedalus's voice is presented to the reader unmediated by any controlling narrator. It is, too, Dedalus 'writing' rather than being written about. However, a diary is not for public consumption: Dedalus, despite his triumphant declaration of his intention to be an artist, is speaking only to himself. At the close of Bowen's *The Last September*, the reader is presented with an image of the burning Big House of Danielstown. Lois Farquar, the main character in the novel, misses this ending, having slipped out of the narrative quietly in the previous chapter. For a novel that dramatises numerous arrivals and departures, Lois's leaving, curiously, is only reported to the reader. The boy at the conclusion of Deane's *Reading in the Dark* has discovered the facts of the secret that has haunted his family, yet he is denied a name and is seen to have gained no true knowledge or wisdom. The striking of a celebratory note that the reader might expect is completely absent. Finally, the narrator at the close of Ní Dhuibhne's novel is singularly unsure as to the import of the story she has just been telling, the narrative finishing on a strangely downbeat note. Each of these endings is disturbing and disruptive; each is radically 'open' rather than 'closed', denying completeness and forcing the reader to reassess what has occurred previously. Of course, all endings are a compromise, an imposed moment of resolution that neatly brings matters to a head, and a finish. But here, there is something other than that kind of concession to formal necessity occurring. Each of these is a profound instance of negation: a reorientation of the entire thrust of the traditional novel form. Each toys with the possibility of undoing the very medium through which the stories are written, each embraces baffled ignorance, signalling certainly the end of things but also the need to begin again. In a culture which has always seen itself as dying or about to die, these endings, consequently, become a way into beginning: beginning to think about the novel in a specifically Irish context.

This history will have a primarily chronological structure. Of necessity, key historical dates and political developments will punctuate the critical engagement with texts and authors, offering a backdrop through which an understanding of the writing can be gained. However, other issues and concerns, besides high political events, will also be an integral element of the contextual background. For instance, changing circumstances surrounding printing and publishing materially connect with the problem of audience in Irish writing, and influence who is being written about and who is being written for. Another attendant frame of reference is the developing critical engagement with Irish writing and the Irish novel that has coloured how the form has been theorised, contextualised and thought about as Irish Studies has evolved as a discipline. Interesting, too, is the ever-changing image and role of the writer in relation to his and her audience, the mutating public masks created and worn at different times for different ends. The first chapter, 'Beginnings and endings: writing from the margins, 1665–1800', considers how Irish novels express the inchoate nature of the Irish scene after the Battle of the Boyne. A new political reality emerges, meaning that identity is fluid and under construction and only from the mid-eighteenth century onwards do Anglo-Irish writers begin to conceive of themselves as such and begin to imagine Ireland as a space worthy of literary attention. Chapter 2, 'Speak not my name; or, the wings of Minerva: Irish fiction, 1800–91', argues that the Irish novel in this period presents an Irish world in a constant state of anticipation, waiting for something, anything, to happen. This chapter also charts the emergence of Catholic writers who struggle to articulate the realities and hopes of their community. Chapter 3, 'Living in a time of epic: the Irish novel and Literary Revival and revolution, 1891–1922', focuses on the position of the Irish novel in this time of upheaval, suggesting that the form's myriad manifestations at this moment – with realism and naturalism, fantasy novels and history novels existing side by side – reflect the national search for a suitable form that might express a new Ireland. The post-independent world and its desire for stability in all spheres of life and culture is the focus of Chapter 4, 'Irish independence and the bureaucratic imagination, 1922–39'. Chapter 5, 'Enervated island – isolated Ireland? 1940–60', traces the emergence of the writer into public Irish life, showing how complicated the relationship between novelist and nation is in this period. Chapter 6, 'The struggle of making it new, 1960–79', sees the Irish novel engage with the emerging energies of the 1960s which reconfigured the modern imagination globally, while also having to deal with what seemed the unfinished business of the past with the explosion of violence in the north of Ireland. 'Brave new world: Celtic Tigers and moving statues, 1979 to the present day' is the final chapter, focusing on novels that perhaps confront one of the most rapid moments of change and transformation in

Irish culture. What is apparent is that the Irish novel remains open to the project of excavating the possibilities of self-hood in this new world, and remains interested in finding a means to express the authentic complicated and contradictory Irish person. Running alongside this wider narrative are eight Interchapters dealing with the anonymously written *Virtue Rewarded* (1693), Maria Edgeworth's *Castle Rackrent* (1801), Edith Somerville and Martin Ross's *The Real Charlotte* (1886), James Joyce's *Ulysses* (1922), Elizabeth Bowen's *The Last September* (1929), John Banville's *Doctor Copernicus* (1976), Seamus Deane's *Reading in the Dark* (1996) and John McGahern's *That They May Face the Rising Sun* (2002). These Interchapters offer the opportunity for a sustained reading of individual texts in the light of the main themes and issues being dealt with in the primary chapters.

The choice of texts and authors to be considered is not by any means exhaustive. The recent work of Rolf Loeber and Magda Loeber, *A Guide to Irish Fiction: 1650–1900* (2006), demonstrates in the form of an itemised and detailed catalogue the range of Irish fiction writing over three centuries. It is an invaluable piece of scholarship. The work gathered together in Margaret Kelleher and Philip O'Leary's two-volume *The Cambridge History of Irish Literature* (2006) and John Wilson Foster's *The Cambridge Companion to the Irish Novel* (2006) also point to a variety of texts and critical approaches and contexts from which to understand the novel in Ireland since the seventeenth century. My intention has been to offer readings of well-known and some less well-known texts – novels which possess some representative qualities that underpin the general thrust and arguments of the study as a whole. It is clear that there is an emerging canon of Irish authors who are returned to again and again by critics and anthologists – writers such as William Chaigneau, Thomas Amory and Regina Maria Roche in the eighteenth century, Lady Morgan, Maria Edgeworth, William Carleton and George Moore in the nineteenth century, and Kate O'Brien, James Joyce, Flann O'Brien and John McGahern in the twentieth. Many of these writers were successful in their own time and subsequently, suggesting that their novels are worth considering. But so too are those novels which existed only in their own moment, their brief flowering offering another perspective to be considered. While this canon will necessarily change and transform quite rapidly in the coming years, it is still useful to have a common set of works and authors to engage with so that students and interested readers might actually be able to peruse texts or selected passages in order to gain a sense of the writers and the issues being discussed. The most contentious choices, perhaps, are those made concerning novelists in the contemporary moment. Here, certainly, all readers will have their favourites, and my choices might not necessarily correspond with theirs. Again, I have chosen novels I believe to be some of the best of their moment and, hopefully, novels and authors that will continue to be read into the future. Of course, I cannot know that they will; but then again neither can anyone else. Each interested critic will have their own list of writers and, indeed, their own list of ideas and concerns that they would wish to concentrate on. I have tried not to be bound to any single theory or literary perspective because that would have precluded so many writers and so many possible avenues of interpretation. It is up to others to continue to excavate particular authors, eras, genres and theories in relation to the Irish novel in the past and in the present. I have also avoided merely mentioning novels and writers to offer some textual and critical engagement with the novels themselves, offering readings that all students and critics might enter into dialogue with.

A history of the Irish novel is a history of ideas and of theories. But, more important than any one theory is how the novel's link to modernity means that it is a site where the emergence of the individual into modernity can be witnessed. For the Irish person, burdened with the often-debilitating effect of the imposed stereotype (meaning that she or he is already always known), the space afforded by the novel form might allow for the complexities of the Irish individual to be played out. Of course, many novels present this as a struggle between the rights of the person in conflict with the pressures of traditional modes of community and shared experience. In Ireland, this conflict is compounded by the fact that, in the depiction of individuals as simply representations of a community and of the nation, the individual person has been habitually overwhelmed. The tension in much of the best of Irish novel writing is between this wish to configure and acknowledge specifically Irish traits and characteristics, and the demand to recognise Ireland as a space where it is also possible to be simply human.

The modern novel's focus is on the everyday, making it strange in the process of being written about. But the writing of a novel also transforms the unusual into the mundane and the commonplace: the very act of telling returning the extraordinary to the everyday. It is this strain, perhaps, that ultimately energises the form. The consequence for the Irish novel, as it is for Irish culture generally, is that it has been and continues to be caught between the desire to be exceptional and the endless possibilities of ordinary life.

Virtue Rewarded; or, the Irish Princess: *burgeoning silence and the new novel form in Ireland*

Laws are silent in time of war.

(Cicero, Pro Milone)

When Dean Rowland Davies – a chaplain with King William's forces – passed through the Munster town of Clonmel in July 1690, he had his pistol and his boots stolen, he believed 'by some Danes quartered there'.[1] This, it might be said, is one instance of lawlessness from the margins of history, and yet it is a detail interesting enough to catch the novelistic eye of Elizabeth Bowen, who mentions it in her family chronicle *Bowen's Court*.[2] It signals a perhaps unconscious tension within the victorious Williamite camp between the Irish Protestant community represented by Davies and those others who have come to Ireland to fight for various reasons – be they personal, political or venal. Dean Davies also talks of having to preach a sermon against swearing to the victors of the Battle of the Boyne. It seems to have been a common complaint among local Anglicans about the Williamite army, who felt that the soldiers seemed

to have banished all but the name of religion, and the only entertainment to be found among the army is drunkenness, injustice, rapine, profanation of the Sabbath, horrid oaths and execrations, and all manner of debauchery: as if they thought their successes were only designed to give them liberty to commit so many great abominations.[3]

If nothing else, the spoils of war should not be corrupted by immoral behaviour. Cruel chance is also on display when Davies tells of how six prisoners about to be executed throw dice to save their lives: 'three of them were executed'.[4] Of interest here is how Davies's narrative uneasily juxtaposes the awful violence and chaos of war with images of calmness, of seeming normality. War is a time of chaos and confusion: a time when, quite literally, all things become momentarily possible. The war of 1689–90 in a European context raised difficult questions about legitimate power: is the authority of kingship divine and absolute or is it something much more bound up in pragmatic human affairs? And what of the relationship between king and individual subject, and who is now truly in the ascendant in the late seventeenth century: monarch or common man? At stake is not simply political gain and territorial advantage: for Dean Davies, and the Irish Protestant victors of 1690, the outcome of the Battle of the Boyne heralds the possibility of a whole new world coming into being.

It is precisely this volatile space that the novel *Virtue Rewarded; or, the Irish Princess* inhabits. Published anonymously in 1693, it tells the story of a foreign prince with William of Orange's army arriving in the town of Clonmel after the Battle of the Boyne as William's army moves towards Limerick.[5] The reality of Dean Davies's journal and the fiction of *The Irish Princess* coincides, accordingly, at an essential level: each text reflects and expresses this powerful occasion of flux and change, each operating out of the tension between order and chaos, between law and lawlessness. This flux in the sphere of politics is mirrored within the novel itself: *The Irish Princess* is crammed full of incident, from the high tragedy of war to the low comedy of drunken soldiery, from the exotic potential of a South American narrative to more mundane local Irish concerns and local Irish colour. Perhaps unconsciously this manifest anxiety with the novel form, shifting between different registers and different places, undermines the hoped- for order that the novel might bring to the Irish scene: the reader's conception of what is ordinary and extraordinary, of where the truly strange might be, is made unclear, and not fully resolved by the story's conclusion.

The conflict of the Siege of Limerick from August to November 1690 is played out and echoed in miniature in the relationship between the two main lovers: a European prince and a local woman. Thus, the macro relationship can be imbued with personal emotions such as love, betrayal, aggression and passivity. Questions of national sovereignty intermingle with issues surrounding personal female independence. The opening pages confirm this, with love and desire being talked of in the language of battle and war, suggesting both the inner struggle of the Prince who must contend between the claims of reason and the heart, and the struggle between masculine and feminine, reinforcing the notion that common to both national and personal spheres are issues concerning power, control and dominance.

The object of the Prince's affection is Marinda, a member of the Clonmel Protestant community. Through her the reader is offered a glimpse of how this group conceives of itself at this point in time, its amorphous codes beginning to solidify round the political power struggle being played out at the battlefields of the Boyne and in Limerick. A maid tells the Prince of

Marinda's various suitors, how the most favoured one is from Dublin: 'When he paid a visit, if any of the rest chanced to come at the same time, the Breeding which he brought from *Dublin*, elevated him so far above them, in his Discourse, his Carriage, and all he did, that they did look like our wild *Irish* to him.'[6] Although only in the process of being constructed, Protestant identity as represented in *The Irish Princess* is far from the absolute citadel of civility, gentility and homogeneity that would become synonymous with the community throughout the long eighteenth century. Clonmel's architecture, and by extension Irish society itself, is also presented as thoroughly rusticated and backwards. While it does allow for 'lively Idea's of Country Freedom, and Country Innocence' (*The Irish Princess*, p. 10), this can only be fully appreciated from the perspective of the metropolitan soldiery. Indeed, the Prince is told bluntly by one of his men that, 'in this island there is scarce one worthy of your high Affections' (*The Irish Princess*, p. 15).

In the midst of the main narrative, an exotic South American story is inserted, as the author declares in the Preface, 'for variety sake' (*The Irish Princess*, p. 3). Its story of the Inca Faniaca's love for a colonial Spaniard means that it can be read as a commentary on the Irish narrative, throwing light on the nature of the relationship between the Prince and Marinda. It operates as a kind of distancing technique, deflecting direct scrutiny away from the Prince and Marinda's affair, allowing the submerged implications of their union to be worked out at a remove. A similar narrative of love blossoming across a cultural divide is presented in this interlude, though here issues surrounding the conflicting claims that love makes between individual desire and demands of family and community are explicitly made. Faniaca's father is said to be a 'Brahmin' – a magic priest who performs what are said to be barbarous sacrificial rites to local gods. Her love for the Spaniard means she must eventually turn her back on her father's traditional culture. Interestingly, in contrast to Marinda's quite passive virtue, Faniaca is presented as much more aggressively active in her pursuit of love and the fulfilment of her desire. In the end, both Faniaca and Marinda make up their own minds as to whom they might fall in love with, no matter what their family or communal loyalties might be. This, of course, is in accord with the emergence of the novel form as being that which best expresses the new modern Enlightenment individual, who is the measure of all things, and the creator of his/her own reality and truth. Indeed, what is being implicitly suggested is that the move into modernity signals an essential act of betrayal on the part of the individual, and that to be faithful to the self means one has to be unfaithful to communal concerns.

But the South American interlude also raises wider political questions. In this narrative, the Spanish are seen as conquering imperialists who take whatever they can in the form of wealth and material. A contrast is established between the military campaign in Ireland and that which is occurring in South America, with Ireland's being – on the surface at least – specifically *not* a colonial campaign. By dislocating the colonial narrative to South America, the author of *The Irish Princess* attempts perhaps to distance an imperial interpretation away from the Irish situation. The fact that William's army is made up of different nationalities – Dutch, English and Spanish – indicates that Ireland is the local site for a wider European ideological conflict that has little to do with colonial expansion.[7] Indeed, even the absence of any detailed description of war and its carnage in the Irish world is of note when compared to Faniaca's narrative that is full of descriptions of violence and death. The horror of war and its consequences are thus transferred to another location, attempting to postpone a thorough analysis of the conflict from an Irish perspective. Yet, it is as if the author is smuggling a colonial critique of the Irish scene into the novel, hinting that for a local Protestant audience what is at stake is not only abstract ideological matters but also a conflict over power, land and material wealth. Thus, there is a double perspective in operation within the novel, meaning that though the war of 1689–90 was fought for far-reaching political, dynastic and strategic reasons, these macro concerns are filtered through much narrower sectarian and colonial interests for the Irish involved. Yet, as the novel makes clear, there is a common mercenary element to both conflicts: most of those caught up in the Irish campaign – including the Prince and his lieutenant Celadon – are said to be there specifically for monetary gain (*The Irish Princess*, pp. 6, 10). As a result, rather than shared motives, what is being presented within the novel is the reality of profound difference between the local Irish Williamites and their European counterparts. The uneasiness noted in Dean Davies's journal is central to the world of the novel too, with a deepening consciousness of confusion and uncertainty becoming more and more apparent as the narrative progresses. In other words, even at this stage, at the moment of decisive victory over Gaelic and Catholic Ireland, a fundamental question is being asked as to the nature of Protestant rule in Ireland: what is it for exactly, and what is the 'project' or purpose towards which it is directed?

The implicit impression remains that despite overtures to moral reform and sentimental feeling on his part, the Prince persists in his dominant position of brutish male power and authority. This reaffirmation of traditional gender relations is seen also in the relationship between those from within Ireland and those from outside, with the tensions between them further elaborated as it is recognised that for the Prince and his men their view of Ireland and the Irish is never far from patronising. In a letter that the Prince writes to Marinda from Limerick, he says: '*We have block'd your Enemies up, won a Fort from them, and daily gain more ground: And O that I were as certain of Conquering you, as of taking the Town! But you, my lovely stubborn Enemy, hold out against all my endeavours*' (*The Irish Princess*, p. 77). The predicament for Marinda and the community she represents is made manifest in the use of the phrase 'your enemies'. The Protestant Irish need the Danes and the Dutch, and their military might, to defeat their foes because they are unable to do so themselves. In other words, Protestant rule in Ireland can only be guaranteed from some other place: final power is always elsewhere from within this culture's perspective, the final arbiter and source of authority is thus constantly deferred from the local space. Again, even after the victory of 1690 what is being hinted at for the Irish reader is an underlying uneasiness about who really possesses power in Ireland.

A bizarre scene takes place in what could be the Franciscan Abbey within the town of Clonmel. After having been robbed of his money and his clothes and plied with alcohol in a brothel, Celadon wakes to find himself clothed in a '*Franciscan* Habit' and 'laid on a Tombstone, by the side of a great Marble Statue (the Effigies of some Great Person formerly buried there' (*The Irish Princess*, p. 25). While this drunken behaviour is in keeping with the bawdy entertainment of William's troops denounced by Dean Davies and other clergymen, the scene's significance lies in the utter disregard for local feeling and sympathy that it displays. In nineteenth-century art, the ruined church or abbey signified the flight of God from the affairs of everyday men and women. Here the reader is presented with a similar situation, though the absence of God from the place has a more political basis: the Franciscan abbey in Clonmel had been closed down by Henry VIII's dissolution of monasteries in 1540. The table tomb that Celadon finds himself on is probably that of the Butlers – the Barons of Cahir and a prominent family in Clonmel. But such detail is of no consequence to Celadon and the other soldiers: Ireland's past or indeed Ireland's present and, certainly, Ireland's future are of no real concern to them. The kind of deeply held religious feelings of the Protestant Irish are of little relevance, thus putting another division between those inside and outside the community.

This colonial reading of the novel with its emphasis on power, control and authority has obvious relevance to the gendered relationship between the Prince and Marinda, but it also pertains to the relationship between the native Gaelic Irish and the new English settlers. Throughout *The Irish Princess*, the Gaelic Irish are notable for their almost complete absence. Nonetheless, from the evidence of a text such as Edward MacLysaght's scholarly *Irish Life in the Seventeenth Century*[8] and John Dunton's *Teague Land: or A Merry Ramble to the Wild Irish* written in 1698[9] with its descriptions of food, architecture and both religious and secular ceremonies, the reality of daily Irish life was infinitely more substantial and rich than that offered to the reader of *The Irish Princess*. Importantly, too, Dunton's text documents the reality of the daily interaction between the different classes and components of Irish society that is practically non-existent in the novel.

There are two scenes of note that take on added significance because of their engagement with specifically Gaelic Irish characters and situations. At the level of plot, these offer curious insights into metropolitan attitudes to traditional culture. The first moment concerns a scene when the Prince visits a spot outside the town of Clonmel where he is lodging. As he sleeps, the narrator says: 'For just by there bubbled up a clear and plentiful spring, of which, from an ancient Irish Chronicle, let me give you this Story' (*The Irish Princess*, p. 27). The story told concerns Cluaneesha, daughter of Macbuanin King of Munster, who is accused of being unchaste with a courtier. Her honesty is eventually revealed when she drinks from a well on a hill outside the town of Clonmel, the water of which when drunk kills those that are deceitful. As with the South American story, this too is another reflector through which to view the action of the main narrative. Its true significance, though, is how it offers the reader a glimpse of, and a connection to, that hidden Gaelic culture so thoroughly absent within the novel's engagement with everyday Irish life. The tale of Cluaneesha would seem to correspond to the 'Dinnseanchas' tradition in Gaelic oral culture that powerfully combines poetry and place lore. Indeed, the fact that the Prince is alone and falls asleep at the well suggests a moment ripe for the kind of vision that a Gaelic Aisling (vision) poem might offer. Such a reading is tantalising in the critical and interpretative possibilities it raises. It is an instance of possible private revelation, the cornerstone of the modern novel, but here that epiphanic insight is denied and suppressed. Gaelic traditions are thus linked to the unconscious, becoming associated with the realm of dreaming. Though there is a well, now called 'Rag Well', outside Clonmel overlooking the town, the story rendered has no actual foundation in Irish folklore or Irish mythology.[10] Significant, then, is not the authenticity of the content of the story; rather, it is the formal implications of this narrative digression into some local colour that is important. Ultimately, it is entirely disruptive of the overall narrative apparatus of *The Irish Princess*.

Neither the Prince nor any other character in the novel has access to this story: it is directly related only to the reader. The narrative frame of the novel is thereby shattered. Claude Lévi-Strauss argued that the 'novel is born out of the exhaustion of myth'[11] and therefore what is witnessed here is the transition from one form to another: from the oral world of traditional Gaelic Ireland to a modern written print culture.

Certainly, there is a power structure set up between writing and the literary, on the one hand, and the oral on the other. What is being attempted is an act of containment. Throughout *The Irish Princess* there are various forms made use of – letters and poetry, for instance. Typical of the novel form in general, this particular narrative voraciously plunders earlier modes and genres, presenting old forms in fresh ways, in its effort to seem both new and simultaneously unthreatening and comfortably familiar. Thus, the new form of the novel hopes to contain and regulate the older traditional form of myth and in so doing make it safe and control it. That the story is an imitation of the form of a traditional local Irish tale is of note too. What the reader is offered *could* be a story from, for instance, Geoffrey Keating's *Foras Feasa Ar Éirinn (A Basis of Knowledge about Ireland)* [c.1634], but it is in fact a total invention. In itself this is a sign of the novelist's newfound power: a demonstration of how the novelist can mimic and consume previous forms, bend them to his/her use as necessary. Once the story is told, the narrator very self-consciously and deliberately declares: 'And now I will no longer tell such Tales' (*The Irish Princess*, p. 29). Demonstrated here is the uneasy and anxious relationship between tradition and modernity articulated at the formal level of the novel. The characters might be protected from the Irish myth but the reader is not. Thus *The Irish Princess* self-reflexively enacts that very moment of rupture between the older world that is passing away and the newer world that is coming into being. Ironically, it is this local tale that is an invented fiction while the exotic tale of Faniaca is based on fact. Perhaps what is being suggested is that the source of real danger, and maybe mystery, is to be found at home rather than in distant lands.

The Age of Enlightenment, of which the novel form is a central element, fears that which is traditional and culturally popular. In Ireland, of course, Enlightenment thinking is inextricably bound up with a colonial cultural enterprise that sets up the stark opposition between what is civilised and what is barbarous. In this paradigm, tradition, superstition and popular culture are to be feared because they are potential channels for what could be subversive, boisterous and disruptive.[12] But even as the Enlightenment imagination demonstrably displays misgivings about traditional culture within Ireland, it simultaneously sanctions the preservation and the collection of cultural artefacts such as those associated with the Gaelic folk tradition, in poetry and music particularly. Of course, this impulse, certainly in an Irish context, comes about only when Gaelic culture can no longer represent any real material threat to Anglo-Irish culture and therefore the engagement is sentimental and nostalgic. *The Irish Princess* anticipates this uneasy situation: the formal nervousness registered in the unusual framing of this story precisely denotes the tension between an old world and a new world, between fear and nervous accommodation. To put it simply, the novel displays a desire to include a Gaelic Irish element for the sake of variety and the interest generated by local colour, and, yet, is unsure exactly how to present that story. The characters' lack of access to Cluaneesha's tale means that its power to influence their development and the development of the plot is neutered.

The other scene of interest is a later one where the Prince happens upon his beloved Marinda being assaulted by Irish rapparees:

The Prince rode up, and commanded them to desist, and let him know what was the cause of their Quarrel; one of them gave him a short Answer in *Irish*, and at the same time made a thrust at him with his Pitch-fork . . . the Prince drawing out a Pistol, returned the *Irishman's* complement with a shot, and laid him dead at his Horse's feet. (*The Irish Princess*, p. 82)

With the death of the man speaking Irish, it is clear to the reader who is in the position of power. Of significant relevance, though, is how the author treats the Irish language: Irish words are reported on but they are not written. The situation is reversed from that earlier at the holy well, when the readers are told the story while the characters remain unaware of it. Here the characters within the novel hear the word but the reader, on this occasion, is sheltered from it. A story that imitates the form of Gaelic folklore is permissible: the story is, in a way, translatable and adaptable into the novel form, but the Irish language is not similarly communicable. At the level of narrative control it seems that another act of editorial manipulation is being imposed: the story will not be contaminated by Irish words, they will not be legitimised in an act of writing.

Irish rapparees posed a very real threat in the countryside of Ireland after the Williamite victories of 1690.[13] It is hard to determine whether they were enemy combatants returning home from war, or simply criminals making the most of the opportunities that war affords for their trade. Roaming the countryside away from towns and cities, they existed outside and beyond the reach of law. Their indeterminate status – which is underlined in the novel – highlights the difficulty for the Protestant community in relation to the Gaelic and Catholic Irish in general, as well as other dissenters from the Anglican faith: are they to be treated as citizens or enemies of Ireland? It is a dilemma that was never fully confronted or resolved satisfactorily, with the contradictions that it underlines concerning the nature of liberty and freedom in an Irish context remaining to trouble Irish affairs throughout the eighteenth century.[14] However, as a counterpoint to the threat of lawlessness and uncertainty, the close of the novel presents the image of three women marrying their lovers: all are rewarded for their constancy and virtue. One interpretation is that Marinda's transformation into the 'Irish Princess' of the novel's title comes about at the very moment when she will depart Ireland and leave her community behind. As far-fetched as it might seem, maybe the 'Irish Princess' of the title refers to the Gaelic Cluaneesha. Paradoxically, she is the only truly authentic 'princess' within the novel.

The novel exhibits a profound sense of ambiguity and uneasiness about an emerging Protestant community: in comparison to the worlds of the South American Indian Faniaca, and indeed the Prince and Celadon, there appears not much to recommend it. Even Gaelic Ireland possesses an intriguing narrative – the myth of Cluaneesha – in a way that the Protestant population does not. The Irish Protestant community's conception of itself thus remains unclear at the close of the novel. The irony of this, of course, is that Marinda and the small-town world she represents might aspire to genteel nobility but are, themselves, thoroughly middle-class and parochial. Even with war occurring on their doorstep, real excitement always seems to be associated with other places and other people. Marinda's choice of husband has little to do with traditional notions of religion or community, and despite the aristocratic labels of Prince and Princess, the Prince is a new bourgeois man not bound by custom or convention but who must begin to reimagine his desires within a new sense of modern polite sensibility. In terms of their relationship with the Gaelic Irish, there is much that remains unresolved and uncertain. Of course, Gaelic culture cannot be ignored even though 'as a rival power structure' it was no more.[15] It is troublingly 'there', brooding menacingly in the background, erupting sporadically onto the page.

At the very moment of its inception, the Irish novel realises the fragility of its own being, under threat from the traditional forms and narratives that it is attempting to supersede. While focused on Irish issues, the novel is European and international with rival voices and stories vying for prominence within the narrative. The Gaelic folktale – though invented and uneasily placed within the narrative framework – is nonetheless offered on an equal basis to all the other stories and voices that are told and heard. The ending of the novel is somewhat ambiguous. If the new Irish Princess leaves at the close of the novel, this points to failure: Ireland is simply abandoned, a site of impossibility. Conversely, if she and her lover are to remain in Ireland, the consequences for this burgeoning Protestant community remain unclear. Her newfound high social status is conferred from outside her immediate society and, because of the Prince's uncertain financial future, this social status might mean very little in the new world of money becoming the only indicator of value. Also, the questions raised throughout the novel about identity, about the possible complexities of the competing power relationships within Ireland, remain unresolved – as do the issues surrounding the subtleties and intricacies within the Protestant community itself as it attempts to imagine itself into existence. The lingering anxiety, though, revolves round how this early Irish novel is unsure of what constitutes ordinary life in Ireland. Life is at once mundane with the expected desires of an emerging middle class being put on display, but beneath that veneer of genteel aspiration, at the level of the unconscious, exist potentially extraordinary narratives and extraordinary emotions.

Beginnings and endings: writing from the margins, 1665–1800

There is no document of civilization which is not at the same time a document of barbarism.

(Walter Benjamin)[1]

Dean Rowland Davies, the chaplain with the Williamite forces who was last seen having his boots stolen in Clonmel, writes in his last journal entry for 30 September 1690: 'This day the residue of our army began their march towards Kinsale; and the magistrates of Cork, resuming their places, proclaimed the King and Queen, and put the city into some order.'[2] After the chaos and the upheaval of war comes the hard task of securing and winning the peace, and of bringing stability back into public and private life. One view of the subsequent eighteenth century is that it is a period of relative calm and certainty, in comparison to the centuries preceding and succeeding it. For W. B. Yeats the eighteenth century was the 'one Irish century that escaped from darkness and confusion'. It is a curious remark and, of course, it is a poet's estimation rather than a historian's. What Yeats, the artist, is attracted to in this century is the 'image of the modern mind's discovery of itself, of its own permanent form'.[3] His assessment suggests that the eighteenth century marks a break with the old in its embrace of the new. Yet, this does not imply that it was an easy, unproblematic transition, the headlong rush into modernity does not necessarily suggest that all of the past, all of history, is left behind and forgotten: trace elements remain to disturb and disrupt the modernisation project.[4] Thus, the prevailing outward appearance of tranquillity hides the turmoil beneath that façade with the ever-present threat of violence lurking to disturb the appearance of passive progress.

Catherine Skeen points out that the eighteenth century is a time of many pamphlets concerning schemes and proposed improvements in agriculture, in coinage, and in trade, banking, canals and bridges.[5] Terms such as *Irish*, *Gaelic*, *Old English* and *English* abound at this juncture, the nomenclature indicating a society in flux and transition. Thus, as Ireland becomes a project of improvement for the Protestant victors of 1690 so too, by extension, does the Protestant sense of identity become a project for the political and cultural imagination. One of the earliest instances of an Irishman in a novel is to be found in Richard Head's (*c*.1637–*c*.1686) *The English Rogue* (1665). Head was born in Ireland, the son of a Protestant minister killed in the 1641 rebellion, and the early chapters of his novel appear to be based on his early life. While the title would suggest that this is a work that should be read and understood within the tradition of the early English novel, these early chapters particularly register vividly the dilemma of this project of self-creation for the Protestant Irish community. The English rogue of the novel, Meriton Latroon, has in fact been unceremoniously born in Ireland: 'By this time my Mother drew near her time, having conceived me in England, but not conceiving she should thus drop me in an Irish Bog.'[6] He goes on to declare:

It is strange the Clymate should have more prevalency over the nature of the Native, then the disposition of the Parent. For though Father and Mother could neither flatter, deceive, revenge, equivocate, *&c*. yet the son (as the consequence hath since made it appear) can (according to the common custom of his Countreymen) dissemble and sooth up his Adversary with expressions extracted from Celestial Manna . . . Cheat all I dealt withal, though the matter ever so inconsiderable. Lie so naturally, that a miracle may be as soon wrought, as a truth proceed from my mouth. And then for Equivocation, or mental Reservations, they were ever in me innate properties . . . This is the nature of an Irishman.[7]

Some confusion is evident here. The accident of birth, or the place of birth, does not rigidly denote nationality: he remains the 'English' rogue throughout. Yet, maybe place does affect character; that is to say, his roguery – his ability to lie and to cheat – is a result of where he is born. It has been argued that Englishness is finally bestowed on the rogue because he repents at the close of the novel and thus Englishness is presented as the reserve of virtue and goodness.[8] But there is an unresolved ambiguous sense of identity here: the hero, at some level, is either Irish or English or, rather, is *both* Irish *and* English simultaneously. Thus the notion of stable national characteristics or racial traits is undermined: being English or Irish is a matter of choice rather than a condition of being born into any particular place or culture. Ultimately, though, it is obviously English identity that is radically destabilised in this novel, because it appears as a set of codes and manners easily accessible to anyone and therefore constantly under pressure from marginalised groups such as the Irish. What is ultimately fascinating about a character such as this rogue is his mobility between classes and nations: his ability to recreate himself at will as each situation throws up new obstacles and challenges. As a picaroon, who aspires to bourgeois comfort while simultaneously deconstructing those codes, he is not only a fascinating character, to be sure, but also a person to be feared. No sense of traditional order or structure or value system can contain him; he transcends those strictures and embraces all the possibilities that the new world has to offer. He wills himself into existence, making it up, and in the process making a self, as he goes along. His existence is one of active forgetting which, in a way, mirrors the form of the novel at this moment, which also, in its efforts to be new and original, must forget or, rather, reimagine the numerous forms and literary genres it hopes to replace.

What is remarkable about *The English Rogue* is how it complicates straightforward notions of national identity. Margaret Doody has said of the early modern novel that, 'Growing nationalism has not yet enclosed [it] within narrow national boundaries. Neither has the temporal boundary found its later strength. In the seventeenth century, as in the sixteenth, there is a mingling of old and new, the remote with the neighbouring.'[9] Thus, the novel was a fluid form, unsure and uncertain as to what it might actually be, but nonetheless a form that a growing number of writers felt was capable of both containing and expressing all that was new in the modern world. In *The English Rogue* there is easy access to the native Irish, as the Rogue possesses a few Gaelic words that allow him to make love to a woman before she cries out and he is discovered. Indeed, language other than the normative English language is presented as exotic and a key for entry into other worlds and other lives. The 'Cant' language of the gypsies is presented as a list of words and their meanings in the novel. For the opportunistic Rogue, knowledge is power, with language being just one more tool that will enable him to get what he wants.

For the Irish Protestant community after 1690, a figure such as this Rogue is exactly the kind of character to be jettisoned owing to his obviously embryonic bourgeois characteristics. Indeed, the novel form itself, tied as it is to all that is new, has a difficult position within Ireland. The novel, with its need to reflect flexibility and its openness to the issue of identity and difference, becomes threatening. Attitudes are hardened in an Irish world where interest in others is replaced with caution and wariness. It has been argued that the eighteenth century did not produce any novels of Anglo-Irish life. Fiction was not a medium through which that experience could be adequately expressed.[10] Certainly, in contrast with later periods, there appear to be very few novels that confront Irish life – either Anglo-Irish or Gaelic – in any great depth. Theatre, for instance, offered a more readily available and very public medium through which to view the issues and themes that dominated the century. As Christopher Morash has argued, the fundamental question of legitimacy – the central issue surrounding the events of the Glorious Revolution – are played out again and again on the stages of Dublin throughout the eighteenth century.[11] The ballad form as well as essays and sermons are additional popular public media permitting comment on and interpretation of contemporary affairs for writers and readers alike. In this context of action and accomplishment – of doing – the novel as an aesthetic pursuit in the early eighteenth century, for either the Irish reader or the writer, appears frivolously bound to the notion of luxurious ease and therefore perhaps not worth pursuing. More Irish novels appear from the 1750s onwards and it can be argued that what is witnessed is a move towards a moment of leisure and ease for the Irish Protestant community, when rather than struggling to become, they might simply be. The modern novel flourishes in such a moment when, as the hero of *Don Quixote* discovers, time is redeemed in the act of doing absolutely nothing.

There were three competing power groups in the late eighteenth-century Ireland: the imperial power of Britain, the Anglo-Irish Ascendancy and the middle-class businessmen who were both Catholic or Protestant. The novel is perfectly placed to chart this society and its internal conflicts. Indeed, there was a growing trade in books at this time, a trade that was not simply centred round the metropolitan areas of Dublin, Belfast or Cork, but had sophisticated networks that allowed book readers dwelling in the more remote parts of Ireland access to the literature of the day. Mikhail Bakhtin argues that the novel emerges at a time when centralised political, linguistic and literary authority is beginning to collapse.[12] What is interesting from an Irish perspective is that during the eighteenth century the exact opposite was occurring at an official level. The strain of projecting authority and control by the ruling Anglo-Irish elite is what is of significance here, and in many ways the novels of the period – written mostly by the Ascendancy class simply because they have access to the means of writing fiction – reflect these confusions and tensions. The ethical vacuum produced by the chaos of war means that, for those who inherit that situation, there is an element of improvisation, of being compelled to create out of nothing. One of the major legalistic consequences of this situation was the Penal Laws enacted in 1695 and subsequently amended and added to throughout the eighteenth century. They were only repealed from the 1770s onwards with a series of Catholic Relief Acts. While there had been laws before this restricting the religious and cultural practices of the Gaelic Irish, these were more far-reaching and pernicious than those which had gone before. Areas of life dealt with were ownership of property, the regulation and education of

priests, education for Catholics in general, and employment by both the state
and private enterprise. The passing of these laws signalled that a new cultural
and political elite was coming into being and that this new elite intended to
rule as it saw fit. Its existence and its application make manifest the ambiguities and uncertainties central to Irish experience throughout this period,
underlining the strangeness and contradictions central to everyday life for
both Gaelic and Anglo-Ireland. This confusion affected both those who made
the laws and those for whom the laws were intended. Each community
recognised a gap between what was law and what was reality. Each community, in their own way, was forced to live a lie.

Despite the Anglican victory of 1691, it can be said that what unites
Gaelic and Anglo-Irish experience of the eighteenth century is that for
each community it was marked by 'uncertainty and ambiguity'.[13] For the
Anglo-Irish, as well as the Gaelic Irish, the Penal Laws and their application
produced a break between actuality and ideology, between the word and
the world. Chancellor Bowes remarked in 1759, 'the law did not assume a
Catholic to exist'.[14] His observation throws up, perhaps, an unintentional
irony: the speaker unconsciously plays on the gap between the laws of state
and the reality of everyday lived existence on the ground. The real site of
conflict in eighteenth-century Irish life, as this emphasis on the rupture
between actuality and ideology suggests, is between the public and the
private sphere, between the inner personal world and the outer world of
communal and shared experience. What is of moment, then, for the novel
form is 'realism': reality itself is a category under pressure in an Irish context
as there is no common sense of what the Irish reality is or ought to be. This
rupture between actuality and ideology, this uncertainty in the relationship
between the private and the public realms, is exploited by Irish fiction in
this period because it is the novel which best registers the real ground of
conflict in eighteenth-century Irish life between the inner and outer worlds.
The novel, then, concerns itself with mapping this new interior space of
sensibility.

For some writers following the Williamite victory, the label of Irish was
seen as detrimental to a successful novelistic career. Mary Davys (1674–1732)
declared that if any reader had knowledge that she was Irish, it would result
in 'a general Dislike to all I write'[15] and moved to England. *The Reformed
Coquet or, Memoirs of Amoranda. A Surprising Novel* (1735) can be thought
of as typical of her writing, as it is concerned with the proper way for a
relationship to develop. Women must choose men who possess sense and
sensibility, as well as outward beauty in order for a harmonious union to
succeed. Interestingly, this was one of William Carleton's (1794–1869)

favourite novels, being the first he ever read.[16] Writers such as the well-known English author Penelope Aubin (1679?–1731?) in her novel *The Life and Adventures of the Lady Lucy, the daughter of an Irish Lord* (1726) make use of Ireland as a space in which a story of jealousy and marital difficulty can be told. Of course, the Dublin and the Dundalk she mentions could be anywhere: the life being lived is very much a British one. Yet, there are hints and gestures recognising Ireland's difference. One particular scene shows the Anglo-Irish characters and the native Irish each cut off from the other because of the lack of a shared language: 'Here I found a poor *Irish* Woman and her Daughter, who spake nothing but their native Tongue, which, though we are all born in the same Kingdom, except the Captain, yet we are not able perfectly to understand.'[17]

William Congreve (1670–1729), better known as a successful dramatist, wrote a novel while still a student at Trinity College, Dublin. Published in 1692, *Incognita* is now famous for its Preface which makes a useful and clear distinction between the newness of the novel and the more traditional romance narrative: 'Novels are of a more familiar nature; come near us and represent to us intrigues in practice; delight us with accidents and odd events, but not such as are wholly unusual or unprecedented – such which, not being so distant from our belief, bring also the pleasure nearer us. Romances give more of wonder, novels more delight.'[18] Congreve's story, though, has nothing to say of Ireland or of the affairs of the contemporary world: it is a parody of the romance form – rather than the novel form – so effective, there is hardly any room for ironic or humorous distance. However, it might be said that Congreve's marginal position in Ireland means that he can critique more effectively the mainstream English novel emerging at this time. One original element is that the novel follows the three dramatic unities of time, place and action, which obviously reflect Congreve's interest in the possibility of theatre rather than prose.

As Ian Campbell Ross and others argue, the difficulty for the Irish novel in this period is that it deals in known and comforting stereotypes. Novels such as the anonymously written *The Irish Rogue: or the Further Adventures of Teague O'Divelly* (1690) and *The Wild-Irish Captain, or Villany Display'd Truly and Faithfully Related* (1692) reproduce negative attitudes towards Ireland and Irishness from the vantage point of British metropolitan power.[19] In the midst of such writing there is published a novel in 1716 by Sarah Butler. Little is known of her, the events of her life are mere conjecture. She may have been the widow of a Williamite captain killed at Aughrim in 1691 but there is nothing to link the author of *Irish Tales: or Instructive Histories for the Happy Conduct of Life* (1716) to any actual event, person or place.[20] Perhaps, and this seems more likely when the obvious Jacobin content of the novel is considered, Butler is a pseudonym. Quite simply *Irish Tales* is one of the more remarkable fictions, indeed one of the more remarkable texts, of the entire eighteenth-century canon of Irish writing. This is so for one reason: Butler offers a version and a vision, a novelisation, of Ireland's past as thoroughly positive and wholly celebratory. Not until the latter half of the nineteenth century and the Irish Literary Revival's rediscovery of Cúchulain and the tales of the Ulster cycle would such an effort be made to bring out of Ireland's past heroic characters and heroic stories that might fire the modern imagination.

While the Cúchulain stories are myth, Butler chose to relocate her narrative to a more recent and factual past: the eleventh and twelfth centuries and the Norman invasions of Ireland.[21] The underlying impulse is to make Ireland's past real, to get beyond the obscuring mists of myth. Whereas the nineteenth-century Revival was a part of a general cultural, economic and political movement that moved towards independence from Britain, Butler's novel – while being republished as late as 1735 – did not generate, that we as yet know of, any immediate imitators in the area of the novel. It stands alone as an indication of a possible route that the Irish novel might have taken in the eighteenth and nineteenth centuries.

Though the novel's main focus is on the story of Dooneflaith, daughter of Maolseachlin II, King of Meath, and her lover Murchoe, son of Brian Boru, the real story is of Irish resistance to foreign invasion. Ian Campbell Ross's essay on *Irish Tales* highlights the numerous levels of revolutionary shock value within the novel, from the title of the novel itself to the story being told, to the time of its publication twenty-five years after the Williamite victory over Gaelic Ireland of 1691, and one year after the failed Jacobite rebellion in Scotland.[22] As Campbell Ross points out, there was a genre of 'secret history' novels written by women in this period: Aphra Behn's *Oroonoko* (1688), for instance, which used 'history' as a deflected means to talk of politics in the present. Butler's novel, though, is far less concerned with furtively commenting on the present state of Irish affairs in this manner. In many ways, Butler's analysis of Ireland's past is not disguised at all and is a candid comment on the present. For instance, the tyrant Turgesius's conquest of Ireland is seen very much in terms of an attack on religion: 'One whose wicked hands have ransack'd all our Holy Temples, demolished all our Altars! burnt our Churches, and raz'd our Monasteries, ravish'd our Nuns, slain our Pious Priests, and thrown the very Host itself to the Dogs.'[23] Readers in 1716 could not have been unaware of the parallels between recent Irish and British history, and the fate of Roman Catholics under the Penal Laws. As with many Irish literary texts of the period, this too is an attack on illegitimate rule: the tyranny of Turgesius is meant to contrast sharply with the authority and kingship of Brian Boru. The message is very clear: if Ireland was capable off overthrowing such oppressive foreign rule in the past, then the same may be possible in the present or in the future.

Of more significance is the source of the story and the formal appendages employed by Butler to frame that basic story: the Preface and her use of novelistic techniques. The *Irish Tales* reads more like a history than a work of fictive prose. Translating this history into the realm of fiction is an act of smuggling into popular circulation the facts of Ireland's past. The author consciously situates her text in relation to Irish historiography, mentioning in her Preface previous historians of Ireland such as Camden, Edmund Spenser and Peter Walsh. But it is Geoffrey Keating's (in Irish, Séathrún Céitinn) *Foras Feasa Ar Éirinn* which is the main source for Butler's history. Important as the stories of Keating's and Walsh's histories are, of more significance to Butler's novel is the tenor of Keating's and Walsh's work. These seventeenth-century writers were determined to present *true* histories of Ireland because Ireland had been continually misrepresented and misconstrued by British writers and historians from the eleventh-century Giraldus Cambrensis onwards. Of significance was not just the correction of fact and historical detail, but also a more overarching concern with representing the general character of Irish people in a positive light. Employing the novel form means that this appeal to history possesses a moral purpose too.

Certainly Butler's narrative shares these concerns, as she writes in her Preface:

Some (upon what Grounds I know not) would needs have their manner and way of making Love, which I have brought as near as I could to our modern Phrase, to be too Passionate and Elegant for the *Irish* and contrary to the Humours, they alledge, of so Rude and Illiterate a People; when all the while they do not consider, that altho' they may seem now, in the Circumstances they lie under, (having born the heavy Yoke of Bondage for so many years, and have been Cow'd down in their Spirits) yet that once *Ireland* was esteem'd one of the Principle Nations in Europe for Piety and Learning; having formerly been so Holy, that it was term'd *The Island of Saints*.[24]

It is a curious mixture of defence and attack; on the one hand, emphasising the worthiness of the Irish as a people and, on the other, making a claim for the value of the subject of Ireland's antiquity. Butler makes the point that Ireland was a site of learning and knowledge. This shift of emphasis from being the object to being the creator of knowledge is truly revolutionary for its time. This is a vision of Ireland as central, not peripheral, to European life and culture. It is a vision of Ireland as the creator and source of its own authority and reality, rather than such categories being imposed from elsewhere.

Butler's project of humanising and civilising the Irish can be observed through the love story of Dooneflaith and Murchoe: there is much weeping by both of them and Murchoe, in particular, shares many traits with that emerging figure in the eighteenth-century sentimental novel – a man in touch with his feelings: 'I love! I love the fair, the charming, virtuous, and all divine Dooneflaith.'[25] As one would expect of an eighteenth-century novel, their love is nothing if not based on virtuousness. Indeed, that Butler consciously employs the novel form itself is a central element in this civilising project because the novel is increasingly becoming associated with matters of bourgeois taste and manners. Thus, along with offering a history of Ireland based on fact, Butler also offers a secret history of Irish humanity with the novel's ability to normalise the world being written about harnessed to powerful effect here. The mode of presentation of the love story between Dooneflaith and Murchoe modernises their relationship and their feelings and sentiments: the medium is, in this instance, the message. In contrast, the tyrant invader Turgesius is presented as an unreconstructed barbarous male controlled by his lustful passions. The stilted dialogue throughout the novel, coupled with the general employment of an overtly ornate style, also performs the function of moving beyond the Irish brogue, so fascinating to the English ear, and throughout this period one of the main signifiers of the difference and the inferiority of the Irish.

What *Irish Tales* suggests is a yearning for a suitable literary form to convey the Irish story. Hugh MacCurtin's *A Brief Discourse in Vindication of the Antiquity of Ireland* published in 1717 is a text sharing many concerns with Butler's novel, not least that desire to correct erroneous versions of Ireland's history. His 'Preface' is noteworthy for his attack on those foreign historians who are unable to distinguish 'which is the History, and which is the Fable': 'And that is what confounds the Foreign Authors in general, touching the Antiquity of Ireland; for they cannot distinguish the true Histories which are Authentick, from the SchoolBooks, and other Romances that were written for Pastime.'[26] And yet Butler's text successfully merges history and fiction, fact and romance. *Irish Tales* exists on the nexus of oral and print culture and she is very aware of what the novel form can allow her to do with her source material: 'And although I have cloath'd it with the Dress and Title of a Novel; yet (so far as I dare speak in my own behalf, that) I have err'd as little from the Truth of the history, as any perhaps who undertaken anything of this Nature.'[27] The metaphor here of cloaking and disguise is of interest because it is repeated within the novel itself. Part of the plan to defeat Turgesius involves Murchoe and his men masquerading as young women in order to gain entry to their enemy's stronghold. Certainly there is a sense in which Butler is examining gender roles within the novel with women being placed in an empowered position.[28] The real value, though, of this scene and metaphor is how it offers the reader an image of how Gaelic culture survives and transforms itself in the new Anglicised dispensation. What is required is concealment and disguise: in that way Gaelic culture's power can continue to exist, though hidden from view. It suggests, too, that in order for this culture to continue it must find, or create, new forms through which it can realise expression. Butler is able to smuggle rebellious ideas into mainstream circulation. Even the title functions as a means of masking the true intent of the novel: *Irish Tales, or Instructive Histories for the Happy Conduct of Life* points towards a story of individual life, whereas it is the communal concern with overthrowing tyranny which actually drives the narrative forward. MacCurtin's difficulties with the difference between myth and history can be transformed into a source of energy for the artist who can creatively play within the spaces between history and fiction. As Ian Campbell Ross has argued, Butler conflates history in her narrative, excising over one hundred years, so that her narrative of invasion resonates more clearly.[29]

While *Irish Tales* is remarkable for its time in offering an English and Irish readership positive, at times revolutionary, images of Ireland, Butler is not content to simply and unquestioningly celebrate the Irish character. The Irish appear often more concerned with perceived slights among themselves than with resisting their foreign invaders. Importantly, too, Dooneflaith's father refuses her permission to marry Murchoe and frustrates their love. That their love ultimately remains unfulfilled is suggestive of a profound failure: a pessimistic counterpoint to the wider story of victory over tyrannical rule. It is a gap between the public sphere of history and the private one of lived experience, registering the need in an Irish context, to realign these two realms in order that the public space is a place that the Irish individual can exist in, and vice versa.

The ten years between Butler's little-known *Irish Tales* and the publication of the widely acclaimed and widely known *Gulliver's Travels* (1726) by Jonathan Swift (1667–1745) saw numerous developments in Irish life. The main thrust of these developments – which are manifested in Swift's *Drapier Letters* (1721–26) concerning the controversy of 'Woods Halfpence' – is the desire of the Irish governing elite to get some real political power into their hands. Since 1692, Irish government, while having some power, was in reality merely a façade for British rule through what is known as 'the Undertaker' system. In 1720, the Declaratory Act was passed which asserted the right of the British parliament to legislate for Ireland. Yet government in Ireland did provide a public focus for political concerns to be played out, as well as a powerful social focus for Anglo-Irish life to revolve round. The term employed by historians and critics labels this desire for real power as 'colonial nationalism',[30] signifying recognition for the need for authority over local concerns, while maintaining the important link with Britain. This, though, implies a well-defined idea of what such a relationship might be and how such a government might actually function. The opposite is actually the case: despite overtures of confidence and the seeming display of unbending rule and authority, what is at the heart of the Anglo-Irish experience at this time is precisely the opposite – doubt, uncertainty and anxiety.[31]

Swift's novel can be thought of as a companion piece to Butler's *Irish Tales* in that as an author he represents the Irish colonial story, not from the colonised perspective, but from the vantage point of the coloniser. Unsure, exactly, about his relationship to the metropolitan centre that is Britain and London, Swift's *Gulliver's Travels* expresses doubt about the nature of his position in Ireland and his role in the ongoing colonial project. For a time Swift had been right at the heart of the British imperial government, writing propaganda for the Tories. His appointment as Dean of St Patrick's in Dublin meant a return to the margins. In many ways, his experience represents the confusion of the Irish Protestant: he is Irish in England and English in Ireland, a member of the ruling class set to Anglicise Ireland, but cut off and denied access to return to the original home place.[32] While his early work, such as *A Tale of a Tub* (1704), is a confident satire on the encroaching mediocrity of the modern world of ideas and books, written by a someone at the centre of power and knowledge, *Gulliver's Travels* – written from the marginal space of Ireland – displays a much more anxious attitude.

Gulliver's Travels can hardly be labelled a novel at all, even at a time when the novel form is quite nebulous. The book lacks an overall unifying narrative force and whatever unity it possesses does not revolve round the development of character. Lemuel Gulliver learns nothing from his adventures, meeting each new episode unburdened by any knowledge or memory gleaned from his earlier encounters. He exhibits no interior life to speak of and this is exactly the new space that the novel excavates so illuminatingly. Instead, the fictional world of *Gulliver's Travels* is very much concerned with exterior realities: descriptions of characters are famously physical and, more significantly, perhaps, the work is made up of surface descriptions of each encountered society's workings, its politics and philosophy. And yet, *Gulliver's Travels* functions so successfully precisely because it mimics the form of the novel, and particularly the travel narrative best exemplified in this period by Daniel Defoe's *Robinson Crusoe* published to wide popular acclaim in 1719. So, even if *Gulliver's Travels* does not operate exactly within the accepted parameters of the form, it still requires knowledge of the novel and how it functions to make its all-encompassing satire work effectively.

In Defoe's *Robinson Crusoe*, travel allowed for a clash of cultures to be represented. Ideas and assumptions about home are tested, with, ultimately, English and European culture being seen as both superior and spectacularly adaptable to the foreign space. This difference is central to the narrative dynamic of travel writing. *Gulliver's Travels* reverses this formula: while the reader is undoubtedly confronted with exotic worlds, these worlds are – in the end – very much like home. Gulliver, rather than bringing back home new ideas from these far-away places, in reality only brings back versions and variations of the home place – brings back only confirmation of what he already knows. This is because the target of Swift's savage indignation is much closer to home, if not the very ideas surrounding 'home' itself.

Irish readings of *Gulliver's Travels* focus on the depiction of the Yahoos in Book Four. Their juxtaposition with the ultra-rational Houyhnhnms – who happen to be horses – mean they appear utterly barbarous and savage in comparison and thus the link to the situation in Ireland is obvious. The Houyhnhnm relationship to the Yahoo race is played out as exemplifying the master/slave, coloniser/colonised dichotomy, even acknowledging the absolute need for the inferior race to exist in order that the superior race can be just that: superior. The Houyhnhnms are said to return constantly to a debate about whether 'the Yahoos should be exterminated from the Face of the Earth',[33] a phrase which anticipates Joseph Conrad's Kurtz and his cry of 'Exterminate all the brutes!' in *Heart of Darkness* (1902).[34] It is the unresolved contradiction at the heart of the colonial project: pure assimilation of native culture is impossible, as is its final destruction, and therefore the desire to recreate perfectly the imperial home in the foreign space is doomed to fail from the very moment that idea is first conceived and acted on.

The real significance of Gulliver meeting the Yahoos is his coming across a mirror image of himself: 'My Horror and astonishment are not to be described, when I observed, in this abominable Animal, a perfect human Figure.'[35] This shocking moment of recognition is central to the entire novel because, for the reader, that is what has been occurring throughout: the minute size of the Lilliputians or the giant Brobdinggnags merely underscores their all-too-human characteristics and petty foibles. Declan Kiberd suggests that 'The world of Gulliver, like the Ireland of Swift, is a place where the observer all of a sudden becomes the observed.'[36] Thus, Gulliver from being in a position of power and control is unexpectedly on the receiving end of observational authority. As Terry Eagleton argues, the principal concept systematically unpacked by Swift is the concept of perspective itself. *Gulliver's Travels* explodes the means by which hierarchal difference functions. The foreign is made look familiar, the familiar made look foreign. Perhaps, in spite of itself, Swift's novel does what any novel should do: make the extraordinary appear ordinary and the ordinary appear extraordinary. Truth itself is 'a matter of proportion and comparison' and the reader is forced – as is Gulliver to a lesser extent – to re-examine some basic assumptions about the world in which she or he lives.[37] Perspective is linked to power and control in the colonial space: its attainment signals possible empowerment for those who had previously been in inferior positions. It is a technique that will be taken up again to great effect by James Joyce in the 'Cyclops' episode of *Ulysses*, emphasising how Ireland is created and invented through discourse. The satire is so successful in *Gulliver's Travels* that no normative position persists by the close of the book. In other words, there is no normalising concept of home by the end of Gulliver's various travels.

Gulliver with his lack of depth, his lack of interior substance, is a disconnected homeless figure. If Daniel Defoe and other novelists of this period celebrated this condition by eulogising the emergence of the 'new man', unfettered by tradition or inheritance who makes his way in the world through industry and graft, the man who can make and remake his home wherever he so wishes, then Swift laments the coming of the new modern age. Gulliver's dilemma, as is Swift's, is that he is not only fundamentally and perilously unsure of where to live but also unsure of how best to live. Underscoring this conclusion is the stylistic feature noticeable in Book Four with an increasing amount of lists being deployed by the narrator, the stylistic equivalent of Houyhnhnm logic: spare and direct, certainly, but overall signalling an enervation and exhaustion. By the close of the novel, Gulliver has internalised the Houyhnhnm view of himself as a worthless Yahoo and that narrational style which marked him off as an individual, as a unique human being, has been eroded and abandoned.

Thus, if Sarah Butler humanised the colonised native Irish by giving them a modernised language and modern sentimental emotions, Swift views the coloniser in less than human terms. Butler is happy to engage with the novel form and how it interacts with a readership whereas Swift fears what the novel can do. The consequences of colonisation, then, are shared between the two groups involved and Swift is one of the first Anglo-Irish writers to make manifest that impact on his community. By reading both these novels side-by-side it is clear at this moment that the novel is formless, still searching for a set of common images and tropes that might be shared between the different elements of Irish society.

These early forays into the Irish novel might suggest, perhaps, a burgeoning vibrancy in Irish prose. That, of course, is not the case in relation to the novel. Histories of the publishing trade in Ireland make clear that, while there is an ever-increasing interest in, and production of, specifically Irish work from the 1750s onwards, the Irish scene is very much influenced by what is being read and published in Britain. That the British Copyright Act of 1709 did not apply to Ireland meant pirated copies of popular English fiction and other writing could be profitably and widely circulated to the detriment, particularly, of Irish writing. Indeed, throughout the eighteenth century, the novel as such was never as popular as other forms and genres of prose. For the lower classes it was a constant diet of: 'histories of robbers and pirates; books of chivalry; books of witchcraft and gross superstition; indecent books; these classes constituted about two thirds of the whole number, the remaining third consisting of useful or innocent books of voyages, travel, history or novels'.[38] Such a list suggests that the Irish were still attracted to texts that connected to stories circulating within the oral tradition. But, the availability of fiction – of all kinds – was to be denounced, one imagines, in general as a bad thing for all readers from every class. James Arbuckle, writing in the *Dublin Journal* in 1725, condemned the reading of novels, attacking those 'fabulous adventures and memoirs of pirates, whores and pickpockets wherewith for sometime past the press has so prodigiously swarmed'.[39] His words are echoed ten years later when 'A Dublin Catholic bookseller in 1735 condemned "the reading of old immoral, ridiculous romances".'[40] What these remarks demonstrate clearly is that the novel remains a site of potential danger and unruliness. The modern world requires something other than the romance, but the vulgar novel merely updates the follies and the lewdness of past forms. Arbuckle hoped that Irish writers might turn their attention to Irish themes and Irish concerns. Such a literature could be used for the ethical enlightenment of the populace rather than mere titillation.[41] These remarks and concerns anticipate in terms of the specifically Irish novel, the latter half of the eighteenth century when there is an upsurge in observably Irish novels with Irish settings, Irish themes and Irish characters. Paul Hiffernan (1719–77) in his *The Hiberniad* published in 1754 takes up that topic and writes about the need for national pride in Ireland, in its people and, importantly, its landscape. It is a remarkable document for its time, offering writers another possible trajectory for Irish writing. His pleas, though, are all but ignored and it would take another thirty years for writers to begin to display an interest in Ireland in the way that he envisaged.

The observable increase in Irish-themed novels after 1750 can be attributed, perhaps, to a growing sense of confidence in Anglo-Irish society particularly, as the community became more embedded and grounded in the Irish world. Certainly, from the evidence of the novels themselves, there appears to be an agreed and accepted sense of Anglo-Irish society, its limits and its boundaries, its codes and expectations. There is, too, the sense that the novel is able now to reflect this society, to offer its Anglo-Irish readers images of themselves – sometimes flattering, sometimes not – and in doing so, solidify that community further. Of course, the question of an audience beyond the local one means that the stock figure of the stage Irishman, which had a long history in the theatre, now migrates into the novel form, reinforcing stereotypes of the Irish as wastrels and schemers, characters far beyond redemption. The link to Britain opens up a ready market for novels with Irish concerns, and yet the problem is one of either expressing or exploiting these concerns for that readership. There is, too, the exploitation of Irish characters and concerns from a particularly British viewpoint – whether written by an Irish or English author does not really matter – which presents curious interpretations of Irish characters and Irish issues and concerns. Swift's consideration of 'perspective' in the colonial world is thus continued and advanced.

Three works in particular manifest this new cultural reality when the Irish novel comes into its own: the anonymously written *The Adventures of Shelim O'Blunder, Esq., The Irish Beau* (1751), William Chaigneau's *The History of Jack Connor* (1752), and Thomas Amory's *The Life and Opinions of John Buncle, Esq.* (1756–66). What can be observed in moving between the three novels is how the Irish character transforms from being a stereotype into something more complicated and interesting. In many ways, these works return to the picaresque world inhabited by *The English Rogue*. After the turmoil of full-scale war and conflict, the world of middle-class material desire and want, the world of chance, desire and opportunity re-establishes itself.

The Adventures of Shelim O'Blunder, Esq., The Irish Beau (1751) is a 'fortune hunter' novel and there were many of these during this period, such as the anonymously written *The Fortune Hunter; or History of Jack Fitzpatrick* (Dublin, 1762), with Jack coming from an old Milesian family, and John Oakman's *The Life and Adventures of Benjamin Brass: an Irish Fortune Hunter* (1765). The figure of the Irish fortune hunter was common to the theatrical stage at this time also. As the sub-title of *Shelim O'Blunder* suggests, 'a few cursory Reflections on the common ingredients of a Teague-land Beau, or Fortune-Hunter. By way of salutary Advice, or friendly Caution to the Fair sex of Great-Britain',[42] this is a novel that positions itself from a British perspective. While the stress throughout is on fun and entertainment, there is nonetheless a serious undercurrent to the novel, especially in how it makes use of national stereotypes which need no justification: appearing well known and widely accepted. For instance, it is said of this Irish fortune hunter[43] that he is, like most of his countrymen, a schemer and that 'He abounded in Hyperboles and his Compliments were constrained, rough cut, and ill adapted'[44] and that he is known in society 'by the genteel Appellation of the Ladies Monkey, or the Hibernian Slave'.[45] The end of the novel neutralises whatever danger or threat this character might offer as he finds himself in debtors' prison. Interestingly, the reader is never made aware if O'Blunder is Gaelic Irish or Anglo-Irish. This lack of interest in distinguishing between classes is frustrating for the Anglo-Irish establishment who desire to differentiate themselves from the mere Irish. From the metropolitan viewpoint the Irish are all the same, and there is no need for the subtleties of such distinctions: the Irish are the perpetual outsider. That is the real significance of novels such as these, perpetuating the image of the Irish as wanderers: homeless agents who are always already beyond the boundaries of acceptable normality.

William Chaigneau's (1709–81) *The History of Jack Connor* (1752) is an altogether different type of work. It is a novel which attempts to take Ireland, Irishness, Irish themes and concerns seriously from a fictional perspective. Written within the form of the picaresque, the novel's hero rambles far and wide in Ireland, as well as in England, France and Spain. The episodic nature of the picaresque genre, aligned with the peculiar passiveness of the picaroon (things happen to these characters, they do not initiate action), allows for an almost objective image of Ireland to emerge from the pages. It is argued that this novel, while following closely the codes of the picaresque, differs in important ways from the usual accepted trajectory of the picaroon. Ian Campbell Ross maintains that the reason for this divergence from the norm is the author's being an Irish Protestant. The need to reassert ethical values at the end and the need to rediscover true, authentic identity is based on the author's uncertain position in Ireland. Connor returns to Ireland – the land of his birth – at the close of the novel and, crucially, Chaigneau has him embody moral rectitude, as well as having him attain the type of social status most usually spurned by the amoral picaroon that more typically inhabited a world of social and moral flux.[46] Despite the picaresque qualities of the novel, and notwithstanding the effort on the part of Chaigneau to present realistic images of Ireland and its people, *The History of Jack Connor* can thus be read as an enchanted moral fable – a parable – for the Irish Protestant community in the eighteenth century. Quite simply, Jack Connor is lost, and then found, or rather forced to find himself, before he can return home and claim his true inheritance.

As with the more famous picaresque novel of Tobias Smollett, *Roderick Random* (1748), narrative energy is generated by constant movement from one place to another, tension constructed through varying nationalities and identities colliding and mixing in heightened situations. National stereotypes abound in both novels, and in *Roderick Random* the traits and the characteristics of the Irish nation are lampooned on an equal footing to all others. However, something altogether different occurs in Chaigneau's novel. At first glance he is trying to render and be true to the complexities of Irish identity in the eighteenth century in a way in which the author of *Shelim O'Blunder* did not. All aspects of Irish experience are gestured towards – Catholic, Protestant, aristocrat and lower classes people the pages of the novel. Jack Connor's identity is thoroughly mixed: his nominal father was a soldier with William of Orange's army, and his mother is a local Catholic serving girl, much younger than the father. But his real biological father is Sir Roger Thornton, a landowner in County Limerick.

In spite of this acknowledgement of the various possibilities of Irish identity, the novel fears the integration of all these differences. For in truth, the Irish appear to corrupt all who come into direct contact with them.[47] While particular individuals may not be to blame, Dolly, Sir Thornton, the comically lascivious Father Kelly who lusts after Dolly's ample bosom, are all part of an Irish world that is itself inherently debased. One humorous example of this has a woman from Lancashire come to Ireland with hopes of reforming 'the Pronunciation of the People' but who, in turn, loses her own accent and is then labelled an 'Irish bog-trotter' and a 'Teague'.[48] Later it is said of an Irish character that 'he writes as he speaks' but 'In spite of the Brogue of his Pen, you find he comes to the point.'[49] Even the act of writing becomes contaminated by Irishness. This becomes a common enough manoeuvre in the Irish novel, especially in the nineteenth century: authors, not wanting to lose the comic potential of the Hiberno-English blunder and bull, have many Irish characters writing as they speak. The idleness and the sloth of the Irish are much remarked upon and it is said when Jack's family are driven away from their farm by the machinations of Lady Thornton, who knows how her husband likes to wander from the marital bed, that 'the Transition from an Irish Farmer to a Beggar, is very natural and common in the Country'.[50] The image of beggary is a notable one because it is an image that is increasingly employed to view the native Irish, confirming a Protestant belief of the fallen nature of the Catholic. There is a widespread idea at the time that beggary is something chosen, akin to a profession. All the negative connotations of begging – uselessness, lack of industry, backwardness – are bound up in the image.[51]

Jack is an innocent bystander in relation to this all-prevailing atmosphere of corruption. Yet, he still needs to shake off the Irish influence in order to prosper. A teacher says to him:

'You have not much of the common Irish Manner of speaking, but let me advise you to forget the little you have, and endeavour to speak like the People you live with, which will prevent you being often laughed at and ridicul'd by the ignorant and Vulgar. Your name is quite Irish, but I shall call you John Conyers in my letters, and henceforward let that be your name.'[52]

Thus 'Jack Connor' (not so thoroughly an Irish name as it might suggest) is transformed into John Conyers, an identity – a mask – allowing all the subsequent adventures to occur. Emphasising this profound shift sees the header of the pages change to 'The history of Jack Connor, now Conyers' as does the title of the second volume. But this rediscovery of his true self, signalled by his return to Ireland and the rehabilitation of his real name, is a conscious move on his part, indicating a desire to be stable and complete: the movement of the novel is from rejection to an acceptance of his intrinsic Irishness.

Yet, this new relationship with Ireland is not a return to the past; rather, it is a relationship set firmly facing towards the future. Perhaps, it can be argued that *The History of Jack Connor* is one of the very first of the Irish 'problem' novels predicting their centrality in the nineteenth century. In these narratives, Ireland is presented as a dilemma: there is something wrong with it – socially, politically, economically. Corrective action can be taken, however, to make a better future for all. The 'new' Jack Connor embraces the possibility and forward-thinking culture of the Irish Protestant elite, cutting himself off from his Gaelic and Catholic origins.[53] Lord Truegood, Jack's benefactor, represents this reforming attitude. It is he who imagines a future for Jack, a future that will see him: 'build convenient Houses for the poor People, and set them a Spinning. You will ... compel them to

Industry and Labour. They will thrive under you.'[54] It is in this way that *The History of Jack Connor* encapsulates a resurgent energy in Anglo-Irish thinking at this time: new beginnings and fresh starts are the order of the day as evidenced by the many pamphlets produced, taking the improvement of Ireland as their theme. Sections of Bishop George Berkeley's *The Querist* (1753) best exemplify this developing attitude, covering areas of interest ranging from trade to culture.[55] The interrogative mode employed by Berkeley indicates Ireland as the site of an ongoing project, a place of unfinished business.

The History of Jack Connor is an Irish novel that sets up codes and images that will be returned to again by numerous writers. The image of the peasant cottage is one that will resurface again and again, as will the detailing of Irish customs such as the Wake, and in the process making these cultural differences seem interesting and exotic to an audience outside Ireland. The focus on the Anglo-Irish Big House as a place of civilising and industrious influence as the centre of possible improvement will be taken up continuously throughout the nineteenth-century novel particularly. The overly conscious working out of identity issues will also become a cornerstone in Irish writing in general. The novel's focus on the future potential of Ireland and the Irish remains a constant in much Irish novel writing, even to the present day, belying the view that Ireland and Irish writing is always concerned with the past: the unknown future is always the promised land in Irish writing.

Thomas Amory's *The Life of John Buncle, Esq.* (1756–66) is more concerned with the present than the future. This unwieldy novel is remarkable certainly for its formlessness, but also in consequence for its wide-ranging interest contained in the many digressions embarked upon by the narrator in the main text and in the numerous footnotes that are scattered throughout. This novel marks a return, or perhaps a rediscovery, of the quixotic principle of the ramble not only in terms of travel but also in terms of discourse. Here, too, as in Miguel de Cervantes's *Don Quixote*, the boundary between what is factual and that which is fictional is purposely played with and made problematic. From the outset, there is confusion between Thomas Amory the author and John Buncle the character.[56] It seems that the character of 'Buncle' is merely a fiction allowing Amory to discuss and digress on numerous topics and stories that he finds interesting. This is truly important: highlighting the uncertainty surrounding the very categories of fiction and reality, of history, and of biography in an Irish setting. The story of the self, of its creation and its persistence, is the only important one and, yet, the truth of that, the reality of it, can only be approached in the guise of fiction. Again and again in Irish prose – from James Joyce to John McGahern – this line between fiction and reality, between biography and fantasy, is negotiated. As Buncle says in the Prologue: 'In justice to myself, as before observed, and that tradition might not hand me down, when I am gone, in that variety of bad and foolish characters, which a malice, that knows nothing of me, whispers while I am living; it was necessary I should tell my own story.'[57] The self is both the object and the limit of his project, but we can extrapolate from the individual character and consider Buncle's statement as pertaining also to the numerous misrepresentations of Ireland and Irishness. What becomes critical in this story of self-realisation is the act of writing itself: writing *is* the story; writing is power and is the means by which Buncle/Amory will create himself.

It is a novel without a plot, meandering from story to story, full of diversions, digressions and crammed with factual information on numerous topics, including history, theology and natural science. And yet, it is, in many ways, utterly realistic because of this inclusion of the mundane and the everyday. A certain Thomas Cogan in his *John Buncle, Junior, Gentleman* (Dublin, 1776) attempted to parody Amory's achievement, saying that 'I am the youngest son of John Buncle, Gentleman of marvellous memory; who leaped Precipices, tumbled through Mountains, found wives and good men.'[58] Cogan recognises how Amory made the mundane extraordinary and wants to mimic that accomplishment. What becomes significant in Amory's novel are the quality of the stories and the digressions on various topics. As Buncle/Amory declares at the outset:

That the Transactions of my Life, and the observations and reflections I have made on men and things, by sea and land, in various parts of the world, might not be buried in oblivion, and by length of time, be blotted out of the Memory of Men, it has been my wont, from the days of my youth to this time, to write down *Memorandums* of every thing I thought worth noticing, as men and matters, books and circumstances, came in my way; and in hopes they may be of some service to my fellow-mortals I publish them. Some pleasing, and some surprizing things the Reader will find in them.[59]

He is his own authority; he does not need anyone to tell him what is of interest or importance. This confidence and self-reliance infuses the entire novel. In Buncle's travels throughout England, he continually meets up with acquaintances from Ireland: these moments are presented as commonplace and unexceptional, reversing the usual image of the English visitor to Ireland. Buncle is a character very much at ease with himself; he feels no sense of inferiority about himself or his home place.

It is Buncle's openness to varied experience which is particularly of note. He says of his youth:

that I was born in London, and carried an infant to Ireland, where I learned the Irish language, and became intimately acquainted with its original inhabitants: – that I was not only a lover of books from the time I could spell them to this hour; but read with an extraordinary pleasure, before I was twenty, the works of several of the fathers, and all the old romances. (Prologue)

This awareness and appreciation of both literary and oral culture means that he is perfectly positioned to offer descriptions of Ireland that are, for the time, astonishingly fair and objective. Perhaps his being a Unitarian with its tradition of freethinking, and thus a dissenter – an outsider – in Anglican Ireland allows him to have such an open perspective. Certainly, this openness is the case with his encounters with Gaelic culture:

As I travelled once in the county of *Kerry* in *Ireland*, with the *White Knight*, and the *Knight of the Glin*. We called at *Terelah O Crohanes*, an old Irish gentleman, our common friend, who kept up the hospitality of his ancestors, and shewed how they lived, when *Cormac Mac Cuillenan*, the *Generous*, (from whose house he descended) was king of *Munster* and *Archbishop* of *Cashel*, in the year 913. There was no end of eating and drinking there, and the famous *Downe Falvey* played on the harp.[60]

Two lengthy footnotes accompany this passage, giving background information on Gaelic customs and culture. Reference is made to numerous sources for Irish history that Amory is acquainted with, among them Geoffrey Keating's *Foras Feasa Ar Éirinn*. As can be observed, the primary form employed throughout the novel is not history but that of the 'anecdote' or the 'told tale'. It is a peculiar Irish form that resurfaces in the short story, especially in the twentieth-century writing of authors such as James Joyce, Benedict Kiely and John McGahern. The anecdote suggests authenticity and intimacy, operating by personalising that which is distant and abstract, making what might seem strange appear known and familiar.

Buncle is equally comfortable in Anglo-Irish company and the surroundings of the Big House world:

As I travelled once in the county of *Kildare* in *Ireland*, in the summer-time, I came into a land of flowers and blossoms, hills, woods, and shades: I saw upon an eminence a house, surrounded with the most agreeable images of rural beauties, and which appeared to be on purpose placed in that decorated spot for retirement and contemplation. It is in such silent recesses of life, that we can best enjoy the *noble* and *felicitous* ideas, which more immediately concern the attention of man, and in the *cool hours* of reflection, secreted from the fancies and follies, the business, the faction, and the pleasures of an engaged world, thoroughly consider the wisdom and harmony of the works of nature, the important purposes of providence, and the various reasons we have to adore that ever glorious *Being*, who formed us for rational happiness here, and after we have passed a few years on this sphere, in a *life* of *virtue* and *charity*, to translate us to the realms of endless bliss. Happy they who have a taste for these silent retreats, and when they please, can withdraw for a time from the world.[61]

There are, to be sure, stark contrasts to be made between the worlds of Gaelic and Anglo-Irish life: the Gaelic scene appears unrestrained and obviously less formal than the refinement of the Anglo-Irish Big House. And yet, neither is privileged above the other: both exist, both are worth experiencing; they are different but have equal value.

Celebration is central to Amory's vision, as is the need for the time to celebrate. His utterly democratic fiction joyously engages with the world of ideas and philosophy, the world of science and technology, the antiquarian Gaelic world: everything has worth and wonder, and everything is deserving of his observation. Amory does not ignore the darker side of life either: a tale of murder is recounted – a true story from early 1700s Dublin, and his own family life is not one of bliss as domestic stability is constantly being denied: his wives keep on dying; and his father leaves his estate, not as one would expect to Buncle but rather to a close relative.[62] It might be argued that the constant frustrating of his desire for matrimonial happiness and the comforts of home sets him adrift, forcing him to wander through Ireland and Britain. Nonetheless, life is worth living: life is an absolute in itself and Amory's novel indicates the primacy of sharing that experience through acts of storytelling. At a time in Ireland, as elsewhere, when entertainment and diversion was becoming increasingly organised and refined for the elite of society – the Phoenix Park, for instance, as a place of pleasure was opened in 1747 and the drawing room scene was still the height of respectability – Amory rejoices in the chance encounter, the moment of diversion and the titbit of knowledge and information. In other words, he embraces the possibility of chance and chaos and this is mirrored in the formlessness of his novel.

Amory desires that Time itself be slowed down, if not stopped completely, in order that life can be savoured and enjoyed. He fears an encroaching modernity that will challenge this notion of leisure. In a period when much fiction writing is busy with rendering melodramatic incident, with the incredible and the exotic, with heightened sensibility and quickening emotion, Thomas Amory's novel quietly affirms that ordinary life – lived slowly – is truly extraordinary. However, the prevalence of the anecdote in the novel highlights the perils of nostalgia, of revealing the world as represented as already being of the past and but a memory in the present. This concern with Time is shared throughout the seventeenth and eighteenth centuries with the Gaelic poets who lamented the loss of the forests throughout Ireland:

> Now what will we do for timber,
> with the last of the woods laid low?[63]

There is an obvious symbolism at work here with the woods representing the political downfall of the old Gaelic aristocratic order.[64] The loss of the woods registers the loss of so much else in Gaelic culture. What the poem really registers, though, is the newness of the Irish world. The landscape must have looked decidedly strange to the native Irish, the bare countryside – being seen for the very first time – reflecting the sense of exposure and powerlessness in the face of this new way of living. The felling of the forests registers also that traditional Time is itself ripped open and exploded. The forests had been there always: suggesting that the Gaelic life they represent had no beginning and no end. Now, with their destruction, a new conception of Time and of culture as something open to change and transformation comes into being. It can be argued that Gaelic culture is in a permanent state of apocalyptic crisis and collapse during this period. The flight of the earls in 1607, the Cromwellian settlements of 1649 onwards, the events of the Battle of the Boyne and Aughrim of 1690 – each signal one more stage in a long, slow decline in status and authority. And yet, the end never finally or definitively arrived, the culture carrying on in new, often reinvigorated ways.[65] Thus, at the very moment when this culture and tradition is under most threat of extinction, it re-energises itself, reimagines itself in order to exist in this new dispensation. Aogán Ó Rathaille in a poem written during his last illness declares:

> Wave-shaken is my brain, my chief hope gone.
> There's a hole in my gut, there are foul spikes through my bowels.
> Our land, our shelter, our woods and our level ways
> are pawned for a penny by a crew from the land of Dover.[66]

Equating his dying body with the destroyed landscape unites communal concerns with the personal. This manoeuvre is one way in which Gaelic poetry developed in the face of change: bringing a personal and individualistic note to what had been traditionally a communal medium, thereby energising the poetry with authentic and real emotion.[67] It is also recognition that in the modern world the site of subversion and possibility is increasingly in that inner realm, beyond the watch and control of wider society.

The ambivalent attitude to Time witnessed in Thomas Amory's writing and in the Gaelic poetry of the period also underpins Laurence Sterne's (1713–68) *The Life and Opinions of Tristram Shandy* (1759–67). *Don Quixote* haunts the writers of this moment because Cervantes achieved – seemingly effortlessly – all that was possible with the new novel form. There is a joy central in Cervantes's work that can be observed, too, in the manner by which Laurence Sterne also plays with the possibilities of the novel. Formally *Tristram Shandy* is a tour de force, dismantling the conventions of the novel, just as the novel form is itself beginning to codify and solidify.[68] Indeed, its widespread popular success can be attributed to how well readers were attuned to what was expected from the novel, thrilling at the ways in which Sterne expertly mocked those expectations. Sterne himself put no emphasis on his Irish roots whatsoever, nonetheless there is a sense in which Sterne's beginnings on the margins of the metropolitan centre afford him the opportunity of analysing and deconstructing the nascent novel form, as only an outsider can do. Everything about the novel form is called into question: its supposed transparency and claims to knowledge and realism – its being a clear lens through which the world can be seen – are undermined. Notions of plot and character are also cleverly and persistently challenged. The hero Tristram, for example, does not appear until volume three of the novel. So, just as the novel appears to be *the* form through which modernity can be engaged with and dealt with, Sterne demonstrates how impossible the form actually is in its relationship to the real world. This is a novel about beginning and beginnings: when exactly do Tristram's 'life' and 'opinions' actually have their source, how far back does the author have to go in order to get to the point of origin? But it is also a novel about how to begin writing a novel. *Tristram Shandy* thus parodies the obsessions and concerns of the established modern novel in that it truly does deal with the everyday, the mundane and the domestic scene in unrelenting detail. It is a timely reminder to its readers, and to other writers, about the precariousness, and the relative newness, of the form.

Time, itself, is a main focus in the novel in that Sterne recognises the gap between the writer writing and what is written, and the impossibility of bridging that gap: words – language – are powerful, to be sure, but in the end they only distance us from that which they supposedly bring us closer to. Thus, beneath the virtuoso linguistic and formal performance, lurks a very dark reality: ideas about objectivity, truth, universal knowledge – those ideas underpinning the Enlightenment revolution are exposed as mere ciphers. Perhaps that is the Irish influence: a distrust of the medium itself – a playful attitude to it, mocking it – or taking the Mick out of it, gently alerting the reader to its limits and its impossibilities. For instance, we never get beyond the childhood of Tristram, and, of course, it takes so long for him to appear at all. It is as if a fear persists concerning the unpredictability of the present and the future, thus the retreat into childhood signals a wish not to get involved in the adult world of action and decision-making. Uncle Toby, too, is a child-like character, caught up with re-enactment, rather than acting, caught up with endlessly reliving the past – in minute detail – rather than imagining a future. Thus, at a time in Ireland when those in power are beginning to project into the future, beginning to assert influence in many ways – from the wide streets commission, to economic and political reform – Sterne offers a story of sterility, of entrapment because a concern with arrested development is an admission of stalled aspiration, of incomplete and thwarted desire.

Despite it being a self-declared Cock and Bull story, this is a novel – through the character of Toby especially – which gently celebrates the power of emotion and fellow feeling between people. While Tristram Shandy himself remains unknown, the reader does get to know a great deal about his father and his Uncle Toby and his manservant Trim. Without knowing it, perhaps, Sterne – like his great hero Cervantes in his novel *Don Quixote* – eulogises the past and a previous generation, rather than giving birth to a future. Ironically, in order to do just this, he is obliged to tear asunder the very form – the novel – that gestures towards and encapsulates that future. Cervantes is important, too, because his novel *Don Quixote* recognises the centrality of human feeling and emotion. Quixote looks back to the heightened emotions of the medieval knights because he observes mediocrity in his own time. What English writers of the sentimental period take from Cervantes is that stress on the centrality of feeling, and, importantly, feeling being open to all men and women, regardless of position or class. The rise of the sentimental novel throughout the eighteenth century is a wonder to behold, but inevitable in many ways. With the publication of John Locke's *An Essay Concerning Human Understanding* (1689) and *Two Treatises of Government* (1689), and then David Hume's *Treatise on Human Nature* (1739), the shift towards individual human feeling is brought centre stage in gauging modern 'humanity' and levels of modern humanness. Feeling is now the basis for Western society's conception of itself: ideas such as compassion, virtue, modesty, sympathy and taste come to be the cornerstone of the individual and the individual's relationship to others. Everything, including nature and the landscape, becomes a means of inciting and evaluating emotion. It does not take a great leap of the imagination to realise the central role of the novel form in perpetuating this cult of sensibility: the novel is *the* form that can truly render this shift towards the human as the measure of all. The novel's plot, in many ways, is merely a conduit for the display of heightened emotions and feelings: a character's worth is no longer centred round what they do, but rather how they feel. Outer action is replaced by inner turmoil. Of course, such sentiment cannot remain private for long and must make itself manifest in the public sphere; indeed, many storylines take that movement outward as their basic premise and thus, sensation, emotion and all that that entails becomes its own begetter, its own reason for the story being told at all.

In this light, Frances Sheridan's (1724–66) *Memoirs of Miss Sidney Bidulph* (1761) was a highly successful novel within the genre of sentimental writing. Sheridan was the wife of actor and theatre manager Thomas Sheridan and mother of Richard Brinsley Sheridan. The novel focuses on a heroine who must suffer the extreme indignities of a ruined love affair and the reader is rewarded with a character whose virtue remains incorruptible in an extremely corrupt world. The emphasis is very much on distress and suffering and how these misfortunes can be met and overcome. The marginal position of women at this point in time is clearly delineated: Sidney Bidulph is distressingly at the mercy of her lover, Anglo-Irish landowner Orlando Faulkland. From an Irish perspective, there are a number of issues manifested particularly in this novel that says much about the Anglo-Irish community's conception of itself at this juncture. It is important that the sentimental novel is possible for Anglo-Ireland, for the Anglo-Irish must be seen as capable of feeling, emotion and sentiment, as is everybody else: proving their worth and their common humanity. There are numerous novels in this sentimental mode. Each is focused on individuals and on families, eschewing any sense of a wider political or contextual world of issues and problems that might have to be confronted. Ireland appears only insofar as there are descriptions of the native peasant Irish, suitably subservient and ultimately insignificant to the development and the fetishisation of feeling that is the main focus.

The other feature of interest with *Memoirs of Miss Sidney Bidulph* is how it manifests the motif of travel and journeying that is such a central feature of Irish novel writing at this time specifically. Characters here are constantly on the move, certainly within Ireland itself, but also importantly between the spaces of Ireland and Britain. In Sheridan's novel, Orlando Faulkland makes an excursion to his estates in Ireland, which situates him as a stereotypical absentee landlord, happy to play in the spas of Brighton and Hastings with the income generated from Irish land. More importantly, however, all this movement reflects the reality of metropolitan power being very firmly centred on England and London. Characters, therefore, are obviously drawn to that centre where action and incident of seeming significance can occur. Ireland, unsurprisingly, is located determinedly on the periphery of such power and authority.

Taken as a whole, novels of this period suggest a desire by their authors (and their readers) to be recognised as connected to the wider cosmopolitan world of feeling and of power: similarity rather than difference is what is being stressed. These novels demonstrate, too, a developing sense of the rituals of middle- and upper-class Irish life becoming increasingly solidified from the 1750s onwards. Novels of the period trace the boundaries of Anglo-Irish life with known, rigid limits and spaces described. The country-seat is one such place, as is Dublin – visited as the centre of colonial rule within Ireland itself offering what is being described as a 'congenial round' of places to meet, congregate and socialise.[69] And, of course, there is the life to be experienced in London and also Bath and other English towns. Nevertheless it can be suggested that what is really at the heart of such imagery is an underlying restlessness within the Anglo-Irish ruling classes, who seem perpetually driven to search for an adequate 'place' that they might feel comfortable occupying, forever shunting between the Irish countryside, Dublin and then London and elsewhere. Significantly, Ireland as home is never presented as the final destination.

Richard and Elizabeth Griffith's *A series of Genuine Letters Between Henry and Frances* (Dublin: 1757–66) plainly demonstrates this desire for sentimental feeling among the Anglo-Irish community. This semi-autobiographical fiction, based on the courtship letters of the two lovers, is intended for the moral benefit of the reader. Critics have noted how Frances's letters concern themselves with marking out possible roles for women as intellectuals and wage earners.[70] Of particular interest, though, is how these letters – this novel – celebrate the inner world of sensation and feeling above the outer, public realm of action and politics. Characters are presented observing those about them, placing them in terms of their knowledge of what is tasteful and acceptable: all of which emanates from the metropolitan centre. When those ideas are applied to an Irish setting inevitably it is a failure: 'nay, I have seen Portico's in Ireland built to the North, and winter summer houses in gardens, with very comfortable fireplaces in them' (pp. 239–240). And even when sensibility is present, there is a want in terms of its realisation: 'This man had observation, but wanted the sense of application' (p. 240). Throughout the novel there is much consideration of literature and philosophy. Henry feels that *Tom Jones* is 'a true copy of human life' (p. 205). The novel becomes a reading list for those who might want to develop their taste and their sensibility: Montaigne is mentioned, as is the work of John Locke. The underlying message is that anyone can be a moralist, a philosopher and a thinker: once they cultivate their minds through education in all matters of taste. As Henry opines: 'All the ideas we have in common with Brutes, I will allow we may acquire, as they do – but no farther' (p. 256). Education is central to this potential transformation.

Experiences that might further ignite emotion are actively sought out. Henry is involved, owing to his status as a landowner, in some Assizes in Kilkenny. He desires to encounter a condemned man so that he may know how he feels as he meets his death. Such moments offer him an opportunity that might 'occasion some useful Reflections' (p. 324). Henry travels the length and breadth of Ireland, observing new techniques and new technology at work in Irish industry and agriculture. Ireland is a place of possibility: not only in the realm of the material and economic, but also – quite obviously – in relation to the development of fine feeling and sentiment. Nothing seems to get in the way of that ongoing project: 'There are forty-seven women and fourteen men, at work round about me, while I am reading Pliny, and writing to you' (p. 334). It seems the Enlightenment project is limited to those happy few who have the secure economic base from which to make that intellectual journey. The kind of restlessness on view in other novels appears absent here, as Ireland is presented as a place of possibility and potential, becoming in the process the premier site of home.

Oliver Goldsmith's (1728–74) *The Vicar of Wakefield* (1766) is also concerned with the sphere of sentiment. Usually read as a parody of the excesses of mid-eighteenth-century popular sentimental fiction, there is still evident at work within the novel a strong strain of nostalgia. In many ways, the hero of the novel – Dr Primrose – is a man out of place and out of time. His hopes for himself and his family are summed up in a vision of edenic plenty and quiet ease, among a people who: 'Remote from the polite, they still retained the primeval simplicity of manners and frugal by habit, they scarce knew that temperance was a virtue. They wrought with cheerfulness on days of labour; but observed festivals as intervals of idleness and pleasure.'[71] Of course, such a life is not possible and the plot of the novel sees all his hopes dashed in the face of an encroaching modernity that lays waste to his world of traditional morals and manners. At times it seems this is a novel with a moral message, offering readers ideas about how life ought to be lived. The problem is that with this emphasis on the 'ought', the lasting suspicion is that is exactly how life is *not* being lived.

Certainly, connections with Ireland as a rural paradise, a pastoral world lived at a slower, less maddeningly progressive pace, can be positively made and the novel acts as a counterpoint to those writers and readers who look to the city as the only site of potential. Everyone is happy in their allotted place: workers and elites live happily and productively side by side. As W. B. Yeats would later write: 'Oliver Goldsmith sang what he had seen, / Roads full of beggars, cattle in the fields, / But never saw the trefoil stained with blood, / The avenging leaf those fields raised up against it.'[72] A happy ending is offered at the close but it is a fairytale conclusion. The lingering sense of an older world of order and rigid class structure coming under serious threat, if not actually disappeared, is what remains.

A more sober novel of this period is *The Fool of Quality; or, the History of Henry, Earl of Moreland* (1765–70) by Henry Brooke (1703?–83), now more famous for being the father of Charlotte Brooke (1740?–93) whose *Reliques of Irish Poetry* (1789) became such a central text in the late eighteenth-century popular revival in Gaelic culture and literature. Heavily influenced by the writings of Rousseau, the importance of education in the improvement and development of the individual is paramount; the relevance of this novel to the Irish situation could not have been lost on contemporary readers. His satire, too, shows the influence of both Sterne and Swift. Again, though, as with the earlier novels of improvement exemplified by William Chaigneau's *The History of Jack Connor*, the issue of the possibility of re-educating and including Catholics into this new world remains problematic within the confines of he novel, as well as in the real world.

If the sentimental novel – as a fictional and recreational offshoot of Enlightenment thinking – intimates a developing world and a developing humanity moving towards possible perfection, the harsh realities of Irish life explode such sanguine conclusions. The development of a Catholic merchant class, as well as the remnants of a Catholic and Gaelic aristocracy, ensured that the thorny problem of the exclusionary and sectarian penal laws become more pronounced in the latter half of the eighteenth century. It has been estimated that between 1704 and 1784 about 5,500 Catholics changed religion.[73] No matter what the reason for such conversions, it is, in truth, a tiny figure in terms of the growing population of Ireland throughout the eighteenth century. The figure highlights, on the one hand, the steadfastness of Catholics of all classes in their religion and, on the other, the uncertainty of the Protestant project in colonial Ireland: if conversion and cultural modernisation of the native population was not being carried out, what then is the purpose of artificially skewing politics in the way that it was throughout the eighteenth century?

The Catholic Committee was formed in 1758 by, among others, Roscommon landowner, amateur historian and antiquarian Charles

O'Connor, opening up a civic space for 'secular Catholic loyalism to the House of Hanover'.[74] Even with this attempt to enter into the world of civic responsibility and thereby the world of sentiment, Ireland was still beset with the very real issue of agrarian unrest with the rise of the Whiteboys and other such groups in, especially, Munster. Thus the realms of culture and lived economic experience throw up varying ideas of what Ireland is and might be. On the one hand, among the marginalised Gaelic aristocracy is a desire to enter into the society that has excluded them, a wish to enter – or re-enter – the world of feeling. On the other hand, there is a world where sentiment and feeling are thoroughly absent and the only means possible of trying to change that world is through violence. Importantly of course, such a debate between the claims of civility and barbarity are not confined merely to one section of Irish society. The Anglo-Irish response to agrarian unrest – and perhaps on an unconscious level a response to the mounting claims for Catholics to be admitted to the body politic – sees the execution of the palpably innocent Father Nicholas Sheehy in Clonmel in 1766 for alleged association with Whiteboyism. His head was impaled on a spike outside the Main Guard in Clonmel for twenty years.

It would seem, then, that the darker underbelly to the Enlightenment knowledge and culture, that which was denied and driven underground, evident all over Europe was perhaps most patently manifest in an Irish setting. This dark side of Enlightenment is precisely that which novelist Charles Johnstone (1719?–1800) deals with in the work he is chiefly remembered now for: *Chrysal; or, The Adventures of a Guinea* (1760–65). Hugely successful and popular in its own time, this novel of circulation – in this instance using the device of a coin, the guinea of the title – Johnstone casts his cynical eye over the world of base men and women. The object of the coin allows him the opportunity to range far and wide, high and low in society, in order that he may observe how all humankind is much the same, united in their avarice and small-mindedness. His novel is an antidote to the celebration of sense and sensibility found elsewhere. Ireland is not Eden, but a place of material opportunity: it is said of Irish peerage titles that they are the 'constant refuge of those sons of fortune, who not being born in the rank of gentlemen, or having forfeited it . . . want to change their name' (vol. II, p. 42). As is usual with a novel of this type, Johnstone's characters are based on real people and thus his fiction becomes a means of commenting on events and personages in the real world. No one person or character emerges with much to recommend them; all humankind is seen to be utterly irredeemable. A later novel of Johnstone's does deal with Ireland. *The Adventures of Anthony Varnish* (1786) is a mad picaresque tale with the eponymous Anthony meeting a motley array of soldiers and thieves, and even some bears and a baboon, on his journey through Ireland and England. Interestingly, Varnish is not identifiable as Irish or Anglo-Irish, Protestant or Catholic: perhaps he is all of them simultaneously. What is observable here is that constant confusion of the Anglo-Irish in England as Irish, highlighting their difficulty in differentiating themselves, or projecting a viable collective sense of identity.[75]

One of the more interesting sentimental novels of this time is Dorothea Du Bois's (1728–74), *Theodora: A Novel* (1770). In an oblique way, it is a comment on the dilemma of who exactly may have access to sentiment. Semi-autobiographical (Theodora is an anagram of Dorothea), it traces the growth and development of Theodora in quite conventional novelistic terms. Her father leaves her mother and remarries, thus bringing issues of legitimacy and illegitimacy to the fore and one interpretation suggests that it celebrates the feminine sphere of the domestic and the solidarity of women who stand against the brute individuality of men.[76] Two sections, however, show up the complexity and the nuances of sentiment and sympathy in an Irish context, highlighting the centrality of power and authority in delineating who exactly is permitted access to modern feeling and emotion. A depiction of an Irish peasant woman – a midwife – offers the reader a glimpse of radical difference in an Irish setting:

> This room was hung with tapestry, the figures as large as life. At first view of them she started back, crying, By my own sweet soul, agrah, I won't go into place where there is so many fine gentry … The servants eased her scruples with regard to the fine gentry, by putting her hand upon the tapestry. This again excited her wonder. Faith, honey, says she, I did not think they were dead people, I thought they were all alive.[77]

The mirth of those gathered together forces the Irish woman to retreat into her own space, enraged at being laughed at: 'she squatted herself down on her haunches by the fire-side, pulled out of her bosom a tobacco-pipe of about two inches in length, black as jet, which she set fire to, and began to smoke so furiously, that she almost suffocate the poor Baroness' (*ibid.*). This image of isolation is telling, as is her confusion when confronted with the tapestry. The meaning is obvious: the old Irish woman is unable to appreciate 'representation'. She possesses no feeling or sympathy for art and its relationship to the real world. She is aware, though, of being patronised and sets herself apart from the others, disengaging herself from their community as a form of rebuke.

Much later, however, Theodora on a trip to Cork has a revelation by the River Lee:

The rocks impending over the smooth surface of a beautiful meandering river, clad by nature with a variety of shrubs, which hang over the wide mouths of the hollow caverns, as if to hide the peaceful retreat of some poor wretched being, detached from all the follies of a busy inconsiderate world on top of a stupendous hill, whose craggy sides are almost inaccessible, stands the beautiful ruins of a castle, or rather a fort . . . a few roods from it, see an ancient church, whose thick and solid walls seem to defy the levelling hand of time. Beneath this hill, a cottage, neat but homely . . . (a mill is nearby) whose awful stroke beats time to the melancholy murmurs of its forced stream. Over this, a little bridge is fixed, which affords a communication with an extensive common, whose verdant carpet, embellished with daisies, primroses, violets, and butterflowers, yields a delightful prospect to the contemplative eye, while the swelling river cutting its way thro' it, adds amazingly to its beauty. (pp. 246–247)

It is a moment, not unlike many such moments in the fiction of this period, when the landscape and the individual consciousness merge in a sublime instant. Increasingly in Irish writing in the nineteenth century, such moments of powerful connection between the seer and the landscape become a means of beginning to celebrate the Irish locale as something distinct, and worthy, from the metropolitan and increasingly urban centre. It is a remarkable passage when contrasted with the earlier one. Immanuel Kant ushered in the modern consciousness with his idea of how the world and mind meet to create reality that is neither wholly human nor natural. Of course, his conception is a compromise that allows for an enhanced role for the human imagination, while also allowing for a world outside that imagination, a world made by God. Thus, in this passage, what the reader witnesses is the celebration not only of the beautiful landscape but also of the mind that can apprehend and truly appreciate that beauty. Theodora possesses the imagination that the peasant woman from the earlier scene does not. The human world is observed in the cottage, the castle and the bridge but it is set side by side with brute nature. The human imagination teases out the form and shape of this particular landscape, humanising the scene, bringing harmony to all its disparate elements. The use of 'as if' and 'seems' enacts this humanising process, the observer creating purpose and design in the scene. In truth, what is on show here is not the landscape, but rather the creative imagination, which makes a 'picture' out of the real.

The irony is that the Irish peasant woman thought the picture was real, but the Anglo-Irish believed the real to be a picture. In other words, nature is to be framed and natural landscape to be manufactured, placed and influenced. There can be no coincidence that the great landscaping of Anglo-Ireland, of placing the Big House in sumptuous grounds, the building of monuments and follies occurs around this time. This literary equivalent registers a number of things. The obvious difference between the civilised and the barbarian is presented in aesthetic terms: between those who can see and discern and those who do not possess such sympathy and taste. The question of power is also blatant: the modern imagination can shape the world in whatever way it might choose. Edmund Burke's analysis of the Irish situation pinpointed the centrality and the authority of language in Irish life – both materially and culturally. Words, for Burke, are extraordinary tools with powerful influence: 'Words ... [are] ... capable of being the representatives of ... natural things, and by what powers they [are] able to affect us often as strongly as the things they represent, and sometimes much more strongly.'[78] Words, in Burke's thesis, are the human link to the sublime and beautiful aspects of nature and the landscape; but, he suggests, words can go beyond the reality they allegedly connect with; words have the power – as do laws – to create new realties.

That the Irish landscape is always curiously depopulated in these images is also significant. It is a recurring feature of the romanticisation of the landscape that stands in contrast to the ever-increasing population of Ireland in the eighteenth and nineteenth centuries. Of import, at this juncture, though, is that it signals the beginning of the abandonment of the project of improving the native Irish. They are, it appears, beyond aid and assistance and the turn is now towards an engagement with the landscape, of imaginatively inhabiting it and possessing it. The Anglo-Irish now begins to emotionally connect with the place of Ireland rather than with its people. Such a manoeuvre, glimpsed in this novel, begins the long and continuing reconfiguration of the Irish landscape for both personal and political purposes. It is out of this inception that the Big House novel comes to be the paramount genre in Anglo-Irish writing, emphasising simultaneously the landscape, the house and the local.

Thus it is only in the latter half of the eighteenth century that Anglo-Irishness begins to be formulated as a distinct characteristic. As W. J. McCormack has argued, it is only in the 1780s that the appellation of 'Ascendancy' begins to gain currency within the Anglo-Irish ruling class, precisely at the moment when that group is most under threat from within Ireland and without, as the political future of the country moves inexorably towards union. Novels of this period, such as *The Irish Guardian* (1776), *The Fair Hibernian* (1789) and *The Irish Heiress* (1797),[79] as well as *Theodora*, also initiate a tentative formulation of this group, although in some cases the title suggests more about Ireland and Irishness than do the plot of the novels themselves.[80] Two novels, in particular, offer an insight into this process. The anonymously written *The*

Triumph of Prudence over Passion; or The History of Miss Mortimer and Miss Fitzgerald (Dublin: 1781) opens with a depiction of a Volunteer gathering. Members of the Protestant ruling class, in order to protect Ireland from foreign invasion, founded the Volunteer Movement in 1778. Outside the control of the British and Irish administration, the Volunteers became a focus for patriotic support: 'I think it warms ones heart, and I really pity lukewarm souls, who can see such a sight without emotion' (p. 5). This patriotic opening sets the tone for a novel that reflects the growing desire for economic and political autonomy in Ireland. Crucially, strong feeling is now linked to a notion of nation. Such independence came to pass in reality in 1782 with the advent of what has become known as Grattan's Parliament. Their position in Ireland is presented as unproblematical: happy tenants are everywhere displaying their due reverence to their social and economic superiors. What problems do exist seem eminently solvable in the sphere of politics.

One of the most popular novels of its time was Regina Maria Roche's (1764–1845) *The Children of the Abbey* (1796). It is a sprawling tale concerning the fate of two orphaned children of an Irish soldier – Amanda and Oscar – who are disinherited of their fortune by an aunt and a cousin. The story moves between Scotland, Wales and Ireland and is thus firmly located on the Celtic fringes, its Gothic undertones striving to make connections with a past and tradition beyond metropolitan and urban centres. Jarlath Killeen argues that there is a Catholic strain running through the novel at a subterranean level and that *The Children of the Abbey* points towards Ireland's future when, in the nineteenth century, Catholic Ireland will once again come into a position of power. Even the title indicates the Catholic basis for Irish and, indeed, Western culture: we are all children of the abbey.[81] More significant is Roche's use of the Irish landscape. Edmund Burke's sublime and Gothic tendencies influence the Irish novel writer's newly found enthusiasm for Ireland as a possible site for the mediation of intense and passionate emotion. Amanda's first view of Ireland prompts this response: 'To contemplate a scene which far surpassed all her ideas of sublimity and beauty, a scene which the rising sun soon heightened to the most glowing radiance.'[82] The lack of nuance or subtlety is worthy of note: landscape in general, but the Irish landscape in particular, gets its significance and worth for being such a site of feeling. It is as if the Celtic periphery has now found its role in Empire.

This role, though, is a very limited one, which fits into the general upsurge in interest in Celtic and Gaelic myth and culture from the 1770s onwards. It is one of the paradoxes of Enlightenment: the march towards reason and rationality, the fetishisation of science over all other branches of knowledge obviously spells the end of an older world and traditional routes to knowledge and understanding. Thus, Enlightenment values bring to an end oral culture, and traditional culture. Yet, it is precisely that Enlightenment drive for knowledge that feeds the reawakened interest in Gaelic poetry and culture and language among Ireland's elite. Of course, the power relationship in such a situation skews the perception of that older culture, and in this instance Ireland and Gaelic culture are always presented without any decisive energy or power in the present moment. In *The Children of the Abbey* this is seen very clearly. A visit by Amanda to Castle Carbery in the north of Ireland offers an opportunity for a Gothic interlude: a decaying castle, and a ruined abbey dominate the landscape. It is clear that the castle and what it might represent are firmly located in a past time:

As she entered a spacious hall, curiously wainscoted with oak, ornamented with coats of arms, spears, lances, and old armour, she could not avoid casting a retrospective eye to former times, when, perhaps in this very hall, bards sung the exploits of those heroes, whose useless arms now hung upon the walls. She wished, in the romance of the moment, some grey bard near her, to tell the deeds of other times – of kings renowned in our land – of chiefs we behold no more.[83]

The Irish past and its culture are exhausted. Here the objects of battle and war are merely anaemic ornaments adorning a wall. Threat and violence is located safely in a mythic, as opposed to a historical past, and is simultaneously relegated to the realm of the aesthetic: the role of the bard is to retell the glories of that now enervated culture. Not unsurprisingly, a harp arrives for Amanda a number of days later and the picture is complete.

The irony of this imagery can be noted when it is recalled that two years after the publication of this novel, in 1798, the United Irishmen uprising occurred. Thus, the positioning of threat, violence and energy in a distant past was shattered. Yet, what is truly remarkable is how this deployment of imagery persists well into the nineteenth century: the Irish landscape, the Irish language and Irish culture generally continue to be signifiers of defeat and impotence. Despite this positioning, however, what is suppressed cannot fully be ignored. On an unconscious level Roche acknowledges all that is being denied overtly within the text. For instance, the convent nearby the castle, while surrounded by ruins, is still very active within its walls. More interesting, though, is how during these moments of romantic and sentimental engagement with the landscape, Roche talks of the surrounding sea and waves murmuring quietly. The obvious link to speech acts in the word 'murmur' is of note, hinting at a steady move towards eventual and full articulacy. Thus, despite the fashioning of a culture bereft of energy and power, beneath and behind that surface broods a force that could rise and overwhelm this polite culture that, in truth, only plays with passion and deep-felt emotion.

It is the Irish novel in the nineteenth century that would begin to articulate that rise.

Beyond history: Maria Edgeworth's Castle Rackrent

In dreams begin responsibility.

(W. B. Yeats)[1]

Critic Seamus Deane declares that *Castle Rackrent* 'is . . . a work of startling incoherence'[2] and certainly, on the surface at least, it is a text that bears deeply the scars of the contextual upheavals of its creation. A major reason, if not *the* major reason, for Irish critics returning again and again to *Castle Rackrent* and its thematic and formal environs is the fortunate timing of its publication in 1800, coming as it does just two years after the violence of the 1798 rebellion and precisely at the moment when the Act of Union between Great Britain and Ireland came into being, formally and legislatively manifesting the colonial relationship between Ireland and Britain. Maria Edgeworth – in the guise of the editor in the Preface – knowingly links the novel to this moment of change, suggesting that 'When Ireland loses her identity by a union with Great Britain, she will look back with good humoured complacency' on the fecklessness of the Rackrent family.[3] The title of the novel also operates in an overly historical fashion, determinedly directing the reader to a time 'before the year 1782': the year in which 'Grattan's Parliament' came into being, ushering in a modicum of independence in Irish political affairs. Deliberately employing such a pivotal date reinforces the notion that this is a novel connected to historical change and development. Being on that crucial historical cusp means *Castle Rackrent* becomes the principal literary text for reflecting and commenting on the nature of that union, as well as being conveniently positioned to be a foundational text for modern Irish writing in general and the modern Irish novel in particular.

The textual history of the novel's creation speaks of seemingly haphazard development over many years towards a final and complete text. The early section of the novel was written in 1794–95 and the second between 1796 and 1798. Footnotes were employed from the early stages but the glossary was included only *after* the complete narrative was written.[4] In many ways, therefore, it is a novel working consciously at the level of a work-in-progress, each additional layer – palimpsest-like – covering, but not quite erasing, what has gone before it. Declan Kiberd suggests that *Castle Rackrent* is 'shorthand notes towards a novel' and that consequently the first supposed modern Irish novel could also, in actual fact, be the last owing to the manifestly provisional nature of the final text.[5]

Of real importance, though, is how *Castle Rackrent* self-consciously establishes itself as something utterly new and original. From the very outset in the Preface, Edgeworth, without explicitly articulating it, suggests that before *Castle Rackrent* there had been nothing: no novel nor memoir that might have enlightened 'the *ignorant* English reader' who will necessarily be 'totally unacquainted with Ireland' (*Castle Rackrent*, p. 4). This studied posture of novelty sets up a pervasive pattern for Irish writing, and more generally Irish culture, for the next two centuries: Ireland, its culture and its writing, is always on the cusp of an ending and a beginning, always imagining and reflecting an Irish world and an Irish reality in the process of transition. Most critical attention focuses on Thady Quirke as the narrator and his position in relation to the story he tells of the Rackrent family and their dissolute decline because nowhere in Irish fiction to this point has an Irish voice been so central to a narrative's telling. The limiting nature of Ireland's colonial position means that the truncated roles of master/servant become central to engaging with the novel.[6] Indeed, this has persisted in much of the criticism on *Castle Rackrent*, which revolves round doubts about Thady's loyalty to his social betters and the reliability, or not, of his oft-asserted attachment to the family. His own preferred label of 'Honest Thady' could, in short, be merely the public front that a disgruntled native must always wear in the colonial world. Thady's narrative traces the decline and fall of the Rackrent family over four generations. Each member of the family possesses his own peculiar vice. Sir Patrick is a drunk, next is Sir Murtagh who is highly litigious but utterly useless with the law. Then there is Sir Kit who is an absentee landlord, preferring to take whatever money the estate can generate and lose it gambling in London and Bath. The theme of mismanagement, irresponsibility and misrule continues with Sir Condy finally having to sell Castle Rackrent to Thady's son Jason who has risen in the world in inverse proportion to Condy's and the Rackrents' descent into penury.

This bare sketch of the plot does little to capture the vibrancy and pace of the narrative provided by the voice of Thady. And, of course, that voice has to be dynamic because of the very localised setting of the novel. There is no travelling in *Castle Rackrent* to divert and entertain the reader, no move to the urban space of Dublin or the metropolitan centre of London. To be sure, they are present in that the Rackrents and their wives come and go (and the wives of the Rackrents, in particular, come and go, leaving their men to wallow in their own ruination), but Thady as a narrator is rooted to the spot. This, too, is a great difference to the eighteenth-century Irish novel which placed a great deal of emphasis on the act of travel, stressing Ireland's peripheral and, at times, exotic status in relation to Britain and Europe. Voice is coupled with location, thereby fixing this as an Irish narrative.

The first part of *Castle Rackrent* is very much anecdotal, with the emphasis predominantly on eccentric incident and the outlandishness of the Rackrent men. This section possesses the tempo of a picaresque novel from an earlier age. Little time is given to delineating or developing individual emotion or sentiment: those elements that the novel, in general, at this time concerns itself with and, indeed, Irish novels up to this point were so at pains to present. The tone of the second section shifts into a somewhat more recognisable novelistic register with moments of real feeling – or the potential for real feeling – marking out Sir Condy and Thady as flesh-and-blood characters as opposed to mere ciphers. Thus, *Castle Rackrent* in its struggled movement towards the discernible modern novel form actually reads as a potted history of the novel. The moral is clear, as are the dangers of the colonial project for the coloniser who might lose touch with the Enlightenment values of empire. Perhaps the imminent union with Great Britain will halt this kind of deterioration.

Important, too, are the formal peculiarities of *Castle Rackrent*. If the narrative displays a certain developmental inchoateness, then it is the dynamic friction between Thady's tale and the paraphernalia framing and controlling it – the Preface, the footnotes and finally the Glossary – where incoherence is perhaps most fully manifest. Thomas Amory's *The Life and Opinions of John Buncle, Esq.* employed footnotes and other thoroughly modern print techniques and, from the more recent past, *The Castle of Inchvally: A Tale – alas! too true* by Stephen Collins from 1796 also makes use of footnotes to explain Irish customs to English readers. That the issue of the union between Ireland and Britain was being raised throughout the 1790s, even before the United Irishmen rebellion of 1798, suggests that such supplementary material is a formal recognition of these proposed closer political ties. Despite this precursor, *Castle Rackrent* with its overly self-conscious use of footnotes and Glossary – in many ways they become integral to the plot of the novel – thus bursts onto the literary scene and at the level of form is something new and original.

The Preface is a variation on many eighteenth-century prefaces: a plea to the reader's sensibilities concerning the benefit of novel writing and, of course, novel reading. And yet, there is more than just the usual soliciting of the reader's attention. The Preface quite clearly positions the narrative on the cusp of historical change: it is continuously made clear that the story of the Rackrents is one of 'former times', set firmly in a distant past and bearing little comparison to the present moment and, indeed, Ireland's hoped-for future. The notes and explanations reinforce this message: they are there to explain the past to the present, and to explain Ireland to England and in the process suggesting that Ireland's backwardness is also of the past. Edgeworth, in a startlingly modernist move – a move that James Joyce would repeat again a century later – initiates her own tradition: ignoring all that has gone before, staking a claim for the complete originality and innovation of her own work. The presence of these footnotes and Glossary indicates how Ireland is entering into history, or certainly a new phase in its history. *Castle Rackrent* thus announces the start of modern Irish history. A new world requires new ways to view it and render it. Even the conceit of Thady's oral tale being transcribed by the editor enacts this shift from one culture to another: from the oral to the written, from the ancient to the modern.

Central to understanding the use of the footnotes and the Glossary is the issue of power: who wields it and who is on the receiving end of that relationship. Without doubt, the most attractive reading of the novel sees the framing discourse of footnotes, Preface and Glossary as an attempt to control Thady's voice – 'regulating and supervising',[7] 'restraining and governing'[8] it in order to prioritise the written over the oral, the rational over the anecdotal, and the English language over Hiberno-English. The editorial voice and the numerous appendages mediate between Thady and the reader: ensuring that his direct voice can never fully take hold in the reader's consciousness. *Castle Rackrent* is thus doubled, reflecting in its combination of Thady's voice and the editor's perspective, the new union between Ireland and Great Britain, acknowledging that there are different audiences who will have different expectations and needs from an Irish narrative. Obviously, this arrangement gestures towards the hierarchical nature of that new legislative relationship.

Critics have outlined comprehensively the type of footnotes employed: how they deal with linguistic peculiarities, or how they enlighten the reader to various peculiarly stereotypical Irish 'characteristics', customs and attitudes.[9] The antiquarian perspective is itself part of that process of constructing Ireland as strange and had been becoming increasingly prevalent in the late eighteenth century among the Anglo-Irish Protestant class, allowing them the opportunity of safely engaging with an Irish and Gaelic culture that was now weak enough to become the object of interested observation. Thus, *Castle Rackrent* appears to not only concern itself at the level of narrative with the imminent Act of Union, but actually performs it in its juxtaposition of two opposed voices. One difficulty with this reading of *Castle Rackrent* is that it is overly prescriptive, making both voices merely pawns in an instructive fable. Each is a nonentity, a 'nobody' in terms of feelings, motives or emotions: they are simply flat characters playing out rigid predetermined roles.

Clíona Ó Gallchoir argues that it is far too easy to set up this hierarchical binary opposition of either/or between Thady and the editor.[10] To take such an easy option implies that Edgeworth is not capable of subtlety or complexity as a writer. A more productive approach is to consider not only Thady's unreliability as a narrator, but also the unreliability of the entire text. Rather than being mere non-entities, in this interpretation *Castle Rackrent's* voices – those of Thady and the editor – display sophisticated characterisation on the part of the author Edgeworth. The editor of *Castle Rackrent does* possess a distinct character and must be thought of as a character within the novel taken as a whole: he/she is not merely objective or impartial, as no editor, despite appearances to the contrary, can ever be disinterested in or detached from the main narrative they mediate. It might seem unusual then, or, indeed, even very modernist or postmodernist to begin reimagining this nineteenth-century novel as a self-conscious and multifaceted expression. Perhaps so, but the interpretation can remain consistent with what has gone before: the conflict of the hierarchical relationship is still central to the novel, but this time with more feeling and emotion being attached to both sides.[11]

All readings and meanings can now be reversed radically. For instance, if the notion of 'character' is applied to the editor, it can be seen how the alleged loquaciousness of the Irish – the tendency towards excess in speech – is actually the preserve of the editor: he/she is unable to be silent, interposing – at great length – with points of information about Irish customs and local interest. He/she shifts roles throughout: one moment being a folklore collector and then later transforming into a liberal commentator explaining the need for the application of Enlightenment values to the Irish scene. And, despite all efforts to contain and control Thady's voice, the editor ultimately fails in this objective: Thady's narrative – especially in the second part of the novel – throbs with life and energy, overwhelming the deadening charms of the tyrannical footnote.

In consequence there is a hint of failure running through the narrative. Early on in the Preface the editor declares that 'Thady's idiom is incapable of translation' (*Castle Rackrent*, p. 4). Of course, this does not deter the editor from undertaking precisely such an act of translation. But, in other ways, the characterisation of the editor becomes more apparent. It is interesting to note those points that he/she chooses *not* to explain. At the outset of Thady's narrative there is a certain instability regarding the name of Rackrent and Castle Rackrent itself: it is named Castle-Stopgap at first and evolves through Rackrent Gap to the final, fixed name of Castle Rackrent. We are also told that the Rackrents had formerly been called O'Shaughlins. That they were so suggests that they were originally Catholics who changed their religion in order to inherit property. Nowhere does the editor try to explain these moments of obvious confusion for the reader. The reader ought to be informed about these 'facts' of Irish history but perhaps the editor is involved in an act of conscious subterfuge, not wanting to acknowledge the reality of Ireland's past. In the Preface, the editor makes clear that this work aims at a truth beyond that accessible by traditional history: the knowledge gleaned from 'secret memoirs and private anecdotes' (*Castle Rackrent*, p. 1) means that the genre of fiction is just as important as history. Though, the presence of so many footnotes and glosses does suggest that the facts of history are never too far away. Still, the editor emphasises the importance of rendering 'domestic lives' and how they are a source of invaluable information about the human condition. And, indeed, Thady's tale is one such private narrative, focusing on a family through generations. In the process what becomes hidden to the reader is any sense of a public shared history: the rebellions of 1641, or 1690, the Penal Laws, Grattan's Parliament of 1782 onwards, the Volunteer movement and the United Irishmen rebellion of 1798 – each moment and event is palpable in its absence and certainly would have been for a contemporary audience. The reality of such a complex history mirrors Edgeworth's own family story and, indeed, her present position in advocating the union. Not unlike the character of her editor, her own act of assertion involves a simultaneous act of elision and a conscious disregarding of facts. For the Act of Union is a sign of failure for the Anglo-Irish: the independence of Grattan's Parliament in retrospect is seen as an unsuccessful experiment. In focusing on individuals in the way she does, Edgeworth allows a class or a group of collective politics to evade responsibility for the wounds of Irish history. Her move into fiction, therefore, is an escape into the realm of the novel, rather than a confrontation with the moral demands of history, and is a denial of history.

Many commentators read Thady as typical of the colonial relationship: his feigned loyalty masking a barely concealed contempt for the Rackrents. But perhaps his loyalty is not contrived and, in keeping with Gaelic culture, his story is a lament for a fading aristocracy.[12] He is their bard and the bardic poetry of the seventeenth and eighteenth century now finds expression through the novel form: its vulgarity being wholly appropriate in encapsulating a debased keen for what is now a degenerate nobility. And certainly the vulgarity of the novel form, in both its expression of the concerns of the common man and its attractiveness to a new middle-class readership, is important to understanding the nature of the dynamic of *Castle Rackrent*. Declan Kiberd argues, in keeping with the Burkean reading, that the Rackrents are really middle-class rather than true nobility.[13] Unquestionably their main interest is that shared by the middle-class reader: money. But, if our focus is shifted away from the status of the Rackrents towards the position of Thady's son Jason Quirke, it can be observed how appropriate this new novel form is to the story being told. For Jason represents the new middle-class man who relies on his own endeavour to gain wealth and position in society. He is a self-made man and his single-mindedness, his astuteness, his business sense and his utter lack of sentimental feeling for the 'family', in short his ruthlessness, mark him off as an Irish character who, like his father Thady, is usually read as a comic caricature. Jason is the future and – both he and that future he represents – is to be feared by Maria Edgeworth and her class. Thus the story of *Castle Rackrent* is not one of racial, cultural or sectarian conflict; rather, it is a story centring on generational conflict. Clíona Ó Gallchoir makes a convincing argument for Thady's confusion and divided loyalties with his being caught between the old feudal world and the modern world that finds expression through his son Jason. A relative of Thady's, Judy M'Quirk, dismisses any notion of a union between herself and the penniless Sir Condy: 'what signifies it to be my lady Rackrent and no Castle?' (*Castle Rackrent*, p. 92) she asks, and the answer is precisely nothing in the new dispensation ruled over by the likes of Jason. Thady is forced to reassess his worldview: 'Well, I was never so put to it in my life between these womens, and my son and my master, and all I felt and thought just now, I could not upon my conscience tell which was the wrong from the right' (*Castle Rackrent*, p. 93). It is one of the rare moments of authentic feeling and emotion within the novel precisely because of this recognition of the complexity of his situation. His painfully real confusion registers this shift into new and uncharted territory and it is the novel that allows such a movement to find expression.

Thus, in many ways, the story told by Thady undermines the attempt at poise and almost academic indifference employed by the editor and, despite his/her best efforts, a real story does emerge from the pages of *Castle Rackrent*. That this friction is a reflection of that moment of literal historical change seems clear. Perhaps not so obvious is how *Castle Rackrent* is a text intersecting with major developments in Enlightenment and romantic ideology.[14] The Edgeworths themselves were imbued with Enlightenment and romantic values. Their interest in their estate in Ireland was based on the principles of matter-of-fact improvement and husbandry but they were, as is evidenced by both Maria and her father Richard's various writings, concerned with a more all-encompassing application of Enlightenment philosophy at the level of culture and education as well as economics and agriculture. What is being played out, then, in the relationship between Thady and the editor in *Castle Rackrent* is a commentary on the fate of these Enlightenment and romantic values in an Irish context.

One of the effects of this is that an economy of knowledge underpins this relationship. The editor must mediate between Thady and the reader, framing his narrative, giving it a context that will make it understandable and palatable to a supposedly refined readership. Thady, and the Irish generally, will always be at a disadvantage because unlike the possessor of a romantic imagination, he and they can never fully know or appreciate the world that they inhabit or, indeed, the stories they tell about that world. It is one of the ironies of Irish writing which celebrates the romantic engagement with Irish culture and the Irish landscape in particular that romanticism, in fact, is debilitating in an Irish context.

Critics, who perhaps unconsciously embody those Enlightenment values in their persistent desire to be sure and certain of his motives, focus on whether Thady knows the significance of the story he tells. Is he both the teller of the story of Rackrent ruin *and* a player in that unfolding drama, intentionally involving himself for the sake of his son Jason? The difficulty, of course, centres on his way of speaking, on his use of language: can he be trusted to know the significance of the story he tells? The editor as an authority figure and as, particularly, an antiquarian embodies the curious doubleness of Enlightenment – as with the doubleness inherent in its cultural by-product, romanticism – in that it both destroys that which it overcomes – traditional modes of living and thinking – while simultaneously preserving that older world in the form of knowledge. In giving voice to that which has been denied and relegated to the realm of silence till now, the editor and, indeed Edgeworth, cannot foresee fully the repercussions of such an act. In other words, though the creation of Thady is initiated as an act from a position of control and authority, unruly disruptive forces are unleashed that go far beyond authorial intention or control. Thus, the liberal Enlightenment agenda undermines itself, as does romanticism, because it gives space and voice to that which it potentially cannot contain and control.

Ultimately this is what is most interesting and significant about *Castle Rackrent*: its doubtlessness, scepticism and its schizophrenia – basically, the radical undecidability about the status of both main voices, or characters, within the novel. The epistemological anxieties about knowledge and who is really in control permeate out from the story itself to infect the ontological status of the entire text. Essentially, *Castle Rackrent* does not really possess a clear sense of what it is: novel, history, handbook to the traits and customs of the Irish nation – it is all of these, and none of these, simultaneously. Nothing is finally resolved by the close of the novel. The nervousness of the final editorial comments about whether the approaching union 'will hasten or retard the amelioration of this country' (*Castle Rackrent*, p. 97) sums up this pervasive apprehension: perhaps Union will not bring about changes for the better after all? The final attempt at a joke is an uneasy one: 'Did the Warwickshire militia, who were chiefly artisans, teach the Irish to drink beer, or did they learn from the Irish to drink whisky?' (*Castle Rackrent*, p. 97). The potential for cultural interchange is certainly present in the prospect of the union between Britain and Ireland but nothing within Edgeworth's novel would leave a reader to believe that it is to be a union of equals. This final reference highlights the lingering suspicion that the union will be a forced one. For, despite their being artisans (a curious detail to include, raising the question of what are the mere Irish in comparison, what label other than servant can they employ?), these men from Warwickshire came as a part of a military operation.

That Maria Edgeworth never again in her fiction returned to a voice like that of Thady Quirke – so dangerously ambiguous/ambivalent – suggests her own awareness of its potential for rupturing the basis of the relationships as they stood within Ireland at the turn of the century. But perhaps the more important character in retrospect is his son Jason. Famously Edgeworth wrote in the 1830s:

It is impossible to draw Ireland as she now is in a book of fiction – realities are too strong, party passions too violent to bear to see, or care to look at their faces in the looking-glass. The people would only break the glass, and curse the fool who held the mirror up to nature – distorted nature, in a fever.[15]

This is an oft-repeated summation of the status of Irish fiction for literary critics on the hunt for realism in the nineteenth-century Irish novel. Of course, for Edgeworth this problem with realism only emerges when the Catholic nation becomes publicly and collectively heard in the 1830s under the stewardship of Daniel O'Connell and his campaign for Catholic emancipation. While *Castle Rackrent* anticipated this emergence decades earlier with the voice of Thady, it is really Jason who is set to inherit the benefits of political recognition.

One major consequence of a novel which centralises thematically the possession of knowledge and, particularly, the antiquarian position, is that anything that might exist outside that system of knowledge, which does not conform to what is already known, remains shadowy and beyond control. Thus, while the reader comes to know Thady and while the editor forces us to know various aspects of Irish culture, Jason escapes being fully drawn and fully known beyond the bare minimum. Joep Leerssen argues that *Castle Rackrent* and other novels of the period reflect nineteenth-century Ireland's position as always already the exotic other: an object to be observed with all the attendant forms and methodology from that cosmopolitan perspective.[16] The difficulty with this theory is that when the object of knowledge refuses to correspond to this preordained template, then dealing with it becomes seriously problematic. In other words, Edgeworth's complaint in the 1830s is about how the Irish are no longer conforming to type. Indeed, as she says 'realities are too strong': but the actual problem is that the Irish now have control of the mirror and are beginning to imagine and create their own realities. The Jasons of this world are content to allow images of the Irish as feckless and comic to perpetuate: it is a distraction permitting him to get on with the task of bettering his lot. That type of Irish person is beyond any knowledge and is therefore truly threatening and truly dangerous.

CHAPTER 2

Speak not my name; or, the wings of Minerva: Irish fiction, 1800–91

> The owl of Minerva spreads its wings only with the falling of the dusk.
> (G. W. F. Hegel, *The Philosophy of Right*)

The dominant paradigm of the nineteenth century in the Western world is one of progression and development. G. W. F. Hegel and his intellectual disciple Karl Marx theorised development on a number of philosophical and economic levels. Charles Darwin, too, famously based man's development on more material and prosaic grounds. In short, progress and progression pervade all levels of thought and existence from the individual to the social and the national. So central is this idea to Western thought that Hegel could declare that those places – such as the entire African continent – which did not share in this narrative of development and progression had 'no historical part of the World; [having] no movement or development to exhibit'.[1] Such regions were outside history. And yet Hegel's words express, perhaps, the opposite of intended superiority, suggesting not the boundless possibilities but rather the limits of Western knowledge. In other words, something *is* going on in a place such as Africa but the West can never know of it or express it because it will always be beyond its thought processes, its system of knowing. Such an interpretation – perhaps only possible in retrospect – moves colonial relationships beyond the merely binary and opens up a more complicated notion of the interactions between differing cultures.

Ireland's position in relation to this paradigm is an interesting one, reflecting the local and particular concerns of an Irish experience of progress and development.[2] Certainly the Act of Union, which comes into effect in 1801, signals a new beginning for Ireland's political status: a clear break with the past and a reorientation towards the future. Or so it would seem. One problem with this easy interpretation, of course, is that union with Britain shifts power and authority to London – thus the future and all that it entails is always somewhere else. Ireland during the nineteenth century is always already outside history, attempting to catch up. With this backdrop of progress being all-pervasive, the representation and stereotyping of Ireland and the Irish, by insiders and outsiders, throughout the nineteenth century are remarkably consistent: linguistically, culturally and emotionally the Irish remain somehow benighted, incapable of entering fully into the benefits of modernity. Emphasising this lack of complexity within the Irish character and Irish culture is the predominance of the desire to 'explain' Ireland to a wider audience, reducing subtleties to types and easy categories that leave no room for ambiguity. Indeed, the novel form at this moment particularly struggles in relation to this paradigm, unable to embrace the human sphere which always seems just beyond articulation as the grand narrative of history becomes central.

The other difficulty with reading Ireland as a simple case of either/or thinking is that running in tandem with the paradigm of progress and development is one of suppression: to move into the future means that the past and all that is associated with the past must be driven underground and denied. And this is true for both Ireland's ancient Gaelic past *and* Ireland's more recent past. The closure of Grattan's Parliament, the United Irishmen rebellion of 1798 and the Act of Union in 1800 obviously signal, on a variety of levels, endings and beginnings. Yet, this catalogue of recent events is shot through with an overarching impression of failure that can only be associated with Anglo-Irish rule. They had singularly failed to allow the majority of the population to begin to share in the possibilities of democracy and, in doing so, they failed to hold on to power for themselves. The implications for the reading of the nineteenth-century Irish novel and the Irish novel in general are varied. The most noticeable shift is that there is now a peculiar urgency to the notion that Ireland and the Irish have to be explained to a wider audience. Indeed, it becomes an absolute necessity to such an extent that the narratives of many novels of the early nineteenth century are almost overwhelmed by the disruptive inclusion of footnotes that point to a world of facts and realities outside the realm of fiction. Indeed, the question of realism as the prevailing mode of fiction generally is bound up in Ireland with this paradigm of progress,[3] with the nineteenth-century novel traditionally being read as one that enacts the move from illusion to reality, from fantasy to fact, and from myth to history.

Maria Edgeworth's famous claim concerning the impossibility of an Irish novel suggested that the novel was hijacked by propagandists who used the form to further their own agendas – meaning aesthetic considerations became secondary to political machinations. Edgeworth's own fiction after the brilliantly subversive *Castle Rackrent* never returned to the possibilities of the Irish voice on display there. Her subsequent Irish fiction can be read, keeping in mind her own comments on propaganda, as an attempt to shore up the ruins of the post-union Anglo-Irish presence in Ireland. Ireland is once again presented as an ongoing project to be worked on and improved. The message to the English and, more importantly, to the Anglo-Irish reader is that this improvement will only come about if the Anglo-Irish regain the initiative lost in the enacting of political union and become, once again, cultural and economic leaders. *The Absentee* (1812) is quite clearly message-driven: the young hero, Lord Colambre, chooses to return to Ireland and his family's estates and to begin to work the land for everyone's benefit. He undertakes a tour, incognito, of well-managed and not-so-well-managed estates, allowing an image of post-union Ireland to emerge. It is an often downbeat picture: political and cultural authority resides – as the title might suggest – elsewhere. Nonetheless, it is acknowledged that there is a burgeoning new middle-classes stratum who are adept at making money: 'commerce rose in to the vacated seats of rank',[4] threatening the traditional power structures of the landed gentry. Revisionist historians make much of the fact that post-union Ireland was a place of economic opportunity: Edgeworth is aware of this but sees Ireland's problems at the level of culture and, importantly, blames the vacuum of authority and power that the union produces. If there is no transcendent guiding principle at work behind the action of making money, it becomes a meaningless and empty pursuit.

The shape and motifs of the novel permit the expected scenes of cultural clash and cultural comparison to occur. Count O'Halloran, based on the real-life Sylvester O'Halloran (a Catholic landowner and Gaelic antiquarian from the eighteenth century), offers access to the Irish perspective, with his home being presented as a museum of Irish collectibles. His home is also, bizarrely, a menagerie of goats, birds and dogs adding to the oddity and grotesque nature of the Irish world, putting pressure on any sense of its normalcy and undermining a comforting realism. The reader is being offered a glimpse of a future Darwinian vision of bestiality with Ireland being transformed into an open-air zoo. As with the character King Corny of the Black Islands in the later *Ormond* (1817), the Gaelic Irish who are worthy of mention are faded aristocrats living a half-lit liminal space, caught between an old order and the present moment where they have access to no real power, influence or wealth. The sub-plot of Lord Colambre's risky love for Grace Nugent – a sign of old Catholic nobility – is resolved when it is discovered that her ancestry is English and thus she is made safe for marriage. In many ways, the conflict in the novel is a generational one, rather than a cultural or political one, with the young Colambre's eventual decision to stay in Ireland being a break with his immediate Anglo-Irish past. Of course, there is absolutely nothing radical or revolutionary in this: his struggle into the future is related to a rediscovery of the Burkean ideals of aristocracy. Much is made of manners and civility throughout, underpinning the need for traditional values to continue to have a place in what seems increasingly to be a vulgar modernity. This stress on the aristocracy and the Ascendancy is an example of how debilitating Irish discourse becomes in the early nineteenth century. The backward glance to an older world order seems thoroughly out of place in relation to the predicaments of modernity; in other words, out-of-date ideas – political, economic and cultural – are being applied to new realities. The result is a form of paralysis. For the novel it meant that Ireland and Irish characters would continuously seem strange and exotic.

Edgeworth's Irish fiction remained interested in national types and the clash of Anglo and Irish culture. The novel *Ormond* (1817), in particular, offers stark images of the choices that need to be made in Ireland between Gaelic and Anglo cultures and, indeed, French culture. But the overwhelming desire is for peace and order and the Irish world is presented as a potential rustic Eden: a place that *could* be a haven of all that is good and all that is proper. There is nothing akin to the kind of questioning and anxious narrative central to *Castle Rackrent*. The formal uneasiness so obviously present in the earlier novel is thoroughly absent in both *The Absentee* and *Ormond*, reinforcing the author's desire for decorum and containment at all levels of her narrative. The rebellious actualities of 1798 and 1803 are to be, quite simply, ignored as if they were an aberration or never happened at all. Rather than the white heat of the contemporaneous as reflected in *Castle Rackrent*, what the reader is presented with in *The Absentee* and *Ormond* is an archaic vision very much bound up in the past: a depiction of the social and political order that is being lost. And yet, these novels could be read as an accurate description of a culturally and politically moribund Ireland in the early nineteenth century: the energies of the rebellion have dissipated, as have the energies of parliamentary reform. The future seems the only place where and when something might happen, but the difficulty for Edgeworth, as it is the difficulty in Ireland generally, is in moving into that future.

Sydney Owenson's (Lady Morgan) (?1776–1859) novels truly capture the popular imagination in terms of the new cultural possibilities that Ireland might offer in the post-union world. Her novels, particularly *The Wild Irish Girl: A National Tale* (1806), plug into the excess dynamism of Edgeworth's *Castle Rackrent*, bringing plot and formal shape to the basic material that Edgeworth so ably presented. Of course, she also inhabits a post-rebellion world – both the 1798 United Irishmen rebellion and Robert Emmet's rebellion of 1803 – and certainly her novels bear the traces not only of union but also of rebellion. Her own immediate Irish-English background – it is argued that she 'literally forged her own national identity'[5] – feeds directly into her novels with the motif of the visitor in her writing mirroring her own desire for a national identity. The active striving for, and the hunting for, genuine Irishness marks out her writing in the early nineteenth-century Irish novel generally by bringing a level of conscious artistic and political decision-making to the literary choices she makes.

In the seventeenth and eighteenth centuries, the geographic space most represented in the Irish novel was Munster and south-east Leinster, reflecting the energies produced by the clash of the Gaelic and English language and cultures, as well as the realities of economic developments. In the late eighteenth and early nineteenth centuries, the perspective shifts and the west of Ireland, principally Connaught, becomes the site most associated with authentic Irishness. Owenson is one of the earliest Irish novelists to exploit this geographic relocation. Her deployment of the traveller as an image enacts this moment, as does the employment of a travelogue perspective. The reasons for this repositioning are varied; certainly the influence of the Burkean sublime means that the Irish landscape of the west can now be read in aesthetic terms, with its barrenness and economic uselessness transformed into a positive asset. But it has much to do with the idea, if not the actuality, of distance – in terms of both space and, importantly, Time – that truly transforms the space of the west of Ireland in the cultural imagination. The image of the visitor is a clear manifestation of this phenomenon: Ireland and Irishness must be found, actively sought out and discovered. Joep Leerssen is correct that this common framing device produced what he labels as the dominant of 'auto-exoticism',[6] which made Ireland always already different. That such Irishness is configured as distant and yet still geographically near enough to be actually encountered by the visitor means that the exoticism of the Irish is anxiously bound up with the peculiarities of the visitor's own cultural needs. Thus, traces of similarity rather than simple difference and straightforward opposition are what actually underpins much novelistic writing at this time.

The Wild Irish Girl takes its cue from all the footnotes, prefaces and appendages of *Castle Rackrent*, setting up competing narratives above and below the line: the two main characters of interest, Glorvina and Horatio, represent the Gaelic and Anglo worlds and their coming together in marriage at the close of the novel signals the hoped-for integration that the Act of Union between Great Britain and Ireland will bring.[7] Running beneath, or parallel to, this plot is a series of often-lengthy footnotes. These resort to personal anecdote in order to lay claim to the truth of what is being presented, while others refer to numerous travel writers, again in a manoeuvre to claim the actuality of the landscape described and the customs of the Irish within that landscape, as well as asserting that Ireland has long been a place of interest and continues to be. The other type of footnote deals with antiquarian knowledge concerning folk belief, ballads, history and language. The sources for this material are diverse but show Owenson's calculated seriousness in terms of her desire not only to tell a love story in the novel form but also to tell Ireland's multi-varied and multi-layered history.

This demarcation between footnote and plot is not wholly rigid however, and there is seepage between the two realms of discourse with various characters breaking off to give erudite lectures on the minutiae of Gaelic culture and its meanings. A contemporary reviewer of the novel commented disapprovingly on this aspect of the work:

Among other defects, we cannot but observe the injudicious manner with which Miss O. has introduced her disquisitions on the manners of the Irish, which compose above one half of her book, and which it would have been better either to omit or to throw into the form of an introduction or of notes. While the tear of sensibility is swelling in the eye of her fair reader at the woes and virtues of the interesting heroine, it is frequently checked by an elaborate dissertation on the Irish harp, or a lengthened argument on the comparative antiquity of the Scotch or Irish poetry.[8]

The complaint is a perceptive one: the reader wishes for and expects to be reading a novel but seems to be reading something else. Owenson's writing sets up a continuing trope in which Irish fiction must grapple not only with personal and local narratives but also retell, again and again, the wider history of the nation. It is a peculiar feature of Irish writing at this particular time when, for instance, British fiction in the guise of say, Jane Austen's *Emma* (1815), can insulate itself from a wider world of the Napoleonic War and politics in its desire to focus on individuals, and does so blithely and brilliantly. It seems that in Ireland, the individual person – Irish or British – can never fully develop in that modern way precisely as an individually complex person, being incessantly framed and grounded in a historical framework. The story, or the history, of Irish fiction revolves around the long emergence of an Irish personality that might be able to exist – even for a moment – outside the burden of stereotype and be themselves rather than ciphers of someone else's propagandist dream. This conscious skirting between genre in Owenson's work – between romance, history, epic – remains an issue of the Irish novelist for a much longer period than it did for novelists of other places. The full possibility of the novel form is never fully embraced by most novelists.

The ultimate union of Glorvina and Horatio is then, at some level, a 'yoking together by violence the most heterogeneous' of cultural opposites, or so it would seem. She, surprisingly, does not have to change, while Horatio must at least begin to change his misconceptions about Ireland and the Irish. Throughout the novel there is a discourse of 'seeing' and 'perceiving' at play, with Horatio trying to get a proper view of his subject. At one stage he declares 'I *now* feel I love!!',[9] indicating that the real lessons to be learnt are not for the Irish but rather for the British person. Of course, this is a reading of Ireland from an imperial vantage point: the Irish are passive, the British active. But Owenson, through Glorvina, does want to celebrate Gaelic culture but can do so only by subconsciously rendering it as defunct. All the references, footnotes and knowledge on display within the pages of the novel are remnants of a culture, disconnected shards: characters within the story, and the reader, can never hope to have a complete, whole image of the Irish world and Irish experience. There is a scene of an Irish wake in the novel (*The Wild Irish Girl*, pp. 182ff.) and not only is the individual being waked but an entire culture that has passed away also is being mourned.[10] As with *The Children of the Abbey* (1796), Gaelic culture – while interesting and exotic – offers no real threat in the contemporary moment. The intention of the incessant emphasising of a Gaelic pedigree that links it to the ancient world of Greece is to humanise the Gaelic Irish, make them in some way compatible with the norms of what is deemed modern society, but actually simply underlines their neutered state in the modern world. Again, as was the case with Maria Edgeworth, this appeal to some past aristocratic grandeur manifests how skewed the Irish world actually is. In Austen's *Emma*, for instance, that older world exists only in the name of Mr Knightly, whereas in the contemporaneous Irish novel feudal rule would seem to be the answer to Ireland's political ills.

There are two ways of reading the work: that it presents Ireland from the outside with an imperial vision being imposed; or, that it presents Ireland from the inside, disrupting the imperial imposition. In a way, *The Wild Irish Girl* is both, as are many novels of this time. The self-consciousness of the Irish novel, the fact its art is not to disguise its art, is a cry for a desire for a new type of discourse that might allow for a real conversation between colonised and coloniser. There is a discussion about MacPherson's Ossian poems at one stage and there is a protracted defence of the source material as being exclusively Irish as opposed to Scottish. Interestingly, as might have been suggested in a novel about authenticity, the poems are *not* dismissed out of hand for being inauthentic. For Glorvina the poems are to be considered very useful because of their 'refined medium' and their lack of 'incongruity of style, character, or manner' (*The Wild Irish Girl*, p. 115). In other words, their being in the English language becomes a conduit into the modern world, making them available to the modern sensibility and giving shape and form where, supposedly, there had been none in the originals. Thus, the death of Gaelic culture might not be a complete death after all if it can continue to exist – revitalised – in other forms, media and languages. It is significant that Owenson focuses on language in this way because, though it will take almost a century for the lesson to be truly learned by the literary revivalists, it will eventually be through the English language that Irish experience will powerfully expresses itself.

The Wild Irish Girl can be understood, then, to be potentially subversive. Certainly there is a dynamic between its desire to tell a story from both within and outside Irish culture. While the majority of the novel is told in the form of Horatio's letters to a friend, the last letter is from his father. This is a device that allows for a concluding frame to be placed on the action and also to bring order – or have order restored – to the world of the novel: 'then, *and not till then*, will you behold the day-star of national virtue rising brightly over the horizon of their happy existence' (*The Wild Irish Girl*, p. 252). Curiously, the father echoes Robert Emmet's famous last words from the dock and, surprisingly, suggests that Emmet's hope for an Irish nation will ultimately come to pass. Thus the hoped-for resolution and the harmonious union suggested through matrimony are actually undermined. The reality of a different narrative and a different solution to Ireland's ills is subtly recognised, even as it is denied.

Two subsequent Irish novels, *O'Donnell: A National Tale* (1812) and *Florence McCarthy: An Irish Tale* (1818), are notable for their heroines being artist figures – the latter actually a successful novelist. The energies and potential of the Glorvina character are thus exploited: the future of Gaelic Ireland becomes inextricably bound up with the position of art and writing in the Anglophone world. In both novels, Owenson continues her attack on British misrule and her critique of the application of anti-Catholic laws in Ireland. Her next major novel to deal with Ireland is *The O'Briens and the O'Flahertys: A National Tale* (1827). The passage of time from 1798 allows Owenson to meditate at a distance on rebellion and revolution with the hero of the story, Murrough O'Brien, flirting with the ideals of the United Irishmen uprising. Of course, she is unable – as no Irish writer during this period is able – to endorse rebellious action and Murrough ends up in the service of the French government of Bonaparte: a faded and melancholy man who pays the price for his youthful action with exile from his homeland.[11] As with the earlier novel, this one is also compelled to tell, in overwhelming detail, the history of Ireland and to offer information on Irish customs and language through numerous footnotes. There is a tacit acknowledgement of the different forms that history and memory may take: oral, myth, place-lore and song are all presented as conduits into the past. On this occasion, though, Ireland's history of invasion, defeat and colonisation is filtered through a densely wrought family history. History is made relevant to the individual: an important manoeuvre because the political moment of Catholic Emancipation which occurs in 1829, two years after this novel is published, informs the action of the novel and its slant on Irish history.[12] Catholics are made human and given human motivations and desires, while the wrongs of an impersonal history are made real and immediate for the reader.

But this is a history novel in another obvious sense: it is clearly set in the past. It is a curious feature of this novel that it is set prior to 1798, as if the trauma of that moment can never truly be confronted or overcome. Owenson's work, then, is a form of wishful thinking, an attempt to reimagine a moment in the past, before 1798, when all possibilities are still open and the right choices might yet be made. For the characters within the novel, the past, in the form of communal history and family history, has a tendency to burst powerfully into the present moment, making claims on the characters and fixing their fate. And, because Irish history has never been complete or satisfactorily resolved, the novel possesses many Gothic overtones, not least of which is the stress on found documents: letters and, specifically, a written history of the O'Brien family, the 'Annals of St Grellan'. Their transcription into the novel ends in 1691: another pivotal moment in Irish history, and another date that cannot be easily or happily accepted.

While the national history is one of emphasising the aristocratic and noble origins of the Gaelic race, the parallel family story is one of disguise and subterfuge with the fate of the O'Brien inheritance bound up in their religion. This emphasis on concealment and mistaken identity suggests a need for suppression of actualities in order to exist. There are echoes of that earlier Catholic British novel, Elizabeth Inchbald's *A Simple Story* (1791), which also concerned itself with the economy of masks and a profound fear of them. Throughout *The O'Briens and the O'Flahertys* there are numerous moments of revelation: shadowy characters are revealed to be friends, and the seemingly empty landscape of Connemara reveals – through images of numerous ruins – the faded glories of the Gaelic past. The landscape becomes a means through which Murrough's undeveloped emotional connection with Ireland can reveal itself. In *The O'Briens and the O'Flahertys*, the deployment of such motifs suggests that there is a real, actual and authentic nation to be discovered.

A very clear picture of Dublin as a colonial city emerges in the novel, acting as a counterpoint to the sublime possibilities of the empty world in the west of Ireland. The geographical co-ordinates of Dublin as the seat of administrative power – Trinity College Dublin, Dublin Castle, Kilmainham Jail and the Phoenix Park – are lovingly detailed as solid images of continuity and human activity, though that human activity is made fun of as a picture of incompetent and indifferent rule is presented. A warning of the transitory nature of all things, however, is seen in the form of the O'Brien house on the quays of Dublin: a kind of comic-Gothic structure that eventually collapses.

Ultimately, *The O'Briens and the O'Flahertys*, in its efforts to gesture towards alternative, hidden histories and its desire to tell Ireland's *grande histoire*, is fundamentally an anxious piece of writing. Owenson's portrayal exposes too many inconsistencies and contradictions, similar to those unresolved issues so evidently underpinning *The Wild Irish Girl*. Basically, she is unable to reconcile the needs of the present with the realities of the past: the Irish are always already a defeated nation in her work despite her wish to represent a vibrant cultural milieu. Her use of history certainly counters the prevailing mood that Ireland is outside history by showing it as decidedly inside its own narrative history. Her difficulty is in rendering any sense of that Irish nation and culture as something energetic and complete. Bits and pieces of the Gaelic past and Gaelic customs and language are strewn about the text – exotic bric-à-brac in comparison to the powerfully solid portrayal of British power and influence. The sprinkling of Irish phrases throughout and the way in which the Irish speak the English language is a sign of their utter impotence. The note being repeatedly struck throughout the novel moves between the comic and the melancholic. Murrough's kinsman Shane, in particular, while certainly brave physically embodies all of these attributes simultaneously – at once melancholy, angry, strong and weak. The presence of the Irish idiom in this novel, and its presence throughout nineteenth-century Irish fiction, suggests realism and authenticity, but serves only to legitimise standard English as the language of power and authority.[13]

It is clear, too, from Owenson's work that the frame through which Ireland is seen is becoming increasingly binary: Catholic or Protestant, Anglo-Irish or Gaelic, Irish or English. Her hoped-for reconciliation between all these opposites no longer holds true.[14] Her desire for the continuance of aristocratic

rule – Gaelic and Anglo-Irish – is also out of date. The room for manoeuvre
and a reimagining of the Irish situation is becoming more restrictive as these
stereotypical designations harden into facts. The lack of a clear-cut conclusion – or solution[15] – to the novel is an admission of her own pessimistic view
of Ireland at this time and her inability to see a way out of its difficulties.
Ireland, once again, is rendered through a backward look, stuck in a past that
cannot be adequately moved away from, while the real concerns of the
contemporary moment are not dealt with.

The kind of anxiousness lurking within Owenson's work, and indeed in
much Anglo-Irish writing of the nineteenth century, about identity and
about Irish history finds one of its most striking expressions in Charles
Robert Maturin's (1782–1824) *Melmoth the Wanderer* (1820). This, simply,
is a remarkable novel: a gloriously labyrinthine Gothic narrative that moves
ever inwards, and backwards in time, in search for the eponymous Melmoth
and a final understanding of his pact with the devil. There are five different
stories within the novel centring on characters that are tempted by Melmoth
to repeat his original sin. Layers of text and plot pile on top of one another,
coherence becoming strained as knotty narrative twists and turns ensure the
text pivots on intense imagery and the depiction of sustained emotional
extremity. The basic Faustian plot gives a focal point around which events
revolve, but increasingly the novel hovers somewhere between order and
chaos, madness and rationality, composure and hysteria. While ostensibly
Melmoth the Wanderer has nothing to do with Ireland and the Irish novel, it
can be argued that, in fact, it has everything to do with Ireland and the Irish
novel.

Maturin's earlier forays into the form were less successful: *The Wild Irish
Boy* (1808) and *The Milesian Chief* (1812) being imitations, but not simply
imitations,[16] of the romantic Gothic as charted by Owenson. Like many
others,[17] Maturin was attempting to profit from the popularity of the
national tale inaugurated by Owenson. Like her, Maturin sees the ills of
present-day Ireland coming from the Act of Union, which signal a significant loss of power for the Anglo-Irish: the dissipated hero of *The Wild Irish
Boy* languishes bored in London with little to excite his imagination.
Maturin's real difficulty, though, is with Irish Catholicism,[18] which
remained for him the real problem in terms of political and economic
development within the country. Such anti-Catholic sentiment was on
the rise among Anglo-Irish Protestants at this time, because of the immi-
nence of Catholic emancipation and a renewed vigour in reactivating
Ireland and the Irish as a project for conversion and improvement to the
level it had been in the early eighteenth century. Numerous novels at this

time take this as their theme. Maturin, too, as a minister of the Church of Ireland is interested in these issues and they find direct expression in his later work, *Five Sermons on the Errors of the Roman Catholic Church* (1824).[19] Here he laid out his belief that Catholicism is not only a force of degradation for the individual but also, importantly, a destructive force for wider civil communities and nations. Unquestionably, such thinking motivates much of the action in one of the main narrative strands in *Melmoth the Wanderer*: that of the character Stanton's incarceration by the infamous Spanish Inquisition. All the lurid detail suggests that the author, while overtly critical of Catholicism, is actually obsessively attracted to the pomp, ceremony, power and colour of its rites and ceremonies. If interpreted in this way, *Melmoth the Wanderer* indicates a deep disquiet in Anglo-Irish culture at this time: totally unsure of its position and authority in Ireland and utterly fearful for its future.

In many ways, the novel can be read as a rewriting of the popular national tale. Certainly it is a sustained attack on the kind of easy romanticism peddled by Owenson and others in the Irish context. The romantic mind privileges the perceiving subject who creates the world in interaction with it – so too with the romantic relationship to the past and tradition. As the aesthetic offshoot of Enlightenment thinking, romantic thought imagines an easy and untroubled relationship, not only with the world of nature but also with tradition: the world and the past are there to be reimagined and textualised in the present moment, to be made palatable and communicable. But there is a darker side to such imagining, usually associated with the Gothic, and it is that world which Maturin inhabits. Thus he generates, and lingers on, moments of transfixing terror, wanting his reader to experience genuine dread at first hand. That he presents these moments in exotic locations geographically and temporally removed from his contemporary moment can be construed as putting some distance between that fear and the reality of present-day Ireland. But the conventions of the Gothic genre undermine such efforts at separation. Literary historian W. J. McCormack is correct to link these moments of terror to very local and historically recent concerns relating to mob violence and rebellion.[20] While the national tale of Sidney Owenson studiously put Ireland's history on display, Maturin retreats from that public sphere into the private realm of the individual. What references to dates there are in the novel point to a peculiarly Anglo-Irish historical narrative: the Melmoth family came to Ireland with Cromwell in the 1640s and the wanderer has been on his travels since soon after that arrival. But Maturin is primarily concerned with offering a history of the individual cut off from the nation, family and community, and alienated from conventional time. Thus the human is constantly stressed: human guilt, human sin and the consequences of individual human choice.

After the opening, and the discovery of Stanton's document, the novel becomes self-consciously textual. It is another means for Maturin to differentiate himself from the national tale that acknowledged numerous oral and folk sources for narrative. Here the written word is paramount in the telling of these individual, but linked, stories. As if to confirm this determined effort to move away from the oral realm, immediately prior to the introduction of Stanton's manuscript a servant gives a pointedly brief, though not untrue, outline of the family myth and the fate surrounding the original wanderer.[21] Her anecdotal account is thus superseded and silenced by the written word. The act of writing itself is being stressed and, consequently, the labour of Stanton and the others in telling their story is shared with the novelist Maturin. And yet a brooding anxiousness remains within the form of the novel: its spiralling ever inwards, towards some moment of truth or revelation that never finally comes, is a challenge to the modern novel as an Enlightenment medium for expression. Here the Gothic has full reign: the supposed progression from past to present collapses into the nightmarish ever-present of the eternal wanderer. Perhaps that is the reason for the withdrawal into the intimate realm of the individual as enacted in this novel: the public world, of public and communal history, is a nightmare of failure, danger and estrangement. Indeed, Melmouth's original sin is bound up with Ireland's colonial past: the family's coming to Ireland with Cromwell in the 1640s[22] and the gaining of land through what Elizabeth Bowen would later label 'an inherent wrong'.[23] The public guilt of that act has detrimental private consequences. The interior world is no better than the public sphere: throughout the novel interiority is echoed in the various prisons and enclosures in which characters find themselves confined. Even the formal framing of the stories within stories implies interiority and separation. Individuality, therefore, offers no liberation.

Maturin's singular achievement is the expression of this interiority, mapping and writing the inner private world(s) that can exist beyond the stereotyping that public life in Ireland seemed to demand of the Irish at this juncture – or perhaps always demanded. In doing so, he energised the novel form in an Irish context, returning it to the sphere of modern human experience. Of course, as a Protestant clergyman he is suspicious of his achievement: the inner life is surely the realm of important potential for spiritual cultivation rather than being the object of a frivolous novel.[24] He remains uncertain about the emotion within his novel, wanting to contain and confine it, but the framed narrative structure of the novel, while promising containment and control, cannot be sustained and the extreme nature of the human experience on display borders on the unbearable as emotions explode onto the page. Nonetheless the novel shocks its readers into recognising the depths of feeling and emotion possible in an Irish context. In contrast to Owenson and others who offered endless factual histories of Ireland, Maturin manages to offer if not a history of feeling in Ireland, then an implication that such a history, hidden though it is, is there to be told if novelists might care to tell it.

With the general upsurge in the publication of Irish novels in the early nineteenth century, there is an attendant realignment in relation to who might be writing the Irish novel. A combination of massive population growth and economic wealth (mainly in agriculture) meant that there was an increasing Catholic audience for Irish fiction. The growing culture of magazines and journals that, among other forms, allowed for Irish fiction to flourish indicates a broad and expanding Irish readership.[25] The end of the Napoleonic Wars brought prosperity to a close: there were numerous local-ised failures of the potato crop and famine. Politically, too, the country was still troubled: no real advances had been made in bringing about Catholic emancipation and the 1820s saw an increase in agrarian unrest, with a rise in violent outrages and a growth in membership of secret societies. Ireland was still a place to be viewed from elsewhere, but now there was a growing interest from a wider readership outside Ireland to encounter life in Ireland from within the burgeoning lower and middle classes.[26]

John Banim (1798–1842) and his brother Michael (1796–1874) represent this new voice in the Irish novel. Consciously, in works such as the collections of *Tales by the O'Hara Family* (1825) and *Tales by the O'Hara Family: Second Series* (1826), they set out to offer accurate depictions of Irish life that might move beyond the debilitating clichés that stunted any real dialogue in Irish affairs. The conceit of their pseudonym, the O'Hara brothers, reinforces the air of authenticity that infuses their work: the image of travellers recounting what they hear on their various penetrations into the real Ireland continuing to frame Ireland and the Irish. That the two brothers come from a thoroughly middle-class background is more impor-tant in terms of their novelistic sensibilities than their religious affiliation: respectability for the Irish in general, but their own class in particular, is what they want to represent in their writing. Of the two, John Banim is the more interesting, with three of his novels worthy of mention: *The Boyne Water* (1826), *The Anglo-Irish of the Nineteenth Century* (1828) and *The Nowlans* (1826). Seamus Deane suggests that the first two novels are

Banim's most important work because they deal directly with the politics of Ireland.[27] In truth, these two works are of interest precisely because of their failure as novels. *The Boyne Water* fails because Banim is unable to register any kind of opposition to the version of history created by those who won the battle, if not the war, at the River Boyne in 1690. He must accept that version and attempts to accommodate the Catholic story to that supposed norm. As Emer Nolan correctly argues, this is a novel concerned with forging a middle-way between the extremes of Irish politics,[28] and though set in the past, this cry for moderation is firmly rooted in the Ireland of the 1820s. Even an early reviewer of the work noted its tired and slavish resemblance to the historical fiction of Walter Scott.[29]

One brief moment from this long novel sums up Banim's predicament. In making reference to the sobriquet 'Shamus-a-Caca' given by the Irish to King James as he retreated from the battlefield, Banim declares it: 'A vulgar, cruel, unmerited Irish expletive, recollected to this day, but rather unsuited to our pages.'[30] 'James the shit' should not be translated and though it is remembered in the popular imagination, it must be forgotten. A passage such as this self-consciously enacts the transition from oral to written culture, from tradition to modernity. What is gained, and lost, is clear: the move should mean a rejection of the vulgarity of the past and, by implication, the acceptance of genteel manners and the future. But 'Shamus-a-Caca' still remains within the text and is not wholly negated by it. Its presence serves to remind the reader that there are alternative histories and disturbing discourses available if only they care to look.

The Nowlans (1826), I would argue, is the work that truly captures that submerged potential of the Irish novel in the early nineteenth century. The later novel, *The Anglo-Irish of the Nineteenth Century* (1828), while scathing in its depiction of the class structure within the Irish ruling classes, is an updating of the kind of hoped-for productive return of some kind of feudal elite envisaged in Maria Edgeworth's *The Absentee*. *The Nowlans*, on the other hand, charts new territory and in the process forges new identities and characters rather than being restricted by types and a desire for conformity. The story centres on John Nowlan, a Catholic priest, who abandons his calling for the love of Letty, an Anglo-Irish woman from the nearby Ascendancy Big House. Complicating matters is that their union is echoed in their siblings Peggy and Frank's relationship. Earlier novels stressed the union between Great Britain and Ireland through images of positive marriage, but this novel offers descriptions of devastating unions. This shift inwards, away from Britain and Ireland, towards the internal relationships within Ireland itself allows for a welcome engagement with the subtleties of

Irish class and life, opening up to scrutiny the standard reductive either/or pigeonholing of Irish experience.

It has been maintained that 'Banim confronts head-on the problem Owenson and Edgeworth evade – Irish violence.'[31] Certainly, there is a lingering impression throughout the novel that there exists a barely concealed world of explosive tension. But it is more than merely an acknowledgement of secret societies and possible political violence, it is also a powerful recognition of the hidden currents of conflict between various social groups within Ireland: the expected conflict between Catholic and Protestant, peasant and Ascendancy is there, but so too is the hostility between an emerging Catholic middle class who are coming into money and readying themselves for political emancipation and those who remain on the margins of economic society. Peery Connolly, for instance, is a buffoon figure, an idiot offering some sentimental light relief. He is also, though, a character reinforcing the claims of the new middle classes for acceptance into normalised and civilised society: he represents the older Ireland that must be rejected. Peery – like the stage Irishman – is afforded no inner life: his consciousness is on public display. The new world, the world of the novel, is the place where interiority is possible and an inner life can be mediated.[32] Peery's presence, then, allows for a comparison between old and new, suggesting the development and the sophistication of the Nowlans and their move into this new space.

The novel consciously attempts to reflect the actuality of lived experience in a country that heaves with humanity as Ireland's population staggeringly increased throughout the early 1800s. Thus, despite the focus of the plot, which turns upon the impossibility of bridging the gap between classes and the Protestant and Catholic worlds, this novel is remarkable in its acceptance and chronicling of everyday lived life, both in the city and in the countryside. The descriptions of Dublin city are remarkably prescient in their depiction of city living: the streets become a maze, reflecting the inner turmoil of John Nowlan after his marriage to Letty. The emphasis on confusion and the alienation afforded by the streets of the city suggest that Banim is aware of the anxieties and uncertainties that attend this movement into modernity:

The coach entered Dublin. Streets and high houses closed around him; other night-coaches passed him coming in from the country; or day-coaches whisked by starting from town. In the trading and manufacturing district of the metropolis by which he entered, that of James-street and Thomas-street, groups of 'operatives' were already in motion towards the places of their daily occupation; the early cries were sung or screamed aloud; carts, drays, and such vehicles ground their way over the stones; from different public-houses, the voices of very late or very early tipplers now and then came in vehement accents; every thing gave him the novel sensation of a morning in a great city. To the young person who, for the first time, experiences such a sensation, it brings – no matter how calm may be his mind and breast, how certain and soothing his prospects – depression rather than excitement; a bleak strangeness seems around him: he doubts and shrinks more than he admires or wonders; he is in a solitude, unlike the remote solitudes he has quitted; in solitude with men, not nature; without the face of nature to cheer him. But, added to this common depression, John Nowlan felt remorse for the past, despair of the present, terror of the future.[33]

The detail that Banim offers of the boarding house John and Letty stay in on the North Circular Road and the pen-picture of the landlord Mr Grimes and his wife are Joycean in intent and execution and could have found their way into *Dubliners*:

Every Sunday [Mr Grimes] appeared caparisoned for church in a complete shining suit of black, taken out of a press, and in a hat, also shining, extracted from one of his wife's early bandboxes; the clothes and the hat some ten years in his, or rather in her possession, and thus displayed once a-week during that period, yet both looking as if sent home the Saturday night before; and, indeed, considering that they had encountered scarce three months of careful wear altogether, namely, the wear of about two hours every seventh day for ten years, it was not after all so surprising they should look so new. Sometimes his wife allowed him to invite to a Sunday dinner five or six old men like himself, all clad in shining black too; and when John saw them come crawling towards the house, or, joined with their host, crawling and stalking about the yard, he felt an odd sensation of disgust, such as he thought might be aroused by the sight of so many old shining black-beetles; the insects that, of all that crept, were his antipathy and loathing. (Banim, *The Nowlans*, pp. 150–151)

That such emotional and economic paralysis is not simply the preserve of twentieth-century Dublin suggests a curious lack of development in the Irish context, indicating how the famine of the 1840s and 1850s stalled Irish economic and social progression so much so that Banim's cityscape and countryside would look very similar, if somewhat more deserted, in the early twentieth-century world of James Joyce and others.

Another novel inhabiting this newly invigorated literary space is Gerald Griffin's (1803–40) hugely popular *The Collegians* (1829). The basic plot of the novel is taken from real life: a notorious murder case from 1819 saw the death of a young peasant woman at the hands of a local Ascendancy man. The ingredients for a commentary on the debilitating structures and relationships in Irish life are obvious. Indeed, this story and its image of an innocent young Irish peasant girl done to death by her social superior is repeated again and again throughout the nineteenth century, finding particularly successful expression in dramatist Dion Boucicault's *The Colleen Bawn*. Of interest, though, is how Griffin reimagines the heroine of Sidney Owenson's fiction: here the Ireland represented through the image of a woman is a passive innocent victim of libidinous Ascendancy misrule. As with John Banim's fiction, the real importance of *The Collegians* is its portrayal of middle-class Catholics. Though the action of the novel is deliberately set pre-1782, at the time of the novel's publication in 1829 Catholics are set to achieve political emancipation and this utterly positive affirmation of their status is meant to dispel any fears a British reader might have of that move towards political recognition.[34] The scene introducing the reader to middleman Mr Daly and his family is said to be the 'most famous depiction of the middle-class home in nineteenth century fiction'.[35] To be sure, it is carefully crafted, even down to detailing the type of acceptable prints that should adorn the walls. The overriding ambience generated in this scene is one of overflowing plenty and comfortable ease. Significantly, for Griffin, religion is not important here: taste is everything and decorum is all.

The middle-class credentials of the Dalys are reinforced when contrasted with the nuanced descriptions of the various layers of Irish society. Peasants, servants, small farmers and artisans populate the pages of the novel in an utterly docile and non-threatening way, their language and demeanour a sign of their acquiescence to the status quo.[36] Even the numerous renderings of Irish folk culture in the form of ballads and songs serve only to present the Irish, in general, as a benign group: the songs are soft, enervated and insipid. Ironically, it is the villain of the piece, Hardress Cregan, who is presented as embodying feeling and passion. It seems that, for Griffin, in order that the sober and restrained Kyrle Daly, and all that he represents, inherits the benefits of the new dispensation, he must be emotionally neutered and politically and culturally disconnected from anything that might be considered disruptive or dangerous. As Dominick Tracy argues, Griffin is caught between nationalism and imperialism, between nostalgia and pragmatism, unable finally to make a choice between them and to follow one path.[37] The close of the novel sees justice being done: Hardress is found guilty and a death sentence is commuted to penal exile. A more transcendent law comes into play when the reader is told he dies on board his prison ship. Importantly, before his death he is forced to look back upon that idyllic scene that opened the novel.[38] Griffin is able to link the losses and the gains within the novel to specific places, thus offering a unifying vision of place, culture, language and class and, importantly, for him, doing

so with great formal ease and narrative accomplishment. And while, as
noted, the novel is set in the past, this final image of enduring peace points
towards a possible future. It is a future, however, that can only come into
being if this Catholic middle class is accepted as the natural site of true
leadership in their community.

With the granting of Catholic emancipation, it might have seemed that at
last the question of Ireland and its problems were beginning to be addressed.
It was indeed a time of change and practical intervention with the National
School System inaugurated in 1831. Such conditions allowed for a writer such
as Samuel Lover to position himself in order to gain from this apparently
overriding sense of plenty and calm. In his two most successful novels – *Rory
O'More: A National Romance* (1837) set in 1798 and *Handy Andy* (1842) – there
is a noticeable shift towards entertainment and diversion, rather than
political propaganda or biased posturing that was the mark of work from a
previous generation of novelists. As Barry Sloan argues, this move towards
light entertainment is important, not only because of the ensuing commercial
success 'but also because in each [novel] the hero is the kind of endearing,
bumbling, good-hearted and sometimes witty peasant who falls into adversity
and out of it again'.[39] W. B. Yeats recognised the power of the humorist's
depiction of the Irish character when he declared about Lover's work,
'The error is with those who have taken from his novels their notion of
all Irishmen.'[40] The usual charge levelled against Lover is that he is the
instigator and purveyor of the stage Irishman figure in the nineteenth century,[41] but that seems unfair as his only crime is to follow in the tradition of
presenting the Irish as comically feckless, which stretches back to at least
the Irish fortune-hunter figure of the eighteenth century. Indeed, that his
novels are episodic suggests a retreat into the genre of picaresque, but here it
seems that whatever lingering sense of danger and menace that such outsider
figures might embody is thoroughly diminished: the Irish never raise themselves above the level of a joke. It has been argued that the picaresque at
this point in time, in its tendency towards universalisation and its subsequent depoliticising of place, possesses an imperial function.[42] Another interpretation is that the picaresque with its endless round of travel and restless
movement, peopled with characters who come and go and, chameleon-like,
adapt to any given situation, points to a lack of identity and any real sense of
home.[43]

Charles Lever's (1806–72) early novels are also usually read alongside
Lover's as perpetuating a horrendous libel on the Irish character. In works
such as *Confessions of Harry Lorrequer* (1839) and *Charles O'Malley, The
Irish Dragoon* (1841), the emphasis is on light entertainment within the

conventions of the picaresque mode: there is much drinking, travel in Ireland, England and Europe and general rollicking. These were hugely successful novels in both Ireland and England, and his connection to the *Dublin University Magazine* raised its circulation at one time to a high of 4,000 copies a month.[44] Sensitivity to representation is acute at this time, though, and fellow novelist William Castleton attacked Lever's success, declaring that he was exploiting Ireland 'for pounds, shillings, and pence'.[45] Young Irelander Gavan Duffy, in a swingeing critical assault in *The Nation* newspaper, accused Lever of being 'unworthy of credit as a witness against the character of the Irish people',[46] his criticism focusing particularly on his depiction of the Irish peasant. Duffy's attack suggests that, in Ireland, literature can never be read wholly in aesthetic terms, and that political relevance is more central to assessing worth. For W. B. Yeats, a generation later, Lever's characters possess all the moral defects of the Anglo-Irish gentry who have no 'sense of responsibility'.[47] His is an astute criticism because he realises that both Gaelic and Anglo-Irish are being characterised as feckless and comedic: the subtle and not so subtle differentiations and gradations of Irish society are of no concern for an English readership seeking only easy distraction and amusement. Military novels such as Lever's were common at this time. William Maxwell (1792–1850), an editor of *Dublin University Magazine*, wrote a number of novels – *Wild Sports of the West* (1832) and *Tales of the Peninsular War* (1837) being the most successful – and was a major influence on Lever's work, with Gavan Duffy going so far as to say that Lever basically plagiarised Maxwell. The use of the military backdrop obviously allows for adventure and travel, and at an unconscious level presupposes an imperial worldview uniting Irish with Scots and English in a common cause. Increasingly from an Anglo-Irish perspective, the role of the military becomes central in their narratives – the institution acting as a social outlet in the form of dances and the opportunity for love to blossom, as well as a forceful presence of order and authority.

William Carleton (1794–1869) is one of the most significant Irish fiction writers of the nineteenth century quite simply because he comes out of the peasant class, whose perspective in the novel had always come from others. Carleton himself was not slow to exploit his unique position in the literary marketplace. His life, and his work, embodies the extremes and the contradictions of Irish experience. Born a Catholic in Clogher, County Tyrone, he studied at one time for the priesthood and had been a member of the Ribbonmen secret society, but he converted to Protestantism in 1818 and began writing anti-Catholic polemic. He also supported the political union between Great Britain and Ireland. His writing hovers uneasily between a fierce, perhaps nostalgic, pride in the codes and rituals of a peasant life that he is fully familiar with, and a strong desire for Ireland to cast off irrational sentiment and superstition and move into modernity. The term 'native informer' is used by critic Julian Moynahan and, perhaps, captures well the tensions at the heart of Carleton's life and work.[48]

While his novels are certainly important, it is for stories and sketches collected in *Traits and Stories of the Irish Peasantry* (1842–44) that he will be chiefly remembered. Of particular interest is his 'General Introduction' to that work where he outlines carefully some central tenets underpinning his writing, attacking the crudity of the persistence of the comedic Irishman in literature and the continual focus on the Irish linguistic blunder. He argues that language in Ireland is in a phase of transition and has been for a long time.[49] With great subtlety he realises that there is energy in this moment of transference that can power his fiction if he can capture it successfully. Here, he prefigures a central element of the work of W. B. Yeats and J. M. Synge, both of whom would succeed in harnessing that linguistic energy for their own poetry and drama. But Carleton is also concerned with the practicalities of publishing and connecting with an interested Irish readership. He believes that a flourishing publishing business in Ireland can reflect the fruits of political and economic development which will find a manifestation in the realm of culture. For Carleton, such a shift would signify that the Irish are writing for themselves and not just for export. In other words, this literary space can allow the Irish to explain themselves to each other, thereby opening up a conversation between different classes, religions and geographic spaces within Ireland. Of course, the contradiction that Carleton desires closer ties with the union – even if he envisages it as a union of equals – undermines his hopes. He is unable to fully disregard an English readership and he is constantly at pains to give the autobiographical source for many of his stories, providing an air of the authentic beyond the dreaded footnote. More interesting, though, is how in this mingling of life with fiction, and fiction with life, Carleton is writing his own story, and his own story, for him, becomes the story of Ireland.

The incongruity of these conflicting perspectives – the far too stark either/or choice encapsulated in Carleton's biography – finds its most telling expression in his novels. His first novel, *Fardorougha the Miser: or the Convicts of Lisnamona* (1839), is said to be his best,[50] employing a more believable plot than some of his subsequent coincidence-driven work. As is fitting for the novel form, the world depicted here is one of small farmers rather than peasants, ensuring that the working through of the conflict between characters and positions is embedded in a society invested economically in the land and property. In other words, there is much at stake in terms of gains and losses for the characters and the choices they might make. Much of the energy within the story derives from the personal conflict of Fardorougha, whose miserliness is at odds with the love for his son Connor. Fardorougha remains something of a ridiculous and grotesque literary character, quite Dickensian in his surface absurdities. That, of course, is the point. Carleton is not concerned with subtleties; rather, all his literary energy is focused on making a clear distinction between father and son, between an old Irish world and the new, modern Anglo world.

Of peculiar interest also is the presence of a Ribbonman secret society in the novel. These secret societies are endlessly fascinating to a British readership: they exist on the margins of acceptability and beyond the realm of the law, hidden from view and dangerous. Their very nature means that they are beyond knowledge and therefore a threat to the power structures of the colonial relationship between Britain and Ireland. Throughout the nineteenth century they are a feature of many Irish novels. Thomas Moore's *Captain Rock* (1824) was enormously successful, and was a means for Moore to outline his view of Irish history and the forms of defiance thrown up by the nature of the colonial connection. Anna Marie Hall, in her novel *The Whiteboy: A Story of Ireland* (1845), would also successfully tap into this undercurrent in Irish life. Obviously what unites each of these novels is their depiction of a less than happy and content Ireland: the continuing presence of secret societies who organise local outrages is a reminder that social normality is not the actuality on the ground. These secret societies – in their literary manifestation at least – act as a representation of the Irish unconscious and its resistance to British rule.

For Carleton, these societies were to be condemned. In *Fardorougha the Miser* they are seen mostly as devoid of ideal or higher purpose, are simply an outlet for petty revenge and violence. And yet, there appears to be another side to these societies: they act as a harmless meeting place for games and banter. For good or ill, the clandestine nature of the gatherings indicates that they operate as a means for their members to connect with their inner selves away from public view, even for a short time. If the conflict between old and new is played out in the public sphere in the relationship between Fardorougha and Connor, then the inner struggle between tradition and modernity is made discernible with the presence of the secret world of the Ribbonmen in the novel: it is the means, in an oblique way, by which the subconscious is approached by Carleton. It can be argued that Carleton's real difficulty is with the unconscious itself. His political and religious beliefs demand that the outer world and the inner world connect without complication: any inner, private turmoil must have a public expression. Thus, there is a noticeable emphasis on physicality throughout the novel. Often overlooked is how the clash between father and son is reinforced in their use of language and their physical presence: Connor is possessed of a 'manly beauty' (Carleton, p. 91) and speaks without a Gaelic lilt. Fardorougha's miserly love of money is merely a transference of superstitious belief into the context of modernity, the grotesque distortions of his body bearing the marks of that conflict and that struggle between these opposing viewpoints. Indeed, throughout the novel various characters feel trauma and conflict physically, as if Carleton is aware of the all-encompassing nature of the transition into modernity for the Irish: it cannot be just an intellectual move, but is rather such a fundamental shift that it is registered in all areas of experience. Mind and body are thus united within the world of the novel. Carleton's contradictory position is that he wants to deny that inner world while simultaneously making public the collective mind of the peasant Irish. Such a position means that he is constantly torn between the demands of the novel and the demands of propaganda. This dual manoeuvre of stressing the body while denying the consciousness occurs at the historical moment when the Gaelic Irish are beginning to be a very real physical presence in Irish life through the political machinations of Daniel O'Connell and his employment of monster meetings. As with the Patterns of a previous generation, and like the secret societies, these gatherings acted as a social outlet on the margins of everyday existence and were to be feared. For Carleton, seeing Ireland and the Irish through the physical body is a means of registering the mob and their awful actuality and presence. The subtleties of the Irish mind, though, remain impenetrable as the scope of the Irish novel remains over-involved in the reproduction of types and the attendant requirement for explanation of these types to an audience elsewhere.

The Irish body in death becomes an encapsulation of the calamity that is the Great Famine in Ireland (1845–49). The horrific reality of this event throws into sharp relief the pervasive ideology of development and the narrative of improvement in an Irish context, disrupting and negating any easy movement into the future for Ireland. The Great Famine has become in the modern moment a contested site of interpretation, of possible meanings and of multiple significances. But even in the contemporaneous moment, the problem of representation, of relaying the truth and the reality of the famine in Ireland, was a very pressing one.[51] By the 1840s, the potato had become central to the diet of the Irish peasant, and its increasing centrality corresponded to a massive growth in population from the early part of the century onwards when the numbers increased from 5 million in 1800 to 8.5 million in 1845, with seven out of eight Irish people living in the countryside.[52] After the famine, Ireland was a different place entirely. Over 2 million people were gone from death and emigration by 1849 and a steady flow of emigration would be the norm from this moment on. By 1891, Ireland's population was 4.5 million.[53] The Irish landscape was once again exposed, as it had been with the felling of the forests in the eighteenth century, and the Irish psyche once more laid bare for all too see.

This massive change (the momentous alteration and the frightening rapidity of it) is what is difficult – then as now – to capture, or even understand, in or through any act of mere writing. Many novels dealt with the famine at the moment of its occurrence but two fictional works in particular, William Carleton's *The Black Prophet: A Tale of Irish Famine* (1847) and Anthony Trollope's (1815–1882) *Castle Richmond: A Novel* (1860), confront this issue of representing and thereby comprehending this acute moment of wide-scale death: one from the perspective of an insider and one from the position of an outsider. Margaret Kelleher's *The Feminisation of Famine* makes the persuasive argument that both writers have recourse to the image of women and children as images of nature, thereby deflecting responsibility for the famine away from human or government action. Even more curious, however, is how both authors have recourse to the law in their respective novels. The issue of conflicting discourses – between legal discourse and the discourse of everyday experience – is obviously of interest, raising questions about the nature of the state and its official functions and dysfunctions in a time of such overwhelming disaster. And, of course, the position of the law in a consideration of Ireland's colonial relationship to Britain is certainly important. Undeniably, Ireland's connection with Britain in the nineteenth century is a legal one. The great issues of the nineteenth century are also filtered through the lens of the law: Catholic emancipation, which comes into being in 1829, and the numerous land acts of the latter part of the nineteenth century. And the famine itself is responded to by poor laws and relief laws, public works bills, poor employment acts, destitute poor acts (Soup Kitchen Act) and so on. Surprisingly, both novels remain very much focused on the individual and the personal rather than being full-scale narratives – critical or otherwise – about the British state's institutional responses to the famine. That the famine is not exactly the main focus, rather being a backdrop for the domestic plots to be played out against, and that, indeed, the law while remarkably central to each plot it is not law as directly linked to dealing with or ameliorating the famine, means that colonial issues are only hinted at obliquely rather than directly confronted in both these novels.

As a contemporary reviewer of Trollope's *Castle Richmond* declared:

It is impossible not to feel that [the famine] was the part of it about which Mr. Trollope really cared, but that, as he had to get a novel out of it, he was duty bound to mix up a hash of Desmonds and Fitzgeralds with the Indian meal on which his mind was fixed as he wrote.[54]

Perhaps unknowingly this is actually quite perceptive: the demands of writing a novel rather than a journalistic piece or an official report means that other factors must come into play for the author. And this holds true for William Carleton also. The problem revolves round the function of the novel as a literary form and the expectations both writers and readers have of that form. Thus the focus on the personal and the domestic sphere is not unusual: it is the accepted space of the modern novel, which develops narratives about modern individual experience. In many ways, the novel form is simply unsuitable in chronicling the horrific scale of the famine. The incessant focus on the single person or the single family who are the suffering victims redirects attention away from the enormous scale of the devastation; and also, for those who try to help, this focus on the individual transfers blame and responsibility away from government and the state. The modern novel is not 'epic' in range or ambition to fully record the scale of the famine. Terry Eagleton's argument that union between Great Britain and Ireland meant 'a metropolitan narrative was overlaid on a colonial one'[55] fits neatly into a consideration of the nineteenth-century Irish novel and particularly here in relation to the famine story. Thus Carleton and Trollope continue to relate a traditional domestic story – the accepted metropolitan narrative – when the real story – the Irish story – of the famine remains untold.

The presence of the law in both plots is a mechanism whereby the domestic, individual and family story can be viewed from a public perspective. The law mediates between the private and the public spheres, allowing the action of both these spaces to bleed one into the other. Thus law becomes a framing device through which to view Ireland at this juncture. But troubling anxieties remain and the failure of this mediation to work thoroughly or properly is never fully addressed by the author. The fact that law appears at all – in whatever guise – is a tacit admission that all is *not* well with the world. Critic David A. Miller argues that the novel as a form is associated with lawlessness: it is new, it is original and it breaks out of the classic modes and forms, offering freedom from the traditional restrictions and traditional rules and regulations governing literary endeavour. Indeed, the novel's early link with the rogue figure is an obvious acknowledgement of this source. Like that figure, the novel makes its own rules as it goes along, utterly provisional and always tentatively temporary.[56] The tension in these famine novels is that tension shared by many novels in the nineteenth century, caught between the disciplinary desire to regulate behaviour and doing so in a form that in its very essence works against such normalising tendencies.

Anthony Trollope's *Castle Richmond* (1860) enacts this imposition of colonial law from without, as it is a novel centred around British attitudes to Ireland and the Irish. From the outset, the urbane narrator makes a plea for the setting of his story in Ireland because 'Irish stories are not popular with the booksellers.'[57] As Melissa Fagan argues, the famine in Ireland forced Trollope, who had lived many happy years in Ireland, to confront his 'otherness'.[58] Thus, the novel is a failure to come to terms with the famine – to fully understand it – even with the perspective that a distance of thirteen years can offer. The famine is tangential to a plot centring on a love interest and an issue surrounding inheritance. The desire for the author to uphold the status quo, to present the landlord class as utterly essential to continued life in Ireland, is blatant and obvious. Famine is the work of God, and while man in the form of government and society can help, it is not a man-made problem and therefore is ultimately beyond man's control. Very clearly the world of God and man is demarcated, and while religion is seen as important – the sectarian divide fascinates Trollope like many British viewers of the Irish scene, whereas an Irish author such as Carleton is more interested in the subtleties of class – the world of action in the novel is the human world. The English lawyer Mr Prendergast wields much power within the world of the novel. In many ways he is the new secular priest: he, and the law he represents, is the final arbiter of justice, and through him all wrongs are righted and normalcy is restored. By the close, the threat to Hubert Fitzgerald's inheritance of Castle Richmond is no more and his plans to marry also move ahead. Order is brought to bear on the hinted-at chaos of the famine.

Central to William Carleton's *The Black Prophet* (1847) is a murder mystery. It is set back in time from its writing and publication: detailing famine from an earlier period, particularly 1817 and 1822. The lessons for the present moment, though, are not to be forgotten. Carleton, in his Preface, very clearly lays the blame for the present disaster at the foot of the British administration in Ireland. He dedicated his book to Lord John Russell, the prime minister, because his name should be placed before a 'story which details with truth the sufferings which such legislation and neglect have entailed upon our people'.[59] Past and present thus merge in the novel: the act of writing being a powerful act of public memory, warning that famine has happened before and will continue to happen if nothing is changed. If the dominating paradigm in the nineteenth century is one of progress, then it seems that in Ireland nothing ever really changes, nothing is ever really past or gotten over. The murder plot itself reinforces this with the final unmasking of the murderer twenty years after the crime itself: the past exploding into and disrupting the present moment.[60]

Throughout the novel, Carleton, as author, intrudes upon the narrative to make clear his analysis of the problems besetting Ireland: it is the failure of the British government, the failure, as he says, of the law. However, he still believes in the law and that, if applied correctly, it can eventually right all wrongs. The solving of the murder after twenty years is testament to that belief. This focus on law means that the cause of famine is man-made; Carleton is not interested in blaming divine intervention. Law thus offers hope, offers a means of solving problems; ultimately, it offers the possibility of justice in the world of men. Law is upheld in other, more obvious ways in the novel. Carleton is at pains to negate violence in his Irish characters – it is not an appropriate response to the famine and their predicament.[61] It is a constant throughout nineteenth-century Irish fiction: the fear of violence and the simultaneous placing of violence beyond the acceptable boundaries of action. The fact Donnel Dhu – the black prophet of the title – was a United Irishman involved in the 1798 rebellion is laden with significance. In the end, order must be upheld and justice must be seen to be done. The difficulty for Carleton is that the law he wants to uphold and believe in comes from elsewhere: the Irish cannot seize justice, they must receive it passively rather than take it aggressively. It is the gift of the British if they choose to give it. The difference between Carleton the insider and Trollope the outside is clear: Trollope's Law is all-pervasive – it is the new religion, the place where all wrongs can be righted, where worldly justice resides. For Carleton, law in Ireland is also something to be cherished, yet his is an anticipatory view: it is something for the future.

Thus, there is an air of anticipation pervading the novel and this is reinforced by many characters having their dreams revealed to the reader. Obviously the 'black prophet' – the prophecy man – embodies this tendency towards the future. Prophecy men were a widespread phenomenon in the early part of the nineteenth century, stimulated by the apocalyptic prophecies of a 'Signor Pastroni' which claimed that Protestantism would be defeated by 1825. For Carleton, these men were symbols of backward superstition; though in his Introduction to *Traits and Stories of the Irish Peasantry* he suggests that, like the traditional storyteller, the prophecy man had entertainment value.[62] In a way, his being an author of novels and stories suggests that he has supplanted the prophecy men or certainly wishes to. Like no other novelist of the nineteenth century, Carleton reflects that deep desire for a better future, anticipating a time when justice will be done and all will be well. Ireland, it would seem, in Carleton's novels is not overly indebted to backwardness. Indeed, his writing signals a movement away from the history novel as a genre but his work still harbours the notion that the past is something unresolved and unfinished in the Irish collective psyche. In a novel such as *The Black Prophet*, at a sub-conscious level, Ireland actively dreams of a better future. The only problem is how that future can be obtained.

In comparison to other subjects and themes, the famine novel is something of a rarity in the latter half of the nineteenth century. However, as Margaret Kelleher argues, the sporadic continuance of the famine as a subject in Irish fiction belies the view that it provoked only wounded silence.[63] Still, its horror remains difficult to confront directly and even when the famine appears in English fiction, such as in Elizabeth Gaskell's *North and South* (1855) or Emily Brontë's *Wuthering Heights* (1847) – if we are to take as given the idea that Heathcliff is a refugee from the Irish horror – it does so indirectly. In relation to the Irish response, as Kelleher suggests, the generic instability of these fictions manifests clearly the trauma that famine produced. Certainly, this one event altered immeasurably Irish experience, giving urgency to the matter of Ireland and its perceived problems. As with the Act of Union a generation earlier, the famine, along with O'Connell's death in 1847 and the Young Ireland rebellion of 1848, marks a pivotal moment when all levels of experience and action are distorted. In truth, the famine as a topic is deflected into other areas: most notably the land question of the 1870s onwards where so many novelists focus their attention. The basic underlying current is one where 'something must be done', but the question always remains, 'what?'

Littérateur Sheridan Le Fanu's (1814–73) response to this question is to be discovered in two novels in particular: *The House by the Churchyard* (1863) and *Uncle Silas: A Tale of Bartram-Haugh* (1864). His is a return to the concerns of an earlier Anglo-Irish generation: the perilous position of the Anglo-Irish within Ireland and the anxieties surrounding the continuance of Anglo-Irish Big House life. The famine – and attendant events – throws into sharp relief those concerns, and these two novels specifically manifest this percolating uneasiness. *The House by the Churchyard* is a novel about nothing: whatever plot there might be holding the entire narrative together is very tenuous and thin.[64] For all that, its praises were 'loudly and persistently proclaimed' when it was first published.[65] Set in Chapelizod on the outskirts of Dublin city in 1767, it is a novel revolving round detailing village life. Le Fanu taps into a narrative structure – in its form-lessness – that captures the realities and concerns of life as it is lived. The very marginality of the year 1767 – in which nothing much of note occurs (the previous and the subsequent years are of more interest historically) – and the focus on the peripheral space outside Dublin reinforce this cele-bration of the ordinary and the everyday. Indeed, many critics link this novel to James Joyce's *Finnegans Wake* which used the novel as a source, making use of a similar locale and sharing some similar concerns.[66] The supernatural is never far away in this work – as it is never far away in any of Le Fanu's writing – and here famously it is quite literally embodied in a disconnected hand.[67] Some might argue that such an image is born out of the recent daily horrors visited by famine, but its presence has more to do with the potentially disruptive energies of psychological trauma made manifest in Gothic moments like this. Behind the façade of better times and a happy community lurks the anxiety of the Anglo-Irish world's ability to conceive of itself as a whole or a complete entity. Thus the emphasis on disconnection, disembodiment and spectral haunting told through a ram-bling narrative points towards the dilemma faced by the Anglo-Irish char-acters in Elizabeth Bowen's fiction of the 1920s and 1930s. She is a critical figure in our understanding Le Fanu's Irish writing. Her remarks about *Uncle Silas* firmly place it in an Anglo-Irish tradition of Big House writing and the Anglo-Irish Gothic: '[It is] an Irish story transposed to an English setting. The hermetic solitude and the autocracy of the great country house, the demonic power of the family myth, fatalism, feudalism and the "ascend-ancy" outlook are accepted facts of life for the race of hybrids from which Le Fanu sprang.'[68] The intense, all-consuming desire for the continuance of property within a family, with its attendant focus on bloodlines and the processes of inheritance (legal and otherwise) coupled with an unflinching concentration on the presence of the bricks and mortar house itself, encap-sulates the increasingly insular perception that Protestant Ireland had of itself.[69] In *Uncle Silas*, the parable of political union through marriage is twisted beyond recognition. Whereas possibility and a better future seemed to offer hope to the Irish situation, the reality now is one of anxious stagnation and impossibility.

Even Charles Lever, who had entertained his readers superbly before the famine, cannot sustain such jauntiness in the aftermath of the great famine's destructive force. His *Lord Kilgobbin: A Tale of Ireland in Our Own Time* (1872) attempts to offer a mix of opinions from within Ireland: from the Anglo-Irish perspective to that of Fenian revolutionaries. The most scathing portrayals drawn are those of the emerging Catholic middle classes, who pose the most real threat to continued Anglo-Irish rule.[70] The majority of Irish novels now follow a prescribed model and trajectory: Ireland remains politically, economically and socially problematic. The Irish question now seems simplified, revolving round a form of Irish independence through home rule, the land and securing rights for tenants on the one hand, while defusing any possibility of violent revolt on the other. The Fenian rebellion of 1867 meant that such political violence was a constant reality in Irish life and would remain so for a long time. The difficulty, though, is how any kind of radical change can come about because any such change would necessarily mean the root-and-branch dismantling of the status quo and the altering of the position of the minority Anglo-Irish ruling class. And yet change did occur through the various land acts from 1870 onwards producing a seismic shift in land ownership.

Charles Kickham's (1828–82) *Knocknagow; or, the Homes of Tipperary* (1873) was a hugely popular and commercially successful novel in its own time and for many years afterwards. The plot is unwieldy[71] but its very shapelessness allows for a remarkably wide-ranging rendering of the nuances and subtleties of a flourishing peasant world. Not since the work of Banim and Griffin had the rural Catholic world with all its divisions and diversity been offered to the reading public. As James H. Murphy argues: 'The key to its success was its capacity to present an oppressed community that was riven with conflict, and yet simultaneously united and harmonious.'[72]

The novel's ability to present an image of the Irish as victims as well as to offer a picture of the emerging middle-class farmer and shopkeeper – the class seemingly set to be the inheritors of whatever new Ireland was going to come into being – meant that it remained popular among this class, whose apparent story of triumph it told.[73] Though the precise historical timing of the novel is unclear, it is suggested that Kickham desires to present an Irish world changed, and continuing to change, radically because of the famine.[74] Thus *Knocknagow* operates at the level of nostalgia in its own time, as well as subsequently.[75] The novel's significance is that it is the most successful of the Catholic novels which hope to present that faith from within its own community. Kickham, at the beginning of the novel, employs the framing device of the English visitor through which to view Ireland, abandoning this contrivance as the novel progresses. This formal shift away from the English perspective is important because it allows his characters to debate the issues of the day, especially regarding the place of the Fenian movement in Irish affairs (Kickham himself was a Fenian) and its relationship to religion and politics, among themselves. It is interesting to observe how he tempers his own extreme political views, aware that he must make them palatable to a wider Irish and international audience.

To an increasing extent, Irish novels begin to slavishly mirror the wider political debates of their time: the Land League, Fenianism, the fate of Landlordism and Home Rule become the staple background to whatever plot is played out in the foreground. Though, as Margaret Kelleher points out, women's writing in this period can be read as challenging some of the easy consensus and status quo surrounding Ireland.[76] Still, the personal fate of many characters becomes entwined with Ireland's history as writers attempt to chart a moral course for their Irish readership, while continuing to explain the Irish dilemma to a wider readership beyond Ireland. One consequence is that character types remain the mainstay of Irish fiction: characters are unable to be themselves, being burdened instead with being representative of a class or a political stance or perspective. There are writers, though, who can read as working against this paradigm. May Laffan Hartley (1849–1916) in novels such as *Hogan, M.P.* (1876) and *The Hon. Miss Ferrard* (1877) has been praised as a 'pioneer in Irish literary realism', opening up the Irish novel to new perspectives on middle-class life away from the usual types in Irish fiction.[77] Born a Catholic who went on to marry a Protestant, she is superbly positioned to offer insight into the various strata of later nineteenth-century Irish urban life. It is ironic that she employs the vulgar novel form as a means of savagely critiquing the aspirations of the rising bourgeois Catholic classes, whom she cuts down to size for their pretensions to gentility and their lack of breeding.

Three novels from this period, in particular, are illustrative of the form that the novel takes at this time: George Moore's (1852–1933) *Drama in Muslin: A Realistic Novel* (1886), Rosa Mulholland's (1841–1921) *Marcella Grace: An Irish Novel* (1886) and Emily Lawless's (1845–1913) *Hurrish: A Study* (1886). All were published in 1886, and thus reflect this period when the land question, Home Rule and violence were all on the agenda within Ireland, and, thanks to Charles Stewart Parnell's political leadership, also on the agenda in British politics. It is a moment when, it seemed, energies were being focused on bringing about a radical change in Ireland's relationship to Britain and a change within Ireland itself that would see a significant shift in power away from minority to majority rule.

Rosa Mulholland's *Marcella Grace* expresses some of the limitations of political Irish vision at this juncture. Her novel sees the ills of Ireland as being the fault of the landlords' careless mismanagement of their estates. Hers is a conception that had not developed much since Edmund Burke's analysis of the irredeemably middle-class nature of the Anglo-Irish in eighteenth-century Ireland. Her solution is to replace a Protestant aristocracy with a Catholic one: authority – political and moral – is a matter of breeding and, ultimately, genetics will out. The eponymous Marcella Grace comes into her rightful inheritance after the death of her mother, who had married beneath her class. It seems that the only way to redeem the Catholic Irish is to reimagine them as natural aristocrats and Gaelic society as one lived along aristocratic lines. The persistence of this feudal solution to Ireland's problems demonstrates the debilitating nature of this notion of Ascendancy in Ireland: real answers are always avoided as the wrong questions are continually posed. While the thinking behind this is surely suspect and utterly simplistic, Mulholland is as aware of the subtleties of class and difference within the Catholic Irish community as were Kickham, Carleton and Griffin. She is at the forefront of that general drive for Catholic respectability. W. B. Yeats, as a representative of the later literary revival, praised Mulholland's work. For him, she is 'the novelist of contemporary Catholic Ireland'[78] – and it is easy to understand why, with her happy recognition – or remembering – of the long-denied noble worth of the Gaelic and Catholic Irish. As Marcella says to her erstwhile lover: 'Oh, how strangely you have known me and yet not known me.'[79] This could be read as the secret code to understanding the emergence of a confident Ireland in the ensuing decades. The cultural revival, and the political move towards independence, were just that: a revival of what had been there all along, an unmasking that allowed the true authentic nature of the Irish person to emerge. For Mulholland, what is uncovered is not something peculiarly Irish but merely an image of the kind of Victorian respectability then predominant in popular culture.[80]

Emily Lawless's *Hurrish: A Study* is a more complex piece of fiction than the fairytale-like work of Mulholland. As with the general tone of the time, the novel focuses on Hurrish and his impossible position in relation to the twin evils of backward landlordism and the threat of Fenian violence. Lawless's work was critiqued as being inimical to revivalist and nationalist thinking at the time and subsequently.[81] *The Nation* newspaper declared that her portrayal of the Irish peasant was 'slanderous' and that the novel was a lie 'from cover to cover'. As Margaret Kelleher says, even W. B. Yeats, in more genteel fashion, damns her work for being 'in imperfect sympathy with the Celtic nature'.[82] The usually astute Yeats misses the point that Lawless notably grounds her narrative very much in a sense of place – the west coast of Ireland in County Clare – so that where things happen is more important than what happens.[83] Despite revivalist objections, this evocation of the local will become a dominant feature in revivalist writing, allowing different writers and characters from differing traditions to lay claim to the Irish landscape while avoiding any overtly political propagandising. For Lawless, the solid presence of the rocky Burren is more enduring than the various political positions held by the characters that play out their drama upon the landscape. In many ways, this interest in the local and in the landscape is a retreat away from the harsh political realities of the day that seem to be irresolvable and a movement into the realm of a personal relationship to people and to places.

George Moore's *A Drama in Muslin*, as its subtitle 'A Realist Novel' subtly suggests, is a conscious reaction to the kind of fantasy fiction with its safely bourgeois solutions, though dressed as a return to a feudal past, peddled by Rosa Mulholland and others in the *Irish Monthly* magazine.[84] Moore was a Catholic landlord, who deliberately embraced European contemporary aesthetic thought, and was perfectly placed to offer a penetrating portrait of an Ireland stupefied by the colonial link to Britain that positioned Irish cultural and political life on the periphery of metropolitan empire. Set between 1881 and 1884 with the turbulent events surrounding the Land League campaign – coercion acts, land acts and Charles Stewart Parnell's increasing visibility as the Irish political leader who would deliver Home Rule – acting as a backdrop, *A Drama in Muslin* presents an image of an Ireland teetering on the brink of profound and radical transformation.

Unlike so many other works of this period, as Declan Kiberd argues, Moore's novel is raised 'to the level of art'.[85] It is so for the simple reason that no easy options or solutions are offered to Ireland's problems, and importantly that the novel form itself – and Moore's anxieties and concerns about the form – are very much bound up with the general apprehensiveness that infuses the work. It has been said of *A Drama in Muslin* that 'there was something in it to offend everyone'.[86] It is a sophisticated critique of contemporary Ireland's ills that the writers for the *Irish Monthly* magazine would not care to offer, and certainly its readers would not care to read. Moore's fiction did not simply reconfirm for its readers what they already knew, or thought they knew; rather, it actively challenges them and their most dearly held beliefs and this is conscious on his part. Certainly, Moore's critique of Ascendancy Ireland is harsh: his focus on the deadeningly insular marriage market to which the 'muslin martyrs' are brought to sell their wares, with its coming-out ball in Dublin Castle and the surrounding social scene, is devastating. With anthropological precision, he delineates the rituals and ceremonies of a culture that, if it continues along this path, will necessarily become extinct. Moore deliberately employs Darwinian overtones throughout the novel,[87] and by having his heroine Alice Barton read *The Origin of the Species*, he connects her to wider Victorian concerns about the nature of culture, civilisation and human progress in the late nineteenth century. Yet, the colonial position of the Ascendancy in Ireland means that such angst about culture possesses particular local resonance: if their role as bearers of modernity and civilisation is abandoned, then what is left in its place? In this reading, where 'the unnatural sterility, the cruel idleness of mind and body of the muslin martyrs' is emphasised,[88] the ceremonies and rites of passage that are the focus become empty, devoid of any real meaning or significance in contemporary Ireland. Thus, rather than ceremonies that allow continuance, these are actually harbingers of doom. But Moore also turns his attention to Catholicism – the Bartons are Catholic landlords – and it too is savagely portrayed. Authentic emotion and feeling is denied, and the individual human person is lost in the embrace of communal action and belief. Thus Alice's dilemma is presented through a complex filter which mixes class, gender and national politics, with each being an element in producing the general paralysis 'in which the whole country was sleeping' (*Muslin*, p. 100).

The detailed descriptions of the urban environment of Dublin mirror and amplify the theme of decay within the novel. The city is full of 'squalor', the 'shops and the streets . . . are but a leer of malign decrepitude' (*Muslin*, pp. 170–171). James Joyce, twenty years later, would continue this exposé of Dublin as a ruinous, grey, uninspiring city. Moore's analysis positions Ireland and the Anglo-Irish as provincials unable to act or think for themselves: for them culture, fashion and manners are always to be discovered elsewhere. Moore's novel itself echoes this condition, being, in many ways, an Irish version of George Eliot's *Middlemarch: A Study of Provincial Life* published in 1872. The similarities between Dublin and Middlemarch as sites of provincial blinkeredness are clear, as are the parallels between Alice Barton and Dorothea Brooke – both of whom challenge the prevailing narrowness and restrictive world of women. But Moore is aware that there are differences too and whereas *Middlemarch* could accentuate, in the end, social cohesion and unity beyond the merely local moments of discord, such a conclusion cannot be achieved in *A Drama in Muslin*.

Throughout the novel images of stark division are presented to the reader: the Bartons and their friends are constantly figured set apart from the crowd, disconnected from the peasants in the countryside and the workers in Dublin:

Never were poverty and wealth brought into plainer proximity. In the broad glare of the carriage lights the shape of every feature, even the colour of the eyes, every glance, every detail of dress, every stain of misery were revealed to the silken exquisites who, a little frightened, strove to hide themselves within the scented shadows of their broughams: and, in like manner, the bloom on every aristocratic cheek, the glitter of every diamond, the richness of every plume were visible to the avid eyes of those who stood without in the wet and the cold. (*Muslin*, p. 171)

Mrs Barton wishes that 'they would not stare so' (*Muslin*, p. 171), as if the act of being perceived by these others had itself become unbearable. Moore, though, is not capable of, or interested in, offering his readers the view from those who stare: we are never in the position to hear their story. The peasant Irish remain ghostly, vague figures who in this act of silent perception unnerve those they view. They cannot be adequately contained within the novel form as it is; they remain just outside his aesthetic reach. However, their brooding presence is a recognition by Moore that their silent threat may well become a vocal reality.

The end of the novel is curious in that it encapsulates failure, suggesting that Ireland is an impossible place, and that its problems are irresolvable. Alice and her husband Dr Edward Reed leave Ireland at the close, a final scene of a peasant family being evicted from their cabin only amplifying their despair at Ireland's lot. Of course, their despair is really for their own position and that of their class. While George Moore was not a prophet, like many others he would have presumed that Home Rule would eventually come about, most probably sooner rather than later, and that this would alter the world of his novel irreversibly. Ineffectual action, stagnation and paralysis are the condition of the Anglo-Irish as portrayed in *A Drama in Muslin*, and not perhaps of the silent majority outside the Big House.

Alice dreams of being an artist, indeed a novelist. Moore's fate for Alice suggests a pessimistic prognosis for the novel form – or particularly the Victorian novel form exemplified by George Eliot's *Middlemarch* – as it might be practised in Ireland. For her dream of being a writer to become a reality, she must escape into a bourgeois life in England. In England, she can become what she already is – middle-class – and, as such, in Ashbourne Crescent, a London suburb where there 'is neither Dissent nor Radicalism' (*Muslin*, p. 325), she can write her novels. Employing that device of Eliot – the all-knowing omniscient narrator – Moore comments upon the happy staidness of this new life, the tone not altogether celebratory or approving. It is as if, commenting on his own position as an artist, he recognises that to embrace the predominant themes of individual advancement and bourgeois desire is to lose some essential connection with Irish concerns. Most damning, perhaps, from Moore's own aesthetic perspective, is how blithely conventional the image of the artist becomes in his portrayal of Alice at the close of the novel: bohemia is just another form of suburbia.

George Moore's *A Drama in Muslin* encapsulates perfectly the anxieties central to the Irish novel form in the nineteenth century, and, indeed, through Alice's desire to be a novelist it manages to dramatise them. In the end, the novel deconstructs all the rigid binaries associated with Ireland and the Irish. The sectarian divide and the stereotyping used to prop up that division from Sydney Owenson onwards is radically challenged and undermined in the novel: it is the Catholic Alice who questions her inner devotion to her religion; it is she who embraces modernity in all its middle-class banality. Rather than the Gaelic Irish being presented as backwards and out of step with the onward march of history, it is the Anglo-Irish who cling hopelessly to outmoded thought and ritual, and who set their faces firmly against change. Alice thus represents a new type of hero for Irish fiction – certainly she demonstrates the possibilities of what that hero might be.

The Irish novel in the nineteenth century reflected the turbulent times out of which it was written, with each novelist groping towards a form of expression, a new frame, that might allow a story to be told adequately. It seems as if some novelists achieved the telling of certain aspects of that Irish story but no novelist came near to giving a full view or account. But suggesting that such a situation is a sign of failure – as many critics do – betrays a fundamental misunderstanding of the novel form. The canon – a creation after the fact – has formed critics' attitudes rather than the novel, as it was constituted in the nineteenth century. In other words, the English novel's stability – that which the Irish novel allegedly deviates from – is only a supposed stability conferred in retrospect. The novel form, from its beginnings, oscillated between the private and the public worlds, between the old and the new: it was always aware of its upstart and improvised nature in comparisons to traditional modes, and certainly the best Irish novels in the nineteenth century remained true to those roots. They are never the finished work of the art, they are never fully complete and fixed; rather, as has been argued, they gesture towards what has not yet come to pass, and are infused with anticipation of that future. In this reading, the effort to express, the struggle to communicate, is what is important.

Edith Somerville and Martin Ross's The Real Charlotte: *the blooming menagerie*

Tragedy is under-developed Comedy, not fully born.[1]

(Patrick Kavanagh)

Edith Somerville (1858–1949) and Martin Ross (1862–1915) were, and continue to be, better known as accomplished comic writers who, with their entertainingly popular series of 'Irish RM' stories, detailed the humorous possibilities of Ireland as a place where the colonial power struggle is played out at the level of hilarious misunderstanding and wry suspicion. The comedic turn in Somerville and Ross's writing comes at the precise moment when their class and caste are most threatened with extinction after the political upheavals of the Land War, various attempts to bring about Home Rule and the numerous land acts of the 1880s onwards forever altered the position of the Anglo-Irish Ascendancy. Such an exercise on their part can be read as a deflective reaction to this reality – an assertion of power in their ability to mock and playfully belittle. And the emphasis is very much on play in their 'Irish RM' stories, with Somerville and Ross recognising the theatrical and performative nature of the colonial relationship for both the colonised and the coloniser.[2]

Yet there is nothing more serious than comedy. Certainly, for Somerville and Ross, beneath the light touch of their brand of social comedy lurks a much more pensive and dark tone. In *The Real Charlotte* (1894) comedy is combined with tragedy with devastating effect. It anticipates some of the Big House themes that would dominate Anglo-Irish writing in the twentieth century, but it would be a mistake to believe that it fits snugly with what some critics read as a long, slow threnody to Anglo-Irish position and power.[3] Here their literary genius is aligned, as it is aligned for many of the Ascendancy class in the late nineteenth century – George Moore for instance or J. M. Synge[4] – with an anthropological desire to unmask the surface workings of society, and in Somerville and Ross's case it is employed in order to debunk the pretensions of an emerging middle-class Ireland.

The Real Charlotte was written between 1890 and 1893[5] and is set in the recent past from May 1887 to June 1888. It is a period when the ongoing national 'Plan of Campaign', combined with localised agitation by farmers against landlords, met with the State response of yet another coercion bill for Ireland and more placatory land acts. This turbulent backdrop punctuates the development of the narrative of Charlotte and her younger and more beautiful cousin Francie: their story charting this particular moment of change and transformation for the Anglo-Irish Protestant world. Somerville and Ross are not overly interested, however, in the details of history: it is made clear that no one in the world of the novel is said to fully understand the various land acts that are being passed and causing a revolution in Irish society. Only Charlotte Mullen possesses the knowledge of what they portend and how they might work. And this says more about the kind of character Charlotte is than being a comment on political manoeuvrings at Westminster. This wilful sidelining of historical events suggests a reorientation of focus away from the past, or what was, towards the unknown future and what might be. In other words, Somerville and Ross know that history comes and goes – that things happen – but that the real story of consequence is the more localised human one. It is furthermore an attempt to understand the predicament of their class as part of a wider, universal phenomenon and not just simply an Irish one. This neglect of history also reorients the novel towards its proper focus, which the authors recognise is the individual within society. Somerville and Ross offer the reader a minute and precise detailing of Anglo-Irish Protestant life, rendering lucidly the subtleties and nuances of class and position. Simply put, the novel is wholly concerned with Anglo-Ireland; the Catholic Irish, the Gaelic peasant world that W. B. Yeats, Douglas Hyde and others involved in the literary revival of this period were so intently engaging with and reimagining, is of no concern to them. One by-product of this is that it explodes any sense of a monolithic Anglo-Irish society as aristocratic.

Indeed, whatever conflict there is in the novel is within the Anglo-Irish community itself, between its different classes and between the old world of position, privilege and aristocratic wealth and a new world where position, power and wealth become spheres for individual enterprise. Traditional power structures are therefore made radically fluid and worryingly permeable. The plot reflects these concerns and anxieties of the Anglo-Irish: it is a story of inheritance, with characters jostling for social position as they manoeuvre themselves in relation to land and money, marriage and sex. Francie Fitzpatrick's attractiveness to many of the male characters, all from different walks of life and class, gives focus to this narrative conflict.

The prime movers in these squalid machinations are Charlotte, who is cheating her cousin Francie out of her rightful inheritance, and Roddy Lambert, who dreams of a much improved financial and sexual future. Their dilemma is that they aspire to old world advantage without new world graft: they want money, power and position but are not prepared to labour for such gains. They do not possess, as no one else in the novel possesses, any interest in the world of industry and commerce. By looking back to a previous generation, they collectively ignore the possibilities that the new world inhabited by the shopkeepers and the mercantile middle classes possesses. Thus, this story of property, inheritance, money and succession is caught up in the nexus between tradition and modernity: between old world values and new world realities. Here the novel resonates beyond the Irish sphere, connecting with a general *fin de siècle* anxiety about cultural and racial degeneration. For Anglo-Irish society predicated on hierarchical difference and superiority, the emergence of a Darwinian world of levelling sameness and homogeneity is to be feared. It has been argued that an unspoken thread running through the novel is that of infertility, with the present-day Anglo-Irish world being unable to produce the next generation.[6] Lineage, then, is hugely significant in a novel where everyone can be known and precisely placed in the world of Lismoyle. No one, save the Dysarts, seems to be of true aristocratic blood, though the name 'Dysart' has a Scottish Gaelic origin. Both Charlotte herself and a certain Julia Duffy are reminders of the dissipation of once aristocratic families. Of course, Charlotte's pedigree explains her attraction towards aristocratic life: she wants to return to the position she believes is properly hers.

In a world seemingly enamoured with patrician values, any deviation from that supposed norm would necessarily appear obvious and awkward. Thus, as is made clear by the narrator, all 'the subtle grades of Irish vulgarity' are on display throughout the novel.[7] Unlike the physical monstrosity which signals the Darwinian beast that lurks within the modern individual to be discovered in much British fiction of this period, Somerville and Ross manifest such theoretical concerns with vulgarity through language. As ever in the Irish scene, linguistic ability and accent remain signifiers of one's position and one's authority.

The reader is first introduced to Francie in the opening passages of the novel, which are set in the northside of Dublin city. The city, as described, is reminiscent of Banim's pre-famine urban scenes while also anticipating Joyce's later use of the same environment. In terms of the wider cultural revivalist movement, Dublin is painted as a dull, lifeless place: 'it is immutable, unchangeable, fixed as the stars' (*The Real Charlotte*, p. 1). The rural scene also reflects this marginal position: the presence of the British soldiers Hawkins and Cruisiter suggesting that real power and authority is situated elsewhere. It is this dead centre of Irish life which Yeats and others want to re-energise with their shift of attention away from London towards Ireland. Francie's Dublin accent suggests 'familiarity' it is declared, which is in itself disruptive of strict hierarchical categories. Roddy Lambert, too, who has his own hopes and desires for betterment in the world, lapses into his native Limerick lilt when under stress. His true self can never be fully denied.

Along with Francie, it is Charlotte who most unsettles socially the ordered Anglo-Irish world of Lismoyle. Unlike those others, whose true identity is never too far from the surface, Charlotte enjoys a linguistic agility, making it hard to fix her to any one place or any one situation. She employs different registers and accents in different circumstances. As one critic puts it, she is 'chameleon like', using Standard English or Hiberno-English, or a male register when she believes it is pragmatic to do so:[8] 'Charlotte had many tones of voice, according with the many facets of her character, and when she wished to be playful she affected a vigorous brogue, not perhaps being aware that her own accent scarcely admitted of being strengthened' (*The Real Charlotte*, p. 11). Certainly, there is a problem with the position of women in this society: they are marginalised and mostly confined to the domestic sphere. Francie's difficulty is that she – quite unwittingly – challenges those codes and regulations with her open flirtation with the English subaltern Hawkins.[9]

It becomes increasingly apparent to the reader that what Francie and Charlotte really represent is modernity itself. Both are figured as modern characters within the novel, but Charlotte especially is *the* modern character. The fluidly of her speech implies that Charlotte can fit in anywhere, and can move around society at will. Possessing brains, ambition and an unsentimental clear-sightedness beyond her allotted station in polite Lismoyle society, she represents the new middle-class Irish woman or man and is thus to be feared. While the narrator states twice (pp. 201, 223) that there is a 'real' Charlotte lurking there beneath the various masks she wears, she actually embraces the possibilities of multiple personalities rather than a singular self. While perhaps feared, certainly distrusted, by her social superiors for this flouting of conventional boundaries, she herself seems always somewhat uneasy. As a truly complex character, and as a modern individual, she recognises that her desires may never be fulfilled, realising that her own position as a new woman signifies the obsolescence of Ascendancy life. For Charlotte Mullen the opposite is also true: in fitting in everywhere, she fits in nowhere and her dilemma is one of trying to discover, or manufacture, a solid place where she can be, and where she can exist. Those she admires simply are, while she strives to be.

Language is not the only indicator of change and decline. In an elaborate ploy on the part of Somerville and Ross, they populate the world of Lismoyle with numerous references to animals. From domestic and farm animals to wild animals, from inside houses to the Big House demesne, this parallel animal universe is very much alive and thriving. And it is consciously presented as a counter realm, a deflected commentary on the world of human habitation, acting as a 'sort of second society'.[10] It, too, is a world operating with an intricate structure. An elaborate hierarchy is in place where each animal vies for space and authority over their fellows. In Charlotte's house, for instance, a recurring motif is the ongoing battle between the cockatoo and Susan the cat for position and attention.

At the beginning of the novel, Somerville and Ross deliberately set out to confuse the reader in relation to the demarcation between the animal and the human spheres. In a fabulously dark introduction to Lismoyle in the second chapter, after the grey descriptions of Dublin, the reader is forced to ponder who, or what, is this Susan – seemingly being talked of as a person but only to be surprisingly presented as a cat. To add to the confusion, Susan is a male cat. All categories – social, gender, natural – are momentarily made porous. If the animal kingdom is anthropomorphised, so the human world is considered in animal terms; for instance, animal imagery is used to describe characters – Mrs Lambert, for example, is called the 'turkey hen' consistently. *Fin de siècle* disquiet revolving round Charles Darwin's evolutionary theories become apparent here. Civilisation and culture as presented in *The Real Charlotte* has developed into an elaborate and rarefied system of codes and rules, but the emphasis throughout the novel is squarely on lineage, heredity and ancestry which, when combined with the presence of this mirroring animal world, suggests that brute instincts of basic survival are what actually prevail.

Acting as a bulwark against 'the filthy modern tide'[11] is the ever-present supercilious narrator whose aloof, controlled, sardonic and knowing voice transcends that of the characters talked of, and indeed the nuances and subtleties of the class structure she is describing. Her consistently unemotional voice throughout stands in stark contrast to that of Charlotte, Francie and all the others. The tone of the narrator presumes a shared range of attitudes with the implied reader: everyone will (or should) see the characters for what they really are. The narrator is highly intrusive, offering comments and asides on characters as well as nuggets of wisdom on the foibles of humanity in general. Subtly the narrator becomes a kind of invisible character actively haunting the text. Early on it is made clear that this is a written narrative (pp. 10, 12), and that the narrator is involved in an act of writing. Through this labour, this work, she is dragged down into the world of the novel – becoming in consequence an integral part of what she talks about, existing at the same level of the characters and not God-like hovering above them. Such a reading works against the supposed superiority of the narrator, exposing it perhaps as a performative pose. For instance, her assertion that there is a 'real Charlotte' amid the numerous versions of her might only be a power play on her part – her hoping to fix and 'know' Charlotte, as everyone else within the space of the novel is fixed and known. It becomes clear that the narrator needs characters such as Charlotte, Francie and Roddy because only then can she be superior in the light of their inferiority.

The self-consciousness of the narrator opens up the possibility of some reflection on the state of literary art in general at this juncture and in this particular occurrence of the novel. Christopher Dysart's interest in the relatively new art form of photography makes him the representative artist figure in Lismoyle. It is an instant form of art, making the exact representation of reality in painting and literature passé. Soon it will be available to the masses, thereby making the mysteries of art open to the coming middle classes. This interest in photography displays the stunted nature of Christopher's character; he is drawn to it as a medium because it is much easier than the hard work associated with either painting or writing poetry. Its accessibility and easiness reinforces his claim to a certain aristocratic languidness. In looking through his scrapbook, Francie is unmoved by landscape portraits of Oxford's streets and chapels, but when confronted by 'an instantaneous photograph of a bump-race, with its running accompaniment of maniacs on the bank' she discusses them 'with fervid interest' (p. 125). Architecture and scenery hold no attraction for her; she is drawn instead to people. In an earlier scene, she stumbles upon a holy well on an outing to Innishochery Island with her flirtatious admirer Mr Hawkins. The potential that revivalists such W.B. Yeats or J.M. Synge might have exploited is left untapped:

a few rags impaled on the spikes of the thorn bush denoted that it marked the place of a holy well. Conspicuous among these votive offerings were two white rags, new and spotless, and altogether out of keeping with the scraps of red flannel and dirty frieze that had been left by the faithful in lieu of visiting cards for the patron saint of the shrine. (*The Real Charlotte*, p. 84)

Tradition and modernity collide, or perhaps elide, here. The holy well is an object whose true significance and purpose are not known within the

Anglo-Irish environment of Lismoyle: it is given no name, and no details as to the healing powers associated with the well are offered. As a tourist attraction it possesses only passing curiosity value: a warning, perhaps, to how modernity can reframe and neutralise the energies of traditional culture. In keeping with the focus on the nature of the new disruptive middle-class individual, Francie and Hawkins use the well for their own very secular and sentimental intentions: they tie two rags to the tree as a symbol of their love.

The difficulty for the narrator is that her own act of writing, her own intervention into the sphere of art, is unable to differentiate itself from Christopher's photography. Throughout the novel the word 'vulgar' is used in almost every conceivable situation and context: people of a certain classes are vulgar, and their manners, attitudes and language reveal vulgarity. The reason for its deployment is clear, setting up a barrier between the multitude – the uncouth and common mob – and the refined codes and taste of the ruling classes. The narrator, as one who writes – as one who labours – would seem to be positioned at an angle to the aristocratically indolent and bored artist figure that is Christopher. Despite positioning herself as one who might speak for the Ascendancy point of view, it becomes clear that she might have less in common with the class and the people for whose future she purportedly fears.

The novel is *the* vulgar artistic form of modernity, possessing none of the rigid rules of classical art and improvising its own set of conventions and codes as needs be. The novel, too, is interested in people – common people; it details the minutiae of their lives and lays bare their innermost feelings and emotions. And, of course, the novel's target audience is those middle classes whose story the novel tells. While the various barriers and boundaries between the characters and the class they represent generate plot conflict within *The Real Charlotte*, the more telling tension is the meta-narrational one of the narrator's ambiguous relationship to the form of the novel itself. It is an ambivalence that remains unresolved: she aspires to a more transcendent world, a more transcendent art, but is condemned to wallow in what by her own estimation she deems vulgar. In other words, the narrator *is* exactly that which she talks of: vulgar and degenerate.

A common critique of the Irish novel in the nineteenth century is that it fails to capture the reality of Irish Catholic life – that Catholicism is inimical to the all-pervasive realism within the novel form.[12] Yet, it seems apparent that the real distrust for the novel form in Ireland in the nineteenth century is not from within the Catholic majority, who happily employ the form in their search for cultural and political respectability, but with the Protestant elite, who, precisely because of their status as an

Ascendancy class, fear its equalitarian levelling impulses. As with Patrick Kavanagh's point about tragedy being underdeveloped comedy, the beginnings perhaps of an absurdist vision in Somerville and Ross's novel can be discerned: it is dark, black humour that is being plumbed in *The Real Charlotte* and not light airy entertainment and diversion. With the death of Francie at the close, all hopes are thwarted; all potential futures come to an end. It is a fallen world that Somerville and Ross, and the characters they create, inhabit – and they know it. As a character in Samuel Beckett's work might say, there is nothing to be done.

CHAPTER 3

Living in a time of epic: the Irish novel and Literary Revival and revolution, 1891–1922

> Ah! when the ghost begins to quicken,
> Confusion of the death-bed over, is it sent
> Out naked on the roads, as the books say, and stricken
> By the injustice of the skies for punishment?
>
> (W. B. Yeats, 'The Cold Heaven' (1914))

Throughout the nineteenth century there was a general expansion in Irish fiction titles being published in both Britain and Ireland and this trend continued on into the 1890s and beyond.[1] Indeed, from the 1880s onwards many English publishers such as Longman, Macmillan and T. Fisher Unwin were increasingly eager to publish Irish writing, including the novel.[2] Within Ireland, too, with the emergence of the Talbot Press yet another outlet for Irish fiction writing was established. How is the reader, then, to understand the relationship of what appears to be the healthy state of the Irish novel in this period in relation to the Irish Literary Revival which has subsequently become almost exclusively associated with the emergence of dramatic and poetic art?

This apparent paradox raises many pertinent questions about the study and reception of the Irish novel generally. At this key moment, a nexus of production and critical evaluation of the Irish novel occurs – both at that moment when many writers consciously attempt to position and place Irish fiction and, subsequently, as the Revival becomes *the* main focus of Irish literary studies. That the Revival period represents a shift in Irish culture and politics is an understatement. The death of Charles Stewart Parnell in 1891 and the failure of the British to grant Home Rule to Ireland, with William Gladstone's final Home Rule Bill being defeated in 1894, produced a concerted effort to reimagine the Irish connection with Britain and to reorientate politics and culture towards Ireland.[3] Douglas Hyde's celebrated lecture, 'The Necessity for De-Anglicising Ireland' (1892),[4] captures perfectly this paradigmatic shift which refocuses the Irish space as a place of innovative potential and possibility. Rather than being anti-English, this energy is concerned with self-help and self-sufficiency in all realms of public life, economics and art.[5] In terms of artistic expression, it was the theatre, especially, which became the site of dynamic creativity, both as a physical space that brought together – created – an audience and as a dramatic location for the public debate and performance of Irish issues and concerns. Its immediacy and accessibility allowed for it, and those involved with it, to imagine momentarily the prospect of epic thought and epic action being united.[6] After almost a century of paralysis, the heroic gesture once again becomes possible.

Against this backdrop some critics suggest that the revivalist project was inimical to the novel, and that the revival as a collective movement deliberately ignored the form.[7] Quoting from a 1940s essay by George Orwell which argues that 'The novel is practically a Protestant form of art; it is a product of the free mind, of the autonomous individual',[8] John Wilson Foster, for example, equates such alleged liberty with the Anglo-Irish Protestant imagination and with realism in art.[9] In doing so, he sets up a dichotomy between a supposed revivalist illusion and fantasy and a supposedly more penetrating realism, between individual conscience and collective cant, between tradition and modernity, and between the urban space and the rural world. His most recent work, *Irish Novels 1890–1940: New Bearings in Culture and Fiction*, revises that rigid either/or division and demonstrates admirably how popular fiction, particularly, ranged between detective novels, ghost stories, New Woman fiction, Great War novels and science fiction. His contention that much of this fiction defies the exceptionalism that many critics employ in their approach to Ireland and Irish literature is a challenging one. Certainly it seems at the level of popular fiction that this might be the case. It could also be argued that such popular fiction perpetuated images of Ireland and the Irish for an English audience rather than an exclusively Irish audience: that the cultural traffic or significance between Britain and Ireland is merely one-way. One of the many difficulties with his argument, though, is the fact that the novel within Britain, that manifestation of the form which Foster links the Irish novel to in his archipelagic understanding of British–Irish relations, is itself not a stable form at this time – its contours and conventions not rigidly set in stone – though it could be said that generally the novel is linked to a notion of safe conformity.[10] And certainly in Ireland, the kind of sweeping generalisation made by George Orwell about the sectarian leaning of the novel form cannot, and does not, hold true. As has been demonstrated in the previous chapters, throughout the nineteenth century the anxieties and the uncertainties of Irish Protestantism find no comfort in the novel form, which in many ways only serves to lay bare their uneasy position within Ireland. Catholic novelists, on the other hand, in their search for respectability for their class and caste have no such worries and are happy throughout the late nineteenth century to offer reassuring narratives cementing the image of a bourgeoisie coming into positions of power and authority.

Other critics also read the revival moment as silencing voices different to those deemed orthodox. The work of numerous women writers of the period, whose writing fits neatly into 'New Woman' narratives of the late Victorian era for instance, also consistently offered differing and challenging perspectives on Ireland's social problems.[11] Quite obviously reading these women writers from a feminist perspective adds yet another layer to the political mix within revivalist Ireland.[12] And certainly it was a very self-conscious moment for many of these writers as they entered into a debate about the nature of the novel and its position within this changing mood in Ireland. Novelist Rosa Mulholland in *The Irish Monthly*, a periodical dedicated to publishing Irish fiction through this period, complained about: 'The noticeable fact that writers who produce one good novel, giving promise of store to come, almost invariably cease to be Irish at that point, and afterwards cast the tributary stream of their powers into the universal river of English fiction.'[13] This admission suggests less a grand conspiracy on the part of revivalists than a pragmatic embracing of market forces on the part of authors. Mulholland's remarks perhaps partly explain her inclusion in W. B. Yeats's *Representative Irish Tales* (1891), which, as an act of canon formation, is another example of the kind of debate occurring in Ireland at this time and subsequently. There is also the point that literary canon formation is a highly complex process that cannot be reduced to either gender or political affiliation.[14] Though, as with William Carleton's list of standard texts a generation earlier,[15] John Hope Hennessy in 'What do the Irish Read?' (1884) indicated how popular histories and sentimental nationalist poetry and fiction were the staple literary diet of the ordinary Irish reader.[16] The same was true ten years later in an 1894 article in *The New Ireland Review*, 'What Our Country Folk Read', which confirmed this trend.[17] Then, as now, literary recognition has little or nothing to do with aesthetic quality.

Much of this analysis surrounding the alleged prohibiting of various voices is predicated on the notion that Irish nationalism and the Revival were unitary movements, straightforwardly unproblematic. Of course, such an idea is a palpable nonsense: it was a time of conflicting ideas and differing agendas, each competing for position and influence.[18] What is truly remarkable about this period is the emergence of a complicated and complicating Irish political sphere that no longer necessarily demarcates itself along traditional lines. The ideologies of unionism and imperialism are in conflict with republicanism and nationalism and there is much productive commerce between individuals and ideas from all these political stances.

A contemporaneous survey of Irish writing by successful popular novelist George A. Birmingham (1865–1950) – the literary pseudonym of Canon James Owen Hannay – supports this view, declaring that 'in fiction, the Irish literary movement is comparatively weak' in relation to the kind of energy and innovation found in theatre and poetry.[19] What becomes apparent is that in comparison to what is happening in Irish theatre for instance, the Irish novel appears moribund and wedded to the past. Birmingham is aware of how distinctive the Irish note being struck in poetry and drama is and how compromised in contrast the novel form is in a commercial marketplace. He would later cause debate and controversy with his novel *General John Regan* (1913) when nationalists attacked it for its satire of Irish provincial life. A stage version of the novel led to rioting in Westport, County Mayo, when produced there in 1914.[20] So many novels of this time perpetuate stereotypes and propound solutions to Irish problems, and Irish questions that were hopelessly clichéd and out of date. There are many novels, for instance, advocating a feudal answer to starkly modern problems. One such example is Alice Milligan's (1866–1953) *A Royal Democrat: A Sensational Irish Novel* (1890) set in the future of the 1940s. The nineteenth-century 'Irish question' remains unresolved: labelled as 'ancient history', an account is given of a revolt in 1895 when the leaders of the Irish Parliamentary Party were killed in battle and by execution. Her anticipation of failure for the Home Rule movement was met by expected criticism from some in the nationalist press.[21] Still, in her vision of the future, Home Rule has not come about and the matter of land ownership still provokes violent opposition from the Irish. The plot centres on Arthur Cormac Christian Frederick, the Prince of Wales, who is supposedly drowned after a shipwreck off the coast of Ireland. The unknown prince comes to know Ireland and the Irish directly. Eventually, after involving himself with a secret society and being arrested, his true identity becomes known to his cousin, now the queen. He is pardoned and Home Rule is granted. Certainly the device of setting the narrative in the future rather than the past, as is the norm at this time, is radically innovative.[22] However, quite obviously the solution to Irish ills as presented is very much bound to the past. Harking back, at least, to Maria Edgeworth's *The Absentee*, the belief that justice will be done *if only* those in authority might be able to see, understand and empathise with the Irish position remains the same. The motif of hidden or disguised authority that cannot but ultimately reveal itself underscores such a reading: the inherent wrongs of the situation and the validity of Ireland's claims will be laid bare for all to see. After the death of Parnell, Alice Milligan revolutionised her own thinking on Irish matters and would stoutly defend hard-line republicanism in the 1920s. Such a political transformation on her part is indicative of how out of date her 1890s Irish parable actually is.

A recently reappraised curio, first published in 1893, captures perfectly the way in which Ireland was generally viewed at this time and the political and cultural torpor associated with the country.[23] Jules Verne, famous for his extraordinary science adventures, wrote an Irish novel *P'tit-Bonhomme*, which would be translated as *Foundling Mick (P'tit-Bonhomme)* in 1895. Having never set foot in Ireland, Verne's descriptions of the countryside rarely amount to more than hard factual details and names more usually found in travel books. This sense of travelogue is reinforced as young Mick's exploits force him on a contrived journey that touches almost all the major towns in Ireland. Verne's political analysis of Ireland's ills is also thoroughly third-hand, with the landlord class, particularly, being presented as melodramatically evil. Verne himself wanted to write a novel in the vein of his literary hero Charles Dickens, and certainly *Foundling Mick* vaguely echoes the Dickensian world but without its charm or its fascinating extravagances. The novel is imbued with a Victorian metropolitan sensibility that singles out the act of begging as, perhaps, one of the more morally repugnant acts for a modern individual to partake in. Such images of the native Irish beggar abounded in the eighteenth-century Irish novel but seem rather out of place in the late nineteenth century. Foundling Mick's innate understanding of this moral code, and his desire to take responsibility for his lot and work, mark him out as the hero of the tale. He is rewarded with riches for his hard graft and with a makeshift family by the close, affirming his entry into the proper world of middle-class society. Though there is little to recommend in this novel – the translation from the French is pedestrian and utterly lifeless – the story of Mick's self-propelled rise in the world does (perhaps inadvertently) connect with the underlying tenets of revivalist thinking: the turn towards Ireland and the self rather than looking elsewhere for assistance surely chimes with Mick's entry into the world of business. Interestingly, it is exactly this aspect of the novel which presumably led it to being republished by the Talbot Press in the 1930s as *A Lad of Grit*.

Overall, the Irish novel reflects a wider malaise in the novel form generally at this time: its popularity as a form and its being bound to the vagaries of market forces levelling any widespread radical attempts at experiment in terms of content or form. The novel form always struggles to be read beyond its moment of production: its link to the 'now' – to the notion of 'news' – is sometimes far too hard to overcome. It is only when Irish novelists begin to learn the modernist lessons of the revivalists, and begin to reinvent the form in order that it may reflect new realities, that the Irish novel is reinvigorated.[24] A critical re-evaluation of the Irish novel of this period must also begin to contextualise the form, not simply standing in opposition to the revival but also as a part of it. If this perspective is taken, the Irish novel need no longer be considered as an exotic offshoot of the British Victorian and Edwardian novel, or indeed as a colourful variant of modernism.[25] Rather, the various interchanges and interlinks between Irish, British and European culture and literary forms opens up the possibility that cultural and literary exchange is not simply a one-way street with Ireland only at the end point.[26] Beginning to read the novel in this way explodes easy categorisation, opening up the potential of reading of competing *modernisms* rather than a single hegemonic unitary movement.[27] In this way, Irish fiction offers – as perhaps all marginal writing offers (if not actually defines) – an alternative history of what has usually been read as metropolitan literary movements.

If mainstream European art was in the throes of articulating the end of things, giving expression to a profound sense of a world – a way of life – passing away, then some of the best Irish fiction of this period positions itself towards articulating possible futures and the beginning of a new way of life. That permeating impression throughout the nineteenth century of anticipation at all levels of Irish life – political and cultural – now gives way to action. Of interest, then, are those novels that attempt to challenge rather than ratify the status quo with narratives that reflect and inaugurate the epic moment.

Emily Lawless's (1845–1913) *Grania: The Story of an Island* (1892) has received much critical attention in the contemporary moment. The novel and its author's fate being considered an example of how narratives other than a supposedly narrow revivalist one have fallen out of favour. Its focus on the Aran Islands and a realistic portrayal of a young peasant woman prefigures later such depictions, particularly of J. M. Synge. Grania's desire for a life other than the traditional one allotted her makes her an interestingly disruptive and oppositional character, allowing for the 'still relevant exploration of the conflict between communal identity and feminine individuality'.[28] More interesting, perhaps, is Grania's inability 'to under-stand or articulate her own plight' – that facility being open only to the controlling narrative voice.[29] So, while an insight into the consciousness of an Irish peasant woman is allowed, it is still one framed to that character's disadvantage. The difficulty, then, is discovering a way of writing that might overcome that prejudicial framing.

Declan Kiberd argues that if it was the case that throughout the nineteenth century Ireland was made and remade endlessly interesting to, particularly, a British audience, then the task of the revivalist period was to make Ireland interesting to the Irish themselves.[30] It is precisely this process which is enacted in W. B. Yeats's (1865–1939) only published novel, *John Sherman* (1891). Prompted by his father to write about real people rather than myth and fantasy, the poet Yeats turned his attention to imagining his own situation through the medium of fiction. He said of the novel that, 'There is more of myself in it than anything I've done.'[31] The resulting semi-autobiographical work develops along the lines of a *Bildungsroman*. John Sherman is confronted by numerous choices concerning his future and marriage prospects, but it is his movement between Ballah – a fictional rendering of Sligo town – and London and his choosing between them which is central to the novel. Yeatsian critics might be drawn to the nascent exploration of some of the poet's theories of doubleness and the mask and the Nietzschean conflict of the inner self. There are also, importantly, numerous references in prose to imagery that would later find its way into his poetry. The basic impulse for his famous 'The Lake Isle of Innisfree' is detailed:

Delayed by a crush in the Strand, he heard a faint trickling of water near by; it came from a shop window where a little water-jet balanced a wooden ball upon its point. The sound suggested a cataract with a long Gaelic name, that leaped crying into the Gate of the Winds of Ballah.

He goes on to talk of his boyish dream of 'building a wooden hut there and burning a few years out, rowing to and fro, fishing, or lying on the island slopes by the day, and listening at night to the ripple of the water and the quivering of the bushes' (*John Sherman*, p. 58). The juxtaposition of urban and rural, of the inhibiting and unwelcoming streets of London with the more open streets of Ballah and the easy access to nature, make obvious the kind of impetus central to the revivalist project. As with the poem, there is the implication that Sherman, in his constant movements to and fro, rather than becoming grounded, is actually a portrait of a man rootless and out of place.

As a result, the novel connects fundamentally with Yeats's other artistic projects at this time. And yet, it is clear that it lacks the power and penetration of his drama and, particularly, his poetry. The description of the lake isle in the novel, for instance, avoids the kind of deep emotional tone on display in the poem: the awareness of the emigrant's profound sense of homelessness on the streets of London and the imaginative return to, and construction of, a home place is absent. In its stead, the reader is offered wooden dialogue and stilted characterisation. It is not a case of Yeats being unable to blend realism with myth: it is a case of it being utterly tedious without energy or impetus. He realised that the novel was, for him at least, unable to capture the intensity of feeling and immediacy that both poetry and drama might provide. He attempted one more novel, *The Speckled Bird*, but abandoned it after working on it unsuccessfully for a number of years. His most successful prose work is to be found in his autobiographical writings, which he learned from James Joyce's *A Portrait of the Artist as a Young Man*, adopting an impressionistic approach allowing him to transcend chronological detail and hard fact for a more idiosyncratic rendering of his life. Interestingly, in the epilogue to the first instalment of his autobiographical writing, *Reveries over Childhood and Youth*, he writes: 'all life weighed in the scales of my own life seems to be a preparation for something that never happens'.[32] For Yeats, perhaps, the only true medium for expression is poetry – all other literary forms (like memoir) remain for him merely a channel towards that final end. His novel, therefore, is but one of those acts on that path to poetry.

Yeats's failure as a novelist has more to do with the form as it stood at this juncture than his own artistic limitations. In truth, the novel was a conservative form at this time: most popular novels were content to uphold conventional mores and conservative values, and the choices Yeats presents his readers seem like the conformist dreams of the average Victorian man intent on getting away from the pressures of city life and settling down in some rural idyll far from the maddening crowd. This conservative strain can be found in many novels of this period, especially among Catholic novelists who desire to secure their social position through narratives which underpin the Catholic faith's middle-class acceptability and respectability. The untroubled form of the novel allows these novelists to advance their cause. Indeed, this is a time which is remarkable for producing a number of religious novels written from the sympathetic perspective of the Catholic priest, and written by Catholic priests. The works of Canon Patrick Sheehan (1852–1913), Canon Joseph Guinan (1863–1932) and Gerald Donovan (1871–1942) were very popular at this time and long afterwards.[33]

Canon Sheehan's work was particularly successful. His *Geoffrey Austin, Student* (1895) and its sequel *The Triumph of Failure* (1899) are overtly didactic tales focusing on education and the nature of religious belief.[34] James H. Murphy's analysis suggests that Sheehan's story, while possessing local interest, is a more universal questioning of Catholicism's internal debate with regard to its positioning in relation to modernity and modernisation. Sheehan's achievement, then, is to internationalise Irish Catholicism through his protagonist Geoffrey Austin's intellectual struggle with various strands of liberal philosophy. His most successful work, *My New Curate* (1900), is a much more leisurely affair[35] in which, in its close portrayal of parish life in a County Cork town and with its two humane priests, Father Dan Hanrahan and Father Letheby, an image of the Irish Catholic faith and institutions is presented as closely tied and central to the rhythms of everyday life. Canon Joseph Guinan's work is far more straightforward, dealing in the glib stereotype of the Irish Catholic peasant as long-suffering and accepting of their lot.[36] In novels such as *The Soggarth Aroon* (1907) and *The Island Parish* (1908), the true relationship of the people with their priest is one of unquestioning loyalty and love. While the priest can become central to country life, taking on roles of leadership and responsibility outside the religious realm, it is a case of the Irish waiting for their reward in the next world rather than betterment in this one. More challenging of this celebratory perspective is Gerald O'Donovan's *Father Ralph* (1913), which follows a young man through the seminary of Maynooth into the real world and his final turning away from the priesthood. His difficulty is with the Church's attitude to modernity; his decision to leave the priesthood is prompted by a 1907 Encyclical of Pope Pius X, 'On the Doctrine of the Modernists', and its affirmation of central Roman authority and its basic challenge to the claims of individual conscience. Ralph's departure from the Church and from Ireland is presented as a quiet human victory: 'I have found myself at last.'[37]

Common to all three novels is an attempt to present Catholicism from within Catholicism, as a faith with intellectual foundation and rigour, open to debate and discussion. As with W. B. Yeats's *John Sherman*, there are many set-piece scenes that allow for discussion of religion and faith. As astutely noted by Emer Nolan, however, Ralph O'Brien, unlike so many other priests in Irish fiction, and indeed ordinary Catholics, does not leave his homeland and his faith for any sexual motive.[38] Here, the dilemma is strictly an intellectual one. The difficulty is, and will continue to be, trying to accommodate that kind of intellectual stance with a faith which will increasingly base its authority in Ireland on loyalty through the heart rather than the head.

Two other novels of this period can be read in many different ways. While both touch upon religion, and specifically the Catholic religion in relation to modernity, their interest with regard to Irish concerns lie in how they express a radical fluidity around cultural exchange that might be understood as undermining and challenging reductive and normalising forms. Oscar Wilde's (1854–1900) *The Picture of Dorian Gray* (1891) and Bram Stoker's (1847–1912) *Dracula* (1897) reflect general *fin de siècle* themes of decadence and degeneration and have become perhaps the most popular expressions of these concerns. However, they can also be read in a more radical way in relation to specifically Irish anxieties. Oscar Wilde uncovers and exposes the hypocrisy at the heart of a Victorian world that stresses the importance of the public appearance of rectitude and morality, while simultaneously trying to control private deviancy. In an attempt to simplify existence by narrowing the gap between public and private, between the inner and outer realms, Victorian life by necessity opens up a world of disguise, masking and, ultimately, hypocrisy. Wilde's novel can be read as part of this overall project to deconstruct Englishness through his sustained assault on Enlightenment thinking and its rigid Victorian manifestations.[39] As part of this assault, he humorously critiqued the worn-out format of the novel in his own time, having a character in one of his plays famously utter: 'The good end happily, and the bad unhappily. That is what fiction means.'[40] Yet, even a cursory reading of *The Picture of Dorian Gray* suggests that this is exactly the kind of novel it is: a straightforward morality tale with the consequences of Dorian's selling his soul laid horribly bare at the novel's close. However, in the Preface he included in the 1891 edition (an in-built critical framework for reading the novel) – after the critical reaction to the novel in its first appearance in *Lippincott's Magazine* in 1890, all of which stressed the filth and the dirt of the world portrayed therein – he makes an effort to break the link between author and work, emphasising the autonomous existence of beautiful art: 'the Artist is the creator of beautiful things ... There is no such thing as a moral or an immoral book.'[41] In this desire to efface authorship – his authorial intention – Wilde connects with the energies of the revivalists and their interest in folk material and folk belief. For, does not Dorian become a kind of modern-day folk character, existing more strongly in the popular imagination at the level of myth than he ever does within the pages of the book in which he first appeared? This is also true of Stoker's famous Count Dracula, who inhabits a peculiar place in the modern psyche, continuing to haunt successive generations' imagination.

More interesting, perhaps, is how Wilde reverses the seemingly age-old motif within Irish fiction that presented Ireland as other and strange, allowing Irishness and all its foibles to be always already exoticised. Wilde simply makes England and Englishness the site of curious fascination. The endless discussions, or rather monologues, of Lord Henry Wotton, while offering an insight into decadent aesthetics, also anatomise English culture for the late Victorian reader: they are a master class in taste. As Jarlath Killeen argues, Lord Henry, far from being a thorn in society's side, does very little to disturb it: his fulminating against it being merely one more adopted pose among many possible poses.[42] He is a hypocrite and England is *the* place of hypocrisy. Killeen also maintains that Dorian, in the passages listing his various interests and passing passions in religion, science and style, hints at his – and thereby Wilde's – interest in knowledge beyond the realms of rationalist epistemology. The end of the novel brings all these different disruptive layers powerfully together. While Dorian must die to restore order, the troubling fact of his life – and the sins he has committed – remain mysterious, though the awful reality of his misshapen and haggard body – a Darwinian body without a soul – is a signal of the inner/private and outer/public worlds being reversed. *The Picture of Dorian Gray*, centring as it does on acts of transformation, itself performs this reversal in its making public what is hidden, making strange what is known or thought to be known. The Irish novel, then, in a manoeuvre such as this can become a site of possible resistance to the imperial norm rather than a site that must simply be an unquestioning conduit for imperial thought and action.

Bram Stoker's *Dracula* has become something of a literary touchstone for the numerous anxieties at work within Victorian society at the turn of the century. The Count can be a signifier for the metropolitan fear of the foreigner and the fear of being overwhelmed by immigration. His presence in London, and his means of gaining sustenance and transforming his prey into fellow vampires, speaks to apprehensions surrounding racial difference and eugenic infiltration: the emphasis on blood connecting with both issues of heredity and contamination. Added to this heady mix are questions about female sexuality and desire, and the proper containment of such possibly disruptive forces. Along with the position of the new woman, the reader is confronted with versions of masculinity under threat, not only from voluptuous women but also from the hyper-masculine Count Dracula who, both literally and metaphorically, is from a different time and place. It has been critically read from specifically Irish perspectives too: 'Among the Irish interpretations, Dracula is said to be Parnell, Wilde or starving tenants; an upstart Catholic miscegenist or Ascendancy bloodsucker.'[43] It seems that

Dracula can signify whatever any particular reader wants it to signify. Yet, some more pertinent readings connecting the novel to the general thrust of Irish writing at this time are possible. Dracula might represent the old aristocratic order of privilege and position, and those that align themselves against him are, mostly, the new middle classes. At its heart is a pulsating uncertainty about the position and power of the new middle classes and, from an Irish perspective, a palpable anxiousness about their relationship to the rule of the old aristocratic order. For, despite their resourcefulness and reliance on the fruits of all that is new and modern, there remains something attractive and noble about Stoker's Count Dracula and that older, traditional world that is passing away.

Despite an emphasis on Edwardian efficiency,[44] in reality it is a mixture of old and new, of folk knowledge in the form of garlic and mirrors and the ceremonies of Christianity combined with the ruthless application of reason (there is, as there always is with decadent literature, the element of a detective story here) that leads to victory over Dracula. The old world – the past – can never be fully denied: Dracula as the undead reconfirms the past's hold on the present. Indeed, as in the cultural movement then well underway in Ireland, this kind of combination, eschewing the reductive limitations of either/or and embracing the possibilities of both/and, *is* the future. As with Wilde, Stoker is aware of alternative ways of knowing beyond the merely rational.

Stoker brilliantly follows Wilde's reversal of point of view in *Dracula*. He advances Wilde's basic premise by taking the well-worn framing device for much Irish fiction throughout the nineteenth century – the visitor to Ireland who necessarily views the place and the people as exotically other – and simply inverts it, making England the place travelled to. In his first novel, *The Snake's Pass* (1890), Stoker had made use of such a ploy himself: Arthur Severn, a young Englishman holidaying in Ireland, gets caught up in an unlikely adventure that mixes local myth, in the form of a bog that swallows anything up, with the more mundane Irish reality of land grabbing. In *Dracula*, it is English culture that comes under such scrutiny. Lacking the levity, and indeed the penetration, of Wilde, Stoker's insight into English life is somewhat clichéd. At one stage Jonathan Harker comes across the Count in his library before his journey to England. It is a room full of texts:

The books were of the most varied kind, history, geography, politics, political economy, botany, geology, law, all relating to England and English life and customs and manners. There were even such books of reference as the London Directory, the "Red" and "Blue" books, Whitaker's Almanac, the Army and Navy Lists, and it somehow gladdened my heart to see it, the Law List.[45]

The primacy of the written word here is obvious: books bring order, books are knowledge, and knowledge is power. This mania for textual coherence is mirrored in the form of the novel itself, which self-consciously is made up of different narrative voices and styles: diary entries, newspaper clippings, even the transcribed voice recordings of Doctor Seward are presented. If that were not enough, this regard for texts – for the act of writing and of reading – becomes integral to the action within the novel as an element of plot. Near the end, especially, a great deal of emphasis is put upon Mina typing up and collating the different strands of the narrative and then other characters reading her text, suggesting how modern knowledge will undo the medieval threat embodied in the Count.

Outside these various written texts is the oral world inhabited by Dracula. He says that he wishes to become proficient in the English language: 'As yet I only know your tongue through books . . . I know the grammar and the words, but yet I know not how to speak them' (*Dracula*, p. 31). Books can bring order, but an act of writing is never enough: there is always knowledge, the intimate knowledge of belonging, outside the realm of the written word. A result of this interaction between the written and the oral worlds is that even as writing attempts to domesticate and make safe and normalise the events of the novel, they remain strange. There is a constant pull, then, between the fantastic and the utter ordinariness of the lives of those portrayed. As a comment on the situation in Ireland and the place of the Irish language and Irish culture within an anglophone world, this suggests a uneasy strain in Irish writing – and in the Irish novel particularly – between form and content, between the story told and the enabling frame surrounding that story. For Stoker, as for Oscar Wilde, this recognition of the move from the oral to the written anticipates that modernist shift towards 'writerly' concerns that will begin to dominate the Irish novel from this moment on.

Dracula is a curiously self-devouring text: the narrative being repeatedly consumed by the characters within the novel in their efforts to possess the whole story. Befitting the *fin de siécle* mood, the novel represents a literature of exhaustion in many ways, with each new style continually being replaced by another in a seemingly mad rush to discover any one particular style that might fix and contain the narrative. But the desire to experiment with form, to mix different registers and genres, to combine fantasy with reality, is *Dracula*'s legacy to the Irish novel, along with the subversive questioning – the dissection – of the unspoken codes of metropolitan empire. Just as Mina takes control of the narrative in the novel, ordering it and producing it, so too with Irish novelists who must now begin to tell their stories in their own ways.

George Moore (1852–1933) is *the* writer haunting Irish prose fiction, and specifically the Irish novel, during the Revival period. His active involvement in the Revival project with his collaboration with Yeats in the theatre, his returning to Ireland in order to connect with the energies of the margins, and his conscious experimentation and embracing of a modernist stance and aesthetic are what make him central to the Irish novel at this time. His short fiction in *The Untilled Field* (1899) and *A Story Teller's Holiday* (1918) is important for its employment of a self-conscious writerly mode that confronts and mediates the oral world of Gaelic Ireland. This literariness is also an important aspect of his Irish novels. In Ireland, two novels particularly are of relevance: *A Drama in Muslin* (1886), which has been dealt with in the previous chapter, and *The Lake* (1905). *A Drama in Muslin* demonstrated the possibility of aesthetic principles underpinning an act of writing, rather than simple didactic motives that continually viewed Ireland as a conundrum to be solved, which had dominated the Irish novel form throughout the nineteenth century. *The Lake* (1905) goes a step further and concentrates solely on an individual and his confrontation, ultimately, with himself. Father Oliver Gogarty (the use of this name perhaps a humorous reference to the writer, surgeon and raconteur of the same name) comes to realise that his religious belief negates life rather than affirms it. His inner argument forces him to come to the conclusion that he must leave the Church in order that he may choose life. This inner struggle is mirrored in his correspondence with Nora Glynn (Rose Leicester in the original 1905 version, which was changed in the 1921 edition) whom he had chastised from the pulpit for having an illegitimate child. His mock suicide by the lake and his swim into a new life at the close of the novel fits with Moore's use of the recurring image of real possibility always occurring outside Ireland. For him, Ireland remains the place of impossibility. The note of exile struck in this work, particularly, reverberates through the twentieth-century Irish novel where the leaving of Ireland, and all that Ireland represents (especially in the post-revolutionary moment), becomes the only action possible.

While this reading emphasising a leave-taking is but one simplistic way of approaching the novel, there are others which complicate it. James Joyce, for instance, derided Moore's pretentious references to European art and culture provided by Nora as she describes travelling through the continent.[46] And Moore is subtle enough to make her a complex character not above trying to make Father Gogarty feel small and wretched in the light of a newly found intellectual arrogance on her part.[47] Gogarty, too, is a complex character – his measured development, see-sawing between ignorance and insight, avoids stereotype. More important, perhaps, is the manner in which Moore conceives of Gogarty's connection to the world of nature, for in this Moore reimagines, expands and revolutionises the possibilities of an Irish relationship to place. It is not a simple love of the home place that is being described, nor is it simply a celebration of nature's beauty. What Moore achieves is a move away from the distanced sublime view of the Irish landscape that had prevailed throughout the late eighteenth century. He humanises that link, opening up the possibility of a truly personal connection with land beyond history, politics and ideology. For Gogarty is shown as truly alive only in those quiet moments of being-in-the-world:

> On a sudden resolve to escape from anyone that might be seeking him, he went into the wood and lay down on the warm grass, and admired the thickly-tasselled branches of the tall larches swinging above him. At a little distance among the juniper-bushes, between the lake and the wood, a bird uttered a cry like two stones clinked sharply together, and getting up he followed the bird, trying to catch sight of it, but always failing to do so; it seemed to range in a circle about certain trees, and he hadn't gone very far when he heard it behind him. A stonechat he was sure it must be, and he wandered on till he came to a great silver fir, and thought that he spied a pigeon's nest among the multitudinous branches.[48]

In contrast, it is the aesthetic world of European culture as described by Nora which seems remarkably artificial, staid and affected. The Catholic world, too, appears utterly devoid of feeling and mystery in juxtaposition to the delicate changes of the seasons traced by the lake and its environs. Of course, this is exactly the world that Gogarty must abandon when he chooses exile. As he leaves, he wonders about the lake:

> 'I shall never see that lake again, but I shall never forget it,' and as he dozed in the train, in a corner of an empty carriage, the spectral light of the lake awoke him, and when he arrived at Cork it seemed to him that he was being engulfed in the deep pool by the Joycetown shore. On the deck of the steamer he heard the lake's warble above the violence of the waves. 'There is a lake in every man's heart,' he said, 'and he listens to its monotonous whisper year by year, more and more attentive till at last he ungirds.' (*The Lake*, p. 179)

What Moore brilliantly does, in a purely modernist gesture and much earlier than James Joyce, is present an artistic sensibility as being democratically open to all. For here Gogarty realises not only what will be lost but also recognises how that loss will fuel his imagination in his new life lived away from this place. He wants to be a journalist (a surrogate artist in the common pursuit of explanation) – which, of course, foregrounds the act of writing, which itself is central to the novel with both Gogarty and Nora coming to know themselves through writing their own narratives in a series of letters. Moore's legacy to Irish writing is not just the introduction of Zolaesque naturalism to fiction,[49] but rather is the establishment of this type of romantic pan-aesthetic – the ability to see and appreciate the world outside the self – wherein imaginative sensitivity is what marks off the individual. What becomes central now is the quality of the imaginative engagement with the landscape as an act of cultural possession. Reinforcing this is Moore's deployment of the interior monologue coming from Édouard Dujardin's (1861–1949) *Les Lauriers sont coupés* (1888). From this moment, the Irish novel will be populated by artist figures who, though they may not all actually be artists, will possess an artistic sensibility which in itself is celebratory and liberating.

Moore's subsequent reputation within Irish writing is a curiously spectral one – at once involved but also aloof. His reputation in Britain rests on one novel, *Esther Waters* (1894), dealing with the life of a servant woman in a non-judgemental fashion – quite a radical manoeuvre for this time. Moore was prepared to take deliberate risks with his art in his efforts to extend the boundaries of his own aesthetic, but the problem is – as with the narrative of *Dracula* – Moore is forever looking for new ways and means to tell his stories. For instance, *A Drama in Muslin* can be read as one of the first modern Big House novels depicting the decline and fall of feudal Ireland that would be returned to again and again over the next century. Moore writes his novel and never makes use of the genre again, though one critic oddly suggests that *Esther Waters* can be read as a Big House novel.[50]

Increasingly, after his early creative dalliance in the world of Irish possibility, his fiction is marked by over-elaborate efforts to be new and, perhaps, intentionally shocking. His *The Brook Kerith: A Syrian Story* (1916), for instance, revolves round the story of Jesus not dying on the cross and his continuing to live happily long afterwards. Christ is shown meeting and debating with his disciple Paul twenty years after his 'death': Christ's thinking has evolved into a humanist perspective that suggests that God is some kind of Kantian projection formed between the individual and his/her interaction with the world. Christ, rather than being God, is just a man. In comparison to his earlier work, it lacks any real depth or dynamic. He wrote it simply because he could write it, and in the hope that it might scandalise a comfortably bourgeois readership. Sadly for Moore, the bourgeoisie were dying in the trenches of Belgium and France and ignored the book.

Though not a novel in any strict application of the term, his autobiographical *Hail and Farewell: Ave, Salve, Vale* (1911–14) charts another fundamental shift in Irish fiction. What is truly innovative in this work is his taking real people, real events and real situations and writing about them as if they were in a novel, using all the techniques associated with fiction at his disposal. While this allows Moore to manipulate his material, offering often meticulously malicious pen pictures of the personalities involved in the Revival – Synge, Lady Gregory and Yeats among others – and reducing the entire movement in the process to the level of personality quirks and clashes,[51] it reflects a more profound aspect of the novel form in Ireland. All fiction, from *Don Quixote* onwards, has flirted with the boundaries between the real and the invented, and in twentieth-century Ireland the novel form increasingly becomes closely linked to realism and its variants. Ireland is not a place of fictional invention – the made-up plot appears impossible and only the stuff of life itself will have the tone of authenticity that might hold a reader's attention: anything else will look like an imposed or convenient compromise. It suggests that, in keeping with a general progression in Irish fiction towards a genuine rendering of the Irish person, now – more than ever – the story of the self is the only important story to be told and perhaps, indeed, the only story that it is possible to tell. Autobiography was one means by which revivalists could come to know themselves, precisely as themselves,[52] but this is accentuated in the proliferation of personalised fiction. It suggests, too, that realism in Irish fiction is not merely a retreat into the conventional modes of representation, but that after centuries of misrepresentation the careful detailing of Irish life in all its aspects was, and continued to be, a revolutionary act. The autobiographical impulse in Irish fiction also makes manifest a shift from the oral world into the world of writing and literary art: as writers insert themselves into their own stories, their struggles to be artists re-enact that movement into modernity.

For Irish letters – and particularly Irish prose – Moore acts as a conduit to European and modernist influences. While opening up various possibilities for his contemporaries who would make more of his ideas and his techniques than he could, most of his own work does not transcend its moment of production because he loses himself in the search for new styles and, ultimately, possesses none of his own. His work, therefore, serves to liberate others if not himself.

The immediate beneficiary of Moore's influence, though he himself would have denied it, is James Joyce (1882–1941). Unlike Moore, however, while his writing taken as a whole voraciously deploys a dizzying array of styles and methods, his interest in his Irish subject matter never waned. In other words, there was always a purpose to his artistic efforts beyond merely stylistic flourish. His early short stories, *Dubliners* (1914), in their patterned development moving from childhood through adolescence to adulthood, from the private micro lives of ordinary men and women to more public and macro political concerns, aspires to the kind of wholeness of vision that a novel might provide. Of note is Joyce's epiphanic technique which foregrounds the ordinary and the everyday, imbuing seemingly casual moments with inscrutable significance. His attention to detail is also important: its preciseness allowing the world to be presented as it is in all its inglorious shabby reality. In a dispute with his publisher, Joyce declared that: 'you will retard the course of civilisation in Ireland by preventing the Irish people from having one good look at themselves in my nicely polished looking-glass'.[53] Many Irish writers – most notably Maria Edgeworth – had reimagined themselves as literary pioneers and Joyce, too, obviously positions himself in that way. Beneath the hyperbole, though, lurks a serious agenda to put an Ireland on display that had not been witnessed to this point.

One central objective of revivalist writing was to offer images of potential heroes and heroism to its audience. Figures from mythology such as Cúchulain entered into the realm of popular culture through the prose writings of Standish O'Grady (1846–1928) and others. That basic template infuses the work of Yeats, who complicated this Cúchulain figure in both his poetry and his drama of this period, giving the mythological figure a contemporary edge. And J. M. Synge's famous drama, *The Playboy of the Western World* (1907), sets about deconstructing this fascination with heroes. Against this backdrop, Joyce's *A Portrait of the Artist as a Young Man* (1916) turns also to the image of the hero, but rather than see the hero outside himself as someone to be perhaps emulated, he places himself in the position of hero in what is a fictionalised account of his growth into an artist. The early version of this novel, published as *Stephen Hero* (1977), makes Joyce's basic autobiographical impulse clear. What remains of this manuscript is set during Stephen's time at university and so this version of himself as hero is infused with all the pretensions of precocious youth finding its way in a precocious environment. It is an earnest, utterly plodding narrative of interest mostly to Joycean scholars for its directness of expression as Stephen bluntly lays out his aesthetic theory – borrowed from Aquinas, and thereby making Stephen a strangely medieval modernist – and his view of the artist as the new secular priest. The transformation of this first draft into *A Portrait* revolutionises the text, layering it with significance and subtleties and, in the process, demonstrating Joyce's ability to match form to content and thereby amplifying his themes and intention.

Joycean critic Andrew Gibson suggests that, 'The dominant tone in *A Portrait* is carefully balanced between the cool, intellectual detachment of the vivisectionist and a melancholy often not far from bitterness.'[54] Thus the choice of the hero's name – Stephen as martyr and Dedalus as cunning and skilful artificer – is perfect for Joyce's act of self-realisation. The novel is broken into five chapters revolving round various set pieces, from earliest childhood to school and university, that allow for a step-by-step consideration of Stephen Dedalus's artistic development. The oppressive 'nets', as they are called by Dedalus, needing to be challenged and overcome are language, nationality and religion. Traditionally, Stephen's rebellion has been portrayed as a modernising one that sees him embrace the freedom which the international and specifically European scene has to offer as he rejects the backwardness and narrowness of all things Irish. Of course, this is a simplification of the nature of Stephen's dilemma. His struggle is not just with Ireland and/or Irishness but also with the move into modernity itself.

As such, Stephen seems always out of place, caught between the Victorian certainties of his childhood and the newer more radically fluid moment of revivalist Ireland. What Joyce manages to brilliantly do is combine this national story with the private story of the Dedalus family's downward movement from middle-class affluence into grinding poverty. The shifting scenes between the private sphere of home and the public world of school, university and the street, only serves to elaborate this intense focus on an urban Catholic bourgeois world in decline. His work, then, is an antidote to all those late nineteenth-century novels that simplistically presented the incessant rise and rise in confidence of a Catholic middle class who waited in anticipation for some form of self-government through which they would wield power. His description of Dublin city – grey, empty and anaemic – and his view of a political culture that offers only 'scenes of tawdry tribute'[55] suggest the kind of colonial stupor that Dedalus must work against. Even Stephen's burgeoning sexuality and the growing awkwardness in the teenage awareness of his body, once again emphasise a certain incongruity in his relationship to the world. Indeed, most aspects of young Stephen's life oscillate between the public and private realms of experience. Though he would declare famously in *Ulysses* (1922) that Irish history was 'that nightmare from which he is trying to awake',[56] in *A Portrait* any overt consideration of history is absent. Indeed, this is a very present-centred novel: it is the recent past, particularly the fall of Charles Stewart Parnell, which offers a political context to the world described. Consequently, what informs the political and ideological territory inhabited by Stephen is a very personal narrative. In keeping with the modernist manoeuvre of audacious originality, Dedalus is shown as having no immediate artistic or intellectual antecedents, and as presenting himself as wholly self-created. So caught up is he in his personal story that his difficulty is actually coming into possession of an objective and wide perspective on Ireland and its history. It is perhaps this bourgeois focus and Joyce's story of the desire for heroism in the midst of bland conformity that a wider international audience finds appealing. From within an Irish context though, his constant move between the private sphere and the public sphere mirrors precisely the mood at the time, with the public realm becoming the site of action and possibility in ways in which it had never been before.

Joyce's real achievement, however, is in his portrayal of an uncertain Stephen who might not, in the end, be a worthy hero at all – and, specifically, in this newly charged public sphere. Too many critics fall into the trap of equating without question Dedalus with Joyce and Joyce with Dedalus, forgetting that *A Portrait* is a novel and not autobiography. Joyce is not above casting a cold eye on his own youthful posturing, and not above making a little gentle fun at his own expense. With regard to the development of the Irish novel, Joyce's *A Portrait* is tied closely to the kind of Catholic problem novels then in vogue, as well as returning to the images of the city seen in the nineteenth-century work of John Banim and May Laffan. In many ways, though, it is also a radical break and departure from what has gone before. Stephen's avowed intellectualism marks an utter rejection of the kind of stereotypical Irish characters that cluttered the Irish novel to this point. Despite an air of alienating pretentiousness, Stephen is presented diligently working through his various problems with Ireland, Catholicism, family and sexuality. It is the novel's particular sensitivity to language, though, that marks it off from its contemporaries. Dedalus's growth is charted through a developing relationship to language and its contours – from a basic understanding and ability with words to a sophisticated and theoretical facility by the close. As the narrative is filtered through the mind of Stephen, the reader is forced to engage with these various styles throughout the novel.

The trajectory of the novel, as the title obviously points to, is a representation of the artist figure: the writer who will remake the world through his own voice and language, resisting the all-pervasive imperial culture by writing against it. Stephen famously articulates his relationship to language in a scene with his Dean of Studies: 'The language in which we are speaking is his before it is mine ... His language, so familiar and so foreign, will always be for me an acquired speech. I have not made or accepted its words. My voice holds them at bay. My soul frets in the shadow of his language.'[57] Seamus Deane argues that for Joyce, 'The supreme action was writing' and that the 'the act of writing became an act of rebellion; rebellion was the act of writing.'[58] What Deane argues is that Joyce's work is not overly concerned with reflecting reality; rather, it is concerned with, through his fiction, 'creating a reality which otherwise would have no existence'.[59] In other words, the act of fiction writing is an act that attempts to get beyond, as Deane puts it, the brute hard facts of history. In this Joyce shares much with the revivalists, who also situate cultural production as central to Ireland's political reimagining of itself. The movement of the novel is one towards an epiphanic moment. This we see in the famous final declaration that closes the book: 'Welcome, O Life! I go to encounter for the millionth time the reality of experience and to forge in the smithy of my soul the uncreated conscience of my race' (*A Portrait*, p. 276). It is the climax: the portrait is complete – Stephen Dedalus is an artist, or, at least, makes a statement of intent of being an artist. Coupled with these final sentiments are other declarations that make up the fifth chapter of *A Portrait*:

I will not serve that in which I no longer believe, whether it call itself my home, my fatherland, or my church: and I will try to express myself in some mode of life or art as freely as I can and as wholly as I can, using for my defence the only arms I allow myself to use – silence, exile, and cunning. (*A Portrait*, pp. 268–269)

What is of significance is that Joyce self-consciously calls attention to the act of writing through his employment of the diary format that makes up the final section of the novel.

The diary's content is significant in that Stephen brings together for final comment and critique many of the themes and issues he has been concerned with throughout the novel. Formally, it is very significant. Dedalus finds his voice in the diary: he is not attempting to imitate anyone else as he has done in the one other act of writing in the novel found in his villanelle, 'Are you not weary of ardent ways?' (*A Portrait*, p. 202). The diary format – a mind allowed to speak for itself and to itself – is a precursor to the stream-of-consciousness technique deployed in *Ulysses*, as if Joyce is blindly groping towards the form that *would* ultimately unlock the conscience of his race. Stephen Dedalus at this moment enters into the zone of action: his act of writing is an act of self-assertion, of self-creation. It seems that the diary might be the beginnings of signifying all that is expressed in his phrase 'silence, exile and cunning'. But Joyce undermines such an overly celebratory reading of the diary precisely because it is a diary. Rather than a public declaration this is, in fact, a very private manifesto: he is talking only to himself, he is not communicating, not connecting, with other people or a wider public audience.

This calls into question the movement of the novel to this point: it is not an end or a resolution, but rather a radically open and ambiguous conclusion in which nothing is satisfactorily concluded. Dedalus himself is perhaps aware of this: '*11 April:* Read what I wrote last night. Vague words for a vague emotion' (*A Portrait*, p. 274). He knows what is at stake in becoming an artist and the isolation that it will necessarily bring. As with George Moore's character Father Gogarty in *The Lake*, there are gains and losses in choosing exile. And, more importantly, Stephen also knows that he might fail. It is a curious feature of Joyce's depiction of Stephen Dedalus in both *A Portrait* and *Ulysses*, in that while Joyce himself at the time of their setting – the late 1890s to 1904 – had begun to write what would become *Dubliners*, Dedalus is never presented as anything other than on the cusp of creation. That anticipatory note struck throughout the nineteenth-century novel still finds an echo here. As with the general political mood, Joyce cannot, or will not, be prescriptive as to what the future might be: he knows, though, that the old colonial world is about to pass away. Like W. B. Yeats, in his 1914 collection of poems *Responsibilities* – where the poet gloomily acknowledges the paradigm shift about to take place at both a public and a private level with the supposed imminent granting of long-awaited Home Rule – Joyce also concedes that such a change is occurring. His portrait of an artist thus becomes a portrait of a colonised artist who is daringly confident of his own abilities because he has absolutely nothing to lose. But Dedalus is also utterly uncertain of exactly what or how his abilities might manifest themselves because the new world about to come into being has no antecedent as a guide.

That he wants to create the uncreated conscience of his race also points to the colonial status of Joyce's artist. Colonisation lacks morality, built as it is on the lie that the colonised can be assimilated into the dominant culture. Curiously, Stephen's and Joyce's rebellions might be construed as quite conservative. Rather than simply desiring to destroy the old world of traditional values, Joyce perceives the old world as fundamentally lacking in a value system and therefore the need for the creation of a new moral order amid such chaos. Such a reading throws new light on Joyce's disdain for his father's generation. The events of Easter 1916 would alter that mood of anticipation and ignorance for good. But the close of *A Portrait* with its radical ambivalence powerfully captures that moment on the threshold when anything might come to pass, when writing in the dark – as Joyce is doing – just might penetrate into a realm of luminosity. Perhaps one reason that Stephen Dedalus towers above other fictional characters of the period is because he is a flawed character: an all too human hero. At a juncture in Irish history when the nature of heroism and the hero was paramount, when the zeitgeist was one of possible epic, James Joyce offers this image of flawed humanity – which will be further developed through the character of Leopold Bloom in *Ulysses* – and it is *A Portrait's* gift to the Irish novel.

James Stephens (1880?–1950) was a writer much admired by James Joyce, as well as George Moore. Stephens's entire writing career manifests the kind of uncertain fluidity of the time. His work moves easily between different styles and genres. *The Charwoman's Daughter* (1912) set in the back streets of Dublin with its intense observation of tenement life suggests that a direct realism might be wed to a social critique of Irish life. But that the main character is called Mary Makebelieve implies that realism as a form and a technique might be limited in its ability to tell the complete story of this young woman's relationship with an older man who is a member of the RIC police force. Her name, too, evokes the fairytale world of Cinderella. The close of the novel reinforces the fable-like reading – happiness is restored as the reader's view is gently reoriented away from Mary and her life:

The world is all before her, and her chronicler may not be her guide. She will have adventures, for everybody has. She will win through with them, for everybody does. She may even meet bolder and badder men than the policeman – shall we, then, detain her? I, for one, having urgent calls elsewhere, will salute her fingers and raise my hat and stand aside, and you will do likewise, because it is my pleasure that you should.[60]

Also in 1912, Stephens abandoned this blending of the real with the romance of fable and wholeheartedly embraced the possibilities of fantasy with his work, *The Crock of Gold*. As a contemporary reviewer noted: '*The Crock of Gold* eludes all the usual classifications of the novel.'[61] And indeed it does. Unlike any other work of fiction of this period, Stephens accepts the possibilities of the revivalist engagement with the world of Irish folklore and myth. The plot is merrily absurd, centring on a journey taken by the philosopher and his wife in search for a young woman of their locality, Caitilin Ni Murrachu. The story allows for a strange, often unsettling, fictional world that mirrors both the real and the mythological. The presence of authority figures such as policemen mingle untroublingly with the world of leprechauns and the great god Pan. Humour is juxtaposed with serious Blakean – and Yeatsian – philosophy in that all things have an opposite and find completion in the double. It is a remarkable feat on the part of Stephens that he can create such a balanced and controlled narrative voice which never tends towards the sentimental or straightforwardly comic. For Stephens, his deployment of the fantastic in this way challenges Enlightenment thinking. Thus, rather than the alleged Irish inability to deal with fact, fantasy becomes an active attempt to acknowledge different ways of knowing in an epistemological revolution.

At one stage the narrator declares: 'A thought is a real thing and words are only its raiment.'[62] Stephens quietly implies that the underlying concerns of the novel are truly modernist in its desire to link the mind with the physical body, action with thought. This novel is a good example, then, of how limiting traditional surveys of literature can be as they position modernism as a purely metropolitan affair with purely metropolitan concerns and issues. Stephens's novel, for instance, is a much more subtly challenging piece than say D. H. Lawrence's *Women in Love* (1920), the modernist credentials of which are quite plainly obvious, sometimes bordering on the laughable as Lawrence searches frantically for imagery that might transcend the banality of life as he sees it. For Stephens, there is no need to make journeys to either the arctic north or the sweltering south, knowledge and wisdom can be found more locally in tradition and myth. Working at the level of symbol, Stephens's *The Crock of Gold* offers the reader a glimpse of an Edenic future beyond the constrictions of modernity with its anti-humanist institutions:

They swept through the goat tracks and the little boreens and the curving roads. Down to the city they went dancing and singing; among the streets and the shops telling their sunny tale; not heeding the malignant eyes and the cold brows as the sons of Balor looked sidewards. And they took the Philosopher from his prison, even the Intellect of Man they took from the hands of the doctors and lawyers, from the sly priests, from the professors whose mouths are gorged with sawdust, and the merchants who sell blades of grass – the awful people of the Fomor . . . and then they returned again, dancing and singing, to the country of the gods. (Stephens, *Crock of Gold*, p. 312)

Freedom is not something given, it is striven for: a work in progress. In his *The Insurrection in Dublin* (1916), Stephens gave a clear, journalistic account of the events of Easter 1916. For him, as for many, that act of rebellion was part of a work in progress towards a better future for all of Ireland's citizens: 'From this day the great adventure opens for Ireland. The Volunteers are dead, and the call is now for volunteers.'[63]

Against the idealistic striving for intellectual and cultural freedom – collective and individual – on display in the fiction of Stephens, Joyce and Moore can be found a more hard-nosed social realism. Certainly there are obvious traces of such a perspective in the work of Joyce, especially in *Dubliners*, though images of urban poverty also underpin *A Portrait* with the Dedalus family presented as drinking their tea from jam jars. That the narrator offers such an image without any commentary implies that, for Joyce, Dublin's position as the poorest city in the United Kingdom was a simple matter of fact.[64] The 1913 lockout pitted workers against economic

power, highlighting the endemic inequalities in Irish life, but though Joyce
does possess an interest in economic realities, these concerns are masked
somewhat by charting the individual's growth and development. The
disparity, though, between Joyce's portrayal and that in a very popular
book by Joseph Edelstein (18??–1939), *The Moneylender: A Novel* (1908), for
instance, sharply underscores the differences between high and low art.
Stephen Brown labelled the novel 'strangely realistic'[65] and Cormac
O'Grada has signalled how the novel captures the detail of early twentieth-
century life for many Jewish Dubliners.[66] Working against such realism is
the close of the book where Moses Levenstein recants, not his religion, but
his profession as he embraces the true tenets of his Jewish faith. The evils of
the entire system are made clear in what amounts to a moral fable.[67] The
book went through at least five editions between 1908 and 1931,[68] suggesting
that the kind of poverty portrayed in the novel did not magically disappear
with the arrival of independence.

Another type of social realism is to be found with the anthropological
note struck, for instance, in J. M. Synge's *The Aran Islands* (1907). Such a
frame becomes quite dominant in the fiction of the post-Revival period,
especially those works centred on the rural scene. Perhaps one of the most
successful early works in this mode is Patrick MacGill's *Children of the Dead
End* (1914). When it was originally published it had the subtitle 'The
Autobiography of a Navvy', and MacGill made it clear in his preface that
his portraits where drawn from real life.[69] It sold 15,000 copies in three
months (MacGill, *Children of the Dead End*, p. vii) and was widely praised
in the press.[70] His descriptions of life in Donegal, the day-to-day existence
of families' precarious economic positions, always one rent payment or bill
away from destitution, is a corrective to the overly saccharine portrayals of
the Irish peasant associated with the revivalist movement. MacGill's depicts
a brutally hard world and his critique moves from the financial system,
which forces the peasant into an endless cycle of making do, to the Catholic
Church, which is seen as much more interested in earthly gain for its priests
than the spiritual well-being of its flock. The image of a child's innocence
being brutally interrupted with the presence of the Hiring Fair – the chapter
is called unambiguously 'The Slave Market' – awakens memories of the pre-
modern world when a child was an economic asset. The move to Scotland
and detailing the work of building roads and picking potatoes, and the
images of the displaced Irish lost in this world of work are powerfully
described. Despite his stated desire for penetratingly realistic writing, it is
here that MacGill's work itself becomes sentimental in the Victorian mode.
The image of himself as the navvy poet – the exotic creature who can

decipher this hidden world for a middle-class audience – finds its way into his fictional version of himself, Dermord Flynn. And while his characterisations never descend into the grotesquerie of Dickens, remaining faithfully drawn from life, they are forced, in the end, to exist as archetypes with characters' individual tragedies becoming representative rather than unique.

Other novels of the period have a more narrowly intense focus, concerned as they are with the sober reality of lower- and middle-class bourgeois Ireland. Two novels in particular capture the condition of these lives and places. Daniel Corkery's (1878–1964) only novel, *The Threshold of the Quiet* (1917), offers the reader an Irish picture of Henry David Thoreau's (he is invoked in the prologue) 'quiet desperation'. Set in Cork, this picture of urban life, as a reviewer for the *Irish Times* noted at the time, eschews the literary possibilities of both the 'quaint, humorous peasant' associated with the revival and the loquaciousness of the stage Irishman of a generation earlier. And, despite the convulsions in the wider political world, it is noted that Corkery has no interest in party or faction.[71] Centred on a group of people who must come to terms with the suicide of their friend, commercial traveller Frank Bresnan, the novel turns on the paralysis of these characters and their 'thwarted ambitions, bridled emotions, [and] unfulfilled loves'.[72] In keeping with the world of James Joyce's *Dubliners*, all possible action is curtailed and the two main protagonists fail to come together at the close of the novel. Lily Bresnan enters a convent and her putative lover, Martin Cloyne, despairingly accepts his fated life of loneliness. This mood of 'acceptance, resignation, and Catholic piety'[73] – a form of destined naturalism – becomes a dominant paradigm in Irish fiction.[74] While such a lack of human agency can be maddening for Marxist literary critics desiring to bind art to politics and history, it is a perspective that in many ways in an Irish context *is* revolutionary. This type of naturalism opens up the possibility of an engagement with the lived pressures of the everyday and the commonplace beyond the realm of ideology: presenting life as it is lived and no more. That no real explanation is offered as to why the characters are as they are and act as they do is indicative of this retreat from empirical knowledge and the modern desire to know: there are mysteries to existence and, perhaps, these can be only be gestured towards rather than fully grasped.

The fame, or notoriety, of Brinsley MacNamara (real name John Weldon) (1890–1963) as a novelist rests on one particular piece of work, *The Valley of the Squinting Windows* (1918). As with Corkery, MacNamara recognises that real life is not lived at the level of politics or history and his novel, therefore, is a work of unrelenting satire directed towards the small-town bourgeois mentality that operates a strict code of conduct working against the all-consuming idealism of post-rebellion national politics. There is humour at work here with the plot developing along melodramatic lines, and the inclusion of a murder to entertain the reader points to an ominous undercurrent emerging in this picture of midlands village life. Power and control, of course, are fundamentally at stake in the bourgeois world, especially at a time of uncertainty and insecurity. No character comes out with much credit in this novel revolving round squalid schemes and intrigues. An array of 'drunkards, liars, thieves, eavesdroppers and black-mailers'[75] populate the town of Garradrimna – a fictionalised version of MacNamara's homeplace of Delvin, County Westmeath. The focus of the town's concerns centre on the relationship between Rebecca Kerr, an assistant primary school teacher, and the wastrel Ulick Shannon. She becomes pregnant by him and is forced to leave the village. John Brennan, studying for the priesthood, actually loves Rebecca and murders Ulick for his abandonment of Rebecca. The sensational twist is that John and Ulick are, in fact, brothers. The outlandishness of the plot might divert attention away from the fact that, as was the case for Stephen Dedalus, the middle-class desire for mastery manifests itself in the realm of morality. Here, quite obviously, the arena of sexuality is the focus and any wayward deviation from supposed norms has devastating consequences. Interestingly, the penalty passes through the generations as if the original 'sin' must be punished. Increasingly, in the New Ireland coming into being, it is the ethics of sexuality which develops into *the* site for conflict between tradition and modernity.

Of note, too, is the reaction to *The Valley of the Squinting Windows*. Unlike the situation with J. M. Synge's drama, *The Playboy of the Western World* (1907), those being lampooned were the ones who actually objected and locals publicly burned the book in Delvin. McNamara's father, a schoolteacher, was boycotted and he subsequently took the parish priest and other locals to court seeking damages. He lost the case. While realism does become the norm in Irish fiction, it can be forgotten how uneasy the writer's relationship actually is to that genre, for the modernist novelist's desire to unmask and unveil the real is one fraught with very genuine dangers. Certainly the legacy of colonisation produces a distrust of all types of representation as misrepresentation. But there is also the issue of betrayal, of making public that which is private, and of saying or telling that which should be left unsaid or untold. This issue of betrayal becomes more and more pronounced in Irish writing as the twentieth century progresses. Linked to the Yeatsian warning that Irish artists must choose between either 'expressing Ireland or exploiting it', novelistic literary betrayal suggests a seriously anxious relationship between the Irish writer and his/her local audience.

The reality of war and the violence of war, at both an international and a local level, bring this concern with betrayal to the fore in the Irish novel at this period. John Wilson Foster highlights how many of these war novels – for instance, St John Ervine's (1883–1971) *Changing Winds* (1917) and Mrs Victor Rickard's (1878–1963) *The Fire of Green Boughs* (1918) – confront the political questions of the day in terms of loyalty to Britain's war efforts and the Easter rebellion. Each is self-conscious in its efforts to present the arguments and the issues of all those involved: Ireland, as it was throughout the nineteenth century, is still a problem to be talked through and solved.[76] Remarkably, such a configuration of characters as mouthpieces will remain a staple in Irish fiction dealing with Anglo-Irish relations for many years and can be witnessed in the work of Elizabeth Bowen, Molly Keane and Iris Murdoch. The liberal mind celebrates the potential of straightforward debate above all else. The motif of travel and the visitor to Ireland also structures these novels. Such patterning can be read as attempting to integrate Ireland spatially and imaginatively with Britain. It might also be a continuation of Ireland as the site of the exotic, forever beyond what might be thought of as the norm. And all this movement to and fro insinuates that, for some, Ireland is a place that can be physically left behind and escaped from.

Eimar O'Duffy's *The Wasted Island* (1919) is one of the earliest literary critiques of the Rebellion of Easter 1916. Focusing on Bernard Lascelles (a thinly disguised version of the author himself), his childhood and his education, O'Duffy is able to draw a clear picture of middle-class Dublin life before the revolution. As with the other war novels, there is much worthy conversation and debate about the pros and cons of the rising, the thinking behind it and, for O'Duffy, the disaster of its coming to pass. The death of so many of the leaders of the rising, and many other young men, is seen as a waste of talent and potential, but even as it criticises the rebellion, the novel closes with the suggestion that all is not lost as a character declares amid all this death and waste that 'we must begin all over again'.[77] Interestingly, two reviews of the work – forty years apart – take O'Duffy to task for not distancing himself from his work of fiction. Katherine Tynan contemporaneously said it was: 'an unpleasant book in many ways. It belongs to the class of temperamental novels and despite the number and variety of its incidents it centres entirely about the personality of the writer, which he is unable or unwilling to get outside.'[78] Author Mervyn Wall, in retrospect, also commented on the faithfulness of O'Duffy's account of his life and times.[79] Wall points out how O'Duffy would have suffered from his less than positive account of the rebellion, of being labelled a traitor when the novel was published at the height of the Black and Tan outrages during the War of Independence. But Wall's review also points to the problem of fiction as invention in the Irish scene, and how dominant is the paradigm of realism in the critique of the novel form, when he offers some of his own personal reminiscences of O'Duffy and his family. Unconsciously, it seems, this review hints at how betrayal in Ireland – while always a political possibility – has more to do with the local and the personal than with the concerns of wider historical movements. All novelists – and their readers – are highly attuned to the nature of narrative and the power it may wield in offering versions of events. In this, it can be argued, the Irish novel's relationship to realism is further complicated as the act of fiction writing gets caught up in a broader debate about the nature of truth, and history writing, between what might be imagined and what actually happens.

Near the close of *The Wasted Island*, during the rising, the hero Bernard has a feverish dream which distorts and exaggerates the sense of destruction and waste that is at the heart of the story's moral: 'In a few hours he went through an eternity of torment. He had lost all sense of time, all feeling of reality. Existence had become phantasmagorical.'[80] Obviously, the dream and the fever combine to momentarily alter his sense of reality. And yet, because of Bernard's, and the author O'Duffy's, political stance, the idea of reality becoming 'phantasmagorical' is a curious one. The problem of the 1916 Easter Rebellion, at its moment and subsequently, is that it actually happened. Action by the Irish – real action – had always been something of a difficulty. Certainly, as has been seen thus far in our survey of the Irish novel, the Irish have been represented as unable to act or unable to act decisively in certain ways. The 1916 Easter Rebellion shattered that pervasive image of passiveness and demonstrated how thought could become action, how what is imagined might become a reality. W. B. Yeats would ponder the mysteries of that movement into actuality in his poem 'Easter 1916'. O'Duffy's character, too, in the very midst of that action, is unable to come to terms with it and, in a way, his fever signals an attempt to deny it. But even so, a new reality has come into being and reality is made phantasmagorical. A paradigm shift has occurred and nothing would be the same again. Interestingly, O'Duffy's response sets up a template for those who would revise the rising throughout the twentieth and twenty-first centuries, attempting to imagine it out of existence. The rebellion's significance is now to be fought over in the realms of imagination and narrative.

The novel in this Revival period truly breaks the mould of what has gone before: splitting into diverse paths and possibilities. Rather than the silencing of voices, the Revival allowed for an upsurge in different, competing ideas of what Ireland might be, and from different perspectives. Though, beyond the scope of this present study, the novel in the Irish language also begins to emerge at this time and gain an audience.[81] The novel, particularly, manifests this diversity between modernist innovation and popular sentiment, between a Catholic middle-class desire for respectability and Anglo-Irish Protestant feudalism. The novel also charts the conflict between an idealised Ireland and the actuality of widespread poverty in both the rural and the urban spheres. Formally, the novel reflects the fluid nature of the period, mingling autobiography with fiction, fantasy with realism, the short story with the novel. Artistically, anything and everything becomes momentarily possible.

This active search for a suitable form or style which might be an appropriate framing device to tell the story of Ireland registers another crucial shift. The debate about realism and naturalism in the Irish novel is no longer confined to critically evaluating the relationship between Ireland and Britain and the international scene, as was the case in the eighteenth and nineteenth centuries. It is now an internal debate: the search for a style mirroring the political debates about the direction a New Ireland might take. For, if nothing else, the Revival and the political upheavals that ran in conjunction with it created an audience now eager for an engagement with the possibilities of Irish narrative, eager for stories that might begin to tell their story and encapsulate their experiences.

James Joyce's Ulysses: *choosing life*

[A]nd even Milton, looking for his portrait in a spoon, must submit to
have the facial angle of a bumpkin.

(George Eliot, *Middlemarch*)[1]

James Joyce's *Ulysses* (1922) is a remarkable piece of experimental prose
fiction. It is at once the quintessential novel, recapturing the energies of the
nascent form – its improvisations, self-consciousness and playfulness particularly – precisely at moment when the form itself is at its most jaded and
dissipated. It is also, of course, *the* anti-novel, superbly critiquing and
exploding the polite form as it stands in the late nineteenth and early
twentieth centuries. It is clear, too, that despite the desire of many critics
to narrowly situate *Ulysses* exclusively within a European context, this piece
of writing could only have been produced during the period of the Irish
Literary Revival. The cultural and political fluidity of that period created a
unique cultural space, allowing a genius such as Joyce to discover the means
of expressing his personal and artistic concerns with the themes of father–
son relations, betrayal, love and the civic responsibilities of life in the
modern city. A contemporary Irish reviewer of the novel, in critically
dismissing *Ulysses*, noted that it was, 'an attempted Clerkenwell explosion
in the well-guarded, well-built, classical prison of English literature'.[2]
Certainly James Joyce wrote *Ulysses* for a reason and not simply, in some
version of decadent aesthetics, because he could.[3] Joyce himself talked about
his desire to hold a mirror up to the Irish so that they might see themselves
as they actually were. In *Ulysses*, his character Stephen Dedalus further
develops this imagery, reasoning that the fractured nature of Irish experience needs something other than a 'nicely polished mirror' and that the
symbol of Irish art ought to be the 'cracked lookingglass of a servant'.[4]
Playing on Oscar Wilde's pronouncements that 'The nineteenth century
dislike of realism is the rage of Caliban seeing his own face in a glass' and the
'The nineteenth century dislike of romanticism is the rage of Caliban not

seeing his own face in a glass',[5] Joyce/Dedalus cleverly gives his art a political edge.

And yet such a reading of the novel is only half the story. The colony is a place of analogy: it is always being compared with places and experiences and supposed realities elsewhere, with the centre of empire, of which the colony can only be but a pale reflection. Joyce's *Ulysses* challenges this predicament and, far from being an example of the Empire Writing Back,[6] what it actually captures is the colonised world in conversation with itself. Samuel Beckett recognised this when he declared that 'His writing is not *about* something; *it is that something itself*.'[7] In other words, *Ulysses* is not equivalent to some other novel or aesthetic vision or cultural perspective: it is not similar to or an approximation of some other thing, genre or style – it is itself only. Consequently, while other writers might employ some of its techniques and engage with some of its concerns, *Ulysses* is, perhaps, entirely beyond imitation.

In having the Irish talk to themselves in their own inimitable fashion, and being consistently true to that throughout, Joyce's very local world is rendered truly universal. Being genuinely universal in this way is the main reason, possibly, that *Ulysses* has generated so much critical interest and commentary. Thus, the arc of reflection of Joyce's cracked mirror is very wide, allowing for many different readings and interpretations of *Ulysses* since its publication. *Ulysses*'s openness to interpretation is extraordinary in that none of these readings cancels out other readings: it can be all of them simultaneously. The novel's emergence just at the moment when Ferdinand de Saussure's groundbreaking *Course in General Linguistics* (1916) was published means that a purely aesthetic reading of the novel would never be possible. De Saussure's dismantling of the traditional connection between word and world inaugurated the modern theoretical turn in literary studies, and as that field of study expanded and developed through the twentieth century, James Joyce's *Ulysses* became *the* theoretical text *par excellence*. The consequent disconnection in time or space of any text from its context meant that *Ulysses* has been read profitably in the light of linguistic theories, structuralist and post-structuralist theories. Political readings have also been applied so that Marxist, feminist and post-colonial theories have enlightened the general engagement with the novel. In many ways, the history of modern critical and literary theory is bound up with the history of reading, or readings, of *Ulysses*. It has been, and continues to be, a text wherein all readers and theorists discover themselves and find their own stories being told and being reflected back at them. In *Ulysses*, they see not James Joyce but versions of themselves.

For Joyce himself, though, *Ulysses* was in many ways quite straightforward:

It is the epic of two races (Israel-Ireland) and at the same time the cycle of the human body as well as a little story of a day (life). . . It is also a kind of encyclopaedia. My intention is not only to render the myth *sub specie temporis nostri* but also to allow each adventure (that is, every hour, every organ, every art being interconnected and interrelated in the somatic scheme of the whole) to condition and even to create its own technique.[8]

Yet such a deliberately 'made' novel suggests how consciously Joyce attempted to layer his narrative so that form and style are of parallel importance to action. Indeed, in the absence of plot – or at least a plot of exciting deeds and daring do – language and style increasingly become the focus as the novel progresses and traditional character development recedes. Thus, the reader's introduction to the immature Stephen, who is still imagining art as opposed to creating it, gives way to the middle-aged ad man Leopold Bloom whose very ordinariness makes him extraordinary. And then the city itself becomes like a character and, from the Sirens chapter onwards, linguistic concerns and literary modes come to the fore. Finally, to comment on all the action, and all the men, that have commented on her throughout the day, Molly Bloom's soliloquy brings the day and the book to a close. Experiment is central to the novel as Joyce plays with conventions and expectations, loosening the restrictions of form and language, and as he playfully employs a dizzying array of different styles and genres in order to render the complexities of Irish life as he sees it. Beginning at eight o'clock in the morning, his characters – through eighteen episodes corresponding to eighteen hours of the day – meander through the city of Dublin, their sauntering *flâneur* status being a combination of the powerlessness of the colonised as well as simple bourgeois desire. Joyce's work, from *Dubliners* to *A Portrait of the Artist as a Young Man*, was infused with the world-weary atmosphere of Mikhail Lermontov's *A Hero of Our Time* (1841), with Stephen Dedalus particularly adopting the pose of the aloof Pechorin's studied jadedness.[9] However, with the creation of Leopold Bloom, Joyce manages to if not entirely dispel the European modernist fixation on the losses and absences within the fragmentation of modernity, then at least to indicate how a new type of hero might manage to negotiate the perils of the contemporary world. That Bloom and the book is future-oriented towards potential and possibility is underlined, perhaps, by the fact that, in contrast to so many of the characters in *Ulysses* who have their originals in real Dublin life, Bloom *is* invented.

The realism of *Ulysses* is important in an Irish context. Joyce's is a hyperrealism, with its emphasis on the quotidian experience of the everyday, the detailing of the habitual and the routine combating the deadening misrepresentation of Ireland in the novel to this point. Indeed, its celebration of the rituals of the daily round differentiates this work from most modernist writing occurring elsewhere, much of which feared the conventions of the commonplace as that which anaesthetised the modern imagination. Joyce's uses of the stream of consciousness technique along with an encyclopaedic method[10] are ways in which this real world is rendered on the page. With its numerous styles, *Ulysses* reproduces Ireland in a manner that no parliamentary Blue Book or official report ever could. And yet as Seamus Deane argues, Joyce's work is not simply about 'reflecting reality'; rather, it is concerned with 'creating a reality which otherwise would have no existence'.[11] In other words, the act of fiction writing is an act that attempts to recover from, as Deane puts it, the brute hard facts of history. Joyce's microscopic detailing of Dublin life in June 1904 is an attempt to portray that reality in order to get beyond it.

On a personal level for Joyce and on a cultural level, 1904 is very much a year of transition. It is the year that the Abbey Theatre was founded, the year that J. M. Synge's great one-act drama *Riders to the Sea* was first performed, and the year when a ten-volume anthology *Irish Literature* was published. It is a moment when numerous possible futures are open to the citizens of Dublin and Ireland. Certainly, in the way that *Ulysses* is written, though the reader in 1922 would know what happens subsequently – the 1916 rebellion and the gaining of independence – Joyce does not in his novel predetermine any particular outcome or fate or destiny for his characters or for Ireland: anything and everything seems possible. This is true, too, for Joyce himself as an artist. The Stephen Dedalus of *Ulysses* is presented as all potential not yet capable of producing even the early stories of *Dubliners* – three of which actually appeared in A. E. Russell's periodical *The Irish Homestead* in 1904 – let alone be the author of *A Portrait of the Artist as a Young Man* or *Ulysses* itself.

From the outset, critical attention has been drawn to Joyce's 'mythical method', with each of his eighteen scenes corresponding to an episode from Homer's Greek epic, *The Odyssey*, so that the first episode pictures Stephen Dedalus, like Telemachus (Odysseus's son), wondering about familial relationships and paternal connections. Or most famously, and recognisably, the 'Cyclops' episode is reimagined in Joyce's work as Leopold Bloom in verbal combat with the one-eyed citizen in Barney Kiernan's public house – Bloom waving his cigar becoming the comically diminutive version of the burning stake that Odysseus plunged into the eye of the Cyclops. This structure of correspondence certainly gives shape to this most plotless of narratives, allowing for varying types of movement and development at the formal level as well at the level of content, beyond the stasis that the singular focus on Thursday 16 June 1904 will necessarily reflect. Of course, certain critics position modernity, Joyce and Ireland as being the reflectors – the receivers – of this foundational Greek text in the Western canon. The insinuation is that modernity lacks the high, grand gestures and heroic possibility of the distant past, that Joyce – like other modernists in the vein of T. S. Eliot, for instance – mourns the passing of the underlying unitary nature of Western thought and culture, and that he, coming from the periphery of the Irish scene, looks outward to a general international source for his novel rather than anything from within Irish culture itself. In other words, whatever meaning the novel may have, or whatever heroic significance a character may possess, is gifted from elsewhere.

While an element of Joyce's use of Homer is playfully humorous, signalling how high tragedy has been transformed into low absurd comedy in the modern world, he is also operating out of profound respect. His has a much more complex relationship to Homer's *Odyssey* than simply one that sets up a crude binary between past and present, tradition and modernity. Stephen Dedalus ruminates about paternity and filial debt in a conversation about William Shakespeare's creativity and originality, and he argues that the great bard was 'Himself his own father'.[12] The implication is that modernity demands self-invention and that the modern artist, particularly, must eschew all that has gone before and be self-made. Earlier Stephen had talked of his father as 'the man with my voice and my eyes' (*Ulysses*, p. 46), which indicates his modernist pretensions and his pompous sense of his own significance. Yet, what both these statements actually signal is not a radical break with tradition and the past, but rather how central a free dialogue is between tradition and modernity, past and present: an empowering reorientation that opens up the prospect that the Greeks were rather like us and not just a case of us being a bit like them. History is made relevant in the present moment with living links being acknowledged rather than disconnection and difference. In other words, Joyce reverses the accepted polarities and, in doing so, creates a truly radicalised space wherein all opposites can exist as dualities. The result is that the modern moment *can* be a place of heroic action and thought, that Ireland – even existing as it does on the margins – *can* be a place of energy, innovation and invention.

Accepting that Dedalus's theory is a central motif running through *Ulysses*, in terms of how the novel is written and what it is about, it is then possible to begin to appreciate some of the manoeuvring undertaken by Joyce in his reaffirmation of the epic as a medium for expression in the contemporary world. In relation to the history of the Irish novel, Dedalus's reversals open up intriguing readings and rereadings of specifically Irish themes and Irish concerns.

One chapter in particular, the 'Cyclops' episode, has become the primary focus for much of the critical debate about Ireland and Irish political, cultural and national concerns in *Ulysses*. The one-eyed nationalist – the Citizen – supposedly embodies all that is narrow and backward in contemporaneous Irish politics. However, Emer Nolan brilliantly argues how complicated the Citizen's politics actually are, thereby challenging any simplistic or predetermined interpretations of Joyce's engagement with contemporary Irish concerns.[13] More thought-provoking, however, and not as overtly obvious, is how a conception of Ireland emerges from the 'Hades' episode, which revolves round the funeral cortege of poor little Paddy Dignam that makes its way through the centre of Dublin city and his burial in Glasnevin cemetery.

The 'Hades' chapter, centring on the funeral of Paddy Dignam, parallels Odysseus's journey to the underworld in Homer's work. As has been noted throughout this study, the Irish wake and funeral have always been of almost obsessive interest to a wider novelistic audience outside Ireland. In many ways, especially in the nineteenth-century novel, all Irish culture was distilled into this one custom. Any one individual funeral became a symbol of the death of traditional Irish culture that could be played out again and again. Personal grief became subsumed into a national funerary narrative of defeat and a general movement towards the end of things. What is interesting, of course, is that the wake and the funeral were always perceived from outside the ceremonies, always looking in from a distance. One consequence is that this national and communal reading was imposed from without and therefore the wake and the funeral became signs of Ireland's backwardness – with its preoccupation with the past, with tradition, with forever wallowing in death and dying. Ultimately, this absorption with the past results in Ireland being unwilling to embrace modernity. Joyce directly interrogates this debilitating legacy in Irish discourse, deconstructing it and offering an alternative reading of Ireland's relationship to its past. In many ways, the blankness of death, of non-existence, becomes another reflecting mirror for Joyce to present different attitudes to Ireland and Irishness.

The 'Hades' episode has been read as transforming the entire city of Dublin into something of a cemetery. Joyce has the ability at times in his narrative to radically depopulate the city. It was a technique he also employed in *A Portrait* in order to emphasise the city's deadening paralysis. And here, in this episode, the city is imagined as a kind of vast graveyard, a monument to the dead. As the funeral cortege moves through the city, from south to north, numerous memorials are mentioned: the statues to Daniel O'Connell, Father Mathew, and the foundation stone for what will become the statue to Charles Stewart Parnell become like commemorative head-stones dotting the barren landscape. Of course, all cities commemorate the past in this way, though, due to its colonial status at this time, acts and sites of commemoration in Ireland possessed no official status. Indeed, their being outside what is sanctioned and permitted is one reason for both the interest in and fear of the wake and the funeral. The astute reader will recognise that this image of the city as graveyard is only a momentary snapshot. In previous chapters, and then in subsequent ones, the same places and spaces are imagined and presented differently by Joyce for different effect. For that is the point: this episode is but one hour in the day and there is no sense in which this funeral and this contemplation of death overwhelms the entire narrative. Death – and all that it may signify – has its allotted space on 16 June, no more and no less.

But death is not hidden in the world of Joyce's *Ulysses*. It is accepted as a proper part of life. As the cortege moves through the city, its journey is interrupted by cattle going to the quays (*Ulysses*, p. 122), giving rise to one of Bloom's many civic-minded thoughts about how everyday life could be improved for citizens of the city who must put up with this weekly rural incursion. Often this moment is read as signalling the backwardness of Ireland – its being bound to an agricultural rather than an industrial economy. Yet, in another way, this is a demonstration of the reality of modern living. An element of capitalist progress is to disconnect modes of production from the end product, concealing that which is unpalatable and unpleasant. But here, reversing the modes of polite society, nothing is hidden from view. Indeed, this could be a trope for modernist writing in general and this novel's manifestation of it in particular. As one reviewer said of *Ulysses*: 'All that is unmentionable, according to civilised standards, has been brought to the light of day without any veil of decency.'[14] Polite society's standards are reversed and challenged: reality cannot be ignored or denied, as the fact of death cannot be ignored or denied.

Bloom is forced to recall the death of his father, who committed suicide in a hotel in Ennis, and the death of his son Rudy, who died eleven days after being born: 'If little Rudy had lived. See him grow up. Hear his voice in the house. Walking beside Molly in an Eton suit. My son. Me in his eyes. Strange feeling it would be' (*Ulysses*, p. 110). There is obviously a sense of regret in his ruminations but Bloom is not paralysed by this memory. Simon Dedalus, on the other hand, is:

– Her grave is over there, Jack, Mr Dedalus said. I'll soon be stretched beside her. Let Him take me whenever He likes.
   Breaking down, he began to weep to himself quietly, stumbling a little in his walk. Mr Power took his arm.
   – She's better where she is, he said kindly.
   – I suppose so, Mr Dedalus said with a weak gasp. I suppose she is in heaven if there is a heaven. (*Ulysses*, p. 132)

The Irish funeral, as Joyce knew, has more to do with the living than with the dead. Here, Simon demonstrates how his wife's death gives him a role to play, one which he happily performs. Simon sees no future for himself, save his own passing away. The perils of such immobilising nostalgia are further developed as Joyce moves from this individual attitude to the wider political scene when the mourners visit Parnell's grave in Glasnevin:

– Some say he is not in that grave at all. That the coffin was filled with stones. That one day he will come again.
   Hynes shook his head.
   – Parnell will never come again, he said. He's there, all that was mortal of him. Peace to his ashes. (*Ulysses*, p. 143)

Ireland's hopes of liberation, of freedom and of self-governance appear to be buried along with Parnell. None of these characters can begin to imagine a political future of potential, possibility or action.

Joyce goes as far as to directly mimic the kind of approach that had been taken towards the funeral in the nineteenth-century Irish novel. Bloom, as a Jew, is an outsider to this particular Catholic ceremony and therefore he hovers in a liminal space, both inside and outside, the burial ritual. This technique has numerous functions. The anthropological note struck in Bloom's perspective offers an emotional distance, puncturing and demystifying the solemnities surrounding the burial of Paddy Dignam. The language of the ceremony is gently mocked or, rather, the language is used as a springboard for stream-of-consciousness musing: 'We are praying now for the repose of his soul. Hoping you're well and not in hell. Nice change of air. Out of the fryingpan of life into the fire of purgatory' (*Ulysses*, p. 140). Through Bloom what might be thought of as familiar to an Irish Catholic readership is defamiliarised: 'The priest took a stick with a knob at the end of it out of the boy's bucket and shook it over the coffin. Then he walked to the other end and shook it again. Then he came back and put it back in the bucket. As you were before you rested. It's all written down: he has to do it' (*Ulysses*, p. 131). Certainly Bloom's matter-of-fact account pokes fun at the sombre sacrament: his materialist down-to-earth words existing in stark contrast to the heightened use of liturgical Latin. But, of course, Joyce's critique is multi-layered and he is also lampooning the limits of anthropological discourse itself and its hopeless inability to truly describe the human and cultural world it perceives. And yet this act of defamiliarisation allows the jaded reader see the ritual again as if for the first time. So, rather than undermine completely whatever mystery this rite contains, Joyce through his character Bloom actually reinvests the ceremony with potential significance.

Paddy Dignam's funeral, far from yet again representing death at a national and communal level in the Irish novel, actually personalises and individualises death. For Joyce, part of the misrepresentation of Ireland was this manoeuvre negating the individual and the deployment of stereotypes. Throughout *Ulysses* the numerous traumas of Irish history are viewed from the individual and the local level. The profundity and revolutionary potential of this move away from the constant desire to represent an entire culture and nation, towards the detailing of the human response to events, cannot be under-estimated in Irish art and culture. This foregrounding of the Irish individual in this manner is a refusal by Joyce to submit to any one particular grand narrative, either imperial or religious. As Stephen will later declare: '(He taps his brow) But in here it is I must kill the priest and the king' (*Ulysses*, p. 688). Thus, Bloom's response to death is an all too human one: a mixture of sadness at his own losses and an often humorous approach which, perhaps, belies his fears and allows him to evade momentarily the pain of those losses. Bloom's reflections on the nature of death itself and on how the ceremonies surrounding death might be updated and improved are all part of his attempt to make death human, to make it a part of his own narrative and, in the words of John McGahern, 'return it to the everyday'.[15]

Bloom's journey to the underworld, like Odysseus's journey, is one where knowledge might be gleaned. In the end, he must accept death as an integral feature of life, and this he does: 'Can't bring back time. Like holding water in your hand' (*Ulysses*, p. 213). It is the natural order of things to live and to die, a natural cycle that surpasses the purely human world. He thinks about the cemetery and its proximity to the Botanic Gardens, which are 'just over there. It's the blood sinking in the earth gives new life' (*Ulysses*, p. 137). He becomes aware too that, as with all things in this world, death is a matter of human perception. They pass the house where Thomas Childs was allegedly murdered by his brother in 1898: 'Shuttered, tenantless, unweeded garden' (*Ulysses*, p. 125). What was once sensational news is now forgotten. The relativity of memory, – public and private and popular – becomes clear: 'People talk about you a bit: forget you. Don't forget to pray for him. Remember him in your prayers. Even Parnell. Ivy day dying out. Then they follow: dropping into a hole, one after the other' (*Ulysses*, p. 140). Nothing can be permanent in human kind's fallen state: even knowledge and memory will change and fade in time. Bloom comes to know this, but does not have to accept it as debilitating or negative. Rather than succumb to death, he chooses life instead:

Back to the world again. Enough of this place. Brings you a bit nearer every time . . . Plenty to see and hear and feel yet. Feel live warm beings near you. Let them sleep in their maggoty beds. They are not going to get me this innings. Warm beds: warm fullblooded life. (*Ulysses*, p. 146)

Death and the past it represents are always a presence but not necessarily a presence that prohibits a move into the future – at an individual or a communal level. Interestingly, it is this attitude that marks off Bloom decisively from Stephen. Bloom's middle-aged pragmatism, perhaps even wisdom, allows him to embrace twentieth-century modernity in a way that is denied Stephen who, despite his affectations to the contrary, is still mired in the Irish nineteenth century. Certainly, his role as one that broodingly anticipates future action suggests as much.

In Homer's epic, Odysseus, on his journey to the underworld, meets Achilles and is told that he would 'rather be a serf in the house of some landless man . . . than king of all these dead men that have done with life'.[16] In choosing life, Bloom is choosing all the trials and tribulations that may come his way. For that moment of seeming triumph, as he steps over the threshold of Glasnevin Cemetery back into the world of action, is followed by an insignificant exchange with another mourner, John Henry Menton. Bloom's outsider status is reasserted as he is rudely put in his place. So nothing has changed for Bloom: he has gained knowledge but he is essentially the same man as he was before. The real mystery is that Bloom chooses his own life rather than wish for someone else's. Is that perhaps what is truly heroic about this ordinary man? There is no answer to this question, of course, and there is not meant to be. Despite literary and critical theory's attempts to fix and to know this particular text, much of what it has to tell us remains beyond Enlightenment knowledge. The greatness of Joyce's novel then, comes not from its supposed modernist inclusiveness, its modernist celebration of the individual artist's transcendent imagination's ability to 'get it all in', but rather with its flirtation with ignorance and the constant possibility of its own collapse.

CHAPTER 4

Irish independence and the bureaucratic imagination, 1922–39

These fragments I have shored against my ruins.
(T. S. Eliot, 'The Waste Land')

The year 1922 marks the coming into being of the Irish Free State in the South of Ireland. This is merely a confirmation of the December 1920 'Government of Ireland Act', passed in the British House of Commons, which provided for the partition of Ireland with two parliaments, North and South. Such legal manoeuvrings occurred parallel to the War of Independence (1918–21) and the subsequent Civil War (1922–23). It is, as John Wilson Foster remarks, a confusing time.[1] While historical dates suggest an uncomplicated worldview of steady progress – a stark moment of before and after – the reality, of course, is that day-to-day life is messy and progress is far from seamless. The novel form, particularly, is best poised to explore that muddled reality. In many ways, in an Irish context, the kind of boundary-making that partition implied, the sense of different spheres of experience and influence – different worlds – permeates into the cultural realm. In other words, there is a serious disconnect between the newly formed state that has come into being and the art being produced within the state: a critical disjunction between a public sense of history and the private exposure to the trauma of change. Perhaps this is the case in all places, but in Ireland, because of the quite conscious intertwining of national and cultural interests through the revivalist period, this disconnect is particularly telling.

It has been argued that the freedom post-independence Ireland offered was limited and limiting. As Seamus Deane writes, 'it was a liberation into a specifically Irish, not a specifically human, identity', and this 'Irish freedom declined into the freedom to become Irish in predestined ways.'[2] It was as if, as Declan Kiberd argues, the energy of revolution had been thoroughly dissipated in the effort to gain physical control of the island of Ireland and once that had been achieved there was no energy left to continue that revolution in the important sphere of culture.[3] What was neglected was the individual – the singular self – as the needs for bedding down the new state became paramount and the bureaucratic mind dominated all spheres of public life.

Some could argue that with the Irish novel, as in Irish literature in general at this period, there is a conscious desire to critique the revivalist impulses of a generation earlier.[4] The difficulty with this assumption is that it radically simplifies the Revival's various legacies in independent Ireland. There is always a time lag with the novel form, which lacks the potential immediacy of poetry or drama. Even the mighty *Ulysses*, when published in 1922, is something of a historical document set nearly twenty years previously and before the quite obvious upheavals in Ireland's political life. Thus, the political differences and debates that characterised the Revival period continued to persist in various forms within the Irish novel as they did in the Irish state. Rebellion, war and independence did not end or resolve those discussions, though the bitter divisiveness of the Civil War meant that many lingering critical positions and ideologies were driven underground. Consequently, a sense of unfinished business endures: a hope, perhaps, that the promised freedom of the revolution would actually come to pass, that the project of remaking Ireland would continue despite officialdom's desire for conservative continuity.

Three texts in particular capture something of the mood at this crucial turning point: texts that look backwards and forwards in their attempts to come to some understanding of what has been gained and lost in the years of revolution. George Russell (A. E.) (1867–1935) in the Preface to his *The Interpreters* (1922) explains what he hopes to achieve with his novel:

Nations conceive of themselves as guided or sustained by a divine wisdom, and I have wondered in what manner impulse might flow from Heaven to Earth. Out of my meditation on this came *The Interpreters*. Those who take part in the symposium suppose of the universe that it is a spiritual being, and they inquire what relation the politics of Time may have to the politics of Eternity. Their varying faiths have been held by many ancients and by some who are modern, but the symposium has been laid in a future century so that ideals over which there is conflict today might be discussed divested of passion and apart from transient circumstance.[5]

Not unlike a Socratic dialogue, setting and characterisation are secondary to the ideas and debates between the characters who are broadly modelled on Russell himself, W. B. Yeats, James Stephens and James Standish O'Grady. Russell explores the origins of the ideas and the ideals that drove his own generation, and that underpinned the revivalist impulses as he saw and understood them. Great dollops of his own peculiar brand of theosophy and spiritualism are presented to the reader in his efforts to explain the universal nature of the Irish cause for freedom. While readers could only be numbed by the tediousness of the debates, they might have been struck by the earnestness in which these ideas are discussed. One legacy of the Civil War period was the turning away from theory and from ideas, as if people could no longer afford the luxury of abstractly thinking about the Irish situation. For was it not opposing ideas that had led to the Civil War in the first place? Russell is very aware of this, consciously moving his narrative into the future in an endeavour to deflect attention away from the present moment. The idealists are, in the end, executed for their part in a revolution. At the close of the novel, a character called Heyt, who represents the modern material world of capital and empire and who has been strangely put amongst these men, leaves 'without a word and went out to make the world in his own image'. As with the philosophy underpinning D. H. Lawrence's *Women in Love* (1920), Russell's worldview is impossible to sustain against the forces of the contemporary moment. The ideas, then, appear quaint and fanciful – ridiculous even – in the bright light that modernity brings to bear on them.

While certainly not a novel in any traditional sense, W. B. Yeats's *A Vision*, the first edition of which was published in 1925, makes use of an elaborate framing device, including poems and stories and references to supposed real characters outside the confines of the text, such as Michael Robartes and Owen Aherne. In other words, Yeats fictionalises the context in which his ideas are presented, edging towards prose fiction as that form of expression which might be able to convey his theories. *A Vision* is a lament for the imaginative act of speculation and a critique of the turn towards materiality in thought and life. It is a treatise on his esoteric system based on automatic writing sessions with his young wife Georgie. Its symbols and imagery are central to the view of history and individuality that would find expression in his later poetry. Interestingly, this form of fiction-making allows him to position his friends and associates, such as Lady Gregory and J. M. Synge, as well as public figures, such as Charles Stewart Parnell, in relation to his own sense of himself, to create a world, or an image of the world beyond himself. In other words, he uses the novel form as a means of creating an imaginative community. As always with Yeats, his central concern is himself but this is coupled here with a meditation on the nature of the creative imagination itself. Of course, this creativity could have as much influence on changing the reality of the world as it would have in terms of producing poetry. Yeats is forced to create a form that will allow his philosophy to be adequately expressed outside his usual modes of poetry, drama and the essay.

Certainly, the work of James Joyce and James Stephens demonstrates to Yeats the possibilities of prose fiction for just that kind of debate. Indeed, because of their work, in an Irish context, the rigidity of the novel form coming from the nineteenth century had been exploded, allowing the kind of experiment that is *A Vision* to come to pass.

A number of Irish writers of this period emphatically embrace the possibilities of experimentation in their fiction. Eimar O'Duffy, for instance, abandons the realism of his earlier novel *The Wasted Island* (1919) and in his *King Goshawk and the Birds* (1926), with very serious intent, enters into the realm of the fantastic in order to fulminate against the absolutes of a globalised capitalist economic system which puts wealth and power into the hands of the few. The novel is the first part of what has become known as the 'The Cuanduine Trilogy', with *The Spacious Adventures of the Man on the Street* (1928) and *Asses in Clover* (1933) being the subsequent parts to the series. Though set in the future of the 1950s, O'Duffy satirises the foibles of his own time. The description of two political parties, which are merely flip sides of the same coin, is a particularly astute reading of what will come to be the reality in Ireland. His fantasy world has a civil war being fought so that Ireland may rejoin the British Empire. Obviously O'Duffy believes that the possibilities of post-revolutionary freedom have been squandered. In having the mythological Cúchulain return to a very dirty Dublin, he makes fun of whatever heroic pretensions the Irish Free State might still possess. Formally, though, he is an inheritor of some of the stylistic techniques of Joyce, with one technique – the imitation of the language of journalism – being particularly humorous and pertinent. As with Denis Johnston's play from the same time – *The Old Lady Says 'No'!* (1929) – O'Duffy highlights how Irish myth, reimagined through the fantastic, possesses the potential to be a source of scathing satire in modern post-revivalist Ireland.

What is truly remarkable about his work is how he places Ireland's ills within an international frame. His attack on global capital is unrelenting and, in a way, he foretells how it is economic realities which drive change and transformation rather than cultural concerns alone. In other words, the Orwellian future he envisages is one of Ireland and Irishness not mattering in a world where such difference has no currency whatsoever. Critics have pointed out that much of O'Duffy's sarcastic ridicule is repetitive and overly laboured.[6] While this is true – the expression of his vision does lack any sustained humour or, indeed, humanity – O'Duffy, like Yeats and George Russell, is overwhelmed by the gravity of the problems he confronts. Each writer is aware of something lost – of an absence in contemporary post-revolutionary Ireland – and all struggle towards an expression or a language that might contain that loss and point towards a future. Each writer essentially fails in his or her efforts.

They fail because they ignore the plight of the individual in their efforts to engage with wider philosophical–theoretical issues and national–international concerns. In a way, they fail to recognise that it is precisely this marginalising of the individual and the possible burgeoning interiority of the individual that is the paramount difficulty in the new state. Each presents public or exterior narratives and worlds that are not balanced by any unmasking of the inner consciousness. And it is that inner consciousness that becomes *the* important site for modern and modernist novelists, as it is there that they enact this estrangement from the grand narrative of Ireland with their focus on the isolation of modernity and the individual's efforts at articulation and expression in the new order.

While the idea that the Free State lurched towards 'rigorous conservativism' is certainly a cliché,[7] it is true the Catholic Church became a dominant force in post-independent Ireland, taking the role of moral watchdog, while the overwhelming desire to normalise life and to achieve some form of civil and economic stability became paramount for government. The application of rigid conformity was a real feature of life in the North of Ireland as well as the South. Censorship, which came into law in 1929, in its efforts to broadly control and set the boundaries of taste and knowledge, became the legal manifestation of this estrangement between the new bureaucratic institutions of the state and the individual. Daniel Corkery's *Synge and Anglo-Irish Literature* (1931) in the realm of literary criticism is also a manifestation of this drive towards stability and normality.[8] The problem is the definition of what might be thought of as 'normal' in Irish life is not very clear-cut. The legacy of colonialism means that the new state operated along similar lines to that which went before it and the models of societal normalcy could also be attributed to influence from outside Ireland. The Irish Academy of Letters created by W. B. Yeats and George Bernard Shaw in 1932 was a direct reaction to censorship, giving a public voice to those who might resist being silenced. Though Yeats's involvement with the fascist Blueshirt movement of the 1930s demonstrates how complicated attitudes actually were for artists who might hold seemingly contradictory political viewpoints in comparison to aesthetic opinions.

Thus the novel becomes a site that enacts this anxiety between the old and the new, between the heroic nature of art and politics in the revivalist period and the more mundane, normalised life of 1920s and 1930s Ireland. Writers are forced to react to a world that up to this point had seemed to change rapidly and which now appeared to be a place where time itself had slowed and come to a halt. The real shift in culture is one from where Irish writers were radically original and creative to one where that energy has been directed elsewhere in order to confront the demands of a new dispensation. Thus Irish writing – like most writing of this period – offers a critique of what is thought of as official and acceptable. The novel, in reaction to these shifts, becomes the place where the plight of the individual human person is negotiated and the fragmented nature of Irishness is played out again and again. Critics have discerned two clear strains in the Irish novel at this moment between realism on the one hand and what may be broadly labelled the fantastic on the other.[9] Rather than opposing forms, though, what is of interest is how these differing approaches have a shared impulse. While the high modernist moment that witnessed the kind of experimentation deployed by James Joyce does not continue wholesale in the post-1922 novel, there are still modernist tendencies to be discerned in both fantastic and realist Irish fiction. To be sure, realism acts as a counterpoint to the excesses of nationalist iconography while also reversing certain strains of revivalist emphasis on mythology. Joe Cleary believes that the realism/naturalism of Irish writing in this post-independent period is in its second phase and that it lacks the radical force of its first incarnation in the late 1880s.[10] Certainly there is a turning away from the *grande histoire* of modernism towards the *petite histoire* of the local and the intimately known, but that in itself is a sign perhaps of the exhaustion within the political and public realm. Realism's hold on the novelist's imagination has more to do with the quiet enthralment to detailing the everyday of Irish life because that is exactly the story which had never been told, only misrepresented. Realism however – as a form of anthropology – demands that those lives that have been detailed will be acknowledged in the New Ireland, will be given expression and validity. Fantasy, too, shares that somewhat radical compulsion in an Irish context and need not be labelled as simply coming out of revivalist modes, carrying on a fascination with Ireland's Celtic twilight past. Rather, the fantastic operates as a site to reimagine the all-too-real world of the present moment.

Of more use, perhaps, than this simple, but compelling, binary division is beginning to recognise the twentieth-century Irish novel in terms of genre. For the truth is that the diversity of the form seen since 1890 onwards continues on in this period. Thus, the realism at work in Elizabeth Bowen's Big House novel *The Last September* (1929) is utterly different to that on display in Kate O'Brien's *Mary Lavelle* (1936), while the use of fantasy in Flann O'Brien's *At Swim Two Birds* (1939) is at odds with Austin Clarke's *The Singing-Men at Cashel* (1936). So, what is witnessed is the emergence of distinct types of Irish fiction – for instance, the Big House novel, rural realism, rural and urban naturalism, and women's fiction – each with its own codes and tropes, each demanding recognition and attention.

Peadar O'Donnell's (1893–1986) two novels from this period, *Islanders* (1927) and *Adrigoole* (1929), demonstrate the difficulty of finding a genre that would contain his critique of the inadequacies of the Free State as he saw them from his own republican socialist perspective. Both have much in common with Tómas O'Crohan's (1856–1937) autobiographical *The Islandman* (1929), demonstrating how pervasive this type of rural imagery is in this period. While drafts of his first novel, *Storm* (1925), were smuggled out of prison, any truly radical attack on the emerging status quo is absent in his writing.[11] As with Patrick MacGill's *Children of the Dead End* (1914) that set the template for this type of novel, the hard, brutal peasant life of Donegal is presented with great detail in *Islanders* and to great effect. As if to reinforce this bare existence, O'Donnell's narrative possesses no stylistic flourishes whatsoever: his use of language is direct and straightforward. A romantic plot does not really trouble what amounts to an anthropological account of this community. An element of the story which revolves round the clash between harsh rural realities and the urban desire for the exotic of the Celtic twilight is a challenge to the bourgeois manufacturing of a certain type of representation of the Irish peasant. This critique is more successfully and substantially continued in his next novel, *Adrigoole*. The final scenes of the work are based on events from 1927 in Adrigole in County Cork, where the plight of subsistence living and starvation conditions was brought to the attention of the Dublin media. The same life is described here as in his earlier work as he shifts the scene to his native Donegal. The life of the hiring fair and seasonal emigration to Scotland is detailed, confirming these particular literary tropes' association with Donegal and the province of Ulster. Patrick Kavanagh, in his own novelistic and autobiographical writing, will make use of the hiring fair imagery, particularly, to lend an air of what he suspects will be authenticity to his own prose narratives.

Adrigoole follows closely the fortunes of a handful of characters over a long period of time. The world of politics and history enters into the text in a distanced, rather dream-like fashion, with references to the Treaty negotiations and the Civil War. What O'Donnell manages to show is how the national question is filtered through the actuality of local concerns about this immediate community's well-being. Thus, the economic consequences of widespread unrest are charted, as well as the uncomfortable discord that this upheaval brings to the characters caught up in taking sides. Brian and Brigit are shunned for their aid to republican soldiers on the run. Brigit and their child die of starvation when Brian is imprisoned and he goes mad in the closing scenes on the discovery of their bodies. The brooding presence of the bog pervades the novel and its brown earthiness is the final end for these characters in death. It is a powerful indictment of official disinterest and neglect of Irish citizens living in hardship and poverty, driven by an obvious political perspective that suggests that the New Ireland is a place inimical to true republican ideals. O'Donnell's critique extends to challenging the kind of appropriation of peasant imagery that the political elite would continue to engage in after the revolutionary moment had passed. But his act of writing is not simply a social realism undermining the romanticism of the image of the Irish peasant.[12] O'Donnell's difficulty is that he is employing *the* bourgeois form that is the novel, and unlike Joyce, for instance, he does not possess the artistic wherewithal to begin to actually defy the modes through which he chooses to express himself. Consequently, O'Donnell performs the doubled act of not only presenting to his readers the real world of harsh peasant life, but also simultaneously perpetuating the kind of imagery of the peasant that he wishes to deconstruct.

At what might seem to be the opposite end of the social spectrum to the rural world of O'Donnell's fiction sits the Big House novel. The nineteenth-century popular version of the genre posited a feudal answer to the Irish question, imagining a central role for the Anglo-Irish gentry as aristocrats in the sphere of governance and politics. Such a view lingered well past its being an actual possibility, but its persistence well into the twentieth century adds a certain piquancy to the representation of faded glory associated with the genre. Some critics see its literary perseverance as highlighting a poverty in the Irish novelistic tradition itself,[13] though this assertion ignores the peculiar conditions of that persistence even into the contemporary moment. Such a view also ignores the amazing adaptability of the Big House genre that lends itself to a variety of positions and readings such as feminist, post-colonial, modernist, postmodernist perspectives. Indeed, the genre of the Big House is the one aspect of the Irish novel which has been very well served critically.[14] A number of reasons can be put forward for explaining its continuing interest for writers, readers and critics.

Certainly, there is a major shift in the post-independence version of the novel. Influenced, perhaps, by a Yeatsian emphasis on the constructed nature of the Big House, there is now a dominant self-consciousness operating within many of these novels. Central to understanding the nature of the Irish Big House novel is that it has no corresponding existence in Northern Irish literature, where the actuality was that the old order was now fundamentally linked to the new governmental structures and also had a central ceremonial role to play in everyday life.[15] The Yeatsian focus on a patrician style, and on an alleged liberal and civilising politics, stands in opposition to the base realities of the newly independent Ireland and the newly empowered Catholic-nationalist middle classes. The sense of an injured pride, of what might have, or should have, been is a perpetual undercurrent in these novels which exploit the notion that the Anglo-Irish are a spent force politically, economically and culturally. Of course, the latter two are not exactly the reality – the enduring presence of the Big House novel suggesting a continuing existence at the level of culture at least. One consequence is the image of a supposed gentry under pressure becomes as much of a stereotype as any other stage image of Ireland and Irishness. So much so, that many Irish novelists, playwrights and poets from different traditions within Ireland have all engaged with it at some time or other in their careers. Thus, in the immediate aftermath of the revolutionary period, rather than the misty-eyed Celtic twilight types, it is the Anglo-Irish who become most tied to a romantic, mythical and illusory notion of themselves. Needless to say, of course, the best of these novels are not simple elegies to the passing of a class and its customs; rather, they are complex interrogations of the very notion of the Anglo-Irish and their links to Ireland as a place and a culture.

Though published under the double authorship of Edith Somerville and Martin Ross, *The Big House of Inver* (1925) was written by Edith Somerville alone, her writing partner having died in 1915. The author's note explaining this, tellingly, uses the imagery of commerce: 'An established Firm does not change its style and its title when ... one of its partners may be compelled to leave it.'[16] For all the focus on gentrified life and culture, Somerville is still proud of the fact that she and Martin Ross were able to make their way successfully within the vagaries of the literary marketplace. Indeed, it is that reality that informs – and not just for Somerville – much of the novel writing of this period. This economic context does find its way into the texts themselves and certainly the financial demands of being a novelist – of making a living from writing – spurs many of the novelistic choices about form and genre now being made by Irish writers. For Big House novelists, what is generated is an uneasy anxiousness about the irony of desiring to produce images of leisured ease while also having a very firm eye on opportunities for their own monetary gain. The novelists' predicament is mirrored in the worlds they create with the juxtaposition of high hopes amid the lowly reality of crumbling masonry.

The Big House of Inver is an updating of their wickedly scathing class comedy *The Real Charlotte* rather than, as some would argue, an updating of

Maria Edgeworth's *Castle Rackrent*.[17] The ambivalent position of Charlotte Mullins is now the burden of Shibby Pindy: the illegitimate daughter of the Big House who – more than the legitimate heir – harbours plans for the Prendervilles' continued prosperity into the future. Her machinations come to nothing and the house is burnt to the ground at the close of the novel. Once again, as in *The Real Charlotte*, it is a fallen world which is inhabited by these dissipated characters. It is Shibby, particularly, who represents this reality: 'The two strains in her blood that were in her, the tough acquisitiveness of the Irish peasant, and the hardy practicality of the English middle-classes, were speaking, little as she knew it' (*The Big House of Inver*, p. 80). The damning detail is that she is thoroughly unconscious of her position, fundamentally unconscious of who she is. It is for this reason that there is little real link to *Castle Rackrent*, which foregrounded, in the character Jason Quirke, a more frightening native Irish person who was very much in control of his own destiny. For this kind of unknowingness, of course, is in stark contrast to the authority of the novelist and the narrator who can see and understand everything. There are still demarcations to be made; there are still codes of difference that need to be acknowledged. The climactic end of the Big House in burning in this novel is played out over and over in other Big House novels, violently reinforcing the shuddering demise of the class and caste associated with the space. But, of course, the real tragedy is not simply to be found in this building's absence, but rather in the comedy that will replace it:

The story of the Big House of Inver is finished. The only noteworthy observation that still needs to be told is that of Mr. John Weldon.
'Sure I had it insured, to be sure! On the same day that we paid the money – and all that's in it, too, thank God!
'I'm an insurance agent, don't ye know!' (*The Big House of Inver*, p. 312)

Despite the linguistic humour on display here, John Weldon is practical enough to have done the proper middle-class thing. Once again, as with many Anglo-Irish novels from the late nineteenth century onwards, it is the question of class which is central above all things, including religion and politics. So, beneath this veneer of aristocratic life not only lurk petty bourgeois concerns about position and rank but also concerns about the reality of money, or the lack of it, and those things that money can buy: the portable property of the Big House that can be bought and sold at auction.

Certainly, an element at work within this novel is its critique from within of the Anglo-Irish themselves and their responsibility for their own downfall. However, to modern sensibilities at least, the unseemly recourse to

racial and eugenic issues undermines that assessment by adding a note of
confusion about who exactly is to blame for the decay of the once great
house and family. A contemporary reviewer felt that the book was 'ugly' and
that foreign readers will think that Irish landlords 'were as gross and
degenerate as the characters of Russian novels'.[18] This unfavourable comparison to characters in novels suggests that the reimagining of the Anglo-
Irish into the realm of literary existence comes at a high price. It is also a
signal, perhaps, that there still persists within that community a distrust of
the novel form itself.

Both Molly Keane (1904–96) and Elizabeth Bowen (1899–1973) would
continue to focus on the Big House in their writing. While Bowen has been
associated very much with the Big House novel, she actually only wrote
two. Her most famous Irish novel *The Last September* (1929) captures
brilliantly the mood of dislocation and disconnection of the Anglo-Irish
in the New Ireland. Though, once again, while gestures are made towards
the faded glory of aristocratic living, the truth is that, at a very basic level, for
the heroine Lois Farquar hers are the bourgeois concerns revolving around
marriage and the possibility, or impossibility, of some sort of worthwhile
career. Certainly, there is much social comedy at work within the novel:
Mrs Naylor at one stage complains that one of the problems with Gerald
Lesworth – putative lover of Lois – is that no one knows where he is from,
and that he cannot be comfortably placed socially. Bowen's fiction generally
is full of movement, her characters constantly in transit. In this world of
perpetual motion, people come and go, arrive, visit and depart. No relationship is ever straightforward in Bowen's writing, couples are forever being
impinged upon by others: mothers, aunts, awkward teenagers, ghosts and
lovers from the past who refuse to stay in the past and who assert themselves
in the present. Human energies are diverted away from each other and into
the numerous objects – the bric-à-brac – that clutter up everyday existence.
She fills her fictional spaces with 'things' so that the human imagination is
unable to dominate and her characters' thoughts are constantly interrupted
by some intrusion of the rudely actual. A table or chair being bumped into,
for instance, brings to an end many would-be philosophical musings, as it
brings to an end moments of connection and communication between
characters.[19]

Bowen's world, then, is a peculiarly modern, and modernist one. *To the
North* (1932) opens: 'Towards the end of April a breath from the north blew
cold down Milan platforms to meet the returning traveller. Uncertain
thoughts of home filled the station.'[20] Her brilliance is to combine her
particularly Irish anxieties about place, position and belonging to general

currents of this period: in the way in which both W. B. Yeats and James Joyce do. So even with her focus on out-of-place children, on the encroaching suburbia of inter-war Britain and her emphasis on flux and the transitory in a work such as *A House in Paris* (1935), she is carving out a landscape and psychic terrain that can resonate with an Irish audience.

Molly Keane, like Bowen, was from the Big House Ascendancy world herself and, because of that intimacy perhaps, also rejects a purely nostalgic view of the Big House and its inhabitants. Her early novels, published under the pseudonym M. J. Farrell, recreate detailed pictures of Big House life, especially the world of the hunt.[21] Novels such as *Mad Puppetstown* (1931) inhabit a similar terrain and time to that of Bowen's *The Last September*.[22] Unlike Bowen who only uses the device of ghosts in her short stories, Keane embraces more fully the Gothic possibilities of Big House declension.[23] The backdrop of the First World War as well as the Irish War of Independence makes clearer the nature of the problem facing the Anglo-Irish. The Great War means that a generation of young men have been wiped out and with them has gone the possibility of a viable, peopled future. Thus, while the figure of Aunt Dicksie represents an indomitable will to continue in the face of all adversity, young Easter and her cousin Basil represent the unclear future for the class that they embody: 'temporary, reduced, and doubtless infertile'.[24]

In contrast to these tropes of decline surrounding the shift in Anglo-Irish realities, the Catholic middle classes had risen into positions of power with the foundation of the Free State. Perhaps one of the best novelists of these altered circumstances is Kate O'Brien (1897–1974). John Wilson Foster argues that her middle-class world is similar to that of the gentrified Big House.[25] To be sure, there are similar problems and predicaments faced by individuals and communities. I would argue, though, in line with Edmund Burke's contention, that the Big House reflects middle-class concerns because the gentry *are* middle-class and not aristocratic. Thus, at the heart of both types of novel, perhaps, is a bourgeois desire to break with narrow convention – be it nationalist or unionist, Protestant or Catholic – and to embrace all the possibilities that the wide world might offer.

One striking difference is that the work of Kate O'Brien possesses a religious sensibility thoroughly absent in the realm of the Big House. Indeed, the work of O'Brien and other novelists of this period overturns the hoariest of Irish novelistic stereotypes. While the authority of a powerful Irish Catholicism is challenged and critiqued, there is yet a constant desire on display for some form of transcendent experience. Indeed, religion becomes central for many of O'Brien's characters in gaining access to emotion and, thus, the judgement on religion is tempered and made much more knotty and complex than simple outright rejection.[26] Needless to say, there is too a moral centre to her work and the lives of the characters she creates, the absence of which is actually part of the dilemma that modernity poses for the characters in the fiction of Bowen and Keane. So, while in the world of the Big House there may not be enough morality, in Catholic Ireland there is too much. The puritanical is what must be worked against. Another distinction is that the kind of violence offered as a historical backdrop to the Big House world is absent here, suggesting, of course, that despite similarities and correspondences, the threats faced by each social grouping are markedly different. While O'Brien herself grew up actually witnessing first hand the violence of her time, her fictional environments are remarkably unconcerned with that public sphere. Her intense focus is brought to bear on individuals – men and women – and families and their entwined relationships. Hers, then, is a psychic history of the Catholic Irish middle classes, an excavation of the turbulent lives being lived below the radar of official narratives.

Without my Cloak (1931) charts the coming into wealth of the Considines and their rise into the mercantile classes of Mellick – a fictional Limerick, homeplace of O'Brien. It paves the way for the much more penetrating novel *The Ante-Room* (1934).[27] Here the focus is on Agnes Mulqueen and her illicit love of her sister's husband, Vincent. This moral conundrum provides the dynamic impetus for the novel as she wrestles with her conscience. Interiority is reinforced by the Ibsenite overtones employed throughout, the novel's being very much like a piece of theatre with its singular concentration on the family, not on society, and the action mostly centred within the confines of the home. The forms employed within the novel amplify the oppressiveness of this space. As Declan Kiberd notes, O'Brien regresses to 'nineteenth-century modes' even as she hints at the stream-of-consciousness possibilities opened up by James Joyce.[28] Thus, a sense of repression and restrictiveness – of the limits of expression – becomes central to the novel.

Agnes chooses not to become involved with Vincent, who melodramatically takes his own life at the close. The pervading impression throughout this tragedy is of lives not being lived, of individuals opting for self-denial rather than indulgence. Though set in 1880, this possesses a very modern and up-to-date sensibility, suggesting that O'Brien feels compelled to deflect attention away from any illuminating spotlight on the present moment or on exposed raw emotion. Even the space within the title of the novel – the anteroom: a room that can open up various doors and possibilities; a room that if one stays in means one is ever on the threshold of these other possibilities and rooms – indicates a decentring of action, a deferring of any final commitment or definitive choice. Indeed, this observation can be carried into her relationship with the form of the polite novel itself, her discomfort[29] – perhaps distrust – with it never finally being overcome, though that anxiety never overwhelms her narrative concerns. Many critics have reread O'Brien's writing in light of feminist theory, perceiving in her negotiation of the constricted lives of her female characters a description of the limited role for women in a new patriarchal Ireland.[30] Her characters also hint at feminine difference and images of liberation, though Agnes's desire for what is taboo and unattainable suggests how certain sexual identities are impossible in Ireland. But, the atmosphere of unfinished business – of incompleteness and thwarted desire – is what finally lingers in *The Ante-Room*.

Mary Lavelle (1936), on the other hand, is more open in relation to its display of sexuality and desire. Set in Spain, the novel is centred on Mary's sensual awakening. She has left Mellick and her fiancé to be a governess in Spain, in order that she may know of something other than being the daughter she was and the wife she is going to be.[31] It is a novel of transition: from childhood to adulthood, from innocence to experience. She hopes to fulfil her childhood dream of being 'free and lonely' and, being set in 1922, her notion of such 'perpetual self-government'[32] takes on an obviously political hue. Echoes of the hostilities of Civil War Ireland are but vaguely felt by Mary, though they do impinge upon her Spanish world, filtered through local and wider European concerns. And, of course, at the time of writing the imminent civil war in Spain, with its conflict between left and right, obviously reflects back onto Irish politics in the past as well as onto the politics of the contemporary moment. It is a feature quite peculiar to O'Brien's fiction in how she effortlessly fosters an international perspective out of which to view both Irish politics and Irish Catholicism. Indeed, there is no prevailing sentiment that Ireland or its majority religion is marginal or inferior in her work; rather, Irish nationalist politics and the Catholic religion actually allow access into other cultures on an equal footing. Of course, there are differences, and the Irish puritanical denial of all forms of sensuality is central to those differences.

Spain is a place open to, and encouraging of, the senses, of intense feeling and passions. Mary becomes enthralled with the aesthetic possibility of the bullfight: 'Here was madness, here was blunt brutality . . . and all made into an eternal shape, a merciless beauty. Here . . . was art in its least decent form, its least explainable or bearable. But art, unconcerned and lawless'

(*Mary Lavelle*, p. 117). Kate O'Brien herself shares Mary's predicament: how to embrace these energies and perhaps control them for her art? Of course, the genteel novel form employed by O'Brien can never fully lose itself to those possibilities. This novel, then, portrays outré and unconventional behaviour and, unlike her earlier work, this is not deflected or disguised. Mary has an affair with Juanito, the married son of the family she is a governess to, and Agatha, who unusually for this period is a candidly presented lesbian character, in turn plainly declares her love for Mary. As Eibhear Walshe argues, *Mary Lavelle* is a pivotal novel in Kate O'Brien's career in that it ends on an open rather than a closed note and contends that this openness becomes a central feature in her subsequent work.[33] Mary returns to Ireland at the end, with the intention of ending her engagement to her fiancé and moving away from Mellick into freedom: 'That was the fruit of her journey to Spain. Anguish and anger for everyone and only one, fantastic, impossible hope. Yet there it was – a real story. As real as the bullfight – and … as beautiful' (*Mary Lavelle*, p. 344). This envisaging of her life in aesthetic terms is curious. Her life has become a book or a story fit for a novel, and is worthwhile because of this. Yet, while Mary does act, there is a way in which she never finally succumbs to Spain and its charms, but only flirts with its possibilities as readers, and writers, can only flirt with the lives of others in novels. In other words, Mary's freedom is a freedom into art – a common trope in Irish writing and something certainly to be celebrated, but perhaps in this instance it is a freedom already charted, already created out of the books and the romances that Mary has read. Still, even the momentary imagining, or glimpsing, of such vistas is extremely dangerous and the Censorship Board banned the book in Ireland. This puritanical turn in Irish civic life becomes more apparent throughout the 1930s and, in relation to fiction particularly, lists of banned and censored books appeared regularly in the newspapers. There is a deadening bureaucratic nature to the act of censorship in Ireland. The absurdity of the situation meant that no reasons had to be given for such action, thus no passion or energy is evident, as the act of censorship becomes just one more mundane task of government. The irony, obviously, is that these lists offered an interested reader a succinct guide to what novels ought to be read; and, of course, they were.

Thus, readers and writers had to police themselves, had to second-guess what was deemed illicit territory and what was not. A certainty to cause offence, obviously, would be anything to do with sexuality and sexual relations, meaning that an austere prudishness began to wrap itself round this aspect of human experience particularly, evolving over the years into something of a stereotype associated with Irish writing in general. The matter of sex was important for writers because the focus on it centred on all that was being denied the private individual, allowing it become the primary channel for rebellious thought and action.

Many writers felt compelled to confront the deadening effects of this new moral order. Austin Clarke (1896–1974), better known as a poet, in two novels – *The Bright Temptation* (1932) and *The Singing-Men at Cashel* (1936) – makes use of Ireland's medieval past to talk of the present puritanical moment. Clarke realises how narrow Irish tradition has become in the new state and how narrow the conception of Christianity. His retreat into a monastic past is a desire for a loosening of the enervating strictures of contemporary morality that, in his view, are very recent – certainly Victorian – inventions.[34] His excavation of the racy sexuality in his version of Gaelic Ireland is a not too disguised attempt to acknowledge the realities of present-day life behind whatever 'official' versions of Irishness were being propagated. His deployment of various mythical motifs and images, while certainly showing deference to the previous generation's use of them, demonstrates clearly how they can be used to critique the false politeness of modernity, giving access not to some quaint tradition but to a fiercely energetic culture. Like Kate O'Brien, his writing is not a straightforward abandonment of his Catholic faith; rather, it is a working through of the tenets of that faith, challenging its austerity.[35] But the prevailing moral code was not interested in such a debate and the censor banned both novels.

A distant past is also the focus of Francis MacManus's (1909–65) *Men Withering* (1939), which is the final part of a trilogy dealing with the eighteenth-century world of Gaelic poet Donnacha Rua MacConmara. It is as if the bitter divisions of the unhealed wounds of the Civil War propel MacManus's imagination into this almost genteel version of the past allowing him to affirm the power of poetry and the fundamental decency and humanity of the Irish as a people.[36] Again, it is the failure of the modern moment, of Irish modernity, that such propriety cannot be discerned in the present, causing this retreat into the past. It also highlights how difficult it is for some to reimagine the Irish as anything other than oppressed and captive, the actuality of Irish freedom finds no parallel form or mode of expression and thus what we witness is the easy recourse to the safely familiar.

Another novel famously banned for indecency was Sean O'Faolain's (1900–91) *Bird Alone* (1936). Stylistically accomplished, with a highly lyrical turn of phrase, this novel describes paralysis for the individual protagonist Corny Crone: 'But then, as I stood there, I realised suddenly that in those years in which I lived, the years after Parnell, the shore of Ireland was empty, too, and would remain empty for a long time, and that I was merely one of many left stranded after the storm.'[37] But the novel itself is anaesthetised: its plot delivered at a deadeningly slow pace, and the narrowness of the world being described infecting the pervading vision of the narrator and tainting the very form of the novel itself. There is a sense of something being withheld throughout O'Faolain's *Bird Alone*, as if he as author is unable to get beyond the constricted lives of his characters: he exists as the one who can both perceive and critique the Irish scene but is also fundamentally contaminated by that world, unable to truly transcend it. The setting of the novel in the past is a symptom of this kind of emotional caution. The post-Parnell Irish world appears as a cultural wasteland wherein the Catholic Church and a narrow-gauge nationalism fill the gap. But why return to a distant past when all has changed utterly since the downfall of Parnell? Of course, O'Faolain's target is his own contemporary 1930s world but he is unwilling, or perhaps unable, to contemplate that reality directly, and the past, however remote it may be, offers a more fixed and dense background for his story to unfold. It is also an indication of the seeming lack of possible heroism in his own moment. This is interesting because O'Faolain himself had fought on the republican side in the Civil War. The return to a previous generation's past suggests that the real moment of action was in that time; that it was the moment of potential and transformation, which his own time cannot sustain or replicate. This retreat into a historical past by many of the writers of this period suggests that despite their desire to open up spaces of difference in Ireland, despite their forward and progressive attitude, there remains a fundamental inability, in art at least, to map an Irish modernity. O'Faolain, for instance, in his critical and commentary writing in *The Bell*, can deal with the present day in a fashion beyond him with this particular novel. Regardless of the lessons of a figure like Joyce, who was well able to confront modernity directly, many of the generation after him curiously failed to do so. Thus everything concerned with *Bird Alone* – at an unconscious level – indicates the numbing actuality of the here-and-now Ireland in the post-independent period.

As will later be seen with Frank O'Connor (1903–66), O'Faolain obviously had profound difficulties with the expansiveness that the novel form might allow, preferring instead the limiting scope offered by the short story, which better suits, perhaps, the kind of restrictiveness that each author wants to emphasise. Neither, though, is actually open to the novel's experimental potential. *Bird Alone* suffers from being brilliantly episodic rather than organically seamless and, as a novel, is a failure. Again, as with other works being routinely banned at this time, O'Faolain's analysis of religion is not a wholesale rejection but instead is the beginnings of an engagement with its principles.

Norah Hoult (1898–1984) in her novel *Holy Ireland* (1935) also retreats into the past, setting the action at the turn of the century. It is a story of patriarchal rule uniting with Catholic dominance to keep youth and the feminine in tyrannical check. The Irish reader, of course, would have encountered this era already in, particularly, James Joyce's *A Portrait of the Artist as a Young Man*. Hoult's take on that historical moment is monocular as Joyce's work is multifaceted. Margaret O'Neil's vitality and intelligence is a challenge to her father's rule as she vainly attempts to live a life other than the one destined for her. Hoult's virtuosity comes through in the detail of her description of comfortable middle-class life, stressing conservative thinking and action at all times. Not much happens in terms of plot, perhaps unconsciously underlining this zone as anodyne and narrow. Having the focus primarily on the family home, too, makes the private sphere prison-like rather than a nurturing space. Margaret MacCurtain suggests that Margaret's father employs the rituals of Catholicism in a legalistic manner in order to wield power over his family.[38] Thus, the rosary becomes a means of exerting control over his family, of keeping his children in an infantile state of arrested development. The local priest, Father O'Flanagan, makes some advances towards Margaret, which though she laughs it off, hints at another repugnant layer to Catholic control.[39]

Though set in the past, there is no question that the work has contemporary significance to the 1930s. It can be argued that this legalistic approach to sacred rituals is another aspect of the bureaucratisation of Irish life in the post-revolutionary state-building years, deadening ardour and feeling, making even the spiritual routine. It is the reality of money, though, that exerts most influence in the lives of Patrick O'Neil's children, for it is only money that offers the prospect of real independence. The son Charlie, who lacks the easy intelligence of Margaret, cuts a sad figure in the scenes with his father on a market day in a small rural town. He is never allowed any adult authority, and is cruelly forced to remain in his father's shadow, childlike, tied to whatever monetary allowance he might be given. Margaret escapes this emotional net by marrying Clem, a Protestant civil servant, whose religion is an affront to her father and his authority. Yet, Hoult's description of Margaret's new home and her family life is a grittily realistic one, signalling that her liberation into lower-middle-class family life is not all that she might have hoped it would be. But, it is not just the contrast in her material world that is telling but also the way she is patronisingly treated by her husband. Interestingly, too, the conflict between Catholicism and Protestantism is not easily worked through in a binary either-or fashion. Clem's religious feeling finds expression in Theosophist thinking, with A. E. Russell a marginal figure in the novel. Certainly Theosophy's feyness is an antidote to a very hard and utterly intolerant Catholicism, but its emphasis on transcendence amid the very material world on display in the rest of the novel means it is presented as something faintly absurd.

The one writer from this period who is able to make something spectacular in art out of the immediate moment, to engage with the staid realities of independent Ireland and do so effectively and successfully, is Liam O'Flaherty (1896–1984). His achievement as a working novelist is that he embraces the possibilities that the form permits in terms of genre. It is a remarkable achievement on his part that between 1920 and 1940 he can produce so much writing which is varied and entertaining. The diverse aspects of his biography connect him with the great historical movements and moments of his era – born on the Aran Islands, he possesses first-hand experience of the Gaelic world, fighting in the First World War allows him to connect with a reality beyond Ireland, his time spent in a seminary gives him access to the codes of institutionalised religion, and his communism and republicanism during the Irish War of Independence and the Irish Civil War give his aesthetic vision a consciously political perspective. This background becomes the 'wild tumult' of contemporary Ireland[40] that creatively feeds into his fiction. More than any other writer of this period, his work captures the energy of the times out of which it is written and, indeed, captures too the dissolution and dissipation of those energies.

Many critics see the writerly reaction to post-independence Ireland as a move towards realist modes in an effort to deconstruct the illusory romanticism of the Revival and the romanticism of Irish nationalism particularly. O'Flaherty's fictional sphere is often a bleak one, but importantly his is a grotesque and melodramatic rather than strictly realist rendering of this brutal world, thus allowing a deeply intense psychological understanding of the trauma of recent Irish experience to emerge from within the pages of his novels.[41] His critique of Ireland is not simple or straightforward, it is rather wide-ranging and consistently angry, even its inconsistencies, and is always deliberately rebellious.[42] While his early work focused on the rural scene for which he was praised by those elites who desired the authenticity of a native voice, O'Flaherty's artistic vision would not be confined by any label or stereotyping. Some of his best work of the 1920s and 1930s lays bare the twilight existence of the underbelly of urban Dublin, concentrating on the lanes and backstreets where a ferment of life persists below the radar of official decorum. His deeply penetrating vision of urban life is seen particularly in *The Informer* (1925), set during the Civil War. It is a remarkably dense piece of writing that at once consciously harks back to nineteenth-century detective novels with its incessant reference to precise time and place over the period of the eight hours of the story,[43] as well as acknowledging the new form of cinema with its emphasis on photographic detail along with overtly physical descriptions of characters and place.[44] This intense focus on the body, especially that of the protagonist Gypo Nolan, is an essential element to O'Flaherty's modernist vision of the animal brutishness of contemporary life. Fleshy instinct rather than the polite manners of so-called civilisation are the driving force of action and reaction in this world. Again and again Gypo's physical presence is stressed to the point of almost Dickensian grotesqueness: his body, as with the bodies of other characters – particularly prostitutes – bears the traces of a life hard lived, his and their moral choices etched indelibly in his skewed and battered face. O'Flaherty's consciously naturalistic and primitivistic aesthetic stands in opposition to, and is an attack on, the political sphere.[45] The references to Karl Marx throughout, as in Sean O'Casey's work of this period, suggests that all such theory is bunkum in the face of the base Darwinian perspective on display here. While revolving round one of the more despised figures in Irish culture – the informer – the real conflict for O'Flaherty is between the head and the heart, between brain and brawn, and the kind of figure that Gypo represents – the proletarian who is only of use as a corporeal presence – will always be punished by the theorists who wield knowledge like a weapon. It is these thinkers, the opposite of the men of action, who the author warns will come into positions of power in the new Free State. From O'Flaherty's perspective, it is clear that these are men to fear.

The famous ending of the novel, with Gypo's symbolic Christ-like death in a church asking for forgiveness from the mother of the man he informed on, serves to underscore the centrality of the body and, ultimately, O'Flaherty's celebration of it as the one thing beyond ideological control. Christ – as God made incarnate – becomes an emblem of all that has not come to pass since Irish independence: bondage of one kind has only been replaced with another type of captivity for the ordinary person. In other words, revolutionary change has not come about.

The absence of authority – political and moral – central to *The Informer* is also on display in *Return of the Brute* (1930). O'Flaherty's own experiences of the First World War allow him to offer what is a contemptuous account of the mad futility of life and death in the trenches. Again, his matter-of-fact style with its emphasis on numbing exactitude is in evidence as he lays bare the conditions in which these soldiers existed. The body, of course, is being punished in this environment and death is never too far away. There is an undercurrent of homosexual attraction in the feelings that Gunn has for the angelic Lamont, though this desire is beyond conscious thought for him. It has been argued that this love is sublimated into the killing of his superior and maybe this is so.[46] However, the corporal dies also because he is thoroughly devoid of any moral centre: he is the most immediate symbol of power and his actions and orders represent the extreme absurdity of this war. O'Flaherty's view, as with many other writers of the time, does not imagine the Great War as a moment of celebration. Here he breaks with the Anglo-Irish view as encapsulated by, for instance, Elizabeth Bowen, which saw the sacrifice of the Great War as a disaster for that community with a whole generation of youth laid waste. Her critique is never a direct attack on the notion of authority, though inevitably such a traditional notion of authority is presented as becoming exhausted in her writing. For O'Flaherty it shows up acutely that instant when the traditional link between the individual and state authority is ruptured: when that old world passed away, the new brutal moment of modernity came into being.

O'Flaherty's *Mr Gilhooley* (1926) also foregrounds the body, but to much different effect than had previously been the case. The body continues to be the conduit through which O'Flaherty's analysis of the ills of modernity is traced. The opening pages present an image of modern ennui, with Mr Gilhooley bored with his dissolute life. He is said to be a voluptuary; that is, addicted to the pleasures of the senses. In a subsequent electrifying sexual encounter in a cinema – the choice of this most modern of places is telling –shows how the modern Irish body needs to be shocked into life and into sensuous feeling.[47] The difficulty is in channelling this much-needed energy, giving it shape and direction. Like all modernists, O'Flaherty discerns that something is seriously amiss in the contemporary age, some-thing ruptured and skewed. The kind of savage delirium that is barely concealed within his characters is his response to that situation, with the underlying destructiveness of his protagonists a symptom of this new disease.

Perhaps *The Puritan* (1932) is the greatest of Liam O'Flaherty's reflections on the often twisted energies driving modern conflicted Ireland onwards during the 1930s. All of his writing possesses a Russian quality, especially seen in the work of Fyodor Dostoevsky and Nikolai Gogol.[48] As with their great work of the nineteenth century, O'Flaherty captures vividly the fears and desires of the petit-bureaucratic mind that now dominates public life in Ireland. Francis Ferriter, coming from a good middle-class family, should be set to inherit all that the new state can offer its citizens. In typical Russian fashion, though, he is a disappointed man and has failed to secure a position suitable to his aspirations. Of course, those desires can never be fully articulated and exist only as a vague sense of entitlement and a persistent hope of a better future; in other words, they represent the typical paranoiac's dream.

O'Flaherty's genius is to take this well-known literary type and wed it to the kind of religious zealot that held sway in public discourse in 1930s Irish society. Indeed, he renders skilfully the nature of the newly established chattering classes: everyone has an opinion on everything – on the Irish character, the failure of Irish economics – whatever might be the topic of the day. All of this is comically rendered in the novel as O'Flaherty clinically dissects the social mores of the New Ireland striving to find its sense of identity. He sees clearly how Ireland's post-colonial position apes what has gone before, merely perpetuating systems of governance and thought rather than radically breaking with them. However, as an author, O'Flaherty is not above criticism himself and there are several moments of self-referential deflation, when the narrator offers his own opinions and comments on numerous relevant 'national' subjects and concerns: '[Vesey] was equally repelled by the religious fanaticism which is part of our unfortunate legacy from civil strife and the frustration of our political ambitions.'[49] Demonstrated here is how acceptable this kind of comment and debate was at the time. Indeed, a cursory glance at the newspapers of the period and recognising the existence of a burgeoning journal culture suggests that such opinion-making was commonplace and de rigueur.[50] The object of O'Flaherty's satiric blade is exactly that type of discourse which had little or nothing to do with the reality of everyday life. His desire is to expose the hypocrisy central to the dominant puritanical mode and its manifestations in censorship and religious observance, to reveal how authentic religious feeling or sentiment has nothing to do with this moral crusade which is simply about the possession and retention of power. Ferriter's 'sacrifice of blood' – his murder of a prostitute – is his attempt to determine God's existence and humanity's divine destiny. Sadly for a true believer like him, the officious nature of puritan Ireland means his mission fails and that he, and those like him, will always be out of place. Ferriter is quite obviously insane but his madness seems to be a reflection of the times and certainly its link to rage was something that the ageing W. B. Yeats found attractive and celebratory in O'Flaherty's art.[51]

Like other writers of the period, O'Flaherty also retreated into the past in his writing. Though his novel *Famine* (1937) – for which he is probably now best known – is actually a historical novel in a way in which the work of O'Faolain or Kate O'Brien is not. It is his interest in the possibilities of different types of novel and different genres that allows him to return to this calamitous moment in Irish history. While his writing to this point is obsessively up to date and bleakly modern in outlook and tone, *Famine* in many ways is an attempt by the author to write a nineteenth-century novel. It certainly possesses the scope and vision of such a novel: his narrative touching on not just an individual or a single family but also the entire community of the fictional Crom on the western seaboard. Thus, the middle classes and the Ascendancy as well as peasants are represented; and the rural world and the urban town come into view as intrinsically connected. None of O'Flaherty's rage is dissipated in this return to the past; rather, it finds similar targets to that which ignited his vehemence in his contemporary novels. Of course, the root of the problem is Ireland's status as a colony, but it is the utter corruption of the entire social and economic system which is at fault in terms of the immediate experience of the characters in their everyday lives. As is always the case in his diagnosis of Ireland's ills, it is the lowest members of the prevailing social order on which most real pain is inflicted. Throughout his fiction, death comes to those who have no real purchase in the communities in which they live, their dying being an indication of their powerlessness. Yet again, it is the body, principally, of the peasant, this time in death as was the case in much nineteenth-century Irish famine fiction, which becomes the signifier of all that is iniquitous in Ireland.

And, as was the case with the nineteenth-century Irish famine novel, the desire for justice is central here too. *Famine* exposes what is most uncomfortable for his contemporaneous audience. The Great Famine of the 1840s might have been a subject farthest from the minds of the bourgeois conservative elites of the 1930s who would wish to position Ireland as changed utterly from that moment. This was the year, after all, that the Fianna Fáil government put a constitution to the people which would create a republic in all but name. Thus the principles of justice and civil equality should be to the fore in public discourse. O'Flaherty's novel reminds his readership of the absolute need for such basic ideas in Irish politics. W. B. Yeats, too, in his 1937 updating of *A Vision*, also suggests that justice should be central to individual and communal experience. In the hands of a writer like O'Flaherty, and later Patrick Kavanagh in his long poem 'The Great Hunger', the imagery and symbolic power of the famine become the means by which a displaced critique of the contemporary world can take place.

While on the surface, at least, there would seem to be little to connect the work of O'Flaherty with that of Samuel Beckett (1906–89), there is a link to be discerned through the image of the body in pain and the body under attack. Beckett's most overtly 'Irish' novel entitled, comically and generically, *Murphy* (1938) has the eponymous character obsessed with transcending the body, with escaping the pain of being-in-the-world. The novel opens with Murphy tied securely with the aid of scarves to a chair: 'He sat in his chair this way because it gave him pleasure! First it gave his body pleasure, it appeased his body. Then it set him free in his mind. For it was not until his body was appeased that he could come alive in his mind.'[52] Existence itself is under pressure in Beckett's writing and the minutiae of being – its aches and pains, its momentary slivers of light amid an enveloping darkness – will increasingly become the focus of his fiction as traditional structuring of plot and character are done away with. His is a prose concerned with absences rather than presences: 'The sun shone, having no alternative, on the nothing new. Murphy sat out of it, as though he were free, in a mew in West Brompton' (Beckett, *Murphy*, p. 5). In contrast to the kind of disconnection endured by the characters in O'Flaherty's novels, Beckett's sensitivity to absences – on levels real and philosophical – has much to do with his Anglo-Irish background and his community's experience of disinheritance and dislocation and powerlessness in independent Ireland. Like Elizabeth Bowen, who shares stylistically much with Beckett, this is usually read as his European modernist/postmodernist tendencies. However, the local world of his own specific Ireland – that hinterland of south Dublin particularly – is never too far away in any of his artistic endeavours.

As a novel, *Murphy* suffers from the fact that Beckett is unsure exactly of the pose he wants to strike as an author: casual or, dare it be said, patrician indifference or a more earnestly serious tone? Comedy is never too far away in the narrative and much ironic fun is to be had with the character Austin Ticklepenny, 'Pot poet / From the County of Dublin' (Beckett, *Murphy*, p. 51) who is a thinly disguised depiction of Austin Clarke. At this juncture in his career, Beckett, it appears, wants to be a part of the Irish literary scene, even if he desires to stand at an amusedly jaundiced angle to it. Thus, Murphy's wish to have his ashes flushed down the toilet of the Abbey Theatre is both an idiosyncratic act of homage as well as being contemptuous. Beckett would ultimately abandon the observable public realm of history on display in these moments and in characters such as Ticklepenny, turning instead to remorselessly excavating the more painfully intimate realm of the self. Beckett's move is usually read as marking the transition from a modernist to a postmodernist perspective and, of course, it is. But it is also a rejection of the overtly Irish world of his youthful art, a renunciation of interest in the grand story, or history, of Ireland – not because he is anti-Irish, *au contraire*, but because for him it is no longer possible to tell that story: there is no means, nor any language to do so. His becomes an art that follows the rule: 'The expression that there is nothing to express, nothing with which to express, nothing from which to express, no power to express, no desire to express, together with the obligation to express.'[53] Beckett's comments point to the fundamental contradiction of a postmodern world-view that embraces impotence rather than omnipotence, ignorance rather than knowledge.

Flann O'Brien (1911–66) also straddles a liminal space between supreme authority and abject powerlessness. However, unlike Beckett's narratives which are increasingly concerned with uncovering essentials, O'Brien's work is playfully fascinated with acts of concealment. His own numerous identities – Brian O'Nolan, Myles na gCopaleen, Brother Barnabas – move him between the personal and the literary. And along with his writing in various media from the novel form to the immediate demands of journalism, to his shifting between the Irish and the English languages, this means that liminality is *the* key to understanding his life and work. He consciously worked against final and fixed definitions, mapping and exploiting in-between threshold spaces, acknowledging not only the possibilities but also the anxieties and the uncertainties that such a move into modernity necessarily affords.

His first novel, *At Swim Two Birds* (1939), inhabits such an imaginative space, offering – as does all O'Brien's work – a genuinely funny and quirky perspective on Irish life. It is a brilliantly subversive piece of writing with the characters of the story wresting control of the narrative from their 'author', thus attacking notions of novelistic as well as other forms of authority. In a specifically Irish context, the playful commingling of genres by placing characters from old Irish epics and cowboys from popular fiction and cinema together registers wonderfully the diversity of cultural reference available in a supposedly backward and narrow Ireland. Indeed, *At Swim Two Birds*, more than any other novel of this period, reflects the success of the Irish state's drive for stability after independence. Only a strong sense of shared cultural values, as well as a clear sense of the machinations of the state and its institutions, could produce the kind of angular engagement with society that permeates O'Brien's work. His day job as a civil servant in local government means that he is perfectly placed to enjoy the deconstruction of rules and codes of all types but especially of storytelling and novel writing, and revel in making fun of the prevailing bureaucratic mindset.

The scenes set around the undergraduate world of University College Dublin, especially, express the intellectual abilities of a younger generation being wasted on the details and minutiae of the absurdities of existence, capturing wonderfully the drudgery of an anti-heroic modernity. It is these students who create the story of Dermot Trellis, the author whose characters desire to be free of his storytelling. The levelling modernist imagination of James Joyce is at work in the novel, as all characters from the past and the present – from the mythological Finn McCool, to the Pooka to the people's poet Jem Casey – coexist without any real discernible distance or difference. As is the case with Joyce, the real heroics are left to the author who can manipulate all of this material – though with a proliferation of authorship within the novel itself, even this seems uncertain. Ultimately, though, for both the author O'Brien and the attuned reader, *At Swim Two Birds* is a celebration of the imagination which can delight in the increasing emphasis on style and form, which is itself a reaction to the established officious vision.

In many ways, in typical Joycean fashion, O'Brien's novel is doubled. It is both a highpoint and a nadir – an example of how liberating the novel form might be – but it is also an example of the profound limits of that form. One of the underlying goals of the modern Irish novel to this point has been the achievement of, and expression of, an interiority for the Irish person. Joyce, for instance, realised that brilliantly in *Ulysses*. O'Brien, though, demonstrates how that interiority can actually become prison-like and a barrier to real action and authentic feeling. The numerous stories-within-stories of *At Swim Two Birds*, the various beginnings and endings, are all a means of deferring any final moment of action or clarity or, indeed, emotion. This conundrum of Beckettian inadequacy is one that O'Brien never finally overcomes in the work published in his lifetime.

W. B. Yeats recognised this new position of impotence and powerlessness in his poem 'Politics', which he intended to be the last poem in his final collection, and in it he signals his intention to hollow out a new space for his poetry:

> How can I, that girl standing there,
> My attention fix
> On Roman or on Russian
> Or on Spanish politics?
> Yet here's a travelled man that knows
> What he talks about,
> And there's a politician
> That has read and thought,
> And maybe what they say is true

Of war and war's alarms,
But O that I were young again and held her in my arms![54]

Critic and theorist Ihab Hassan talks about the movement away from the
modernist desire to create and engage with a *grande histoire* to the postmodern realisation of the impossibility of sustaining such a Grand
Narrative.[55] In its place is an elevation of the *petite histoire*, or a more
intimate focus for the artist and writer: anything else can no longer be
told. Yeats, at the end of his life, embraces the possibility of this rather than
be defeated by it.

Just at the moment when Yeats reconfigures the limits of the modernist
imagination in his poetry, James Joyce, interestingly, in his final novel – or
maybe it is an anti-novel – *Finnegans Wake* (1939) appears to still hold to
modernist tenets in his efforts to imagine all stories as connected, all history
as shared, all languages as essentially one language. Thus *Finnegans Wake* is
not about one thing, it is about everything. The local story of HCE, or
Humphrey Chimpden Earwicker, or Here Comes Everybody, and his wife
Anna Livia and his children Shaun, Shem and Issy, and HCE's alleged
transgression in the Phoenix Park, becomes the basis for a narrative which
itself transgresses all rules and regulations and expectations. Myth and
reality, history and story, orality and the writerly, Ireland and everywhere,
are combined and deconstructed, put to rest and resurrected again and
again: 'Almost everything, from Fall narratives, whether of Humpty
Dumpty or in the Garden of Eden, to the Egyptian Book of the Dead,
has gone into its making.'[56] The encyclopaedic method employed in *Ulysses*
is taken even further here in a Casaubon-like act of fusion. All things
– words, actions and characters – have correspondence, come and go, are
told and retold in variety of ways repeatedly. The end of the novel:

End here. Us then. Finn, again! Take. Bussoftlhee, mememormee! Till thousands-
thee. Lps. The keys to. Given! A way a lone a last a loved a long the[57]

forces the reader to return to the beginning:

riverrun, past Eve and Adam's, from swerve of shore to bend of bay, brings us
by a commodius vicus of recirculation back to Howth Castle and Environs.
(James Joyce, *Finnegans Wake*, p. 3)

Flann O'Brien recognised the novel's duality, how it takes on the serious
task of putting the 'incommunicable night-mind' on display while also
bordering on farce by being a playful example of 'silence, exile and pun-
ning'.[58] In many ways, Joyce's *Finnegans Wake* is truly the last magnificent
utterance of the nineteenth-century mind. Joyce, being the product of a

colonised culture, wants to both centralise the Irish experience by showing how it is like everywhere else – how its stories and myths have the same source as all other nations' stories and myths – and, in this act of reverence, destroy that system of knowledge which has been used to oppress and silence. Consequently, as with his *Ulysses* and its microscopic detailing of Thursday 16 June 1904 which was a means of finally overcoming and liquidating that past – that all too present reality – so too with *Finnegans Wake*, which in its effort to say everything that can be said is another way of Joyce attempting to put all that knowledge, all those things that are being said, behind himself.

The humanist impulse towards solidarity central to Joyce's writing[59] would be severely tested when the knowledge of the gas chambers at Auschwitz and Buchenwald come into public view in the 1940s. Ireland's neutrality during the Second World War would also test its sense of solidarity and connection with the wider international scene. Certainly there is a very real sense in which the energies and possibilities of the novel form become decidedly limited and limiting in the immediate aftermath of Joyce's final words.

Elizabeth Bowen's The Last September *and the art of betrayal*

As with many modernist writers, Elizabeth Bowen's art is typified by a certain poise so that her characters who desire to manage emotion, to be in control of themselves within the subtle codes of modern society, mirror her own conception of the novel form that revolves around containment and restraint. Hers is an art of constant deflection and deferral, of making the bric-à-brac of the contemporary world – all the objects and stuff of modernity – the reservoir of all those intense feelings that cannot be admitted in the human sphere. In her Irish writing, much of this acute emotion is bound up in the bricks and mortar of the Anglo-Irish Big House: its centrifugal presence is the centre round which, and through which, its inhabitants circle and find meaning. Bowen's most well-known Big House novel, *The Last September* (1929) set in the autumn of 1920 during the Irish War of Independence, can be read as a multifaceted and sophisticated response to the reality of a newly independent Ireland from a writer emerging from within the class who had been dispossessed of political power and position. Writing a preface in 1952 for an American edition of the novel, she remarked that though the fictional Danielstown burnt to the ground, the real Bowen's Court survived; however, she goes on to say: 'so often in my mind's eye did I see it burning that the terrible last event in *The Last September* is more real than anything I have lived through.'[1] Quite obviously the image of the burnt-out Big House becomes the anxious embodiment of all Bowen's fears and her uncertain sentiment about her past and her future.

What is curious, though, with regard to *The Last September* is how its heroine, Lois Farquar, is absent from that final moment of immolation and therefore impervious to the potency of the destroyed Big House symbol. Her departure from the novel is merely told to the reader and not drama-tised within the plot itself. For Bowen, it is of a piece with her hope for distance and control: an effort to redirect any decisive moment of confron-tation when either she or her surrogate self might have to face up to the horror of that scene of destruction. It leaves open the possibility that Lois escapes into a life away from the deadening and ghostly ceremonies of Anglo-Irish existence. But Lois's leaving might also signal a future of dislocation from home and family, with her condemned to be a homeless wanderer rather than be rooted to a single place.

It may be that what Lois escapes is any final definition of what she is and what she might be. Throughout the novel, this is exactly what she avoids. She wants the freedom not to be fated: 'She didn't want to know what she was, she couldn't bear to: knowledge of this would stop, seal, finish one.'[2] In conversation with her cousin Laurence, she asks plaintively: 'what do you think I am for?' (*The Last September*, p. 161). She is, in many ways, a nascent artist figure or certainly her predicament is filtered through artistic tropes of control and perspective. There is one piece of art seen in *The Last September*.[3] It is a stanza from Robert Browning's poem 'Pippa Passes' (1841) transcribed by Lois onto the cover page of her drawings and her art:

> I am a painter who cannot paint;
> In my life, a devil rather than a saint;
> In my brain, as poor a creature too:
> No end to all that I cannot do!
> But do one thing at least I can –
> Love a man or hate a man
> Supremely –   (*The Last September*, p. 97)

Lois cannot write or author herself, cannot speak her own predicament, and uses the shelter of somebody else's words to express her dilemma at the crossroads between childhood and adulthood, innocence and experience. It could be argued that this short stanza impels Lois along a certain path of action. With no clear idea of what she wants to do with her life, and certainly no idea of the means by which she can begin to even think about her future, she happily accepts this literary voice as an imperative: she internalises these assumptions. Consequently, she can either love or hate a man; there are no other options as a woman open to her, except perhaps for loving Marda.

In the absence of any final definition for her, Lois takes on various roles: she thinks she loves Hugo Montmorency who had had a relationship with her mother, and then she seems to strike out on her own and believes she loves Gerald Lesworth, an English solider. Lois would happily be anyone else rather than herself: as she declares when she tries on Marda Norton's coat, 'Oh, the *escape* into other people's clothes!' (*The Last September*, p. 76). Lois's dilemma, then, is one of trying to make an intervention into the realm of action. It is a problem shared by all who live in Danielstown. Early on a furtive lorry disrupts the silence of the evening at Danielstown as it crawled 'with such a menace along the boundary, marking the scope of peace of this silly island, undermining solitude' (*The Last September*, p. 31). The limits of the demesne are identified: there is a clear and unambiguous sense of what is inside and what is outside this space. Increasingly, however, that boundary is breached. Directly after this moment Lois comes across an Irish soldier making his way through the estate: 'there passed within reach of her hand . . . a resolute profile, powerful as a thought. In gratitude for its fleshiness, she felt prompted to make some contact' (*The Last September*, p. 34). Usually read from Lois's perspective, this non-encounter is evidence of her inability to partake in the world of action. From the IRA man's perspective, however, what the reader witnesses is his utter lack of awareness of Lois's presence: she does not exist for him. And encroachments are made by the English as well: Gerald drops into lunch unannounced and uninvited; Mrs Vermont and Mrs Rolfe arrive one morning to a comically frosty reception from the entire household. The Naylors are powerless to keep these unwanted visitors at bay.

Lois's experience of marginality is accentuated in her relationship with Gerald. It is also a means of gauging Britain's colonial relationship to Ireland. Gerald, representing the English perspective, likes things 'square and facty' (*The Last September*, p. 84). A situation where there is a place for everything and everything in its place. This directness and confidence has a wide arc of influence for him:

He sought and was satisfied with a few – he thought final – repositories for his emotions: his mother, country, dog, school, a friend or two, now – crowningly – Lois. Of these he asked only that they should be quiet and positive, not impinged upon, not breaking boundaries from their generous allotment. (*The Last September*, p. 41)

Gerald brings this imperialistic poise to his relationship with Lois.[4] At one stage Lois equates Ireland with being a woman, saying 'no wonder this country gets irritated' and then going on to claim that she does not know why women should not be hit or saved from wrecks 'when everybody complains they're superfluous' (*The Last September*, p. 49). Gerald replies that it would be 'ghastly' if these things were lost. Lois says she does not understand his attitude and she *is* a woman. This reply leaves Gerald pondering:

Which was . . . exactly why it wasn't expected or desired she *should* understand . . . She had one limitation . . . she couldn't look at her own eyes, had no idea what she was, resented almost his attention being so constantly fixed on something she wasn't aware of. A fellow did not expect to be to a girl what a girl was to a fellow . . . so that the girl must be excused for a possible failure in harmony . . . When he said: 'You will never know what you mean to me,' he made plain his belief in her perfection as a woman. She wasn't made to know, she was not fit for it. (*The Last September*, pp. 49–50)

Here is an example of the male gaze, of the masculine imagination producing an image of the female that has no input from the female side whatsoever. At one point Gerald picks up a newspaper and reads an article on 'Unrest', making him think of Empire:

He looked ahead to the time when it all should be accurately, finally fenced about and raked over. Then there should be a fixed leisured glow . . . as on coming in to tea . . . with his mother . . . He turned in thought to confident English country, days like the look in a dog's eyes, rooms small in the scope of firelight, neighbourly lights through trees. (*The Last September*, pp. 87–88)

What at first might seem a benign, indeed ineffectually romantic, view of Lois in particular and women in general can be seen to be linked to the view of the world that aggressively imposes its own value systems upon other people and other cultures. Even a cursory glance at the language shows us that Gerald's world is a rigid one: a place where ideas are fixed and immutable; where progress inevitably will lead to an 'end', when finally everything will be 'fenced about and raked over'. Empire's function is to bring order: that is its ultimate goal. Gerald sees this 'end' in terms of a homely garden image: of a space with its boundaries firmly set in place, and within this garden all aspects are finally arranged and completed. Of course, this imagery of home and gardens can be linked to the Anglo-Irish Big House itself, except that its function for bringing order is being undermined as its position in Empire is being aggressively challenged.

In the midst of this ideological conflict, Lois is presented as having, at least, the potential to create in an artistic manner. In her dealings with men, she seeks a proper distance from them. The young soldiers 'block her mental view' by 'their extreme closeness' and are thus 'numbing to the imagination' (*The Last September*, p. 13). One reason for her flirtation with Hugo Montmorency is that no matter how 'much he might loom and darken up the close-up view, he would never be out of focus' (*The Last September*, p. 13). The same difficulty is found in her relationship with Gerald. She desires to discover the proper distance from him so that she can bring him into 'focus', and also – crucially – so that she can have room enough in order not to 'stifle imagination' (*The Last September*, p. 52). In addition, Lois wants to achieve a proper perspective of an Irish landscape, which is configured as separate from and threatening to the Big House throughout the novel. Her desire is for a way of seeing that might mean her own individual place is secure within that countryside. She imagines that: 'There must be perfect towns where shadows were strong like buildings, towns secret without coldness, unaware without indifference. She liked mountains, but she did not care for views' (*The Last September*, p. 99). She imagines a utopia – a no place – somewhere where she can exist and be herself. Lois's hoped-for place is presented in very uncertain terms. Indeed, in comparison to the 'square and facty' nature of Gerald's vision of peace, for instance, Lois's dream appears somewhat inadequate. Lois's utopia could be said to be an attempt by her to move away from the rigidness of masculine constructions, to offer a feminine counterpoint to Gerald's patriarchal imagination. Thus, her dream place does not conform to the strictures and conventions of masculine language and imagination: it challenges these conventions and tries to move beyond them and imagine something 'other'. Her utopia, then, is a rejection of the male/imperialist culture she is forced to inhabit.

Events at the mill mark the turning point for Lois. She is transformed by the experience: her and Marda's encounter with the Irish soldier, which results in Marda's being shot at and slightly grazed, is an experience frighteningly real, and because of that thoroughly liberating. Afterwards, Lois is no longer enslaved to someone else's narrative. Thinking of what she might be doing at the same time the following day, she says: '"Funny," said Lois. "Queer." Her heart thumped, she looked at her watch. "Half-past six," she said. "It's harder, for some reason, to imagine what I'll be doing or where I shall be"' (*The Last September*, pp. 128–129). Suddenly the unknown potential and possibility of the future challenges Lois: she is now master of her own destiny because of the fact that she does not exactly know what that destiny might be. She is, in other words, free now to choose her own role to play – to imagine her own future, no matter how uncertain it may be – instead of having other roles thrust upon her.

Not only is the Big House destroyed at the close of the novel but, more importantly, there is a palpable repositioning of power in the text with the inhabitants of Danielstown becoming a part – insignificant as it will turn out – of someone else's story:

A sense of exposure, of being offered without resistance to some ironic un-curiosity, made Laurence look up at the mountain over the roof of the house. In some gaze – of a man's up there hiding, watching among the clefts and ridges – they seemed held, included and to have their only being. The sense of a watcher, reserve of energy and intention, abashed Laurence, who turned from the mountain. But the unavoidable and containing stare impinged to the point of a transformation upon the social figures with their orderly, knitted shadows, the well-groomed grass and the beds, worked out in this pattern. (*The Last September*, p. 119)

Being – their existence: who they are and who they think they are – is now conferred upon them by the Irish. Authority has been passed, like a torch, to others. The linkage to landscape is made clear here with the encroaching threat of the Irish landscape upon the orderly gardens of the Big House revealing the shift in control.

At the very beginning of the novel, the arrival of Hugo and Francie Montmorency is described as a 'moment of happiness, of perfection'. Lois wishes 'she could freeze the moment and keep it always. But as the car approached as it stopped, she stooped down and patted one of the dogs' (*The Last September*, p. 7). At work throughout *The Last September* is a discourse of Timelessness – this being but one example of it. It is linked to an attachment to unquestioning tradition. And yet, even with this strategy of avoidance, there is profound awareness. For that moment of happiness and perfection is already lost. This early observation concerning transience shows that the beginning bespeaks the ending, for this is what Bowen comes to understand – the transient nature of all human things that were once thought permanent. Thus, the discourse of Timelessness is also a tacit acknowledgement of universal currents of change and transformation: all things come and go and all things rise and fall. For Lois, as for Bowen herself, it is that shock of recognition which means she can break out into the difficult business of living.

Critic Robert Tracy suggests that Lois, and by implication Bowen herself, are by the end of the novel freed into art.[5] It has been the point towards which Lois has been moving. Such an achievement can be read as a form of betrayal on numerous levels. Clearly their personal survival is at the cost of communal survival, for both women ultimately retreat from the Irish conflict and escape its deadly consequences. The turn towards art is itself a betrayal of the political realities of late 1920s Ireland. Bowen's deliberate setting of the novel back in time – the only one of her novels to do so[6] – is an indication of her reluctance to enter into the political domain of the contemporary moment. Much better, and safer perhaps, to retell the story of that moment of far-reaching change and make that the story of the cultural legacy for Anglo-Ireland. Thus, Bowen's artistic version of the Big House betrays its continued reality in the Free State with the Big House under pressure and descending rapidly into debilitating stereotype.

What Bowen truly exposes, though, is the arduousness of Irish modernity: Lois's many masks – and her escape into art is but one more of them – offer her a sort of freedom. But in the constant necessity of trying to convince people of the mask's validity, as well as convincing oneself, something essential is lost. The real tragedy for Lois, and the dispossessed Anglo-Irish she represents, is that they are set adrift in a world of betrayal and treachery; their dilemma, in the end, not simply a political one, but a deeply personal one too.

CHAPTER 5

Enervated island – isolated Ireland? 1940–60

Ireland? Things may not be what they were in that unfortunate
country.

(Elizabeth Bowen, *The Heat of the Day*)[1]

The drive for political and social solidity that coloured all aspects of Irish life
in the post-revolutionary aftermath had become more of a reality from the
late 1930s onwards. In other words, a certain stability in the civic workings
of the independent state had come to pass. The implementation of the
1937 constitution reflects the success of bedding down the fledgling state
constitutionally, giving textual legitimacy to the notion of an independent
Ireland. Ironically, what reinforces Ireland's relatively sedate status is the
advent of the Second World War. The official reaction to global war –
Ireland's decision to remain neutral – became the outward public sign of
what had been an almost private individual introspection.[2] Ireland's neutral
stance, for some, is the most tangible indicator of Ireland's cultural and
intellectual isolation and backwardness at this time. Calling this period the
'Emergency' indicates how even the use of language conspires to distance
Ireland from the actuality of the devastation of war, bestowing an air of
unreality to Irish life. However, much recent scholarship has begun to
reassess this hackneyed view of Ireland as politically and culturally isolated,
demonstrating clearly that the consequences of this first tangible assertion of
an autonomous foreign policy were far from straightforwardly negative.[3]
Critic Joe Cleary is correct in arguing that the presumed benightedness of
this historical moment is actually an invention of the more recent Irish past,
which of necessity demands a fixed negative idea to repudiate in order that it
may assert its positive distinctiveness from that past.[4] Nonetheless, there is a
palpable shift in Irish art at this moment and many writers openly acknowledged that a new era was dawning.[5] The political posture of insularity is
compounded by the fact that while the long shadow cast by such luminaries
as W. B. Yeats and James Joyce did not disappear with their dying, the

reflected glow from their achievements was now lost to a generation forced to reimagine themselves and their role as artists on their own terms. This, then, is a period of contradiction and anomaly, the first moment perhaps when a real gap between 'official' Ireland comes into conflict with the realities of Ireland on the ground. Writers, of course, and their work reflect these internal conflicts and public disagreements, uncomfortably attempting to come into some creative relationship with the nation. It is also, importantly, the moment when some writers, in their role as critics, begin to theorise the position of the novel in an Irish context.

Flann O'Brien's (1911–66) *The Third Policeman* (1940/1967) perfectly reflects the ambiguities and contradictions of Ireland's situation at this particular juncture. While the author claimed that he had misplaced the manuscript in a pub, it was, in fact, rejected by his publishers in 1940 and only published posthumously in 1967. It is, while undoubtedly embracing the comic possibilities of the absurd, a deeply dark and ultimately disturbing novel. In describing Detective Lavan's garrulousness in *The Puritan* (1932), Liam O'Flaherty, said: '[he gave] air to [his] opinions; a habit common with policemen, who have a craze for using obscure language and toying with abstruse problems which they only vaguely understand, in order to pose as learned people'.[6]

It might be argued from this that Flann O'Brien's fantastical story of policemen and their bicycles is, in fact, a documentary slice of Irish reality. Certainly he is poking fun at these figures of state authority, making them in the process ridiculous as he makes all notions of authority ridiculous in the novel. In keeping with his own position as a civil servant, he highlights the bizarre logic at work at the heart of the state, its impersonality and baffling expediency. Knowledge itself and the methodologies of knowing are exposed to a mad process of deconstruction through these images of bureaucratic officialdom. In the wake of Joyce's work and his celebration of the totalising imagination, *The Third Policeman* revels in critically demarcating the limits of the human imagination and human language. Fluidity of gender is also a focus of the novel and for critics. Twisting and turning between the realm of the real and the utterly fantastic, this is a work inhabiting a liminal borderland between classic modernism and an emergent postmodernist perspective.

The reader discovers at the close, in a formal manoeuvre similarly employed in *Finnegans Wake*, that the protagonist, who is never given a name, is in fact dead and will have to experience again and again what has already occurred in a Nietzschean purgatory of eternal recurrence, except that there is no element of choice or joy in this version of eternity. Like W. B. Yeats in his play *Purgatory* (1938) and Samuel Beckett later in his novel *The Unnameable* (1952), O'Brien allows the dead to tell their story. Clearly this says much about the nature of a moribund Irish reality, as he perceives it, as a place where the past and memory in the form of the dead crowd out the world of the living. His is a nightmare rendering of Ireland's modernity: an image of inner and interior exile that must be endured by the artist rather than chosen.

The presence of a parallel world in the footnotes about the enthusiastic, if idiotic, thinker and tinkerer De Selby and his various critics and biographers is further evidence of O'Brien's comic and playful dismantling of the epistemological realm of ideas and ontological notions surrounding the nature of the novel itself. This narrative carried on beneath the main text means there is a kind of seepage between that which is above and that which is below the line. The story of De Selby and of the academic conflict between his numerous critics is an amplification of the main story: there are masks and shifting identities, and the continued scrutiny of the relationship between observable reality and theory, between language and the world it supposedly talks about. As the novel progresses, the footnotes threaten to overwhelm the main narrative, but increasingly, as their pretence to academic distance falls apart, they reveal the impossibility of writing itself. While all of this mischievously confirm O'Brien's postmodern concerns, what is of real interest in relation to the development of the Irish novel is how this academic objectivity gives way to descriptions of De Selby and his band of critics full of the personality and human foibles that, in many ways, is thoroughly absent from the main narrative. What occurs below the line is a strangely dynamic counterpoint to the purgatorial nightmare of no-man's journey with the Guards, brimming over with those elements a reader would expect from a traditional novel – plot and incident and character development.

Here, then, is an attempt at articulating the real crisis in the Irish novel at this moment: how to find a way to reconnect with, and express, authentic feeling and emotion. O'Brien is aware, it seems, that the Irish cultural future is one where that re-engagement with the energies of feeling will be a necessity for the novelist. In other words, he recognises that the Irish writer is now faced with the problem of renegotiating his or her relationship to their material, in imagining a new role for themselves in the New Ireland. The irony is that his cautious tale could not be read when it was written. Subsequent critics have overlooked this element as only a subversive reading is concentrated on, as if the time of its publication in the late revolutionary 1960s represses the actual context in which it was produced.

Two writers, Sean O'Faolain (1900–90) and Frank O'Connor (1903–66), approach this conundrum each in their own way, viewing the lot of the novelist in a self-consciously discouraging fashion. O'Connor's 1942 essay, 'The Future of Irish Literature', suggests a bleak future for Irish writing because, basically, the writer is being denied the opportunity to compose a necessary and 'fundamental quarrel with his material'.[7] The certainty of the past, even in its uncertainty, offered Yeats and his contemporaries in the literary revival movement an opportunity of a conflict to work with and work against. For O'Connor, there is no conflict in the present moment, and the cultural apparatus of the state, particularly censorship, makes the writer irrelevant and invisible. He ends by saying that the Irish writer 'must be prepared to come into the open'.[8] Later in 1949, Sean O'Faolain similarly complained that everyday Irish life was a debilitatingly unexciting one for the Irish fiction writer: 'Our sins are tawdry, our virtues childlike, our revolts desultory and brief, our submissions formal and frequent. In Ireland a policeman's lot is a supremely happy one. God smiles, the priest beams, and the novelist groans.'[9]

This is a curious statement in a many ways, pointing to the numerous confusing anomalies and contradictions that this period produces for both the writers of the time and subsequent literary critics of the Irish novel. For O'Faolain, it appears that Ireland offers the would-be novelist no suitable material to work with, or to stand in opposition to: that the Irish world is far too fixed and far too rigidly conformist. This is ironic because both his and Frank O'Connor's celebrated assertion pivot on the notation that the novel form required a stable and fixed social order in order that it might flourish.[10] As O'Connor said: 'The short story not only attracts marginalised individuals and groups, but Ireland itself could be conceived to be marginalised in much the same way without the concept of a normal society the novel is impossible.'[11] O'Faolain's real difficulty, as it is for Frank O'Connor, Flann O'Brien and many other writers, is in discovering an appropriate public role and persona as a writer in modern Ireland. Previous generations looked for a suitable form that might express the reality of Ireland and the Irish character, now the significant shift is towards the writer's relationship to that society. The possibility of the grand gesture or the grand thought seemed appropriate, perhaps even an obligation, in the past for Yeats and his generation. Now Ireland's reality seems to be a mean and backward one, with any lingering energies or radical potential generated in the post-independence period utterly dissipated.

O'Faolain's comments, and his various activities at this time – journalist, critic, man of letters living by his pen – suggest a variety of roles he might choose to play. Here, for instance, his argument is not with the novel form itself – its aesthetic possibilities or impossibilities in an Irish setting – rather his criticism is with Irish reality and its supposed lack of development into modernity. He is acting the part of social critic – of public commentator – rather than simply the artist.[12] Indeed, his involvement in *The Bell*, the monthly literary and cultural journal published between 1940 and 1954, is an extension of the public role of the liberal intellectual, bringing a searing light into the dark recesses of Irish life and culture. The predicament, though, is that in choosing such a public role, of continuingly complaining about Ireland's narrowness,[13] O'Faolain and O'Connor and others ignore their own engagement with the form of the novel itself. While O'Faolain's *Bird Alone* (1936) became a *cause célèbre* for being banned,[14] it was a novelistic failure. Frank O'Connor's *Dutch Interior* (1940), also banned, was a failure too, certainly in terms of form.[15] Critic Thomas Flanagan declares that it is: 'a bleak study of provincial decay, the decline of intellect, the withering of character into mere personality. It is a savage, tearing, and lonely book, a chronicle of spirit wasted and wasting in a provincial backwater.'[16]

This tells us what the book describes but says little of how that story is told. Nothing, it seems, has altered since the time of Joyce's *Dubliners* and *A Portrait of the Artist as a Young Man*. Yet Joyce's Dedalus managed to transcend his situation, to escape those stultifying ideologies thrown against him. No such outcome is afforded O'Connor's characters, who remain rooted to the city of Cork at the close. O'Connor's narrative succumbs to this deadening Irish world. He is clearly powerless to move beyond the short story form in which he is supremely adept, using similar techniques which, rather than producing suggestive characters and scenes shuddering in their brevity, forces his narrative to wallow in an impenetrable vagueness. If his characters suffer from a narrowness of vision and perspective, are unable to see, then O'Connor is himself unable to see his characters, to make them real or to make his reader have any empathy with them. In other words, O'Connor as a novelist has no remedy for the ills he detects, but his writing is, rather, tainted by that of which he speaks.

Clair Wills makes the point that the difficulty for the novelist in reimagining their connection to their Irish audience is complicated by being disconnected from wartime Britain and Europe. On a very practical level, the link to British publishers and a wider audience becomes somewhat fraught. Forced, as Wills puts it, into 'a dialogue with the plain people of Ireland', these writers must test their liberal ideas and, from their perspective, Ireland does not pass the test. But that very liberalism becomes distorted in the process, as once again ideas of Enlightenment and modernity are presented as the domain of others. But, as events are unfolding at a rapid rate amid the flames of Europe, these liberal–humanist ideas look decidedly out of date even in a supposedly backward Ireland. A kind of schizophrenia becomes the norm for Irish writers in that a certain distance comes into the relationship between writer and their material, between writer and their local audience. Ireland is now being made strange to itself as well as to an international audience. This also, in part, explains the whole-sale abandonment of a formal or aesthetic consciousness in relation to the novel and the enthusiastic embracing of documentary realism as *the* mode of expression in Irish fiction. Thus *The Bell* champions a European sensibility that is being destroyed wholesale in the war, and O'Faolain's desire for a rapprochement between Anglo-Ireland and Gaelic Ireland is made precisely at the moment when Anglo-Ireland's sense of loyalty is being sorely tested and made more complicated than it had hitherto been.[17]

It is, then, a time teeming with contradictions and incongruities, with writers looking both inwards and outwards, creating art at the same time as they are creating versions of themselves as artists for public performance and public consumption. It is no coincidence that despite this being usually presented as a dark and bleak cultural moment, it has simultaneously been celebrated as an innocent golden age of the Irish writer as a public person-ality.[18] And if formal experimentation is mostly absent from the Irish novel in this period, the place where experimentation flourishes has shifted out-wards onto the artistic personality, as writers proceed to dismantle the distinction between art and life, between the public and private, making fiction disguised memoir, and memoir another means of recreating the self as an artist. As a result, many writers of this period move easily between the social critique associated with journalism and the aesthetic considerations of art and also shift between different forms of literary expression, poetry and the novel, theatre and the short story, while mixing comedy with brooding and dark tragedy, satire with a pointed realism.

Kate O'Brien's two novels written in the 1940s, *The Land of Spices* (1941) and *That Lady* (1946), demonstrate her own continued commitment to making links to the European imagination without resorting to a self-serving tone. *The Land of Spices* is overtly concerned with marking out once again feminine experience in an Irish world, with the obvious counter-point to the aspirations of middle-class nationalist Ireland being made clear. The subtle and not-too-subtle gradations of the Irish class system underpin the finely tuned descriptions of the wants and desires of Catholic Ireland. It was banned in Ireland, becoming a text central to a 1942 Senate debate on censorship where it was bizarrely claimed that 'the aesthetic motif of the novel was sodomy',[19] which obviously refers to the one line when the young Helen Archer, who in the contemporary world of the novel is the Reverend

Mother, stumbles upon her father 'in the embrace of love'.[20] To be sure, there is a strain of homosexual love coursing through all O'Brien's writing, testing the rigid gender boundaries of her time,[21] but such a sensational claim obscures what is, in fact, a thoughtfully religious book. The story of Anna Murphy's time in a convent school allows for a meditation on the possibilities and lack of them for women in the twentieth century, though not just Irish women. The novel possesses a broad European feel, imaginatively inhabiting and connecting Ireland, Britain and Belgium particularly. The reality of Ireland's position in Europe, despite neutrality, is quietly but forcibly made here. More important for O'Brien, though, is how Anna's poetic sensibility is stressed from early on,[22] allowing her to make a special connection to the Reverend Mother. It is said of the Reverend Mother that: 'After all, a nun knows more than you or I about devotion to an idea, or an ideal' (*The Land of Spices*, p. 207). O'Brien remains dedicated to an aesthetic vision, though she remains unwilling to present that vision in anything other than a historical setting, with this novel being set between 1904 and 1916. Nonetheless, she actively imagines her heroine as a surrogate artist figure who just might be able to live according to her own lights. For once O'Brien is capable of matching her own expression to that of the story she tells. It has been praised as her 'most beautifully written novel'[23] and certainly it is her most controlled piece of writing, the poetry at the heart of the story echoed in her own prose and in the rhythms of the inner thoughts of those characters which are on display for the reader. The religious world – while limiting and limited – opens up drab everyday reality to beauty and gives that beauty form and shape, and because of that, the religious sensibility cannot be easily dismissed.

That Lady, another historical novel, on this occasion being set in sixteenth-century Spain, again offers an image of a strong woman, wedded to ideas and ideals and prepared to suffer for them. Based on the life of Ana de Mendoza, it is not a 'historical' novel as such, with O'Brien at pains to point out that hers is 'an intervention arising from reflection on the curious external story of Ana de Mendoza and Philip II'.[24] It is, then, a fiction that permits O'Brien to create a sympathetic woman: autonomous and strong, and prepared to act on that independence. It was Kate O'Brien's most commercially successful novel, being made into a Hollywood move in 1955.

Molly Keane's (1904–96) *Two Days in Aragon* (1941) offers a more overt description of male and female sexuality than either Kate O'Brien or her contemporary Elizabeth Bowen, focusing on varying notions of sterility and fertility.[25] There is an earthy emphasis on lushness and fecundity in the novel. The Big House demesne of Aragon is constantly described in terms of abundance:

The scent of azaleas caught in the back of her nose like a fog of honey and pepper. The harsh almost animal breath that is behind its scent was not here yet, only the wild pungent sweet of its earliest flowers. Great groups almost grown to the size of trees flowered along the wide grass borders of the avenue towards the house. . . . Above the house again, the hill climbed up nursing the sun in its hollows and elbows, sheltering the rare trees, and the rhododendrons, and tender magnolias, and camellias that flowered so freely along the side of the valley.[26]

Keane also stresses colour: almost every description of a place, and especially Aragon itself, has a mention of vibrant primary colours. There are no shades or half colours here, no creams or greys. Perhaps all this focus on colour can be thought of as lurid, in the sense of being sensational and excessive. Certainly, there is an impression generated within the novel of wildness and unrestraint being associated with the flowers and these stark colours. Untamed and uncultivated nature can be thought of as a place that may harbour danger if left unchecked. In the basement of the house is a sexual chamber of horrors. The threat of very real violence associated with Aragon is intimated here. The implications in terms of the relationship between men and women remain broodingly subterranean and concealed. This secret and repressed history, however, can be connected with the all-pervasive use of lurid colour in that an unbridled sexuality and lust pulsates throughout the entire Big House of Aragon, from both the man-made structure and from nature. As a comment on the nature of the relationship between the residents of the Big House and the native Irish, Keane's novel leaves nothing to the imagination.

Maura Laverty (1907–66) and Mary Lavin (1912–96) also marked out the lives of women in Ireland. It has been argued that Mary Lavin's *The House in Clewe Street* (1945), which tells the tragic story of Gabriel Galloway and servant girl Onny Soroghan, while certainly detailing the minutiae of middle-class Irish life as it attempts to move away from a narrow provincialism, is also a 'relentlessly scathing social commentary' on that middle-class world,[27] thereby complicating the hoped-for movement into modernity. The male bourgeois gaze of Gabriel can ultimately be seen as destructive with Lavin eschewing any embrace of sentiment. Maura Laverty's *Never no More: The Story of a Lost Village* (1942) was hugely popular on its publication. This nostalgic view of life on the Bog of Allen conjured up imagery that even produced a favourable response from hardened republican prisoner Brendan Behan.[28] Though playing on a sentimental desire for community and rural rituals, it found favour with Sean O'Faolain who serialised it in *The Bell* as it did attempt to portray a contemporary reality with references to tuberculosis and illegitimate children. Nonetheless, even as it depicts a version of reality, this is a book allowing for an escape from what is obviously an even harsher reality. In this Laverty, and her readers, are in touch with a common mood in wartime Europe where concepts of sustaining peace become essential amid wholesale devastation and destruction.

Elizabeth Bowen, in her family history *Bowen's Court* (1942), talks self-consciously of her act of writing as a necessary antidote to the destruction she witnessed in London:

Yes, here is the picture of peace – in the house, in the country round. Like all pictures, it does not quite correspond with any reality. Or, you may call the country a magic mirror; reflecting something that could not really exist. This illusion – peace at its most ecstatic – I hold to, to sustain me throughout war.[29]

Only in a time of extreme anxiety is there a corresponding shift into the mode of nostalgia. Here Bowen's private family imagery is offered as a possible communal and public picture of what is at stake in war, of what, for some, is being fought for. And famously, Eamon de Valera, also at this moment of crisis, in a radio address on St Patrick's Day 1943 offered another image of peace and frugal harmony for his listeners to contemplate:

That Ireland which we dreamed of would be the home of a people who valued material wealth only as a basis of right living; of a people who were satisfied with frugal comfort and devoted their leisure to the things of the spirit – a land whose countryside would be bright with cosy homesteads, whose fields and villages would be joyous with the sounds of industry, with the romping of sturdy children, the contests of athletic youths and the laughter of comely maidens, whose firesides would be forums for the wisdom of serene old age.[30]

Of course, as with Bowen's image, this too is an illusion: it is what past Irish leaders had hoped for and not, perhaps, what had actually come to pass. As is the case with Bowen, de Valera's image is meant to appeal to a community, to be an image of desire in a time of threat and not a statement of official policy. Both are ostensibly images originating from the urban world looking backwards into the rural realm. Interestingly, de Valera's dream is full of people and action, whereas Bowen's is bound up in bricks and mortar, intimating perhaps a fundamental difference between Anglo and Gaelic Ireland's priorities. Both sets of images find articulation just at the moment before they will be forever altered, if not swept away. The Big House's distance and disconnection from Ireland will become more pronounced, while the rural idyll of the Gaelic imagination will be decimated by emigration. Crucially, though, extinction in reality will actually ensure their cultural continuance and significance in the realm of imaginative art.

Elizabeth Bowen's *The Heat of the Day* (1949) reinforces this impression, as do her wartime short stories set in Ireland. Robert Tracy claims that: 'Ireland is portrayed with the kind of nostalgia as a place where the order of the past still survives – or has been restored – and so as the embodiment of certain positive values.'[31] Ireland is a dreamscape, a place outside time:

She had forgotten that by travelling west you enter longer days: this hour, as she stood looking down the length of the room at a fire distantly burning inside white marble, seemed to be outside time – an eternal luminousness of dusk in which nothing but the fire's flutter and the clock's ticking out there in the hall were to be heard. (Elizabeth Bowen, *The Heat of the Day*, p. 176)

And yet, Bowen's attitude to Ireland and this picture of sheltered peace in a time of war is ultimately a conflicted one. Her predicament is one of divided loyalties, which are manifest in a 1941 letter written to Virginia Woolf: 'If there's to be an invasion of Ireland, I hope it may be while I'm there – which I don't mean frivolously – but if anything happens to England while I'm in Ireland I shall wish I'd never left, even for this short time.'[32] She needs to be where the actuality of action is, not on the unreal margins of inaction. Central to *The Heat of the Day* is a story of espionage. Stella's lover Robert is passing information to the enemy and Stella becomes entangled in his underworld dealings. Masks and betrayal are the modern themes meditated on and Ireland's neutral position – a 'muddle' (*The Heat of the Day*, p. 81) – complicates this consideration of loyalty. Bowen's own intelligence activities for the British Foreign Office, when her visits to Ireland became opportunities to gauge Irish opinion to the war, suggest that such complications were not, for her, merely material for fiction. Here Bowen's position as an Irish writer offering readers images of Ireland, mediating Ireland to a wider audience, merges with her role as an intelligence gatherer. Like many Irish writers, then, Bowen's bind is one of expressing or exploiting her material, and recognising that in Ireland, perhaps, to express *is* to exploit. She knows that to be a writer in Ireland is to run the risk of betraying, and thereby losing, that which is held most dear.

Other writers, however, did not imagine themselves in such an extreme position or relationship to their material or their audience. Mervyn Wall's (1908–97) *The Unfortunate Fursey* (1946) and *The Return of Fursey* (1948) are two very good examples of a form of writing that seemingly abandons nostalgia only, in truth, to embrace it from a distance. Eleventh-century

Ireland and the monastery of Clonmacnoise is the focus of these novels. Fursey is an anti-hero of sorts, comically setting himself against ecclesiastical authority. Of course, the tone is a modern one, as is Fursey's unfortunate fecklessness: things happen to Fursey rather than being instigated by him. He is a version of the modernist Chaplinesque tramp, who is himself a version of the picaroon, buffeted helplessly this way and that. As if to emphasise this point, in *The Return of Fursey* our hero cries out, 'I have no purpose!'[33] Very popular with the Irish reading public, these are novels dealing in gentle comedy rather than, as some have argued, hard-biting savage satire.[34] Obvious criticism and fun are being made of the Church and, particularly, of censorship, with the presence of a Church censor who finds the Old Testament itself quite indecent and who has eyes that work independently of each other: one to find dirty words and the other to read everything else. As is fitting in a bureaucratic age, Hell turns out unsurprisingly to be similar to the civil service. Much fun is made of the notion that medieval Ireland – the much-trumpeted land of saints and scholars – was a pristine place, morally upright and sexually chaste. Rather than being timeless,[35] this is a novel caught up in a widespread escapist fantasy of the moment, its mild humour playing on the pretensions of a comfortable middle-class readership who will get the joke without threatening to challenge the authority maligned. Interestingly, the Censorship Board did not ban these novels. In short, it is as illusory an engagement with Ireland as the obviously nostalgic versions of rural space being peddled by others.

The sentimental rendering of the Irish rural world as a place of hardy spiritual endeavour and authentic Irishness is savagely undercut by Patrick Kavanagh (1904–67), who declared that the Ireland imagined by the revivalists was 'a thoroughgoing English-bred lie'.[36] His long poem 'The Great Hunger' (1942) possessed the kind of unflinching gaze that the realist novelist might envy, with its depiction of the enervating life of Patrick Maguire whose humanity is sapped by his link to the land. Kavanagh, though, is careful to signal that his critique is far from a simple attack on the smallness and backwardness of the rural world. He perceives that Ireland's difficulty, and the difficulty of the Irish artist, is one of succumbing to a deadening provincial vision:

Parochialism and provincialism are direct opposites. The provincial has no mind of his own; he does not trust what his eyes see until he has heard what the metropolis – towards which his eyes are turned – has to say on any subject. This runs through all activities. The parochial mentality on the other hand is never in any doubt about the social and artistic validity of his parish. All great civilisations are based on parochialism.[37]

Yet, curiously, Kavanagh in his prose work, both in his autobiographical *The Green Fool* (1938) and in his sole novel *Tarry Flynn* (1948), is not beyond pandering to the stereotypes that would keep an urban middle-class audience entertained. And, for expediency's sake, he was also happy to write light journalistic pieces about the rites and the rituals of country life, to be the 'green fool' of his autobiography. But later, in his journal *Kavanagh's Weekly* (1952), he was prepared to rage against all aspects of modern Irish provincialism. Indeed, Kavanagh's entire writing career is one that manifests acutely the quandary of creating a viable artistic persona that would operate in the public sphere as well as energise and nourish the art itself. For Kavanagh's output veers, at times wildly, between that which powerfully acknowledged both the pain and the pleasure of the land and the individual imagination's possession of the land and place, and that which was throwaway doggerel. His work and his life were a mass of unresolved contradictions.

One fixed aspect of much of his prose work – be it fiction, essays or casual journalism – is how he used it as a means of creating, promoting and sustaining an image of himself as a poet. The proper end, of course, and the hoped-for achievement is poetry, but the journey towards that goal can only be recorded in his prose writing. *Tarry Flynn* is that journey presented in the novel form. The novel form also allows him to move beyond the primary exploration of the poetic imagination seen in his poetry and to consider the socio-economic world of his homeplace. Kavanagh claimed of his novel: 'I am humble enough to claim [it] is not only the best but the only authentic account of life as it was lived in Ireland in this century.'[38]

Of course, this self-congratulation is plainly wrong: there were many novels before this that detailed the life on the land. Yet it is one of the first rural novels to be just that – a novel – and to be concerned with the individual within a community: to detail the urges, petty jealousies and desires that underpin what, surprisingly appears to be, if not materially then culturally, a thoroughly middle-class world. If Kavanagh, in his later poetry imaginatively remade the city of Dublin into a rural paradise by the banks of the Grand Canal, it appears he reverses that manoeuvre by suburbanising the countryside in *Tarry Flynn*. Kavanagh emphasises how each member of this world is engaged in an act of surveillance of everybody else.

He brilliantly challenges the stereotypical view of mid-century Ireland ensnared to the will of the Catholic Church. Certainly, the Church is presented as wielding power; but, in truth, the peasant relationship to the Church is a wholly pragmatic one, taking what is needed and disregarding the rest. The Church is not the only institution concerned with the community's moral well-being, the community themselves are keeping each other in line. What emerges, then, from this detailing of an economy of observation and gossip is a rural scene with typically middle-class concerns and in the midst of it his hero Tarry Flynn's battle to emerge as a unique individual. The author is at pains throughout to present his hero as markedly different from the rest of the locals, standing apart from his family and his community, as a poet. It is clear that there is danger in being an artist, putting his character in the way of misunderstanding and ridicule. The reader is offered an insight into the workings of this small rural society and the codes and regulations by which these people live and breathe. Kavanagh is particularly good at capturing the stifling manners in which communities operate in order to denounce those that are different, with Tarry often humiliated by his neighbours and the priests for being 'odd' and 'strange' and being a 'dreamer'. The underlying tension in much of Kavanagh's writing stems from this disconnection, this sense of betrayal, with the poet wanting to be a part of the wider community but remaining steadfastly wary of its ignorance, and thereby enduring its suspicious gaze.

Kavanagh declared that, 'Tragedy is underdeveloped comedy, not fully born',[39] which marked, for him, the transition from earnestness to casualness. Yet, in a novel such as *Tarry Flynn*, tragedy cannot be wholly overcome. Much of it stems from the harsh economic realities of 1930s Ireland during the height of the economic war with Britain in which the novel is set. Tarry, as a poet, unlike his counterpart Maguire in 'The Great Hunger', confronts this grey, deadening world through the power of his poetic, transcendent imagination. In the end, Kavanagh and his alter ego Tarry, are romantics. To be sure, the novel celebrates the beauty of the countryside but it is also a celebration of that poetic imagination which can perceive the beauty of the countryside. By the close of the novel, in Joycean fashion, the world of the creative individual is embraced as the local community is left behind. That world can be the source of art, but he is unable to reconcile his creative imagination with the reality of his rural existence: he cannot be both inside and outside this world simultaneously. What the novel does is present the birth of the poet, as Yeats and Joyce had done before him: art is born out of loss; reality has vanished, only to be replaced by the imagination. Tarry, like Kavanagh, will now be able to fashion his rural world, the world of Inniskeen and Mucker, in whatever way he chooses. He is no longer beholden to the real and can soar poetically from this moment on.

By Night Unstarred (1977),[40] in fact two unfinished novels written in the 1950s and spliced together by the poet's brother Peter Kavanagh, deals directly with the world of commerce and money. By far the more interesting part of this novel is the first, focusing on the rise of a countryman into wealth and social respectability. For Kavanagh, this rise into power is a mystery in a way in which his celebration of the romantic transcendent imagination is also mysterious. Perhaps unconsciously he makes a link between the entrepreneurial spirit and that of the risk-taking artist. Certainly, within the Irish world, both inhabit a peculiar position of being both inside and outside their community simultaneously. Kavanagh harbours a deep, abiding suspicion of his fictional businessman: the kind of suspicion that he himself registers being endured by Tarry Flynn. Both risk their place in the world for their dream. Though the execution is wanting, the intention is highly laudable. Kavanagh recognised that there was a story to be told of such a character but was unable to tell it adequately. His failure has been the failure of many Irish writers, none of whom have been truly able to tackle this subject of commerce and success effectively.

While Patrick Kavanagh asserted that he alone had rendered life as lived on the land in Ireland authentically, it was in fact another Ulster writer who could genuinely have made such a declaration if he had wished to. Sam Hanna Bell's (1909–90) *December Bride* (1951) is a story of country life in which the chords struck – in terms of story, descriptions and character-isations – ring resoundingly true. Unlike other writers of this period, Hanna Bell is not interested in the public persona of the writer, in creating and projecting himself into the public imagination as an artist. Set back in the early part of the twentieth century, the novel tells a story of a woman living with two brothers that is not, in the end, overly sensationalist or provoca-tive. Indeed, in many ways, the plot of their unconventional sexual and familial 'woven through other'[41] relationship is not the most important or interesting aspect of the novel, though that relationship dispels numerous belittling stereotypes of the Irish Protestant character in fiction by acknowl-edging the human complexity of the three people involved. Supposedly its source came from a comic story in his mother's family, but the result steers well clear of the kind of breeziness that Kavanagh is unwilling to avoid. This says much, perhaps, about the difference between the cultural and political development of North and South in this period.

The natural world is that which moves the characters, who are more wedded, at times, to the Ards peninsula landscape than to each other. However, the human sphere of people, with all its subtleties and nuanced silences, is well rendered in what has been described as a 'bleakly humane novel'.[42] Sean O'Faolain in its praise said that: '[T]his faithful novel of Ulster life ... owes ... something to the growing nationalism of the Six Counties, contains .. the manners and customs of the North of Ireland ...

the dour morality of a people as distinct from their southern fellow-countrymen as chapel is from church.'[43] Such a suggestion of North of Ireland uniqueness is utterly disingenuous, first, because the novel is set in a united Ireland before partition and, second, because the life on display here has similarities to other work by, for example, Patrick Kavanagh and later John McGahern. The novel shares with McGahern's work, especially, an emphasis on the human, rather than political, experience within a frame-work detailing the rhythms of the day and the seasons. There are, of course, references to religious difference suggesting how this divide is what really matters in an Irish setting. Though, a visit to the city of Belfast shows clearly an urban–rural divide too. Nonetheless, the brother's Presbyterian back-ground is shown, as the Catholic faith is shown in much Irish writing, to be interested only in curtailing joy and expression. Gatherings of energetic youth occur under the baleful and watchful eye of the minister (*December Bride*, p. 174). The separateness of the Catholic and the Protestant exists at the level of instinct: 'Deep down … the centuries-old enmity against the papist stirred, and neighbourliness and a more ancient kinship were for-gotten' (*December Bride*, p. 162). But that apartness is also fiercely real too, operating for this community in terms of place and locale. Bridie Dineen's status is made clear: 'Outside her own house she spoke to her neighbours with that courteous but evasive briefness that marks the Catholic in a Protestant district' (*December Bride*, p. 120). Hanna Bell realises how insular and isolated country life can actually be and how speech itself becomes truncated and limited in this world of inherent and inherited distrust. Rather than the loquaciousness of the stage Irish stereotype, this novel operates at the level of authenticity, with its descriptions of accepted silence and acts of communication tied to need: 'And as the outside world thawed and the sound of running water was heard once more in the dykes, so speech began to move again, sluggishly at first, between the brothers' (*December Bride*, p. 96). Hanna Bell is alive to the delicate moments of interaction between characters, both the tender and the harsh realities of people living in close quarters. Sarah emerges as one of the more powerful female characters in Irish fiction: her drive for survival, and the force of her maternal love, are at no time presented as maudlin or sentimental.

Sam Hanna Bell is obviously interested in universal truths which might transcend a particular time and place. He was certainly successful because the images he created would, in the 1990s film version of the novel, be reimagined compellingly in the global language of cinema. His setting of the novel back in time only reinforces this tactic on his part. However, like so many novelists of the twentieth century who focus on the rural scene, their writing of that world gestures in many ways to its passing away, even if that world would linger on for a while yet.

Two Irish novelists, Francis Stuart (1902–2000) and Samuel Beckett (1906–89), who had direct experience of the Second World War, make the sombre actuality of Europe-wide physical and psychological devastation central to their writing, producing disturbing and disruptive texts in the process. Francis Stuart's reputation as an Irish novelist in the 1930s was seen to be radically orientated towards the future according to his great champion W. B. Yeats. For a time he even edited a short-lived journal entitled *Tomorrow*: its title, if nothing else, suggesting his forward-looking credentials. However, his time spent teaching in the University of Berlin during the war, his radio broadcasts to Ireland for the Nazi Party during that time and his subsequent brief imprisonment meant that his most interesting writing would subsequently be focused not on the future but on the past, and specifically his own personal past. His actions and his writing have been the source of controversy in Irish literary criticism meaning that, sometimes, the aesthetic merits of his artistic work have been forgotten. He, himself, put his art and his artistic persona in a central position to understanding his actions. His is a very strange career in writing[44] in which he promoted a self-image of the artist as existential outcast, a figure on the edge of society: 'He fits into the niche he has created for himself, that of the "ghetto writer", as he puts it, "of being on the outside, always on the losing side".'[45]

Art, for Stuart, functioned for an elite, a chosen few, who through a necessary process of spiritual destruction, suffering and degradation would come to witness the old wasted world falling away and a new dispensation of higher feeling and purpose coming to pass.[46] While before the war this would have seemed unexceptional in the general crisis delineated by modernism, continuing to tell such a story, especially for one who had been on the side of those who lost that war, propels this existential angst into a completely different realm. His writing, far from being the celebration of the *Übermensch* who regrets none of his choices because there can be no transcendent consequences for any action, is in fact a writing that quivers with a profound anxiousness precisely about choices made and choices that now cannot be unmade.

Two novels, *The Pillar of Cloud* (1948) and *Redemption* (1949), deal with the immediate aftermath of the war. While there are autobiographical elements in each, it is the later novelised autobiography, *Black List Section H* finally published in 1970, which deals, in a curiously and tellingly indirect way, with Stuart's own life. *The Pillar of Cloud* is set in the ruins of a German city where Irish poet Dominic Malone ekes out a living with two sisters.

The horrors of war are filtered through this need for personal redemption: a kind of endurance test that will necessarily lead to a new life: 'I needed more than that. I needed a war and hunger and cold and imprisonment. I needed all these things before my eyes were opened.'[47] The intensity and earnestness in which these ideas of spiritual renewal are expressed in a language that is quite childish and ghoulishly comic highlight the author's ambivalence about his hero. Malone hopes to make a grand heroic gesture, the type of thing one would expect in that old world he wants to escape. In truth, that *is* the predicament of this novel: its arrogant insistence on the primacy of the individual who tries to create his or her own reality seems simply incongruous amid the rubble of a bombed-out city and the detritus of a humanity scrabbling to simply survive.

The action of the second novel, *Redemption*, takes place in a small town in Ireland where Ezra Arrigho pitches up after his wartime experiences. The world of war that produced a heightened sense of living is replaced with the comings and goings of a much more muted existence. In Stuart's religious schema of death and resurrection moving towards final deliverance, perhaps this is meant to be purgatory. Once again there is an insistent valorisation of subjectivity.[48] The hero lacks any humility, betraying little anxiety about his corrupting actions. Underpinning this is a spare style with no rhetorical flourish, a version of the reportage employed by the modernists. One aspect of Ezra's characterisation is of interest though: his predilection for gambling. For it is in this focus that Stuart attempts to allow chance to enter into his very controlled narrative, gambling being that element within the modern world which gives access to a momentary negation of rules and regulations. And yet the committed gambler is, as Walter Benjamin says, 'driven by essentially narcissistic and aggressive desires for omnipotence'.[49] Indeed, the link between erotic desire and the pleasure of winning means that gambling becomes, perhaps, the pre-eminent signifier of the bourgeois imagination, allowing in a managed and socially acceptable way access to that which must be denied.[50] In other words, Stuart's hero is more bound to the middle classes than he would care to admit, his flirting with the extremes of pure existential thought and action merely a bourgeois pose.

Each of Stuart's novels can be broadly read as a defence of his actions based on a philosophical and aesthetic existentialism: a modernist desire to choose alienation over deadening convention. Of course when Stuart, and his fictional versions of himself, went to Germany, he and they had no idea that the Nazis would lose the war, despite his own declaration of always choosing the losing side. Thus, rather than siding with the marginalised and the underdog, he positioned himself at the centre of what then imagined

itself to be an empire that would last for a thousand years. At that level, the
story he tells is basically a dishonest, self-serving one. Rather than encounter
authentic being and nothingness, his writing attempts to negate the hard
fact that he had actually been something: a fascist. His existentialist pretensions are an attempt to allow him to avoid any genuine moral scrutiny of
his actions.

Stuart's novels are essential reading because they make uncomfortable
those who might have been smugly unaware of the effects of the war in
Europe. Ultimately, though, they represent a failure because of his unwillingness to truly shine a light on his actions and his consciousness: his is a
writing of concealment rather than revelation, a process of obfuscation
rather than excavation. Theodor Adorno's famous dictum that 'It is impossible to write poetry after Auschwitz'[51] suggests a reappraisal of the link
between art and civilisation, between art and ideas of refined and polite
cultural progress. It is modernity itself, then, which comes under scrutiny
after the holocaust, or should do. Stuart fails to recognise this: his hoped-for
visions of the future expressed in his language of transcendence are, in
reality, very much grounded in the world he wants to escape. Like so many
modernist writers, his work is infected by that which he wants to cure. Sadly
for him, and for many of those who championed his work, he does not
recognise that serious flaw at the centre of his own aesthetic. A writer such as
W. B. Yeats, in his great late play *Purgatory* (1938), is attuned to that
dilemma and is, therefore, assured a level of greatness that Stuart could
never achieve.

Like Yeats, Samuel Beckett also exposes his art to this kind of profound,
perplexing failure. In direct contrast to the work of Francis Stuart, his art
'has no faith whatsoever in redemption': 'Refus[ing] to turn its gaze from
the intolerableness of things, even if there is no transcendent consolation at
hand.'[52] A transitional work for Beckett is his novel *Watt* (1953), which
begins his move away from traditional literary form and expectations.
Something of a parody of the Anglo-Irish Big House novel,[53] *Watt* dis-
mantles the language of Beckett's class and its rituals, laying bare its
constructedness and its imminent dissolution. Whereas Elizabeth Bowen
turned to the solid nature of the Big House in a time of crisis, Beckett's
wartime thoughts anticipate the end of ceremonial existence. That separate
characters – Watt and Knott, for example – seem to be versions of a single
self (that the master can become the slave and the slave the master) suggests
the collapse of a world based on difference and hierarchy and the underlying
homogeneity of modern experience. 'No symbols where none intended',[54]
the last line of the novel, is a warning to both his readers and himself,

proposing that his project might be a shared one. But then again, the novel's inscrutableness might suggest that this can only be a personal undertaking. In truth, that conundrum becomes central to Beckett's fictional oeuvre: the possibility, or impossibility, of moving beyond the realm of an embattled subjectivity.[55] Indeed, that inner world, the zone of consciousness itself, is where the traumas of modernity are played out again and again in Beckett's writing.

His trilogy (though, in fact, it might not actually be one) *Molloy* (1950), *Malone Dies* (1951) and *The Unnameable* (1952), written first in French and then translated and published in English in 1959, mark a paradigm shift in the novel form in a way that James Joyce's *Ulysses* had done a generation earlier. Beckett himself realised that he was engaging in new territory: 'The kind of work I do is one in which I am not master of my material ... I'm working with impotence, ignorance. I don't think that impotence has been exploited in the past.'[56] The emphasis is now on the processes of knowing rather than the end result, 'the event of knowing' is privileged over 'the fact of knowledge'.[57] In other words, Beckett's focus is now on the imagination itself in the moment of its imagining, on how stories are created and how these stories are all that there might be. The move ever inwards, away from the world, is a move towards something basic and essential. On that journey, words and language become strained as they are forced to say what, perhaps, cannot be said, forced to express what, perhaps, should not be expressed. In negating language, Beckett obliges us to attend to the fragile nature of words and their infinite subtleties. In an apparent contradiction just at the moment of extinction, both ontological and linguistic, he rediscovers the poetic rhythms inherent within language, shunning as he does so that realist tendency towards blunt reportage: a compensation of sorts, a final release of energy, for the often despairing truths he exposes.

The characters Molloy, Malone, Moran and so on are all creations of a singular imagination, or versions of a singular self, or so it seems. The final voice – the voice in *The Unnameable* – could be the voice of the dead, condemned to speak forever without end. In negating the self, Beckett compels us to recognise, to re-know and remember, what it is to be human, what it is to be:

You must say words, as long as there are any – until they find me, until they say me, strange pain, strange sin, you must go on, perhaps it's done already, perhaps they have said me already, perhaps they have carried me to the threshold of my story, before the door that opens on my story, that would surprise me, if it opens, it will be I, it will be the silence, where I am, I don't know, I'll never know, in the silence you don't know, you must go on, I can't go on, I'll go on.[58]

Beckett's vision is a truly devastating one. It annunciates a new reality where all the certainties of tradition have melted away, though obviously they are not forgotten and mourned in the memory of them. Conversely, Beckett's vision is a truly liberating one: it annunciates a new reality where all the certainties of tradition have melted away, though obviously they are not forgotten and celebrated in the memory of them. His trilogy is both an end and a beginning. For the Irish novel, particularly, Beckett's fiction consciously did not allow for imitation: it was a dead-end in terms of offering either a stylistic or narrational ground for a continuing tradition. Like so much Irish fiction of this period, these three works are so bound up with the persona of the author – real or imagined – that, were others to write likewise, it would necessarily lead to caricature.

Samuel Beckett's sense of desolation and dislocation is certainly influenced by his Anglo-Irish background: that class and caste's experience of cultural and political dispossession becomes a template for him to comprehend a universal emergence into a new postmodern conception of authority. This background is shared with Elizabeth Bowen and while not often considered in conjunction with Beckett, much of her Irish writing has very strong links to his work,[59] certainly sharing this awareness of disinheritance. What is most dear to her, the Anglo-Irish Big House, is lost – and in a way found again – in *A World of Love* (1955). While critics disagree as to its worth in relation to Bowen's oeuvre and question its genre,[60] *A World of Love* remains a troublingly magnificent meditation on the obsolescence of the Big House symbol in modern Ireland that manages to simultaneously announce the end of a certain tradition of living, while opening up the possibility, with all the attendant anxieties, of an unknown future.

Montefort is what the Big House of Danielstown in *The Last September* would have become if it had survived that final conflagration. However, the threat from fire remains a symbolic actuality with the action of the novel taking place over four days of an intense summer heat wave. A foreboding impression of possible combustion underlines the exploits of all the characters, young and old. The unusual heat wave is also the cause of a drought. The implication is clear: like the land, the lives of the Anglo-Irish are arid and desolate, in need of revitalisation. From the outset the reader is presented with a world where lives and living appear stifled and sterile. The heat is at times unbearable and produces in the characters a languid torpor that appears impossible to overcome: the very act of existing, of being, is exhausting. A legacy of the Anglo-Irish's colonial past is that their sense of being is bound up with their being perceived and, like many of Beckett's characters who inhabit an environment heedless of their existence, modern Ireland is 'absolute in its indifference to [them]' (*A World of Love*, pp. 88–89).

The façade of the Montefort is described as possessing 'a ghost of style' (*A World of Love*, p. 9), suggesting that the past relationship to the present is one based on haunting. The Big House's Beckettian endurance in spite of all demonstrates how Anglo-Irish powerlessness still finds a means to go on in a ghostly fashion, haunting the Irish landscape and psyche.[61] 'A ghost of style' might also refer to Bowen's poetic language in the novel: a language that manifests her own uncertainties and ambivalences at this time attempting to express the ghostliness of absent presences and present absences. The disruptive force within the novel, the channel through which the past explodes into the haunted present, are Guy's letters to an unnamed lover discovered by Jane in the attic of the house. The entire household is in thrall to their uncertain power. Guy's violent and sudden death in the First World War left too many unfulfilled possibilities of what might have been. His phantasmal return raises uneasy questions about inheritance, about legitimacy and illegitimacy. Interestingly, it is the trauma of the First World War and not the more recent Second World War that is the issue for Elizabeth Bowen and her conception of the Anglo-Irish dilemma. Hers is a recognition of how Ireland's peculiar status to, and relationship with, international affairs mean that Time – and the significances that Time imposes – becomes profoundly relative. And this despite the constant presence of Big Ben as the regulatory image of normal Time that comes up again and again throughout *A World of Love* as an obsession of Maud's, Jane's younger sister.

While Antonia's and Lilia's response to the resurfacing of the letters is one based on their memory of Guy, Jane is not beholden to the past in the same way, and therefore she can be creative with it in ways that are not possible for either of the older women. The death of the author is in this instance the birth of Jane as a creative reader. Jane learns from her experience with Guy's letters and is ready to 'no sooner look but love' by the novel's close. The reader is presented with numerous versions of Guy competing against one another and none cancels out any of the others. By the end of the novel, the reader is no closer to the truth of Guy than at the beginning: he still remains a mystery, elusive to the last. In the end, the novel is a remarkably postmodern one: an endless labyrinth of fictions reflecting one another but never reflecting any final reality.[62] Throughout reference is made to an obelisk at the front of the house and for most of the novel there is no explanation as to what the obelisk actually signifies or commemorates. It appears to be a sign without a signifier or a sign radically set adrift from its signifier: whatever memory it was first erected to, now appears no longer relevant or is forgotten. Thus, in correspondence with Beckett's work, these characters are condemned to tell their stories into a void. Their narratives are meagre attempts to overcome the inevitable isolation and alienation both from the past and from each other. Similarly with Guy: the real Guy is always just beyond reach, the story of this mysterious woman to whom the letters were actually written would have been so different, coming from him, from any of the stories created by Antonia, Lilia or Jane.

Jane at the close of the novel, on her journey to Shannon airport, orientates herself towards the west and America rather than the east, Britain and Europe.[63] Bowen recognises clearly the place where the future is located. At a dinner party attended by Jane, an older man, Terence, a remnant of the old order, says of the past that it is 'rotten old romancing and story-telling: you make the half of it up, and who's the wiser?' (*A World of Love*, p. 63). In a wonderfully self-reflexive moment, Bowen is offering an auto-critique of the Big House novel itself, signalling that, for her at least, it cannot continue in any meaningful way or vital manner into the future. The shrewd Terence declares that the new age is a material and pragmatic one: 'These days one goes where the money is . . . Those days, we went where the people were' (*A World of Love*, p. 64). As critic Robert Tracy argues: *A World of Love* 'is not a requiem but an exorcism'.[64] This was to be Elizabeth Bowen's last Irish novel.

Another manifestation of impotence is on display in Brian Moore's (1921–99) *The Lonely Passion of Judith Hearne* (1955). The argument that naturalism is the dominant paradigm in Irish fiction in the twentieth century,[65] while it possesses obvious merit, suggests that its apolitical concerns signify a lack in Irish writing. Certainly, a writer such as Moore shuns the grand political gesture, leaving that to others and concentrates instead on individuals.[66] Shifting his focus in this fashion suggests that politics is a dead-end artistically, that there is an urgent need to tell more human stories, to connect with a narrative strain that transcends the narrowness of the political sphere. Moore recognises, as later writers such as John McGahern and Edna O'Brien would recognise, that politics is but one mode of existence, and that the authentic human life is lived at various levels and at a variety of intensities. Of course, such a manoeuvre into a politically neutral realm is in itself political: scorning the traumas of ideology to embrace the pleasures and the pressures of lived experience.

Moore's best-known novel, *The Lonely Passion of Judith Hearne* (1955), demonstrates clearly the aesthetic advantages of this repositioning of the writerly focus towards character. Dealing with a middle-aged unmarried woman who finds in alcohol a way of ordering both her life and her losses, the novel captures well the provincial world of urban Belfast. All the characters that Judith comes across, in her bed-sit and beyond, are individually hateful in their own unique ways. Their petty and selfish fancies sprawl across the pages of this novel in a manner not fully articulated since James Joyce's short story collection *Dubliners*. And Joyce's meticulous meanness is on display here too: there are no moments of transcendence or illumination, no wavering from a direct, plain style that renders brilliantly this world and its inhabitants.[67] The only aesthetic flourish is Moore's allowing for different voices and perspectives to enter briefly into the narrative,[68] giving the impression of the wider community in which Judith lives: her single story but one story out of many. A novel such as this punctures smug conceptions of what constitutes modern life, shining a chink of light into experiences and feelings that bubble away beneath official images and narratives. In a very unassuming way, Brian Moore sets up a template that will become increasingly popular with Irish writers.

In contrast to both Elizabeth Bowen and Brian Moore, Benedict Kiely (1919–2007) would seem to embody the world of middle-class confidence of those who came into possession of political power and position in the new dispensation.[69] In his critical account of modern Irish fiction, Kiely stated that after war and civil war, 'The time for heroic gesture was over and the future must be as prosaic as building a wall.'[70] In many ways, his writerly orbit is one where a barrier is being built, one that firmly segregates past from present. In this period Kiely, as well as the grind of everyday journalism, writes a history of partition, *Counties of Contention: A Study of the Origins and Implications of the Partition of Ireland* (1945), a study of William Carleton, *Poor Scholar: A Study of the Work and Days of William Carleton* (1947), and a critical appraisal of contemporary Irish fiction, *Modern Irish Fiction: A Critique* (1950). These are the works of a self-assured young man imaginatively taking ownership of his cultural and political heritage, surveying the scene and staking his claim not just to the past but, more importantly, to the future.

Such poise is also to be found in his prose fiction, none of which manifests the kind of linguistic anxieties on display in the work of either Bowen or Beckett. Also absent is any sense of disquiet regarding the form of the novel as a means of expression. Because a plot needs such things, there are indeed crises for his characters to contend with, but they are not of the ontological or existential kind that profoundly troubles the characters of *The Trilogy* or *A World of Love*. Still, though, there persists the air of sluggish apathy that filled Bowen's last Irish novel. So much so that in his early work such as

In a Harbour Green (1949) and *Land Without Stars* (1946), despite being set in Omagh in the North of Ireland and using the backdrop of the Second World War and local IRA engagements, the atmosphere is one of quiet untroubled existence. Rather than politics or religion being central to his artistic concerns, the emphasis is on the individual's growth into maturity through the Joycean filters of sexuality, morality and intellectual development. Indeed, in relation to what would happen in the late 1960s when the tension within the North exploded onto the streets, for Kiely it is not religion which divides people, but rather it is class which keeps communities apart. And class is central to his vision of contemporary Ireland and his work is endlessly open to the subtle, undeclared class codes within Irish society that separate country from town, farmer from civil servant. Of particular interest is how he positions attitudes to republicanism along class lines, offering an oblique warning of how the middle classes with some material stake in society have much to lose by allying themselves to their socialist cause.

However, what allows even a riven society to operate is that bourgeois liberal trait of tolerance, and Kiely's novels celebrate it – even through those moments when his authorial perspective wryly bursts pretension and pomposity. His work is littered with references to songs, stories and anecdotes and this will increasingly become a major thematic concern in his later writing and, indeed, influence his experimental approach to the novel form from the 1960s onwards. These cultural details are clustered round local places and landmarks, depoliticising them out of the reach of wider nationalist or unionist narrative and, as such, are an attempt to create a shared sense of the past and culture that might transcend difference and that all sides of the political divide might lay equal claim to.

Kiely's mapping of the empowered Irish middle classes is what is of note in *The Cards of the Gambler* (1953). It juxtaposes a modern, contemporary narrative with a folktale, one becoming a comment on the other. This is a curious and interesting novel – certainly a move away from the serene naturalism of his earlier works as he ventures into the realm of the fantastic and the magical. It weaves together the traditional Irish folktale, of the gambler who makes a pact with the devil and the European Faust theme. In doing so, Kiely is capable of dealing with existential and ethical issues, rather than being compelled and obliged to consider simply Irish matters. The hero, a gambler, makes a deal with the devil so that he may never lose at cards again. Gambling, of course, is a means for deferred desire to find an outlet, and the protagonist's wish to neuter that channel for excitement, and that opportunity for chance further deadens his existence and his experience. There is a sense, then, that the ennui experienced by the hero is a deep and self-perpetuating one, a general malaise of dissoluteness that cannot be escaped. And when the gambler finally dies and enters into the afterlife, Death imparts to him the knowledge that 'hell is homelessness'.[71] The twist in the tale, of course, is that the hero has lost that which he most despised in life: the mundane comforts of home. More noteworthy is how anxiety now revolves round those things celebrated in his Northern Ireland novels of the 1940s and 1950s: the stability that humdrum bourgeois ritual might bring to a divided society. South of the border, it seems, such commonplaces are transformed into a source of numbing tedium and monotony. Certainly, there is a different perspective from the rural to the urban scene, altering how such attitudes might be taken up. More significantly, however, this is a good example of how Northern Ireland developed at a different pace and in a different way from the Republic declared in 1948. Unconsciously, Kiely shows how partition operates at a cultural as well as a political level and how even those sympathetic to unification became desensitised to its consequences.

Kiely's next novel, *There was an Ancient House* (1955), is based on his own experiences when he went to the Jesuit novitiate in Emo Park, County Laois for a year. The absence of colour is what marks it off from the world outside the demesne walls. The book opens with: 'It was a white world . . . All the whiteness made him afraid. Was it black or white was the absence of colour?'[72] It ends in a world of glorious colour: 'This world was a multi-coloured arc. It was black and white, grey and white, blue and red' (*There was an Ancient House*, p. 240). McKenna is the artist figure, and Barragry is the worldly-wise and world-weary journalist representing the two strains within the author Kiely himself. In his own undemonstrative way, Kiely perceives that the ills of religious life spring from these eager, energetic and spiritually idealistic young men being forced to live apart from the world. The walls of the ancient house are there not only to keep them in, but also to keep the world out. This stark division is what truly separates these religious men from their flock: the world of life, of experience and of existence is the fallen world and these young men are forced to have a foot in the otherworld well before their time.

A novelist writing about us would scarcely need to label the little snippets of dialogue that novelists must use to avoid boring their readers by long stretches of description, or philosophising. When I get back into the world I'll write a novel about this place: the lake and the tress, the seclusion from everything, even newspapers, the prayer, the charity, the peace, the blues, the noonday devil, the fear for perseverance. (*There was an Ancient House*, p. 67)

McKenna, like Stephen Dedalus before him, transfers his religious sensibility into the realm of art. Kiely's overall purpose here, as it was in his earlier work, is to rejoice in this world rather than disparage or mock it. While he sees faults and offers criticism of this Catholic institution, he does not, nor does he want to, jeopardise the status quo. In the end, the religious life is transfigured rather than wholly abandoned. Tolerance once again is paramount.

While on the surface his gentle realism manifests no unease, Kiely's position of being a part of the establishment and also wanting to be at an angle to it in order to create vital art is a precarious one. Patrick Kavanagh penned a bilious attack on many of his contemporary writers for their obvious success in furthering their careers in foreign journals and magazines such as the *New Yorker*:

> I mean to say I'm not blind really
> I have my eyes wide open as you may imagine
> And I am aware of our boys such as Ben Kiely
> Buying and selling literature on the margin.[73]

The poet recognises the unsettling position writers such as Kiely, Frank O'Connor and Sean O'Faolain were actually in, even if they could not see it themselves. On the one hand, they write and want to write out of a realist commitment to social critique and analysis, to expand their literary horizons into zones other than the Irish stereotype, to give voice and expression to those lives that had hitherto not been heard. On the other hand, at a more practical level, they are forced to sustain literary narratives and images that would find a welcome with a readership not necessarily appreciative of a caustic commentary on the modern state of Ireland. They needed also to meet the demands of new technology and outlets for their art, translating a literary sensibility into the realm of, particularly, radio. More and more, this will become an issue for many Irish novelists who must juggle their many public roles within Ireland and outside it. Irish publishers also had a role to play, but failed to provide a space for Irish writers who were forced to look to Britain as an outlet.[74]

One particular novel that attempts to seize this precise moment when the artist as public figure is at its zenith is J. P. Donleavy's (1929-) *The Ginger Man* (1955). With its focus on the bohemian world of Dublin's pub and drinking culture with thinly disguised portraits of some of Ireland's better-known writers of the 1950s, it makes a virtue of debauched living. In the milieu of Sebastian Dangerfield, an ex-GI studying in Ireland, the only real peril is to one's morals. Banned for its lurid details, the novel is in reality a very light and airy excursion into Irish life. Nonetheless, its vision of a carefree world peopled by outrageously larger-than-life characters has become the nostalgic image of an Ireland that operates powerfully both within and outside the country. It is an image as debilitating as it is liberating. Even as Donleavy's book was published and was gaining a reputation, and as he reimagined it for the theatre in the late 1950s and early 1960s, the Dublin he wrote of was already gone and the energetic characters he recreated were succumbing to the harsh realities of alcoholism.

Brendan Behan (1923–64), perhaps, is the most famous of these writers who lived in the public view. Not since a figure like Oscar Wilde, it might be argued, does an Irishman move so easily between the life and the work, between the genius of creating a persona and the talent of writing. The source material for much of his writing was his life in inner-city Dublin and his experiences in various prisons because of his republican activities. His autobiographical *Borstal Boy* (1958) is rendered in the form of a novel: its plot, its language and characterisation, its numerous revelations, far too perfect to be an exact account of reality. It is read little in the contemporary moment, its afterlife – and that of its author – guaranteed through many stage versions stressing its origins in Behan's own life, its force coming from the unifying power of his personality. Like Irish novelists before him, Behan's subject is the growth of the individual from innocence to experience, except that his *Bildungsroman* occurs neither in the domestic space nor on the streets of the city, but in the confines of prison. Despite the location, the protagonist does come to learn the classic liberal lessons of the world. After being caught on a bombing mission for the IRA in Liverpool, the young teenager spends a number of years in the British Borstal system for youth offenders. His republican ideals are tested as he questions his actions and their worth. The real revelation, though, is that he comes to understand that there is common cause between Ireland and Britain, indeed between Ireland and the world. Questions of nationality fall away when each of his prison mates can be said to be 'chums' with the others: difference remains, but equality and justice are paramount. In other words, Behan reconnects with the socialist roots of republicanism, clearly recognising that the future – or the 1960s at least – would move to the left politically and culturally in the West.

Certainly, it is the future rather than the past which the novel orientates itself towards by the close. After his experiences of the wide world, of different people from different places, and of having his cultural horizons exposed to new ideas, he is sent home to Dublin. It is a reversal of what had become the formulaic route for the Irish artist, which was a move away from Ireland and into exile. Rather than departure at the close, the reader is offered a sublime moment of return:

There they were, as if I'd never left them; in their sweet and stately order round the Bay – Bray Head, the Sugarloaf, the Two Rock, the Three Rock, Kippure, the king of them all, rising his threatening head behind and over their shoulders till they sloped down to the city . . . I had them all counted, present and correct and the chimneys of the Pigeon House, and the framing circle of the road along the edge of the Bay, Dun Laoghaire, Blackrock, Sandymount Tower, Ringsend and the city; then the other half circle, Fairview, Marino, Clontarf, Raheny, Kilbarrack, Baldoyle, to the height of Howth Head.

I couldn't really see Kilbarrack or Baldoyle, but it was only that I knew they were there.[75]

Truly an act of imaginative repossession is performed here: even the places he cannot see become a part of his topographical reclamation. An immigration officer then greets him:

He looked very serious, and tenderly enquired, 'Caithfidh go bhfuil sé go hiontach bheith saor.'
'Caithfidh go bhfuil.'
'It must be wonderful to be free.'
'It must,' said I . . .   (*Borstal Boy*, p. 384)

While some might quibble for the need of translation at all, at least Behan acknowledges his dual inheritance *and* acknowledges the autonomy that it might afford him. In this final moment of the novel, he tells us, and performs for us, how Ireland can again be a location for art and possibility. No longer do energies have to be diverted into an act of exile, better to put those potential exertions into an art that will possess a European and a universal sensibility because it is centred in Ireland, and not in spite of it.

Behan's writing and career encapsulate the contradictions and the tensions inherent within an Ireland emerging into the possibilities of the post-war international scene. As a poet, a playwright, short-story writer and memoirist, moving uneasily between the English and the Irish languages, he looks backwards to tradition while simultaneously looking forwards into uncharted territory. All of his work registers this position, being full of references to songs and stories, while formally oscillating precariously between the haphazardly improvised as in the plays and the more highly wrought work on display in a novel such as *Borstal Boy*.

As was the case for the revivalists before him, his life and work – because of this reorientation towards Ireland – operates in a remarkably post-colonial space. Thus, while Behan's work is local, his vision is global. His life and work stand as an example of the kind of dynamism needed to break out of Ireland into the international scene, and a warning of the inherent dangers in that manoeuvre. To achieve entry into this global orbit there are gains to be made and losses to endure. Like no Irish writer before him, he had access to a variety of media outlets, such as television in Britain and America, which meant that he could create an audience for his writing. Of course, this would ultimately be his great tragedy, that some of his best work would be lost in the instant of the barroom quip.

Behan's position is an urban update of the peasant poet of a generation earlier. Even his revolutionary background is tamed with his entry into the circus of success, merely adding a whiff of chic sulphur to his work and his public performances. And, like all self-publicists, the constant need for more attention meant that his outrageousness descended rapidly into stereotype. Despite this, his urban working-class background punctures elite pretensions surrounding bourgeois art and throughout his career Behan remained, mostly, aware of how to use the media. One major lingering difficulty, however, is the problem of cultural translation. The difference and the gap between his 'broth of a boy image' outside Ireland and his reputation within Ireland can never be fully bridged and overcome. Thus, he exists in a space that is at once comic and tragic, simultaneously invigoratingly embracing stereotypes as well energetically deconstructing expectations.

For those novelists who came after Brendan Behan, Patrick Kavanagh and Flann O'Brien there would be a more knowing and measured relation-ship to the public world, though they too would cultivate particular images that would allow them to continue to write and help in the reception of their work. For many, though, the shift is towards a sense of the novel as a site for high art and serious expression.

John Banville's Doctor Copernicus: *a revolution in the head*[1]

No motion has she now, no force;
She neither hears nor sees;
Rolled round in earth's diurnal course,
With rocks, and stones, and trees.

(William Wordsworth)

None of John Banville's (1945–) writing to the point of his publishing *Doctor Copernicus* in 1976 could have indicated how brilliant this particular novel would be. Not unlike the stammerer's obsession described in the novel: 'searching . . . for that last elusive word . . . that surely would make all come marvellously clear',[2] Banville's career to this moment was a groping towards a narrative and a way of presenting that narrative which might manifest most powerfully his intellectual disquiet regarding language and form, along with his thematic interest in the modernist/postmodernist story of the plight of the modern individual imagination's engagement with the real world. The achievement of a certain authorial poise, a stylistic control and distance, utterly absent in his previous novel *Birchwood* (1973) which positively revelled in its own chaos, conceals the anxieties central to *Doctor Copernicus*. Playing, as it does, with the fundamental contradictions of a modernity which oscillates between desire for the certainties of an older traditional world and the recognition that such certitude is no longer possible. Indeed, Banville's discovery of a means of masking disorder in his aesthetic pursuit of the well-made sentence becomes the keynote gesture of his art from this moment on.

John Banville's art is one of concealment rather than revelation, one of striving towards objective expression rather than self-expression. This is reflected in a novel such as *Doctor Copernicus* where, on the surface at least, Banville self-consciously positions himself within a European and international literary framework, figuratively escaping from what might be thought of as the narrowness of Ireland and Irish concerns. The great scientist wished to transcend the disorder of the world and contemplate the harmony of the heavens and Banville, too, wants to find solace away from the disorder of his own world in this retreat into the distant past. However, a primary motif in his writing is that of failure[3] and, in truth, the hoped-for escape from the confines of the Irish world is never fully effected. For the mediaeval world of Copernicus is surprisingly familiar to an Irish audience, rife as it is with national intrigue and sectarian division.

The backdrop to Banville's writing of the novel in the mid-1970s is one of political catastrophe in Ireland. After what seemed a golden moment of palpable cultural reform in Ireland, and obviously everywhere in the Western world during the 1960s, when everyone and everything seemed open to the endless possibilities of the future, the 1970s marked a grinding halt to such progressivist thinking. The conflict in the North of Ireland was at its worst and it was as if the unresolved past exploded into the present, shattering any complacent concept of Irish historical development. The subsequent benumbed response that years of being exposed to outrage had not yet come to pass, so that the onslaught to the senses of the daily horrors of murder and mayhem still possessed the raw power to shock. It is little wonder, then, how attractive this turning towards what seemed the distant past and a remote medieval Europe would be to an author who worked as a copy-editor in *The Irish Press* newspaper at this time and had to deal with the reporting of shootings and bombings over and over again, night after night.

There is a keen sense of the cultural and political milieu out of which Copernicus operated that allows Banville to comment obliquely on his own place and his own time. Throughout the novel, Copernicus is given numerous names: Nicolas, Nicolas Koppernigk, Herr Koppernigk when in Italy, Caro Nicolo when he is with his friend Girolamo, and Canon Koppernigk when he receives his doctorate in Canon Law. When he is resident with his uncle, Bishop Lucas, at Heilsberg, he is called upon to declare his nationality but discovers 'that he did not know what it was'. His uncle, however, resolves the conundrum for him: 'You are not a German, nephew, no, nor a Pole, nor even a Prussian. You are an Ermlander, simple. Remember it' (*Doctor Copernicus*, p. 106). There is an obvious tension here between nation and self, between communal and personal identity. The demands of one betray the demands of the other. In an Irish context, the development of the individual sensibility would have seemed to come to a shuddering halt with the very real violence in the North of Ireland calling into question once again issues of communal identity, which many would have believed, and hoped, were a concern of the past. After the quickening of history in the 1960s, it appeared that in Ireland progression was being replaced with regression. The dilemma was one of revealing a way to transform this reality, to regain the energies that might begin to propel the self and the world into the future.

The ready-made story of Nicolas Copernicus became a means for Banville to explain his own dilemma and frustrations with what seemed to be a society stuck in a moment and unable to move forwards. All his writing is concerned with the act of writing itself: it is a self-conscious, self-aware, and ultimately self-reflexive art. Thus, in the character of Copernicus, Banville discovered a protagonist who, though a scientist, is a surrogate artist figure through which he can meditate on his own position as a writer writing fiction. Deconstructing the boundaries between science and art is central to Banville's project: laying bare the imaginative impulses common to both spheres of action, and in the quantum age, humanising the scientific mind while simultaneously redeeming the artistic vision as something to be celebrated rather than scorned. More important perhaps, are the affinities of empathy as a person that Banville creates for his Copernicus: one of 'those high cold heroes who renounced the world and human happiness to pursue the big game of the intellect'.[4] For, despite the claims of atavistic nationality made by his uncle and despite being what he is told to be, the authentic person remains true primarily to the project of making the self rather than simply the production of his theory of the heavens. He is aware that national identity, like all those other identities which make demands on him, is but one more mask. Behind all those masks, in truly artistic fashion, is to be found his essential self that no name – be it son, brother, friend, – or, indeed, nation can claim: 'He was *Doctor Copernicus*' (*Doctor Copernicus*, p. 106).

Banville's choice of Copernicus, particularly, is important because of his centrality in producing ideas and theories foundational to modernity itself. Certainly Copernicus's theory of a sun-centred universe is a paradigm shift in thought that forever changed our conception of ourselves. A time before this cannot be imagined now, so momentous a change is it. Its influence is not simply confined to the realm of science and astronomy, but also reverberates through all levels of modern experience. Copernicus, then, is a man perched on the cusp of the modern world, looking backwards and forwards simultaneously: desiring a future but fearing its advent nonetheless. Of specific interest to Banville are change and transformation and how change and transformation come about. As a child of the 1940s and 1950s in Ireland, he wishes to reimagine and remake his world anew, to propel it into the future. In returning to these moments of transition in the past, he is able to confront directly the dilemma of modernity and post-modernity in the present moment. In this he connects with the writing of James Joyce and W. B. Yeats before him, both of whom contemplated deeply the nature of the transformative impulse, and the possibility of harnessing that impulse, in a moribund Ireland.

Banville's story of Copernicus's life follows a conventional movement from childhood to death and is broken up into four parts. The first section, 'Orbitas lumenque', deals with Copernicus's early life and his religious and academic education in Prussia and Italy; the second section, 'Magister ludi', is mostly focused on the scientist's troubled relationship with his wastrel brother Andreas; the third part, 'Cantus mundi', breaks with the omniscient third-person narrative employed up to this point, offering a version of Copernicus and his book from the perspective of his student and disciple Rheticus; the final section, 'Magnum miraculum', restores the third-person narrative and tells of Copernicus's final years, ending with his death. The central concern moving the plot forwards is Copernicus's theory, which proposed that the earth was not at the centre of the known universe, but that the sun was the axis round which the earth and the planets revolved. Suddenly man is no longer at the centre of creation, and is forever con-demned to be on the periphery of things, bemoaning that loss of a privileged position. Such a theory in a time of civil and religious upheaval was bound to upset many powerful people. For this reason, Copernicus was reluctant to publish his findings, only relenting to do so after many years. His fears were twofold. First, the religious implications of his banishing of man to the margins of God's creation were profound at a time of schism. Second, he felt that his theory had no mathematical basis, that it was only an 'idea' without any grounding in fact.

It is this latter element that permits Banville to weave his postmodern concerns with language, writing and authority round his vision of this medieval scientist. Copernicus desires that astronomy become a system 'for verifying the real rather than merely postulating the possible' and that to achieve this 'Nothing less than new and radical instauration would do, if astronomy was to mean more than itself' (*Doctor Copernicus*, p. 94). But how is one to break out of a closed and self-reflexive system, referring, as it does, only to itself and nothing beyond itself? The solution lies in a 'radical act of creation' (*Doctor Copernicus*, p. 95). Only then will the 'mere hack-work' (*Doctor Copernicus*, p. 96) necessary for proving this act of creation follow. Copernicus is now an artist and not unlike an artist he can sit back and delight in his handiwork: 'He turned the solution this way and that, admiring it, as if he were turning in his fingers a flawless ravishing jewel. It was the thing itself, the vivid thing' (*Doctor Copernicus*, p. 96). The palpable gap that separated the word from the world is overcome in this act of imaginative creation. But it is only a momentary healing of this division. Once the initial idea has been formed, the problem now facing Copernicus is one of matching the numbers to his idea. It is a question now of writing, of textualising, his thought. The difficulty is in discovering a language that will encapsulate his theory.

The initial euphoria of creation is replaced by the recognition that, perhaps, the promise of change and originality can never be truly fulfilled because the words, or the numbers, being employed to 'say' this new reality are very much of the old world. Copernicus realised that in attempting to work out his theory, all he was managing to do was move further away from his initial idea. The same is true for Banville's art, which acknowledges the impossibility of his writing bridging the gap between itself and the reality with which it so desperately wants to connect. Not unlike Copernicus, then, he stands on the intersection between past and present, tradition and modernity, power and powerlessness.

These anxieties are reflected in the form of the novel itself. The novel begins with a stable third-person narrator: somewhat sympathetic but ultimately aloof and distant. As the first part of the novel comes to a close, this distance starts to disintegrate subtly: the narrator begins to be intrusive and voices other than the narrator's also interject and disrupt the telling of the story. Then the narrative further disintegrates into a series of letters – the epistolary form – with the third section of the novel, 'Cantus mundi', seeing the introduction of a previously unheard-of character, Rheticus, who completely usurps control of the narrative. The interjection of the letters and this new narrator brings into sharp focus the act of writing itself, further developing the link between the action in the novel and Banville's self-conscious interest in his own art. Banville employs the intertextual technique often in his writing, acknowledging as he does so the other works out of which this particular work comes, setting up a reverberating dialogue with other texts. Interestingly, he is open to both high and low art, and a feature of his work are cinematic references adding another layer of texture to his sense of a shared cultural tradition. It is also an admission of how cultural reference develops and changes and how aware the contemporary author needs to be of other media beyond the written word.

In early drafts of the work, Banville intended to conclude by unmasking entirely the novel's fictive nature with a narrative that would see Banville's own journey to modern-day Poland, his impressions of the place and his continuing search for the real Copernicus.[5] That he did not succumb to this kind of obvious postmodern trickery says much about Banville's aesthetic: in the end, he does not wish to fully embrace the apocalyptic vision inherent within that postmodern perspective and still hopes for a word that might actually make all come marvellously clear. When confronted with its complete demise, he still has some faith in the form of the traditional novel. Thus, abject failure is never contemplated or surrendered to, the expectations of the established novel still offer the reader, and the author, some solace despite this experimentation with the form.

At the end of Rheticus's narrative, he declares that despite his bringing into the public realm the upheavals of Copernicus's ideas, the world has not been diminished in any significant way: 'The sky is blue, and shall be forever blue, and the earth shall blossom forever in spring, and this planet shall forever be centre of all we know' (*Doctor Copernicus*, p. 232). There is something of a truth here. Nothing has really altered because the human imagination can only perceive the world and the universe from its own limited and subjective vantage point; anything else is mere fancy and speculation.

And yet everything has changed, changed profoundly. Here, the issue returns to the question of the self, and the project of making and remaking the self in the modern world. The world might look the same but has undeniably changed for the individual who, now armed with this newfound knowledge, looks upon that world differently. The epigraph to the novel is lines taken from Wallace Steven's poem, 'Notes toward a Supreme Fiction':

> You must become an ignorant man again
> And see the sun again with an ignorant eye
> And see it clearly in the idea of it.   (*Doctor Copernicus*, p. 9)

Copernicus's achievement is that he has looked at the world again and imagined it anew. That is what art, and certainly Banville's art, attempts to do. By calling into question the very language that is used to talk about the world, Banville can, like a poet, revitalise that language, reconfigure man's connection with it in order to continue in the ongoing project of attempting to say the world. With *Doctor Copernicus* Banville enacts a human drama wherein the security of the ways in which we traditionally view the world are deconstructed. There is, undoubtedly, tragedy in that loss, but there is also the challenge to begin again. Banville realises that the real revolution is that which occurs in the head, in the individual imagination, and not in the wide communal sphere. Indeed, he recognises that in the Irish situation it is the unfinished business of making and expressing the individual self which most needs a revolutionary makeover. This postmodern move from grand narrative to the *petite histoire* suggests a return to that basic need, a turning away from the world of politics and national affairs towards the private and the intimate scope of the self.

What is finally asked of Copernicus, and of the reader, is to accept the world with all its faults, imperfections and chaos, to accept the world as it is: 'There is no need to search for the truth. We know it already . . . We are the truth. The world, and ourselves, this is the truth' (*Doctor Copernicus*, p. 252). Truth cannot be uttered, and yet the paradox remains that we desire to say it nonetheless. But this abandonment of fiction is itself a fiction. Andreas tells his brother that: 'It is not I who have said these things today, but you' (*Doctor Copernicus*, p. 254). Copernicus conjures up an image of his dead brother in order to tell him what he already knows. Of course, this also intimates that there is no essential self that can be fully expressed: all identity is necessarily a series of interchangeable personae. This revolution in the head is an ongoing and endless act of self-creation and recreation, of deconstruction and reconstruction. For a previous generation of Irish writers, this was an exhausting task to be endured. The difference for Banville, and for his characters, is that, unlike his predecessors, this is a state of being to be playfully exploited and revelled in.

In a character such as Copernicus, with all his anxieties, can be discovered a template for Ireland's uncomfortable negotiation between tradition and modernity, between the past and the future in the contemporary moment. If a fundamental aspect of the history of the Irish novel is uncovering the developing portrayals of the Irish person as a complex and self-aware individual, then Copernicus would seem to have achieved that state of being. He is a self-made man after all and has struggled to be so – he is the pinnacle of modernity, a figure to be lauded and celebrated. And yet he is haunted with a persistent sense of deep loss. As a later character of Banville's would declare: 'The self-made man has no solid ground to stand on.'[6] There are consequences, then, for this revolution in the head: new knowledge undoubtedly comes only at a very high price.

CHAPTER 6

The struggle of making it new, 1960–79

> Poets with progress
> Make no peace nor pact
> The act of poetry
> Is a rebel act
>
> (Michael Hartnett)

Poet Philip Larkin observed that 'Sexual intercourse began / In nineteen sixty-three / Between the end of the "Chatterley" ban / And the Beatles' first LP'.[1] Despite the claims of many literary and cultural critics to the exceptionalism of Ireland's supposed backwardness, particularly its sexual benightedness, and its assumed belated progression into modernity as evidenced in the cultural sphere by the persistence of censorship, it would seem from Larkin's reflections that this was a darkness shared by the entire Western world. On the face of it, this twenty-year period between 1960 and 1980 appears to be one of profound change and rapid transformation in Ireland, as it is elsewhere. If until this point Irish historical development had appeared, even as it was being experienced, as plodding, then in this era, in contrast, events moved swiftly. Living through this moment has been likened to moving from monochrome into multicolour, as if this brave new world now offered everything – especially individual feeling and emotion – at a heightened level. While in broad terms this narrative of a straight trajectory into the future seems unproblematic,[2] the truth is that it is a time of stark incongruities.

In Ireland, this zeitgeist's manifestation can be traced to a handful of major developments in the early 1960s particularly. While the arrival of Radio Telefís Éireann in 1963 allowed Ireland to view a world beyond itself, it was also a means – as radio had been before it – for the nation to imaginatively connect with the disparate elements of its own makeup. John F. Kennedy's presidential visit to Ireland, also in 1963, was important

225

in reconfiguring Ireland's position on an international political stage.[3] And yet, JFK's story of success was also read as having deep local resonances. His obvious embodiment of youthful hope, of the future itself, struck a chord of change for many ordinary people, precisely marking the generation gap between youth and age. Economically, too, Ireland opened itself up to the fluctuations of the international marketplace, which would materially drive development and progression.[4] The manifestation of this new economic reality was Ireland's joining the then EEC in 1973. Culturally this was significant in that it reimagined Ireland's relationship to the world beyond the simple binary of the colonial relationship with Britain on one side and America on the other. Of course, this move into the future was, in fact, a remembrance of Ireland's past and its position within a Europe of which it had always been an integral part. Other incongruities emerge with the opening up of the Irish world, which actually brings into extreme focus the old arguments surrounding tradition and modernity, altering what had become the redundant either-or terms of the debate. Advances in travel and technology made the world a smaller place and easier to access; but it also made Ireland, as an atavistic homeplace, easier to access. And while wealth did come to the country, it existed side by side with 'squalor and neglect',[5] making even more palpable the class divisions within Ireland.

With regard to Irish writing, there was a prevailing sense that it, too, might transform itself within this all-prevailing mood for change. Academic Augustine Martin in his wide-ranging and confidently argued essay 'Inherited Dissent: The Dilemma of the Irish Writer' suggested that the New Ireland now emerging demanded a new relationship between the artist and her/his world, one more subtle than the total opposition which appeared to be the dominant paradigm for the previous generation. Only with this new relationship might new forms come into being and new creative energies be unleashed. Importantly, too, Martin realised the dire need for a native tradition in literary criticism, juxtaposed with the work of the writers, which might shape the arguments and the terms by which that work could be read and understood productively.[6]

What marks this period off from others is the sheer diversity of the novels being written from romantic, realistic and postmodern positions.[7] Undoubtedly many writers self-consciously attempted to reimagine the limits of the Irish novel, openly embracing experimentation with content and form, trying to harness some of the energies of the moment. Benedict Kiely's (1919–2007) *Dogs Enjoy the Morning* (1968) captures the vigour unleashed in the rapidly changing Ireland of the 1960s when, it seemed, anything might be possible. Kiely returns to the verve of the early picaresque genre with realism being gleefully abandoned, and Ireland becoming the site of the fantastic, a place of mad freedom and escape.[8] Myth and legend are easily interchangeable with the realities of life in the invented midlands town of Cosmona, wonderfully situated between the poles of Irishness: the city of Dublin, the west and the North. Of course, Cosmona is a version of Cosmos and thus the town is meant to be a nowhere and an everywhere simultaneously and most definitely connected to a wider world:

But we got enough Art said, to fill a book or the *News of the World*. All human life is here. Count our many blessings, count them one by one. A white cock that can shake hands. A darling girl that saw a ghost. A tinker woman can dance on the seat of a chair while her husband holds the back-rung of the chair between his teeth. A dying man who was kicked by the Japs into the River Kwai. A Peeping Tom performing in full view of all.[9]

Such formal free rein reflects that newfound confidence in an Irish culture caught between modernity and tradition, with the mood being one of unambiguous celebration.[10]

The ultra-modern world of journalistic television in Ireland's RTE is the focus of John Feeney's (1948–84) *Worm Friday* (1974). Feeney mixes Marxist theory with Catholic doctrine in his efforts to offer a heady critique of little Ireland and its petit-bourgeois desires. But, as a contemporary reviewer pointed out, Feeney's novel is impressed with that provincialism he sets out to attack.[11] It is a novel clearly demonstrating the difficulty of being too up to date, and rather than being art it becomes a medium for settling personal scores and gently mocking the chattering classes. Francis Stuart continued to carve out his own peculiar existentialist space. Mirroring his own life, his characters take up a series of extreme positions as in *Memorial* (1973) and *Hole in the Head* (1977). *Black List, Section H* (1971), a fictionalised account of his youth and his wartime choices and activities, demonstrates clearly his inability to actually confront himself directly by creating this third-person narrative in order that he may distance himself from this previous self. His fictional evasions continue to fascinate because they offer an insight into a truly flawed humanity. It is the reader who for once possesses more knowledge than the novelist. Still, there is a whiff of real danger and real sulphur from his writing because of the obvious comparisons that might be made to the violence of the North in this period. Bryan McMahon's (1909–98) *The Honey Spike* (1967) also tries to embrace a certain vitality with its focus on the world of the Irish traveller: the honey spike of the title being a lucky hospital that Breda Claffey wants to reach in order to give birth to her first child. It says much about the development of

Irish society – its progress towards normalisation – that this particular social group's travails are of interest, their everyday struggles being so obviously alien to the middle-class reader. Originally a play, the emphasis is on the language of the travellers, its idiosyncrasies and rhythms. The poetry of Synge has been updated and shifted to a marginalised group which now becomes the focal point of exotic interest for the urbane reader.

Others writers of the time, such as Anthony C. West (1910–88) in *The Ferret Fancier* (1963), dealing with life in the rural world of Northern Ireland, is content to continue telling stories of youthful sexual awakenings, linking fertile nature with the ripe emotions of puberty.[12] Anthony Cronin (1928–) in his novel *The Life of Riley* (1964) celebrates the mad bohemian life of the 1950s Irish literary scene, continuing to manufacture and promote that hard-drinking image of the writer that would become so popular subsequently. This novel and the much more interesting memoir *Dead as Doornails* (1976) paints a picture of the male artist (there are no women writers of note) being anecdotally embedded in his world and culture. Even as he presents this impression of a world vital and energetic, it is a public role that the new generation of Irish writer would warily renounce. Christy Brown's (1932–81) *Down all the Days* (1970), a fictionalised version of his life, which had already been the focus of his 1954 autobiography *My Left Foot*, is another reimagining of Dublin in the rare old times. The poverty is undoubtedly real and his disability is real, but in many ways the novel perpetuates a type of sentimental Irishness that would appeal to a wide bourgeois audience in search of a gritty realism combined with lyrical acuity. Indeed, there is a great emphasis on the power of the imagination to transcend the bleak actuality of the world, reflected in Brown's diversions into poetry and the dramatic form.[13] Nevertheless, this is basically an urban revision of the sturdy romantic peasant that had such a grip on the literary imagination from the early nineteenth century onwards.

What marks off these works is the retreat into the past, into the 1940s and 1950s, as if attempting to drive a wedge between the world that was then and the world that is now. Elevating that particular moment in recent Irish history to the level of the searingly authentic and the site of heroic endurance is a view that still persists into the contemporary moment. More worryingly it indicates a resolute indifference – by the reader and by the novelist – to here-and-now realities. Always, it seems, the Irish novelist – in the main – appears unable or unwilling to contemplate the present moment with the same kind of penetrating intensity that the past warrants. But, of course, in a world of rapid change even the present and the recent past become historic very quickly.

The fiftieth anniversary of the 1916 Rising put the act of commemoration centre stage in Irish culture in the mid-1960s. Public acts that celebrated Ireland's history and the women and men who fought and died for independence were actually a stark reminder of modernity rather than a wilful wallowing in the past. Commemorative acts are a mechanism allowing for a clear demarcation between what is done, and of the past, and the myriad tasks of the here and now and the future.[14] Novelists, of course, reflected this general interest and, as James Cahalan argues, the sense of prosperity and confidence meant that the Irish past and historical events in the form of reassuring, affirmative images might be viewed in a more detached manner than had previously been possible.[15] A consequence is that Irish history is made safe for cultural consumption at home and abroad, as the broad sweep of public memory becomes the site of personal narratives in the novel form: Irish history, in short, is demythologised as it is humanised. The contradiction is that as the past becomes more distanced and unfamiliar, it is repackaged in a form that necessarily brings the reader closer to events and to emotions. But a consequence of making history intimately familiar within the novel is that the motivations for action – personal and political – have their source in the moment of writing rather than in the historical past. Something is gained – access – but something is also profoundly lost in these acts of writing.

Iris Murdoch's (1919–99) novel *The Red and the Green* (1965) offers a family story amid the backdrop of the week leading up to the 1916 Easter Rebellion. All the divided loyalties between England, Ireland, republicanism and nationalism are brought to the fore with the often-stilted lessons of Irish history being offered as dinner table conversation.[16] The demands of various plot lines – love affairs across class and religious lines – jar with the preordained movement of wider public events. For all the characters, though, from all sides of the argument, the pertinent moral question is the Yeatsian one concerning the realm of action and how to be a part of it, and being a part of transformative history. Margot Gayle Backus reads the novel as a companion to Elizabeth Bowen's *The Last September*,[17] through the liberated figure of Frances Bellman who equates, as Lois did, Ireland with being a woman: 'Everyone says you're important and nice, but you take second place all the same' (Murdoch, *The Red and the Green*, p. 32). While reading gendered relations as a means of commenting on and subverting the status quo of both nationalist and imperial Ireland is useful and certainly the hint at incestuousness is potentially explosive, what is most apparent is how Frances destabilises not only gender but also the rigid sense of class and position within the world of the novel which seems to conform to the various limited types of character permitted in Irish literature: among them Anglo-Irish, Catholic working-class, and rebel. Her attractiveness to many of the male characters suggests the destruction of this simple framework and the emergence of a much more varied and complex reality. She is yet another disturbing character in the mould of Edgeworth's Jason Quirke and Somerville and Ross's Charlotte Mullen: a character who disturbingly exists everywhere and nowhere simultaneously. The Yeatsian influence returns with the Rising itself presented as a casual comedy: an act that appears incomprehensible to ordinary Dubliners, an act that is but a moment away from farce.

James Plunkett (1920–2003), because of his own background in the labour movement, brings to his historical novel *Strumpet City* (1969) a raw sense of grievance at the injustices done to the proletariat, reminding his readers that even though the cause of nationalism became the dominant paradigm in the Irish grand narrative, there were other important stories to be told, other realities that required thought and recognition. The 1913 lockout, when capital crushed labour and when the intricacies of an Irish class system exploded the idea of national consensus, becomes the focal point for Plunkett's humane rendering of history. Plunkett's attempt at a panoramic vision of Irish society, a vision that would move easily between the high and low, is achieved through the juxtaposition of different narratives that, as the novel progresses, come together and unify.[18] The main interest though is on exposition and any overtly conscious aesthetic is absent: this is a story that must be told without any interference or obfuscation. This directness, perhaps, is what made the subsequent television adaptation hugely popular.

As James Cahalan contends, there is a pedagogic undercurrent in much of the historical novels of this period, linking them to the early nineteenth-century novel which was compelled not only to tell its own particular story but also the story of Ireland. The work of Walter Macken (1915–67) in his *The Silent People* (1962) and *The Scorching Wind* (1964) and Éilís Dillon (1920–94) in *Across the Bitter Sea* (1973) and *Blood Relations* (1977) conform to this formula, making use of footnotes, explanatory prefaces and glossaries to signal the explicitly historical nature of their narratives. Their work is thereby made accessible not only to an international audience but also to a new Irish audience: that of children.[19] Dillon's work also opens up a challenge to a merely male view of historical activity, focusing attention on the world of women and their acts of survival.[20]

Thomas Kilroy's (1934–) only novel, *The Big Chapel* (1971), attempts to deal with the nature of the Irish historical past in a much more sophisticated manner. It is a novel of ideas based on true events in nineteenth-century Kilkenny, showing how a certain conception of hegemonic Catholicism came to the fore from the 1870s onwards, obliterating any local input. This incident had also been the focus of Francis MacManus's *The Greatest of These* (1943). Cleverly Kilroy acknowledges the source of modern debates surrounding Church power in contemporary Ireland, seeing this local concern with a priest refusing to accept the edict of papal infallibility as a moment in time when a modern notion of Irish authority and Irish rebellion manifested itself.[21] The impossibility of the individual human voice, or mind, existing in such an oppressive milieu is made clear. Significantly, Kilroy shifts readers' focus away from the well-known historical signposts of famine and political rebellion towards a minor and marginalised story. Obviously, in a story such as this, the great currents of history manifest themselves as a local variation on a wider theme. Yet Kilroy, through his conscious mingling of different types of narrative – diary entries and letters – and acknowledging local folk narratives concerning the events, suggests how material realities of the past are made present through different narratives, and how history can never be sourced in one narrative alone. The result is a questioning of truth, a critique of how history is written as fact, and an opening up of the possibility of alternative truths and histories. In other words, this story of papal authority is a catalyst for a consideration of the notion of authority itself. Kilroy's dilemma, as it is for other writers of this period struggling to bring the realm of ideas into the novel, is to still be true to the demands of a form that prioritises the personal. At times, characters become mere ciphers for concepts, and therefore too predetermined to be vulnerably human. It is an ironic contradiction of the postmodern – in the realm of literature and of theory – that authors may enact chaos, randomness and indeterminacy: they can talk about it, but they, themselves, should not actually succumb to it or want to succumb to it. Thus, control of the material is essential, leaving very little room at times for any real challenge to the dominant epistemological position of progress and Enlightenment values. Where Kilroy would fail, other novelists would, however, succeed.

Seamus Deane argued that the continued existence of the Big House novel in Irish writing was an indication of a basic poverty in the Irish novelistic tradition itself.[22] Certainly, by the 1960s, whatever themes and concerns had been central to the Irish Big House novel of writers such as Elizabeth Bowen and Somerville and Ross seemed hopelessly out of date in a more egalitarian age, seemed to be narratives of a historical past rather than the demands of the immediate present. Yet, that image of style, even as it existed spectrally in the form of faded grandeur, continued to have a powerful hold on the popular Irish imagination as well as in the novel: the shell of the once despised Big House becoming the empty site of desire for the rising middle classes now coming into wealth and position. The poverty that Deane condemns is an imaginative one where nothing new is made within the vacated space and the past is uncritically mimicked in the present: the comfort of the known and the familiar far outweighing any wish to be challenging and innovative.

Nevertheless, it is precisely this reassurance of the conventional and the well known that attracts novelists of this period to the image of the Big House as they begin to critically engage with the novel form, begin to self-consciously test its boundaries and assumptions in an Irish context.[23] The Big House also became, consequently, the prism through which the past, or a certain version of the past, could be accessed. The established etiquette of the Big House novel offered a stable scaffolding that could be dismantled and deconstructed and reinvented at will by a writer such as Aidan Higgins (1927–) in his novel *Langrishe, Go Down* (1966).[24] Using the pervasive air of decay surrounding the Big House, Higgins's story of a 1930s Ascendancy family in decline transcends any local concerns and also transcends the labours of merely telling a story – which he does do, and does very well. His novel becomes a multi-layered narrative with Imogen, her sisters and her lover Otto, commenting on and critiquing the nature of public history and private memory, a metafiction concerned with analysing the act of writing itself.[25] The kind of distance from the material offered by this move towards metafiction by Higgins is of interest because it signals a challenge to the easy assumptions of knowledge and facts and the grand narratives that communities and individuals necessarily live by. In an Irish context, this exercise can be seen as an element of the revisionist approach to Irish history – then coming into vogue in the 1960s – that confronts the myths of nationalism exclusively. However, unlike the historians, the novelists suggest that there is no objective truth, no reality behind the myth being deconstructed.[26] Higgins's interest is in interrogating the processes of history as well as self-consciously interrogating how those historical narratives and myths are created. On a more intimate level, language and words are interrogated, their failure to connect with the world is eloquently highlighted.

Langrishe, Go Down was Higgins's most successful novel, after which his writing becomes far too guileful, far too painfully self-conscious of its own fictionality. He is unable to truly overcome the solipsistic corner into which his writing necessarily retreats. Other writers, though, were able to play with and consider similar themes and issues, while continuing to forge meaningful links to an audience. Such self-consciousness is on display in J. G. Farrell's (1935–79) novel *Troubles* (1970), the first of his Empire trilogy, linking his story of the dissipation of the Irish Big House to a 'wider post-modern and post-colonial discourse'.[27] One critic argues that Farrell's anxieties connect him to the powerlessness on display in Samuel Beckett's work.[28] Crucially, though, the local concerns of the novel in its bald recognition of the Anglo-Irish connection to Britain situate the Big House's deterioration to the decay of the British Empire itself.[29] Empire's link to modernity as a narrative of progression means that the Big House image becomes amenable to these postmodern/post-colonial readings: the perfect architectural structure wherein 'modern anxieties and displace-ments' can reveal themselves.[30] William Trevor (1928–) makes displacement central to his 1960s work – *The Old Boys* (1964), *The Boarding-House* (1965) and *The Love Department* (1966) – moving his focus to London and characters striving to feel at home.[31] In *The Silence in the Garden*(1988), he also turned to the Big House, offering a masterful engagement with the well-worn contours of the genre. This is an often self-conscious narrative about the nature of narrative itself, with different forms and discourses being employed in an attempt to map this singular family tragedy. Newspaper references mingle with local history, personal memory competes with the language of law and religion, and Sarah Pollexfen's diary punctu-ates the narrative as a constant reminder of the primacy of the personal realm and the search for an appropriate language and form that might contain all her losses. Silence, of course, as the acceptance of the limits of the human imagination and knowledge is never too far away. And silence, too, suggests the end of things, certainly the passing away of the Rolleston family. One area of particular interest is how Trevor, unlike most other writers who deal with the Big House, manages to represent the vibrancy of the world outside the demesne walls, acknowledging perhaps the dissipation of what Elizabeth Bowen labelled the centrifugal force of the Big House in Irish life and culture. All Trevor's writing is marked by a delicately pene-trating prose, its quiet exactitude mirroring perfectly the often quiet lives under scrutiny.

The other major factor at this time influencing both the production and the critical reading of the Big House novel, and of course, the Irish novel generally, is the explosion of violence in the North of Ireland from the late 1960s onwards. Any easy and unproblematic movement into the promised land of the future was brought to a shuddering halt. The Troubles infected all aspects and levels of Irish life and society, politics and culture: the very real violence of the times spilling over insidiously into the realm of ideas and discourse. Indeed, in many ways all other discourses and realms of activity in Ireland, North and South – economic, cultural and political – were to a greater or lesser degree dominated by the Troubles, colouring every action and every reaction.

That the reality of an Irish literary criticism began to materialise in the 1960s and 1970s, alongside the work of artists, is important because a major consequence of the Northern situation was that much genuine debate was sidelined in favour of appallingly extreme thinking. Historical revisionism, which also took in the realm of literature, came to prominence, with Ireland's past blamed for the horrors of Ireland's present. Tenuous links were made between Ireland's history and the present moment of conflict and were transformed into hard immovable facts. Thus, the kind of culture wars that went hand in hand with the emergence of critical and literary theory in the Academic world of the 1960s, 1970s and 1980s possessed an extra layer of meaning and interpretation in an Irish context. The result was, and in many respects still is, that literary issues became bound irrevocably to political concerns, often distorting any proper engagement with art in general and the novel in particular.

The unleashed energies of the conflict in the North of Ireland injected an urgency into the Big House novel that, as evidenced from the recent work of Elizabeth Bowen and Aidan Higgins, traded on varieties of languidness and lack of exigency that echoed their critique of a people and a place out of time. Jennifer Johnston's take on the Big House, in *How Many Miles to Babylon?* (1974) and *The Captains and the Kings* (1972), must be read from this present-centred perspective to be fully appreciated. Though set during the First World War, *How Many Miles to Babylon?* offers the contemporary moment a way to imagine Protestant and Catholic, Anglo-Irish and Irish coming together in a shared humanity that might be a way for unionism and nationalism to find an accommodation in the North of Ireland. Yet, the novel ends with the death of Catholic Jerry and the probable death of Protestant Alec: their relationship across the divide cannot be allowed to be. Despite the desire for connection and unity, the imagery of the novel indicates only how strange their being friends actually is. At home, the site of their companionship is the outdoors, away from the oppressive architecture of the Big House, away from the gaze of the village community. As in *The Captains and the Kings*, there is a hint of homosexual love between the protagonists, never consummated but a palpable undercurrent none-theless. Of course, this subversive gendering of the contact between the two undermines the rigid vision of both empire and nation, but also serves to situate any potential link between the two communities as something that might occur only on the margins of the exotic and erotic. The wish for a normative image is lost in the midst of a relationship made utterly exceptional. This is compounded with the figure of Alec from the Big House being an artist figure – thoughtful and sensitive – while Jerry remains, mostly, a Dionysian figure of action. In other words, even as Jerry wishes for the republican ideal of bringing all the disparate elements within Irish culture and politics together,[32] the hoped-for form of union and rapprochement remains simply aspirational. It is the same by the close of *The Captains and the Kings*, the relationship, the love, between the boy and the man made wholly strange, and thus union remains beyond the realm of possibility.[33]

That both novels revolve round the First World War says much about how that event looms large in the Protestant imagination within Ireland: the consequences of its fated devastation of a generation reverberating into the present. The Great War is presented as fatalistically tragic while in *How Many Miles to Babylon?* the rebel cause in Ireland escapes deep scrutiny, suggesting, perhaps, an unconscious support for its aims of liberation. Johnston's technique is unadorned and direct, a powerfully dispassionate perspective recording without judgement events and emotions. Still though, the impression is one of the Great War being presented as a myth, a sacred object, the actualities and reasoning of it outside the zone of questioning and critique: it just is. Irish republicanism and the Easter Rebellion, on the other hand, are very much within historical discourse and their rights and wrongs are to be opened up to discussion and debate. Of course, these novels themselves become an element in the process of mythologising not only the First World War but also, more crucially, the relationship between Protestant and Catholic, nationalist and unionist, within the Irish space, suggesting that these types – aristocrat and peasant – are the only roles conceivable. All the implications of this relationship – master versus slave, style versus chaos – are thus re-inscribed, taking on the power of a natural force.

The Big House novel is not alone in being invigorated by the violence of the North. Elmer Kennedy-Andrews demonstrates how the 'Troubles' novel exploded into view from 1969 onwards: the violence of the times allowing for politics and romance to profitably intermingle in the sphere of literature. He shows how remarkably defined genres are mapped onto the Northern conflict: the political thriller, or the 'romance across the barricades', for instance, moving the novel easily between high and low themes and concerns. Thus what Kennedy-Andrews labels as the 'trash' literature of Gerald Seymour's *Harry's Game* (1975) or Jack Higgins's *The Savage Day*

(1972) can exist side by side with the more aesthetically engaged work of Terence de Vere White's (1912–94) *The Distance and the Dark* (1973) and Benedict Kiely's novella *Proxopera* (1977). While many of these works obviously widen the focus of relationships beyond aristocrat and peasant, the basic colonial assumptions of that template still dictate the approaches to the North by novelists and by critics alike. Kennedy-Andrews's illuminatingly succinct introduction to his work offers a very useful overview of varying critical perspectives on the Northern Irish novel.[34] The issues he focuses on, surrounding the deployment of realism in the novel – identity and misrepresentation, humanism, postmodernism and the position of women – are not exclusive to the six counties of Northern Ireland however. Rather, the extremity of the situation brings these concerns to the fore, demonstrating how ideas, assumptions and positions that seem so clear and unproblematical elsewhere do not operate with the same alacrity in the Irish scene. Thus liberal theories and aesthetics fail to find purchase in an Irish world where the colonial hierarchies are still being played out for real on the streets of Belfast and Derry in the 1960s and 1970s. How to render violence, either as something acceptable or unacceptable within the novel, causes incongruous positions to be taken as no writer or reader can find an appropriate distance from which to view the unfolding political and personal narratives of the North. The question, then, is one of civility or barbarity, as writers and commentators try to understand the failures at the level of politics and culture that leads to such violence in the modern moment.[35]

Thomas Flanagan's (1923–2002) *The Year of the French* (1979) returns to the revolutionary moment of 1798 to consider the differences and conflict in 1970s Irish life from a historical detachment and framework. As an Irish-American academic whose *The Irish Novelists 1800–1850* (1958) was one of the earliest critical engagements with the novel form, he brings his formidable knowledge to bear upon his story of rebellion in County Mayo. His narrative consequently possesses knowledge of the density of society at the moment being written about, ranging between the last remnants of the Gaelic world, new middle-class Catholic characters, Anglo-Irish and English perspectives. The technique of employing different voices to tell the story from these different worlds, and consciously allowing different types of writing – from journal entries, to memoir, to an 'impartial' account – to be the vehicle for the unfolding narrative, interrogates not only the processes of history but also how history is mediated to us through writing and myth. His fiction is open to the nuances of the various power struggles between class and religion underlying much of the tensions within Irish society. While Flanagan, at times, is somewhat overly self-aware of his knowledge, knowing that the use of characters such as the historical George Moore might titillate his colleagues in the academic world, he does attempt to imitate the forms of the nineteenth-century novel. As was the case with the work of Lady Morgan for instance, Flanagan and his various narrators are unable to simply focus on this moment in time but have to frame it in a historical context. Even the self-conscious reference to the eighteenth-century French picaresque novel *Gil Blas* is an imitation of so much eighteenth- and nineteenth-century novels which were painfully aware of the need to allude to other, better-known, work. Certainly Flanagan's novel shares a tendency to the kind of luxurious long-windedness possessed of nineteenth-century writing.[36]

In many ways, a novel such as this, which struggles towards an epic overview, can be read as a secret history of the Irish novel itself, encapsulating all the themes, anxieties and techniques that have bothered Irish novelists from the nineteenth century to the present. The major impression given, of course, is that there is no such thing as a neutral narrative, nor are there any unbiased perspectives from which to write: the conflict of the 1798 rebellion and its violence continues on after its historical moment in the realm of ideology and discourse. The real conflict or power struggle within *The Year of the French* is centred around opposing versions of Ireland and Irishness and, ultimately, with an eye to the contemporary troubles, a questioning of the legitimacy of revolutionary violence itself. For the reader in the late 1970s, Flanagan's historical novel and its various levels of conflict would have seemed strangely and troublingly familiar. The Enlightenment notion of history as progress is shattered with the realisation that the debates and the issues of 1798 remain unresolved, continuing to torment the political and cultural scene in the present. Brian Friel's contemporaneous play *Translations* (1980) would also make this brilliantly obvious.

John Banville (1945–) also recognised that history was the site of nightmare in the Ireland of the 1970s. Avoiding the epic structure employed by Flanagan, he turned to the more local and potentially intimate image of the Big House precisely because it afforded him a convenient structure through which he might carefully contemplate his postmodern concerns with language, the act of writing and the ongoing dissolution of the modern person. The product of this is *Birchwood* (1973), perhaps one of the more incoherent Irish novels since Maria Edgeworth's *Castle Rackrent* (1800).[37] Despite Gabriel Godkin, the hero and narrator, being afforded a number of truly luminous revelatory moments and providing the novel with some of the more lucid sentences of recent Irish fiction, these cannot be brought together into a unified whole and the overriding impression is one of utter chaos. Banville is unable, or unwilling, to bridge the gap between the individual consciousness of his narrator and the objective world, and thus each lies on one side of an open wound throughout. The novel is quite blatantly a fiction, eschewing any pretence to realistic modes, at times bordering on the cartoonish.[38] The extremity of this points to an underlying crisis in Irish fiction and culture at this juncture. Other novelists such as Thomas Kilroy and Thomas Flanagan might hint at it, but consistently shy away from fully acknowledging it by still holding to the rules of shape, order and comprehensibility. *Birchwood* displays a very fluid sense of history, moving easily between different time periods, referencing numerous historical staging posts such as the famine and the War of Independence as occurring simultaneously.[39] The chaos of the novel reveals the anxieties of its moment: the supposed order of the Big House genre only serving to accentuate the fragile nature of authorial control within and without the novel. Gabriel Godkin's narrative is ultimately about the nature of writing and its relationship to that which is written about:

I began to write, as a means of finding them again, and thought that at last I had discovered a form which would contain and order all my losses. I was wrong. There is no form, no order, only echoes and coincidences, sleight of hand, dark laughter. I accept it.[40]

Control – authority – on both a communal and an individual level is what is central to *Birchwood*. That they are absent says much about the sense of catastrophe in the Ireland of the 1970s. The novel's obvious absurdity; its hovering on the limits of credulity being an indication not simply of postmodern playfulness but also of the inadequacy, the utter failure, of the forms, even the language, available to confront the realities of modern Ireland. History, the reader is being told, is not the site of nightmare, as it always is in the clichéd story of Ireland; rather, it is the present that is all too terrifying.

An obvious conclusion to be drawn from the work of John Banville is that history is a fiction – not that things did or did not happen, but that the past as mediated to us in the present through unstable acts of writing must be interrogated rather than blithely accepted as the truth. Another conclusion to be taken from Banville's writing is the reconfiguration of the public image of the Irish novelist. From his earliest writing to his most recent work, he focuses on, in various guises from the medieval scientist to the actor, writers writing fictions. It is a typical postmodern trope. However, this self-conscious concentration on the figure of the writer as serious artist is a counterpoint to the clownish figures of a generation earlier embodied in

Behan, Kavanagh and O'Brien. For if nothing else, Banville presents his characters, and by extension himself, as purveyors of high art and not merely entertainment. Thus, in an age when universal popularity is the only gauge of success, when the mass media of cinema and television necessarily communicate in broad terms to the widest of audiences, Banville champions a modernist return to an elite conception of art and writing. Of course, there exists an anxious uneasiness between these pretensions to exclusivity and a desire to engage with the economic success possible in the literary marketplace. While this is certainly something to be considered from the author's perspective, its most telling manifestation is with the critics of the novel acutely altering their critical engagement with the form in Ireland. Coupled with the ever-growing celebration of James Joyce as the most important international novelist in the twentieth century, this new conception of the novel as high art means that its important connection to the immediate moment, to 'news', is lost as a very rigid sense of what is high and low art is applied as a measure of worth. In that, however, Banville connects the contemporary Irish novel and novelist with the oldest of problems for the vulgar author who was always torn between the heavens and the earth, between the desire for a transcendent art and the realities of the completely disposable.

Still, the notion that novelists, and writers in general, need to take themselves seriously and need to be taken seriously within popular culture is an important one. For despite the amount of diverse fiction that was being written in this period, amid all this exciting change in the 1960s and 1970s, the view still persisted that the Irish novel form was in some way inadequate. Banville's novels manifest, and make as their theme, this sense of defectiveness and failure of art in the face of chaos. Sean O'Faolain, writing in 1962, continued to bemoan as he had done twenty years earlier not just how the novel's formal demands failed to reflect Irish realties but how that Irish reality itself does 'not supply the *dramatis personae*, ready for the hard conflicts'.[41] Yet, he also attacks writers who, as potential men and women of genius, might 'accelerate the processes of time for their country' for their collective inability to confront their material in new ways. Significantly, he declares that exile is no longer an option, nor is the sentimental celebration of Ireland and the Irish peasant or the Irish poor. O'Faolain is groping towards articulation here, striving for words or a formula that might effectively give shape to his diagnosis of the ills besetting Irish writing. He declares that an 'artist must, in some fashion, love his material'.[42] The implications of O'Faolain's concept of love in relation to the Irish novel has profound reverberations, not only colouring how writers have written in the last forty years but also, importantly, how commentators on Irish writing have framed those writers' efforts critically and theoretically. While he is unable to follow through on his own argument, it seems that for O'Faolain writers must possess some degree of respect for their material, some deep sense of its value and its worthiness for literary treatment. He recognises that Ireland's post-colonial positioning and its island status, always looking elsewhere for influence and ideas, means that the world beyond can easily become the object of an Irish writer's affection, the final and hoped-for destination of his or her art. But, for the writer to take, as he declares they must, 'the local . . . and universalise it', as James Joyce had brilliantly done,[43] then a newly minted regard for Ireland and Irish themes needs to be rediscovered.

Three writers of this period, particularly, John McGahern (1934–2006), Edna O'Brien (1930–) and John Broderick (1927–89), embody this new confidence, this belief in the value of their subject matter and the stories they have to tell. One reason for this, perhaps, is how these writers reflected the palpable shifts in wider culture by moving their focus away from the travails of the nation as evidenced in the historical fictions of this period towards the sovereignty of the individual. Thus their desire to present coherent individuals as heroes means, necessarily, that their stories insist they be taken seriously. And yet, this moment is also marked by a profound tension between the demands, and indeed the rights, of the individual in the context of a wider society. All commentators acknowledge that this era is one of social revolution, when governments and policy-makers began to enact changes in the way in which different sections of society should be treated. This is a time when people believed that there was such a thing as society and that its betterment was an achievable end.[44] The effect on the novel is that, rather than dealing with a singular hidden Ireland, its proper focus is multiplied and hidden Irelands and the individuals who escape traditional labels and stereotyping are now the object of the novel. Here, the growth of an Irish literary criticism and the coming of theory into the academy means that the interest generated by any given writer in this period can become compartmentalised into issues surrounding, for instance, gender, sexuality and history; or on the continued division between rural, urban or official versions of Ireland. Literature, then, for the critic cannot fully escape the mode of dissent that Augustine Martin perceived in the artist, its worth bound up in its challenges to conservative Ireland and its ability to be co-opted to polemic.[45]

Of course, for writers themselves, there is so much more to their work than being tied to this manufactured image of a crusader for justice or their work being yet another opportunity for public therapy, even if it is how they have been figured in both the popular and the critical imagination. Edna O'Brien's early trilogy, of which *The Country Girls* (1960) is the best known, is read as uncovering the reality of Irish life for a young convent-educated woman and her growth into sexuality. Certainly her picture of a male-dominated world whose authority, in all areas of life from the privacy of the home in the form of the father into the public world of Church and state, belittles the place of women and stifles their possibility for independence and expression.[46] Yet, what is disappointing is that, at one level, O'Brien merely apes the form of the Irish *Bildungsroman* as set out by an acknowledged hero of hers,[47] James Joyce in *A Portrait of the Artist as a Young Man*: sexuality and the sexual act being the central manifestation of growth and development. Unlike Molly Keane, for instance, who is capable of registering the very dark side of male and female sexuality, uncovering the real threat in sexual relations, Edna O'Brien even though she fulminates against patriarchal power actually re-inscribes it by slavishly viewing the world of sexuality from a male perspective, as if it were the only form of rebellion possible. She appears too bound to the potential of the scandalous and the shocking, just as many writers in this era of de rigueur sexual permissiveness strove to shock throughout this decade with references to the still taboo realm of sex.[48]

More significant, though, is how O'Brien, in the words of Declan Kiberd, through the 'unerring accuracy of her eye and the deft rightness of her phrase convinced many that here were believable, fallible, flesh-and-blood women, neither paragons or caricatures'.[49] This is her genuine achievement. In *Girl with Green Eyes* (1964),[50] some of the most striking passages are those detailing Baba and Kate's new life in Dublin, away from their homes in Clare. In her description of the loneliness of urban life, of the often deadening routine of work and the improvised nature of entertainment, O'Brien encapsulates brilliantly the drab reality – the fears and the anxieties – of everyday bourgeois existence. In reality, it is that life – in all its shades of monochrome – which her characters so desperately want to escape and not any specifically Irish world of repression. Part of O'Brien's success is her ability to tap into this general malaise and show how the act of rebellion can ultimately be an empty gesture. The real problem for Kate and Baba is not just that their world only offers limited roles for women but also that their access to a range of images of rebellion and possibility is also limited. Theirs is a failure of the imagination: they possess no radical model of emulation, other than some vague notions gleaned from romance novels of what life ought to be and how life should be lived. The consequence, then, is this single-minded pursuit of men and Kate's particular search for some kind of romantic hero who will remake the world anew for her. Other women writers would be more assured in their feminist critique of the male world. Julia O'Faolain (1932–) in *Godded and Codded* (1970) puts on display women who do come into power over the male world, whereas her *Women in the Wall* (1975), set in medieval sixth-century Gaul, shows the dire consequences for those who fail to do so.[51]

John Broderick's *The Pilgrimage* (1961) is a remarkable piece of writing largely because of the austere control the author exerts over his material. That the main character is gay and that his wife finds distraction in seedy sex, that indeed this is a world full of gay men and a world where the sexual act appears to be occurring everywhere, seems almost secondary to the detailing of this outwardly staid bourgeois existence. The pieties of Church must be publicly respected, as must the codes of decorum that bind the people of small-town Ireland together, even as they are being so obviously flouted in private. Certainly his writing is meant to shock, but at its core is not caricature or didacticism;[52] rather, it is marked by a quiet yet determined understanding of the real ambiguities that underpin modern Irish experience. The unmasking of hypocrisy is obviously an element of his writing,[53] and yet Broderick's genius is found in the way in which he expertly depicts the contradictions within all these characters, each of whom cleaves to opposing ideas and actions without rendering themselves utterly immobile.

Michael, the husband, is bed-ridden with crippling arthritis and his planned pilgrimage to Lourdes for a cure is the ghostly presence driving the action gently forwards. Of course, most of the characters do not believe that any cure is forthcoming: after all this is a modern, rational age and the power that pilgrimage has over the contemporary imagination is little. Even the priest, illuminatingly drawn by Broderick with the detailing of his verbal and physical tics, retreats into the mantra of hope rather than expectation. Reinforcing this decided lack of the potentially miraculous is the depiction of the drab claustrophobia of Michael's room, the house and the midlands town of Athlone. The reader, perhaps subconsciously, desires that this trip to Lourdes take place, as it would offer, at least, an exotic variation or vacation from this all-too-gloomy Irish reality. That hoped-for relief never arrives, though the final one-sentence chapter is devastatingly brilliant: 'In this way they set off on their pilgrimage, from which a week later Michael returned completely cured.'[54] The seeds of a magic realism are evident here with this ending highlighting how the miraculous and the mundane can coexist. Of course, it is not followed through, as if to emphasise formally the repressed nature of Irish life. Broderick himself felt that the Irish Catholic bourgeoisie had never been truly captured in the novel form and that his own work would do so.[55] Thus, despite the desire to lay bare double standards, he also wants to concede how complicated Irish Catholicism in the contemporary moment might actually be. In other words, while hypocrisy is undoubtedly central to the world being rendered here, it is not wholly conscious. Rather, these characters do not have the privileged access to the knowledge of their duplicity that the reader possesses. Theirs, perhaps, is a sincere insincerity, the ambivalence of their belief making them entirely ordinary, and utterly human.

Joe Cleary believes that the naturalism of these novelists is simply not radical enough to represent adequately the contemporary age, that rather than enact any real moments of liberation these works actually reflect, in their aesthetic and formal conservatism, the grim reality they wish to defy.[56] Such an interpretation is possible – indeed completely valid – only if it is accepted that the proper object of the artist and their art is to engage only with social and historical commentary. Cleary is aware that what is being enacted is a 'repudiation of history and all its false hopes and empty promises',[57] but is unable to accept that this might be anything other than a sign of failure on the part of the writer. In reality, of course, the artist does not have to embrace the role of social commentator. George O'Brien also suggests that this generation of writers' work is marked by the move away from the public sphere into the realm of the private, away from plot towards personality.[58] This, in itself, is an act of rebellion in a country where the prospect of privacy seems impossible within the often claustrophobic confines of a culture that demands conformity to public codes – both secular and religious. The need for a private space is obviously a sign of modernity and the construction of an authentic character, or self, becomes the object of the individual, artist or not. Needless to say, despite the overt rejection of public history in favour of private histories, the tension in much of this work comes from the pressures that both realms make on the other. History, or context, can never be fully denied, but neither can the basic absurdities of the human condition, a condition that never perfectly fits into any system or theory.

Perhaps the best writer to exemplify these tensions is John McGahern (1934–2006). From his earliest writing he hollowed out a fictional world – in both the novel form and the short story – that reflected his desire to simply tell his readers about the world 'as it is', with all the precision and the clarity that his well-chosen words might generate. In the short story 'Swallows', a character declares: '[We] don't have to concern ourselves with the justice or the injustice. Only the accurate presentation of the evidence.'[59] In many ways, this is a comment on McGahern's own technique, giving voice to ordinary life as it is lived in Ireland and allowing that life to be offered to the reader unmediated by perspective or comment. Certainly, a function of art is to do just that: to capture and to hold on to visions of the world and the human engagement with it in the face of the constant ebb and flow that is existence. And yet the irony of his writing is that rather than simply uncovering, or laying bare, he manages to reinstate a sense of mystery into existence, hinting at that which lies outside language – a knowledge that hovers dimly beyond consciousness – however exact the words chosen. His first novel, *The Barracks* (1963), focusing on the death of Elizabeth Reegan, can be understood to operate on the level of metaphor: her physical death from cancer is mirrored in her spiritual death amidst an intellectually arid environment.[60] But it is the fragile nature of human existence itself, with life being but a thread that can snap at any moment, which comes to dominate the novel. Elizabeth recognises, just at the moment of her death, 'This sense of belonging' both to the world of nature and to each other, which is central to being-in-the-world. But there is a stark difference between knowing and definitively articulating that knowledge, for she asks a question for which there is no final answer: 'What was she doing? What was it all about?'[61] People have no real knowledge of the natural world that goes on without them, goes on existing in spite of them. Yet that natural must be mediated nonetheless: through acts of saying. This anxious sense of essential requirement is the energy that drives all McGahern's writing: there is nothing else to be done in this all-too-human world. Elizabeth's death is a falling away from the appreciation of worldly attachment. The final scene is set in the barracks kitchen with Elizabeth facing her extinction alone. The once central presence of her being fades in the last chapter of the novel, the world of the living and their rituals cruelly turning attention away from her life, and her death. McGahern's vision is not of some sentimental secular humanist reconciliation with the world that must be simply accepted and loved.[62] Rather, what his readers come to recognise is that the world is a harsh, often brutal, and certainly vicious place and that any final reconciliation may never actually be possible.[63]

The Dark (1965) furthers this analysis of the individual self, its narrative technique of moving between the 'I', 'he' and 'you' to tell the story of young Mahoney, suggesting the complex flux of identity not just in youthful formation but also as it is in motion within the world.[64] Like Joyce's Stephen Dedalus, Mahoney is paralysed by the prospect of having to choose a life and thereby bring to an end infinite possibility. His inability to enter the life of the university is an inability to move from the private world of the family into the public realm. It is but one instance of the failure of the national idea in McGahern's work. The family is the fulcrum round which his stories operate, and for McGahern each family is its own republic, with its own authority, set of codes, language and manners. The collective idea of nation can have little purchase in this reality. *The Dark* presents a male-dominated world,[65] the effects of his father's sexual, physical and psychological abuse perhaps obscuring any clear insight or epiphany that young Mahoney may be offered at the close of the novel.[66] This flirting with the impossibility of knowledge and revelation, this epistemological gloom, adds another layer to the darkness that pervades the work. It quietly, yet disturbingly, challenges the expectations of the traditional novel form that accelerates towards exposure.

McGahern's writing is popularly linked to the midland locations of Leitrim and Roscommon. To a certain extent this is true of the novels, but his short stories – in an interesting way – seemingly possess a wider scope charting both the rural scene and the urban world of Dublin. His stories deal with the loves and the frustrations of the middle classes: the civil servants, the teachers, those who have inherited an independent Ireland after revolution. Yet, McGahern is consciously aware of the profound links between the urban and the rural space in Ireland and in his writing the supposed differences between countryside and city melt away. This is most apparent in his novel *The Leavetaking* (1974/rev. 1984), which deals with the sacking of a young schoolteacher from his job. The revised edition of the novel stresses the importance of the action taking place on a single day. The teacher mulls over his own youth, and particularly the death of his mother, while also considering his more recent past in London and his falling in love with and marriage to an American woman. Thus in Joycean fashion, one day becomes everyday, possessing all the significance that any life might possess. What is of interest is how his wife Isobel's story is similar to that of the protagonist, in that her father is a selfish man, as is the protagonist's father. Significantly, though, there is the detail she offers of an instance when the father masturbated himself against her in bed when she was twelve years of age.[67] This is what happens to the young boy in *The Dark*, though the act is never given a name. Beneath the surface differences between the sophisticated world of New York, of modernity and wealth, and the life of rural Ireland is the same story of base instincts at work.

On a number of occasions throughout the novel it is stated that: 'It happened this way and no other way' (McGahern, *The Leavetaking*, p. 151). While this might be simply read as signalling the dominance of a naturalistic fate that cannot be overcome, it is also an acknowledgement that McGahern desires that his art be true to the pressures of life as it is lived. His writing returns a sense of the quiet importance of the world and the human life in that world to the act of Irish writing, recognising that mystery and significance is not to be found elsewhere, but in the here-and-now reality of the everyday. In this excavation of the individual, and his focus on a single day and the overt absence of the grand narrative of history, McGahern hints at a radical move towards a new type of narrative, a new type of novel. He understands that conventional plot is far too predetermined, too fixed, and too teleological for Irish reality. Rather than embrace some form of novelistic destiny, McGahern is attempting to render an authentic openness to the world, and a profound openness to experience, in his writing.

Seamus Deane's Reading in the Dark *and the rebel act of interpretation*

Remember me when I am gone away,
Gone far away into the silent land;
When you can no more hold me by the hand,
Nor I half turn to go yet turning stay.

(Christina Rossetti)

Confusion is at the heart of Seamus Deane's (1940–) only novel, *Reading in the Dark* (1996). It hovers elusively between numerous narrative genres – the ghost story, detective fiction, the Gothic, and *Bildungsroman* – never finally settling on any single one. This uncertainty is central to the story itself with knowledge and knowing being the objects of desire in Deane's novel as his unnamed narrator searches for the truth at the heart of the secret that troublingly haunts his family. Amplifying this ambiguity is how Deane chooses to render his story through the conventions of the novel form and not as an autobiography or memoir, despite the story's genesis in reality and lived experience. In this manoeuvre, perhaps, can be discerned Deane's main preoccupation in *Reading in the Dark*; namely, a meditation on the nature not only of how stories are made but also the centrality of the act of reading and interpretation. In this latter concern, the author is being true to his day job as one of the pre-eminent literary critics of his generation. In a brilliant rethinking of the Irish scene, Deane recognises how debilitating the image of the stereotypical Irish person as artist figure has been in Irish writing: the figure who is the romantically sensitive type, the spendthrift with words, an unthinking poet who creates unknowingly, unthinkingly, leaving the important act of understanding and interpretation to others. There is power in creation, without a doubt, but there is also sovereignty to be located in the acts of reading and analysis.

This novel, of course, must be bound to the realities of the world out of which it was written, and the oppression – economic, cultural and sectarian – of Derry in the 1940s and 1950s depicted here obviously brings into sharp, pristine focus concerns with power and authority central to the novel. A talk by a British army priest given to the boy and his classmates goes to the heart of the struggle: 'Were you to view the Foyle Basin from Binevenagh ... you would begin to appreciate both the beauty and the strategic importance of the dramatic landscape and seascape in which your city rests.'[1] The title of this particular vignette, 'Political Education', makes clear what it is at stake: the power to see, to know, is conditional and the implication is that boys in the class will never have such a perspective because of their position of subservience and obedience.[2] Whereas the priest, with his grand perspective, can easily soar over all obstacles and barriers, those not afforded such a point of view must necessarily deal with the constraints of borders, thresholds and crossings of which there are many in the novel. What the narrator is forced to contend with is a constantly encroaching geographic world – real life experienced at street level – with various landmarks dotting the scene, looming large in the imagination, demanding to be negotiated.

Critics are drawn inevitably to evaluating *Reading in the Dark* as a novel of the Northern Troubles, a novel that will necessarily reflect Deane's background (coming from nationalist Derry) and his political concerns as expressed in his acts of criticism: the autobiographical strain suggesting, perhaps, the desire to connect his personal story, his family story, with the story of Ireland itself. Yet, the moment of the contemporary Troubles comes only at the end of the novel, rushed over in the final pages as if the author wants to telescope these events and move away from them, acknowledging his failure to find a language or form that might contain them. Indeed, in a novel that plays with various types of haunting and where the spectral is always palpably present, it is worth noting that one of the more strange images comes at the close of the novel in the 1970s when the narrator, now a grown man, wakes up on a return to his Derry home to the clip-clop sound of horses' hooves outside his bedroom window: 'As though in a dream, I watched a young gypsy boy jog sedately through the scurf of debris astride a grey-mottled horse' (*Reading in the Dark*, pp. 232–233). The present is not a place of hard facts, and as with the past it, too, is a site of potential ghosts and strange disconnected apparitions. It is a feature of the novel as a whole that it lacks the unity expected from the traditional novel: a certain sense of coherent progression is lacking. While the story of the family secret offers the underlying and binding pattern of order to the book, the book is still a gathering together of disjointed and fragmented scenes that have little or nothing to do with the progression of the novel as whole. Episodes such as 'Rats', 'Maths Class', 'The Facts of Life' and 'Katie's Story', for instance, are interesting in and of themselves but with apparently nothing to do with the wider tale being told. There are many names to grapple with, many different stories to encounter and contend with, such as Katie's story of Frances and Francis whose connection with the narrator's story is not fully apparent at a first glance – if there is a connection at all. Numerous types of stories are embedded in the main story, with many references to myth and legend: the folklore surrounding Grianan fort, for example, as well as Katie's story. There are, too, many times to consider: the present, the past and how they relate to one another, if at all. The title of one chapter is 'Rats: November 1950' but the first sentence begins: 'It was the winter of 1947, the snow had covered the air-raid shelters out in the back field' (*Reading in the Dark*, p. 77). One date appears to challenge and undermine the other. Each chapter and episode is laboriously dated: the narrative is set to move inexorably into the future along a strictly chronological line from beginning to end; and yet, undercutting this progress are these various narratives mentioned and the fact that as the main story moves forwards, the young narrator is drawn ever more backwards into the past and the unearthing of his family secret.

As with so many Irish novels, an integral element of *Reading in the Dark* at the level of meta-narrative is how it traces the struggle towards being a novel. These episodes are like short stories, offering only limited and intimate sketches of the young boy's life. The boy's dilemma, as it is Deane's, is in coming into the position of authority, power and perspective that a global vision might provide. Yet, the emphasis is always on the act of reading rather than creation or writing. In other words, while the critics desire to make grand statements about the novel's concerns and themes, the novel itself acknowledges its failure to supply such a viewpoint on the violence of the Troubles.

Part of the problem is the continuous requirement for the boy to negotiate a world that is in constant motion. *Reading in the Dark* is obviously self-consciously concerned with the act of storytelling itself, as it is with reading. What is interesting is that none of these stories cancel the others out: all are possible simultaneously. For example, the myth surrounding the 'Field of the Disappeared':

There was a belief that it was here that the souls of all those from the area who had disappeared, or had never had a Christian burial . . . collected three or four times a year – on St. Brigid's Day, on the festival of Samhain, on Christmas – to cry like birds and look down on the fields where they had been born. Any human who entered the field would suffer the same fate. (*Reading in the Dark*, p. 53)

These legends reinforce the power and hold of the boy's own family mystery on his imagination: they are, perhaps, comments on his own story, as his is a comment on these myths and legends. In the chapter 'Reading in the Dark', the young boy talks of the first novel he ever read, *The Shan Van Vocht*, and its tale of heroes from the past. Juxtaposed with this type of story is a model essay read out in school by his teacher. The extraordinary is placed next to a detailed vignette of the ordinary and the everyday of an evening in a country farmhouse: 'Then there would be no talking, just the ticking of the clock and the kettle humming and the china dogs on the mantelpiece looking, as ever, across at one another' (*Reading in the Dark*, pp. 20–21). The young boy is drawn to this 'Dutch Interior' as he calls it. Perhaps its tranquillity is attractive in comparison to the flux of his own world, and while this picture of a country kitchen encapsulates a certain stillness, it still throbs with the energy of life as it is lived. It is a lesson for the boy, and for the reader, that despite the appearance of adventure and excitement in the story of his uncle Eddie's disappearance, a more authentic story might be found in the mundane world of the everyday.

What becomes very clear is that acts of criticism, of interpretation, are continually required: stories are never just simply stories. The Field of the Disappeared, for instance, takes on an added resonance as the main story unfolds and is afforded an added layer of meaning when related to Uncle Eddie's disappearance. Myth, which may seem distant, has reverberations much closer to home. Some of the parallel stories show that stories do not necessarily lead to the truth; rather, they deliberately obscure truth. Stories can conceal, as well as reveal. Thus the myths surrounding the various landmarks and places are narrative layers laid over original actualities, making painful reality palatable or, perhaps, communicable. The ghostly presences and hauntings within the novel also act in this way, suggesting how the past is never over and done with, how it necessarily lingers on to trouble the present.[3]

Central to *Reading in the Dark* is the slow uncovering of Eddie's story. It might be expected that the end of the novel when all is made clear for the boy would be presented as a triumph: that he, and the reader, should celebrate his discoveries and thus his maturity. This, though, is not allowed to happen. Eddie's story, of course, revolves round the issue of loyalty and betrayal, of informing against his comrades. But betrayal and loyalty are also central to the boy's own act of reading. As he says: 'Staying loyal to my mother made me disloyal to my father' (*Reading in the Dark*, p. 225). Gaining knowledge only results in driving a wedge between himself and both his parents. Stories, as acts of communication, are usually thought to connect people, not set up barriers between them. The boy's persistence alters his relationship with his parents. The father tells the narrator and his brother Liam some more of the 'truth' surrounding Eddie's disappearance: 'For once I knew more than he did. Than either of them did. It was like being a father to both of them, knowing more' (*Reading in the Dark*, p. 133). It is a curious remark: hinting at power, control, and dominance. The traditional roles are reversed quite starkly.

Despite the obviously negative connotations for the society which this story comes from, the narrator of *Reading in the Dark* is the real informer because he tells the story and the act of doing so betrays his family: betrays their trust. And yet, he is being loyal to himself, loyal to his own desires and his own need to know and to understand. He is, then, being both loyal and disloyal. So, in order for him to gain power, to be himself, he must betray others. In a very subtle way, Deane challenges the expected trajectory of the modern bourgeois novel that celebrates the growth and development of the individual imagination above all else. Like James Joyce did in *A Portrait of the Artist as a Young Man*, Deane recognises the awful vista of alienation opening up for the narrator: an alienation that is initially chosen but must, in the end, be simply endured. Underscoring this is how the narrator is never given a name, as if the act of betrayal and disloyalty means that he is not deserving of one. The hoped-for final moment of empowerment, the triumphant naming of the self, is withheld.

It has been suggested that all of Seamus Deane's acts of critical writing are acts of autobiography.[4] Of course, to say that is to presume that the one who declares such a thing is above autobiography themselves, that their writing is supremely objective. Certainly Irish literary criticism and history over the last forty years has been very much bound to the political realities of a modernising Ireland and the advent of, or rather re-emergence of, the Troubles in the North of Ireland. It is natural that Deane's only novel would be read in the light of his own prominent critical interventions into Irish literary studies. To be sure, in this novel there is a powerful and significant confluence between art and the act of interpretation, so that the kind of power struggles inherent in all acts of saying and writing are interrogated and deconstructed. What becomes clear is that *all* acts of writing and saying might be thought of as disguised acts of memoir, as are all acts of reading: innocent detachment is never fully possible.

In the colonial relationship, it is the coloniser who perceives history as impersonal because it is a view that allows power to be wielded as a law of nature rather than an all too human construct. The narrator declares that:

'Hauntings are, in their way, very specific' (*Reading in the Dark*, p. 225). What the boy comes to know is that the grand narratives of history are never impersonal, nor should they be. His own story is a failed attempt to write history: all those precise dates suggest as much, but as the final pages acknowledge, it was something other than dates and facts that was the real goal. For in spite of the narrator coming into the realm of knowledge, he forfeits wisdom. At the close of the novel, the narrator is able to painfully admit failure in that he is still unable to fathom his father's silence, his innocence: 'I reconstructed his life out of the remains of the stories about his dead parents, his vanished older brother, his own unknowing and, to me, beloved silence. Oh, father' (*Reading in the Dark*, p. 226). The words 'Oh, father' – a stifled cry – betray the emotion that has been, at some level, curiously absent or repressed throughout. It is a signal, perhaps, of his own profound and stunned confusion: he now does not know what to think. Regardless of all his efforts, the boy still does not possess the significance of his discovered facts: truth, for him, can only be hinted at, as in that emotive intrusion into his narrative, and will always be just beyond his cognitive reach.

It is ironical that one of the major publishing phenomena of the contemporary moment in Irish writing has been the memoir and autobiography. Mostly these are closed to interpretation as the writers authoritively impose exact meanings on their past: their image of themselves is always heroic, conventional and unproblematic. Deane, however, chooses to do the opposite in his autobiographical fiction, and by being capable of interrogating himself and his own artistic and critical processes, truly opens up his version of the modern Irish hero to critique. And it is precisely that openness which is important in *Reading in the Dark*. While it has been said that the novel narrowly operates within a 'remarkably parochial and sectarian frame of reference',[5] this misses how Deane recognises fully the emotional and cultural limits of his narrator's perspective. Reorientating his vision towards the personal in this way is to begin to repossess the reins of narrative power, but to do so in a manner that complicates rather than liberates the individual.

To do this at the moment in the 1990s when it might have been thought that Ireland, in the midst of the developing peace process, had come into a position of objectivity to its past – had come to a moment when a reconciliation with its diverse pasts was possible – is to indicate the ongoing trauma of Irish colonial history. For that is the real lesson of *Reading in the Dark*: that we are all readers now. As the boy says about his own excited youthful reading: 'I'd switch off the light, get back into bed, and lie there, the book still open, re-imagining all I had read, the various ways the plot might unravel, the novel opening into endless possibilities in the dark' (*Reading in the Dark*, p. 20). The boy's story is not history but merely one human story among many possible human stories. While uncertain of wanting to make, or even the possibility of making, links to the wider Irish narrative, the implications are clear: Ireland's history is not fixed, finished or complete, there are always more stories to be told and more stories to be read.

CHAPTER 7

Brave new worlds: Celtic Tigers and moving statues, 1979 to the present day

> [C]onfusion is not an ignoble condition.
>
> (Brian Friel, *Translations*)

The last thirty years have undoubtedly been a time of rapid and concentrated transition within Irish society and culture. Every event that occurred over these years in the realm of culture, religion, politics and economics can be read as both a beginning and an end, heralding both the death of an old Ireland and the birth of the new. Certainly the language of progress and modernisation has dominated public discourse as a talisman of desire in the 1980s and the subsequent consensus that something of a break with the past, with tradition, had occurred in the 1990s: that the Irish world was now as it has never before been.[1] Of course, the more mundane truth is that every generation, being so close to events, cannot but view its own time as a moment of profound upheaval, as entirely and painfully new: thus modern Ireland's experience has always being presented as one of transformation and transition. Nonetheless, the rapidity of this change is notable not alone as an Irish but as a global phenomenon. In Ireland, as a consequence, there persists a perverse fascination with excavating the present moment as thoroughly unique in its manifestations of uncharted confusion and trauma. As a result, not since James Joyce articulated the peculiarities of the late nineteenth-century renaissance moment as both the familiar and the foreign has the present seemed so very strange.

The novel form, in its original manifestations so bound as it must be to the new, is perhaps best suited to deal with and register these fluctuations. While it would be easy to declare that there has been an upsurge in the production of the Irish novel in this period – because there has been such an upsurge – mirroring economic growth, more interesting is how seriously the contemporary Irish novel is now taken by critics who, in acquiescing wholeheartedly to the zeitgeist, cannot escape the pervasive impression that all has changed utterly.[2] It is remarkable how studied and theorised the contemporary novel is when compared to novels from previous times and centuries, the implication being, of course, that Ireland has developed enough – matured into modernity enough – to allow the novel to flourish where it could not flourish before.[3] Owing to its basis on a progressivist model, this fetish for what appears invigoratingly fresh and original, despite its claims for the opening up of the novel to new themes, issues, places and characters, actually announces not a beginning but an end to the Irish novel. The difficulty, of course, for these critics and theorists is attempting to impose some form of order on what is an always-mutating subject: with the resulting danger being that what is now thought of as new can very quickly become outmoded, what are now being celebrated as essential works of art might turn out to be merely manifestations of mediocrity. The real problem is in discovering a common critical framework through which to view the contemporary novel because, as was the case with the novel of the 1960s and 1970s, what the reader is presented with is a diverse body of fiction continuing to mine out areas of what had been once been the hidden Ireland, continuing to offer a vehicle through which the Irish character might emerge as something serious and complicatedly human. There are, though, perhaps two observable areas that might contain the novel of the contemporary moment: time, as in attitudes to the past and its relationship to the present; place, as in the changing nature of the local in an increasingly globalised culture.

In many ways, the 1980s in Ireland were much like the 1970s, only worse. And they were worse because there was no hope in any public or private discourse: the same problems persisted, amplified, as if nothing has changed or developed. The North of Ireland remained a seemingly intractable dilemma. While the issues raised by the conflict in the North – identity, power, the nature of the state, memory and the past – permeate deeply into all the Irish writing of this period, both directly and indirectly, writers from the North obviously respond to the Troubles overtly. Eugene McCabe's (1930–) *Death and Nightingales* (1992) set in the 1880s connects with the present in its depiction of how sectarian division develops; but, as Gerry Smyth argues, despite been configured as separate, these communities are fundamentally 'enmeshed',[4] each requiring the other to exist. Bernard MacLaverty (1942–) in *Cal* (1983), for instance, offers what has been labelled a liberal humanist view of the Troubles: both loyalist and nationalist violence is without any worthwhile reason, is presented as beyond acceptability and normality. This is necessary in a novel striving for some notion of civilised consensus that can be pitted against the horrors of everyday beatings and killings.[5] More interesting is how MacLaverty focuses on

Catholic notions of sin, guilt and redemption,[6] as he had done in his earlier work *Lamb* (1980), suggesting that even the ultra violence and immediacy of the Troubles must still be viewed through concerns that seem out of date and out of place, more attuned to the sensibility of a previous generation. Of course, religion is an integral element of a conflict that could never be simply seen in political terms because of the sectarian nature of the political framework in the North of Ireland. Thus, the extreme versions of Catholicism, like that of reformed sinner Matt Talbot, are presented as options in the modern world.[7] As with many of the novels dealing with the North, the war is never simply between differing communities and groupings, but is funnelled through an internal quarrel of the protagonist, who attempts to find a way through the positions of a poisoned politics always already fixed and immutable.[8]

Glenn Patterson (1961–) writes from inside the Protestant community in the North, interrogating that community's myths and narratives in *Burning Your Own* (1988), exposing communal bigotry and prejudice alongside individual tolerance.[9] Central to his writing is the classic terrain of the nineteenth-century novel: of the individual pitted against the conventions of his/her community, of the manoeuvrings between the private and public spheres of action and thought.[10] His next novel, *Fat Lad* (1992), focuses on the changing geography and cultural landscape of Belfast as the old discourses of identity and belonging meet the new world of capital and money-making.[11] Each of these novels makes clear how the past connects with the present through various rituals and traditions: how these must be negotiated and reimagined in the present if they are to be defused of their explosive danger. Robert McLiam Wilson's (1964–) mad and irreverent *Ripley Bogle: A Novel* (1989) wilfully abandons the traditional inert signifiers of Northern Irish identity, embracing the postmodern possibility of shifting identities and deconstruction of opposites and boundaries. Importantly, it holds up for scrutiny the British, or English, element in the mix of the conflict in the North, acknowledging how the figuring of Ireland's dilemma as one of two tribes at war is dangerously misleading. Of course, there is always the threat that with all this shifting between various positions and identities Bogle will imagine his essential self out of existence. That he flirts with the marginalised world of the London homeless acknowledges this almost Beckettian vision of modernity.[12] It is a smart, clever and knowing narrative and Bogle's declaration of a singular identity that is in essence multiple – Irish, English, Protestant, Catholic – would, ironically, be the foundation of the emerging Northern Irish peace process.

Sean O'Reilly (1969–) offers yet another angle on the North in *Love and Sleep* (2002), with the backdrop of Derry being just that: a backdrop. His focus is on a single character, Niall, who is simply angry with the world at large, and angry with everyone in that world. A war-battered Derry and the breakdown of the IRA ceasefire of the early 1990s merely offer a reflecting mirror to his own inner turmoil. O'Reilly's consciousness of form is important, as much of the power of this novel resides in the uneasy and anxious relationship between his often lyrical prose and its use to describe quite sordid acts. There are times when a reader might hardly notice the nature of the action being presented because of the seductiveness of the style being employed. Niall's tragedy is that he is unable to connect with others, and especially his ex-girlfriend Lorna, and though he 'tells' her story – or that part of it which he knows – he is incapable of truly coming to know her. His lyricism, then, is like a bandage used to cover and heal a wound, except in this instance it is inadequate; and rather than being a source of healing and compensation, his style instead becomes a barrier to fuller understanding. O'Reilly offers an existential drama of the individual person: the Irish past and its demands are insignificant as the burden of being is shifted onto the fragile self that throws itself at the world in an effort to make some kind of impact.

More often than not, though, the Irish novelist of this period perceived the past as nothing but traumatic in the present moment, debilitating any proper move into a future. Benedict Kiely's (1919–2007) *Nothing Happens in Carmincross* (1985) captures, perhaps unintentionally, the nightmare of continuing violence and the bankruptcy of a politics that is unable to imagine solutions and thereby a future.[13] The frolicking form of his previous novel, *Dogs Enjoy the Morning* (1968), with its easy shifting of tone and register between the various textures of Irish culture in song, anecdote and history, is rendered as a manifestation of abject failure in this later novel. Mervyn Kavanagh, an academic historian plying his trade in America, returns for the wedding of his niece and undertakes a picaresque jaunt through Ireland, his mind alive to, or perhaps burdened with, the numerous narrative layers of the past continuing in the present. While tragedy ought to be the tenor struck amid the constant anxious reality of violence, his jaunty insouciance suggests that the comedy of the absurd is never too far away. Kavanagh's inability, and indeed Kiely's, to put some coherent shape on the chaos, suggests a loss of authorial control, of the narrative itself being blown this way and that, as the reverberations of the final bomb work back to disturb the entire project. The novel attempts to give an answer to the problems besetting Ireland, but is, in fact, a manifestation of those problems: while it desires to enact power and authority in the face of violence, it is, in fact, a chronicle of powerlessness and impossibility, with the form of the novel itself disintegrating in the face of violence.

The confusion within *Nothing Happens in Carmincross* comes from an undoubted love for Irish culture and history being put alongside a diagnosis suggesting it is precisely Irish history and culture which are to blame for the Troubles. Its scrutiny of the violence focuses solely on one side of the conflict, its final judgement being vehemently anti-republican and anti-nationalist. Critics signalling the emergence of a post-national culture and a post-national novel at this time are, in fact, simply registering this anti-nationalist bias.[14] This conflation of nationalism with the grand narrative of Ireland is a common one in this period, fermenting what became a war on the Irish past as the source of all ills in the present. In a way, a novel such as *Nothing Happens in Carmincross* records the final futile attempt at writing the grand cultural narrative of Ireland, past and present: one last gesture towards an epic form that might contain each and every nuance of the present moment and its textured relationship to the past. Certainly, many novelists of this period, and not just in Ireland, embrace consciously or unconsciously the postmodern dictum that the kind of all-encompassing narrative promised by the epic perspective is no longer sustainable. Yet, it is still the Irish past, particularly its nationalist past, which exercises many novelists who continually rewrite history's centrality to the dilemmas of the present moment. What can be observed is how this investigation of history consciously becomes an element of the narrative of the Irish novel in this period and not simply in the writing of historical novels as such. Rather, the break with the past is enacted within the novel itself, either formally in the mode of a split narrative between then and now – emphasising that rupture, that difference – or as an integral element of the story with a character, for instance, actively contemplating his/her past, contemplating their growth and development away from that past. It is as if Ireland has accumulated enough of a past, of a history, which now makes this kind of meditation possible and, indeed, necessary. It is also a stark manifestation of the supposed 'newness' of the territory for the novel: the retreat into the past can be seen both as desire for a simpler, less complicated time and as a means of displaying – by virtue of making the past utterly strange, foreign and disconnected – the absolute originality of the contemporary moment. Also, and perhaps fundamentally, this prevalence for history in novels – in whatever guise – demonstrates how Irish history became *the* site of cultural and intellectual conflict in these years.

The Whereabouts of Eneas McNulty (1998) by Sebastian Barry (1955–) is one such novel reflecting this particular zeitgeist and was approvingly celebrated on its publication. On the surface its story of Eneas's perambulations through Ireland, Europe and Africa in the twentieth century offers a picaresque opportunity to review Irish history. Among other things, it traces the development of the present-day IRA back to the Irish War of Independence, but also makes explicit, through Eneas's involvement in both the First and Second World Wars, Barry's desire to offer alternative histories to a simplistically nationalist or official history. The use of lyrical language touches all Barry's writing, in prose as well his drama; his characters' striving towards poetry mirroring their innate moral superiority to the world about them. It also deflects attention away from what are quite stark political interpretations, as if poetry might be above such grubbily material concerns.

On closer inspection, *The Whereabouts of Eneas McNulty* is an utterly strange piece of fiction, operating in a realm between abject passivity on the part of Eneas as well as blatantly holding to a quite fixed and reactionary politics. What the reader is presented with in Eneas McNulty is a Forrest Gump type of character,[15] wholly without agency and buffeted through history without imposing his will on events. Things happen all around him, and to him, but he is unable, or unwilling, to intervene productively in any of these goings on. Completing this 'gumpification' of Eneas is his adherence to no firm belief structure save for utterly naïve platitudes. Unlike the traditional picaro who enacted a subversive deconstruction of bourgeois codes of community by being usually self-centred and self-interested, Eneas's wanderings are basically aimless. Of course, as with the movie character Gump, Barry is attempting to mediate history to his readers through a character so devoid of any 'character' that his version of history might be considered objective.

Yet Barry engages in a sleight of hand and this can be observed most clearly with regard to the manner in which he presents death and murder in the novel. McNulty is involved in both of the World Wars, but does not actually witness any action. It is a way for Barry to sidestep the hard questions surrounding any act of killing. If Eneas were to kill an enemy soldier himself, he would soon discover that all such acts are, when viewed close up, unpalatable and problematical. Instead, the author opts for the easy option of portraying only the violence and chaos associated with acts of rebellion. The enemy are those who would choose freedom from the British Empire. Of the rebellion in 1950s Nigeria it is said: 'Bloody politics! Deathly, killing, seducing politics. Feckin ould freedom anyway.'[16] The problem is that the vision set against such 'dreaded freedom and politics' is little more than a passive acceptance of the world, not as it is but as it was in a very distant past. What is being implied is a return to a colonial pre-independent Ireland.[17] Running intuitively counter to the general thrust of the modern novel form which celebrates the emergence of the individual into history as an active participant in that history, Eneas McNulty, as a character, in his actions is unable to gesture towards any type of personal freedom or future. He sides unthinkingly with the might of power, never once questioning the violence that is at the heart of the order he so yearns for.

Barry wants to uncover those silenced stories of Irish allegiance to Empire and for him it is a rich seam which he returns to again and again in his writing. His *A Long, Long Way* (2005), set during the First World War and the 1916 Easter Rebellion, is a more measured and nuanced exploration of divided loyalties. Still, what is entirely lacking in his writing is any desire to critically examine his own stance or, indeed, self-consciously examine the power relations inherent within acts of writing itself. Poetic language cannot compensate for this lack.

Such self-awareness and self-reflexivity is a basic ingredient of John Banville's (1945–) fiction and his work manifests a serious and worthwhile effort to consider the contradictions of Ireland and its history, to critique the very possibility of the unquestioned grand vision that underpins the fictional world of a writer such as Sebastian Barry. Banville's continued his interest in dismantling the very notion of the grand narrative in *Kepler* (1981), his second novel set in the world of medieval science. It is another brilliant portrait of the modern imagination coming into being. Joseph McMinn declares that while *Doctor Copernicus* (1976) dealt with 'the tragedy of personality; *Kepler* is about the triumph of character'.[18] All Kepler's transcendent theories of the skies are revealed to him in the midst of 'myriad and profligate life',[19] gained despite his complete immersion in the all-too-human world of desire. Order and harmony, a congruity and accord that might match God's intention, is what Kepler seeks with his mathematical equations. To echo this quest Banville employs an elaborate formal scheme to contain his narrative:

I have already conceived the form of my projected book. It is ever thus with me: in the beginning is the shape! Hence I foresee a work divided into five parts, to correspond to the five planetary intervals, while the number of chapters in each part will be based upon the signifying quantities of each of the five regular or Platonic solids which, according to my *Mysterium* may be fitted into these intervals. Also, as a form of decoration, and to pay my due respects, I intend the initials of the chapters shall spell out acrostically the names of certain famous men. (*Kepler*, p. 148)

Kepler never undertook this himself, though this is the structure on which Banville weaves his fiction. It is a kind of madness at work, trying to banish chance from the novel: an ornate joke even in its inflexibility. For rather than perfection, this form actually reflects the shortcomings of the human imagination. The attentive reader comes to realise that the order and harmony that Kepler gains a glimpse of are only man's creation, not God's.[20] Once more in Banville's fiction, his hero is transformed into a figure of fun, a silly diviner for a truth that no longer exists. Banville himself was unable to sustain his own first intention to deal with the great European scientists in his tetralogy, abandoning the original schema with his next novel, *The Newton Letter: An Interlude* (1982). Here he returns to the Irish scene, bringing the ideas he gleaned from the previous two novels to bear upon more local concerns. It is, perhaps, his best novel: its brevity powerfully concentrating the reader's attention on his surgical deconstruction of modern Irish confusions. His unnamed historian is bewitched by what he believes is Big House style, which, even in its faded glory, captivates the imagination. He conjures up an entire romance with himself at the centre, his intention of writing a biography of Isaac Newton becoming less attractive as he weaves his present-day fictions. Of course, while the focus is firmly on this individual's mad misreading of the world, the wider significance is clear: the stereotyping of Irish character and Irish history have made certain notions of barbarity and civility into hardened, immovable facts. The burden of the contemporary moment is to try to see beyond what is immutable and fixed: the historian fails to do this and, at the end of the novel, he has learned nothing and will repeat again the same mistakes.

Only in retrospect, perhaps, does a novel such as *The Book of Evidence* (1989) capture the absurdities of its time of production. Based on the 'grotesque, unbelievable, bizarre and unprecedented' events of the infamous Malcolm Macarthur murder case of the early 1980s, Banville manages to render, through the character of Freddie Montgomery, a skewed Irish world out of place and out of time, or seemingly so. For nothing is as it seems in this novel, there is always another layer to be peeled back, uncovering another reality. Banville is aware that beneath Ireland's stereotypical public façade of conservative constraint lurks a nether world of private passion and desire. In other words, in contrast to the notion that nothing happens in Ireland, he is aware that everything happens and has been happening, but just below the public radar. Freddie, for instance, might be gay, though it is undeclared, as was Copernicus's homosexuality in the earlier novel. Sexual identity is one more area of the self in need of masking and disguise.

The frenetic pace of the plot is countered by Freddie's desire for stillness, for moments of peace. Science is replaced by pictorial art as the conduit through which Banville can continue to self-reflexively muse on the vagaries of the postmodern imagination. From this point on, it is clear that Banville has been telling a variation of the same story in all his novels: a story of the limits of language and the human imagination, a story of failure.[21] References to art will remain a constant in his work, but his characters change occupation from being a spy in *The Untouchable* (1997) to an actor in *Eclipse* (2000). The move is away from the wider communal concerns of society and the world, ever inwards into the singular consciousness of the individual self. This self-consciousness can, as in the Booker Prize-winning *The Sea* (2005), offer luminous exposés of the human heart's yearning for connection with others and a sense of completion within the self. Always in Banville's writing, the work of self-making is an anxious, weighty encumbrance to be endured and it is an act that will end in disappointment. In many ways, from a peculiarly Irish perspective, Banville captures a feeling of intense fatigue with the burden of possible pasts, of personal and communal histories, that make constant claims on the business of being here now. It is return to the *fin de siécle* listlessness of a century before, signalling the need to begin again, the need to reinvigorate the tired old modes of thinking and living. There is, then, still some lingering notion of gallantry, of quixotic nobility, in this recurring image of failure: precisely because it is so bound to everyday human desires and needs. For Banville himself, who in his fiction often employed the figure of the double and the twin to manifest his sense of rupture, the obligation to artistic selfhood and authorship was itself exploded when he began to write in the thriller genre under the pseudonym Benjamin Black with *Christine Falls* (2006) and *The Silver Swan* (2007). While his decision to enter into this thriller marketplace could be argued to be a materialisation of a crisis in identity that is so central to his ever-doubling heroes, it has more to do, one imagines, with a desire to connect with a lucrative wider readership. It might also be understood as a tacit acknowledgement on his part that all his work, which toys with expectations and with the form of the novel itself, actually operates under the strict guidelines of genre.

Colm Tóibín (1955–) covers somewhat similar ground to Banville in his fictionalised focus on the life of American novelist Henry James in *The Master* (2004). More than simply a work of literary mimicry, he captures the nuanced desperations of this writer whose homosexuality can never come into full view. This portrait of a life of self-denial, of controlled restraint, offers an insight into James's art that, itself, hovers menacingly on the edge of a self-possession that hides swirling passions beneath the surface. At a time when younger Irish writers such as Keith Ridgeway (1965–) in *The Long Falling* (1998) and *The Parts* (2003) and Emma Donohue (1969–) in *Stir-fry* (1994) could openly present gay and lesbian life in contemporary Ireland, Tóibín presents readers with a portrait of a time when an emotional life was buried and could only be lived in the closet.[22] Tóibín's *The Heather Blazing* (1992) is also concerned with notions of concealment, with charting the currents of hidden desire. A split narrative between the past and the present, it is at its best in detailing the quiet moments of reflection as Irish High Court Judge Eamon Redmond reassesses his personal and private world with that public realm where he dispenses the law and justice. The parallel commentary on Irish concerns, on offering a revisionist critique on the nature of the Irish Republic through this representative of the constitution, is at times obvious.[23] Having Charles Haughey enter the fictional world of the novel makes the links between the past and present momentarily laboured and overblown. The painful recognition of the limits of language and the difficulty, if not impossibility, of real communication is what Redmond really comes to know.[24] This is the site of the real rupture and crisis within the novel, between the analysis of the state and the nation with the more urgent dilemma of the individual person who must come to some form of reconciliation, not just with the wider world but also with himself.

John McGahern (1934–2006), of course, recognises that a conscious meta-narrative of the nation is not what exercises the mind because he knows that the human perspective, as it is lived, is concerned with the more immediate ambit of self and family. He remarked that perhaps there is no one republic in Ireland, but thousands and thousands of republics as each family unit operates by its own set of codes and manners. *Amongst Women* (1990), perhaps one of the most successful and popular novels of this period, continues to see McGahern working through the traumas within twentieth-century Ireland. One reading of the novel suggests that in its depiction of Moran's descent into old age and powerlessness it 'signals the coming of age of Irish society and the eclipse of old-fashioned patriarchy'.[25] This makes it a narrative enacting the drama of Irish modernisation, that uneasy and anxious move from tradition into a new world.[26] Yet, to imply that the novel registers a complete break with the past and with tradition is simply wrong because, in a very strange way, what is presented is a nervous accommodation with the past. Near the close of the novel, Moran is able to see the Great Meadow again, as if for the first time:

They found him leaning in exhaustion on a wooden post at the back of the house, staring into the emptiness of the meadow . . . To die was never to look on all of this again. It would live in others' eyes but not in his. He had never realized when he was in the midst of confident life what an amazing glory he was part of.[27]

Moran has been a brutal tyrant in his home, overbearingly controlling his family both physically and emotionally. The centrifugal force of Great Meadow as the site of the home which his children continually return to can be viewed as a limiting negative influence: it, and the father, can never be fully escaped. The wider public and civic space of Ireland offers a post-revolutionary figure such as Moran no opportunity for growth or development and the world is retreated from, and thus his domineering persona is allowed to evolve unchecked in the private realm. Yet, despite his depiction as a violent bully, this acceptance of the world of nature beyond the human sphere allows Moran a glimpse of redemption: even he, as awful as he is, is permitted a transcendent vision at the end, is permitted to feel the potential of love.

The close of the novel, after Moran's funeral, is most bizarre: 'Their continual homecomings had been an affirmation of its [Great Meadow's] unbroken presence, and now, as they left him under the yew, it was as if each of them in their different ways had become Daddy' (*Amongst Women*, p. 183).

Sheila then comments: '"Will you look at the men. They're more like a crowd of women", remarking on the slow frivolity of their pace' (*Amongst Women*, p. 184). It is a curious remark highlighting a profound lack of closure within the novel, gesturing to an ambivalence towards any straightforward acceptance of the past and tradition.[28] The women are now in a position of power, but it is as if the daughters have internalised the patriarchal brutishness of the father. In releasing themselves of their feminine vision, they acknowledge the elemental skill of survival in a harsh, unforgiving world. It is yet another moment of disturbance and disruption within McGahern's fiction: a troublingly strange and unresolved ending, raising questions rather than answering them.

While McGahern's novels tease out the rituals of a rural Ireland on the verge of collapse, the cityscape was left for a younger generation of writers to make their own. What is surprising is how again and again the city is presented as a place of impossibility, where characters are tragically alienated from themselves and their fellow city dwellers. It is curious because in the great novel of the Irish city, James Joyce's *Ulysses*, the urban space offered not only the opportunity of modern living – of experiencing certainly the trials and tribulations of modernity – but also the possibility of experiencing deep and authentic life as it is lived. Joyce, it seems, for many contemporary Irish writers, is a negative force. Ferdia MacAnna, in his

1991 essay 'The Dublin Renaissance: An Essay on Modern Dublin and Dublin Writers',[29] encapsulates this view of Joyce because he has mapped all levels of Dublin experience, thus leaving nothing for the emerging writer to write about. He declared that: '*Ulysses* ... is a nightmare from which Dublin is trying to awake.'[30] MacAnna blames academics for elevating Joyce into an untouchable realm. Yet, from the 1960s onwards, the image of Joyce so frightening for MacAnna is an image created by international critics who view Joyce as the universal artist, far beyond the practical reach of the ordinary Dubliner and the emerging Irish writer. One of the ironies, of course, is that MacAnna's essay implicitly celebrates and cherishes cosmopolitanism, as opposed to the parochial backwardness that he sees Dublin and Ireland suffering from in the 1980s. He fails to notice, though, that it is such metropolitan sophistication which he is attacking Joyce for possessing. MacAnna's thinking on this subject is obviously muddled, but nonetheless telling in that the same confusion can be observed in much contemporary criticism that quite simply views the Irish world in a Manichean fashion: the past is bad, the present and the future are good but only in so far as they can disentangle themselves from the negativity of Irish history. In the Herculean effort to lionise the 'new', many critics fail to actually engage with what contemporary writers are actually writing, which is far more interesting and thought-provoking than some of these critics might suggest. Despite the obvious flaws within his critique, MacAnna does begin to articulate how the place of Irish writing, how the topography of the local, becomes configured in the cultural and economic discourses of the global. This reimagined sense of place becomes the means by which much Irish writing of the contemporary moment can be approached and gauged.

Roddy Doyle (1958–) is perhaps the single most successful novelist of this period, gaining an audience far beyond the environs of Dublin's Northside where most of his writing is set. Along with the emergence of rock group U2, Doyle represents a brash generational shift, a confident certitude in his generation's worth and ability. His literary focus is not exactly the urban world; rather, it is the suburban world. Not, however, the suburbia of the middle classes in their mock-Tudor houses with names offering imaginative vistas of lawns and downs. Doyle's is a suburbia devoid of bourgeois fripperies and manners. The places of his writing are the numerous: anonymous satellite towns that have sprung up on the ever-expanding edges of the old city of Dublin. They are villages without a centre, or a past: there are no traditions of living other than the immediate codes of survival. These are displaced, disconnected communities: more examples of hidden Ireland. There is strong evidence of a social conscience within all

Doyle's writing, a recurring aspiration for justice and fairness, which can at times work against the aesthetic merits of the work. Mostly, though, Doyle is content to show rather than to tell.[31]

What has become known as the Barrytown trilogy – *The Commitments* (1988), *The Snapper* (1990) and *The Van* (1991) – has become iconic in Irish culture. Centred on one family, the Rabbittes, Doyle makes reference to current events such as the 1990 Soccer World Cup, and in dealing with the issues of teenage pregnancy and unemployment, he captures the mood of a nation requiring something light and entertaining amid the economic and cultural gloom of the late 1980s. Technically direct, with the emphasis on dialogue rather than description, there is little time for self-conscious reflection or a rendering of an interior life working through neuroses. In this some might suggest that Doyle is merely offering another version of the stereotype of the Irish person as public jester. Undermining such a reading, though, is the basic decency of the characters depicted and their biting wit, which acts both as means of deflecting away any serious analysis of their lot and as a powerful weapon to put down those who might patronisingly position themselves in a zone of superiority. Though this emphasis on the interaction in the outer world does mean that a certain possibility for intimacy is lost. What is interesting is how Doyle's fictive world, lauded as groundbreaking and pioneering, actually possesses quite a conservative worldview. While the teenage pregnancy of *The Snapper* is somewhat unconventional, it merely reflected the social reality, not only of working-class Ireland but also of the middle classes at a time when the political realm was being constantly buffeted by demands for a liberalisation of the constitution with regard to both divorce and abortion. Thus, the conventional Irish world of supposed norms and family roles is re-inscribed through Jimmy Rabbitte, who will be both grandfather and father to the new child. There are, therefore, certain ideals – traditional forms – that are to be aspired to and worked towards. *The Commitments* is often interpreted as an attempt to redefine Irishness: the link to soul music a way of internationalising a provincial sense of identity. Of course, the Irish have always operated in such a way, as perhaps do all cultures, taking what is needed from other places in order to aid self-discovery. More important is how in this novel, and in the later *The Van*, there is a powerful fatalism at work subverting any real opportunity for revolutionary change and transformation within characters' lives. The band falls apart at the end of *The Commitments* and Jimmy's chip van business is a failure in the later novel. What is remarkable from the vantage point of post-Celtic Tiger Ireland is how rapid was the dating of Doyle's Dublin, which was vanishing into a world of work, jobs, success and money even as it was being written about. Certainly, Doyle's is a diagnosis of communities operating in a vacuum: the state and the traditional moral and social strictures of the Church have no leverage in these novels, and when a world beyond the local is referenced – the world of popular music and television – it merely confirms that all action and opportunity occurs elsewhere.

That all three of these novels were made into hugely successful movies meant that their influence on international perceptions of modern Ireland were enormous. The visual impact of grey tower blocks has more to do with the movies than with the novels themselves. Their success also added, perhaps, to a misconception that Roddy Doyle only dealt in the realm of broad comedy, and moments of real gloom might be easily overlooked. Doyle's involvement in cinema becomes an integral part of many contemporary novelists' engagement with their audience. Whereas the stereotypical trajectory from James Joyce onwards was to write a book of short stories before moving on into the form of the novel, it has now become the norm to write novels that will eventually become movies. Indeed, the interconnection between cinema and literature is particularly fertile at this time. A writer such as Neil Jordan (1950–), whose novels *The Past* (1980) and *Dream of the Beast* (1983) did not live up to the brilliant promise of his first collection of short stories, *Nights in Tunisia* (1976) (perhaps the most coherent vision within the short story form since Joyce's *Dubliners*), turns to film and brings a literary sensibility to all his movies, mirroring how he brought a movie-like visuality to his writing. His artistic antennae are attuned to the nuances of particular places and this shows through particularly in his Irish movies. Jordan's involvement in bringing the work of Patrick McCabe (1955–), for instance, to the screen demonstrates how rapidly altering technology now demands that any given artistic production, or narrative, can potentially be repackaged and resold in different formats: novels become movies which come with a CD soundtrack and might also be made into a video game. There is no doubt that Ireland's artistic community has been to the forefront of this worldwide phenomenon, with Ireland being lived locally and imagined globally. As Walter Benjamin suggested, the advent of mass production signals a distancing of the art from the artist,[32] and so too with the contemporary moment and the globalisation of the novel. The problem is that the Irish novel can become alienated from itself as it begins to mean something on the global stage as opposed to the local one. Again, as in that Joycean phrase already alluded to, what is familiar becomes foreign in the process of making the everyday exotically strange.

Roddy Doyle himself, though, did not ever fully embrace that globalised perspective, still preferring to work out his concerns in the local arena of Dublin's Northside. *Paddy Clarke Ha Ha Ha* (1993), which won the Booker Prize for that year, is one of the best of his novels and certainly one of the best novels of this period. A *Bildungsroman* of Dublin's suburbia, Doyle brilliantly matches the growth of his protagonist with the building of new housing estates in the 1960s and 1970s that registered the emergence of a New Ireland. Told from Paddy's perspective, the adult world of the home and the wider world beyond the child's immediate surroundings are vague and just on the edge of comprehension. Paddy's anxieties about fitting in with his friends echo the uncertain position of these new estates that amounted to an experiment in living. The cultural milieu is an improvised one of a hotch-potch of television and English soccer with obscure renderings of Irish myth. Emphasising how a younger generation encode their world with their own references, the landmarks in Paddy's Dublin are not those like College Green or the GPO, those public and nationally shared images. Rather, his landmarks are more intimate and local: the Raheny Public Library and Reynolds Newsagent shop having relevance and resonance only for the few. Indeed, what is truly significant about this novel in particular is how Doyle, like the revivalists a century before him, signals that the Irish space of suburbia is worthy of aesthetic contemplation: that lives of feeling, of celebration and frustration, are being lived there and can be the object of serious artistic reflection.

As with his previous work, there is much humour to be garnered from the boyish rituals of growing up. But there is, too, an acknowledgement of something more disturbingly dark in this picture of family life. His parents' marriage is breaking up and the uncomprehending Paddy must somehow accommodate that pain, render it normal in whatever way he can. There is also a scene when Paddy sets ablaze lighter fluid on his younger brother Sinbad: a brutally violent moment that is offered without judgement or explanation, a thoroughly disruptive challenge to any attempt to read the novel as a simple celebratory, and comic, evocation of childhood.

The Woman who Walked into Doors (1996) is another intense drama, stressing the claustrophobia of family as well as the claustrophobia of the imagined Barrytown space that is always already a place of hopelessness. Having his character Paula Spencer, battered wife and alcoholic, be the conscious writer of the narrative is a recognition by Doyle of the need to move beyond simple realistic reportage and dialogue, however vibrant, to begin to explore the more intimate inner realities of his characters, consciously complicating perhaps the stylised and simplistic rendering of his art in the popular mind to this point. Another example of his desire to expand his literary horizons, to engage with the wider themes of Ireland, can be seen when in 1999 Doyle embarked on a planned trilogy focusing on Henry Smart, whose life would span the twentieth century and through whom the history of that century might be viewed. From his focus on the present and his depiction of a reality outside the major currents of Irish history, he turns to historical subject matter as if he feels he must give a context to the Barrytown world he had rendered so capably in his earlier fiction. The ambitiousness of his intention can be seen with the first instalment, *A Star Called Henry* (1999). Henry Smart, the hero of the novel, is from the worst slums of Dublin city. Doyle's description of the city is heavily indebted to research, which he lists at the end of the book. Such learning intrudes upon the narrative flow, as does the attempt at a magic realist rendering of Henry's early life. Henry is drawn into the 1916 Easter Rising because of his connection to James Connolly, who has been a father figure of sorts to him: he has taught him to read and given him something to believe in and, ultimately, fight for. But Connolly has been hoodwinked by the bourgeois nature of this Catholic rebellion and whatever ideals he hoped for perish at the very moment they are being espoused.

Ironically, just as revisionist history was being vigorously challenged in the Irish academy, Doyle re-inscribed it in his fiction. Most of the usual stereotypes remain undisputed: the 1916 leaders were dreamy English-hating poets with an unhealthy fixation on religious imagery; Sinn Fein are racist, murderous bigots with an eye for opportunist propaganda. James Connolly and the Citizen Army are presented as admirable but ultimately naïve participants in someone else's war. All Ireland's contemporary ills, as depicted in his Barrytown work, stem from this single event. He is unable to view the past as anything other than a nightmare and a disaster. The past for Doyle, therefore, is not a site of potential or possibility in the present; rather, it is something to be jettisoned and abandoned. Yet, Roddy Doyle does offer a vision of how to cope with an indifferent world and, quite surprisingly, it is a vision akin to the 'On your bike' Thatcherism of the 1980s. The sense of communal spirit in his earlier work is replaced by blatantly individualistic concerns and desires in the character of Henry Smart. Paradoxically, even as he attacks bourgeois thinking and ideology as it might manifest itself in the Easter Rising, Doyle actually returns to the original middle-class concerns of the novel form and its focus on the unique individual, celebrating the individual's ability to get ahead of the mob. In the subsequent novels in the series, *Oh, Play that Thing!* (2004) and *The Dead Republic* (2010), Henry Smart's Tory anarchist stance confirms the systematic breakdown of the power and influence of traditional Irish institutions such as school, Church, and government. In the modern world, and in modern Ireland, there is nothing left to believe in save the dominance and self-perseverance of the extraordinary self.

Another writer labelled a Northside realist and centrally involved in the Northside renaissance of the 1980s and 1990s is Dermot Bolger (1959–). Like Roddy Doyle, he has not confined himself simply to the novel form, working in drama and poetry as well as encouraging writers with his involvement in the Raven Arts Press and also, in typically renaissance fashion, offering an ongoing critique of, and framework for, his art through essays and introductions.[33] *The Journey Home* (1991) encapsulates powerfully Bolger's aesthetic and social vision. This is a story of 1980s Ireland: a bleak time as detailed here with economic, sexual and political corruption rife. Two friends, Shay and Hano, get caught up in this underworld and pay dearly for their involvement. It is at its best in its descriptions of the uncertain passage between the world of adolescence and the adult world: the tentative and often difficult journey away from family, towards independence. It is, though, a novel marred by its confused polemic linking, and deriding, the rural and the traditional while simultaneously being nostalgic for a world and a time before the advent of dual carriageways and housing estates. His characters have become estranged from what they thought of as home as their landscape becomes a part of another narrative of development and opportunity. Like the characters in Roddy Doyle's fiction, they are unable to enter into the currents of change and transformation, history passes them by and they are victims to its movements: power is always elsewhere. Surprisingly, for all its efforts as rendering an austere new realism, the novel closes with something akin to a Yeatsian celebration of the Anglo-Irish Big House.

Finglas, once an ancient village on the outskirts of Dublin and now a part of the general urban sprawl, is central to Bolger's imagination, because it registers so many different histories and landscapes simultaneously. In *The Woman's Daughter* (1987), a mother who keeps her daughter hidden in her room for twenty years becomes the catalyst for a meditation on the nature of relationships and repression within the parameters of family and a wider world. Numerous voices and perspectives from different times in the nineteenth and twentieth centuries are brought together powerfully and poetically. The locale of Finglas allows the past and the present to exist side by side with descriptions of an ever-changing and utterly fluid landscape. As in *The Journey Home*, there is a palpable sense of loss pervading the sections set in the present: a syrupy nostalgia for a simpler time when the notion of home matched a specific known place. The shifting time frame of the narrative savagely undercuts this backward look by suggesting no time – in the past or the present – is ever simple or straightforward.

The writer who truly made his own this new in-between space between past and present – this liminal region of the borderland between city and country, the modern and the traditional – is Patrick McCabe (1955–). *The Butcher Boy* (1992) vividly delivers to the page the psychic trauma of Ireland's modernity through the madly bad Francie Brady who becomes a version of the butcher boy of the traditional song, wishing in vain to be young again when he and the world were innocent. Indeed, that motif of some moment in the past when all was perfect and unsullied runs through his entire fictional output. Again, the implication is that despite the obviously energetic innovation of the work, there is still quite a conservative vision of normality which is taken for granted as the object of desire. McCabe's not inconsiderable gift is the ability to capture and create vivid voices that act as a guide and filter to a world made fantastic by the author's wonderfully wicked vision. *The Butcher Boy* playfully interweaves gloriously trashy literary, musical and cinematic references with confidence and ease. Francie Brady's imagination registers the postmodern reality of being bombarded and shaped by a variety of texts and stimuli. While being a murderer, Francie retains the reader's sympathy because of the way in which he negotiates these disparate forms and mediums, ultimately allowing an authentic voice to speak as it moves between fear and knowledge. The blackly comic vision and the deadly serious both work in tandem to produce a multi-layered novel of mental disintegration within a dementedly alive portrayal of Irish small-town life, where the population are seen awaiting the arrival of the Virgin Mary in these apocalyptic times.

McCabe continued to tell similar stories in various guises in his later work, the most successful of which was *Breakfast on Pluto* (1998) with Pussy Braiden another memorable borderland, and borderline, character. However, with novels such as *Emerald Germs of Ireland* (2001) and *Winterwood* (2006), what had been exciting and challenging at first became quickly tired and formulaic. The emotions plumbed in *The Butcher Boy* and *Breakfast in Pluto* possessed a genuine dynamic: all the references to pop culture and Irish ballads and country and western songs becoming a conduit for the characters to connect with those buried feelings, bringing them to the surface. In what became subsequently labelled as 'bog Gothic', because of the dark hues being exploited, transformed itself into 'bog Baroque' precisely because it becomes increasingly evident that all these references are a means of denying any access to genuine emotion from entering the narrative. And once cut off from that energy source, the stories become little more than jokey diversions reflecting not the wide world of pop culture but an emotionally devoid bubble that cannot be escaped from. What had earlier allowed a diagnosis of contemporary Ireland's neuroses has now become a symptom of those ills.

James Ryan (1955–) in *Home from England* (1995) uses the trope of emigration to begin to deconstruct rigid notions of modern Irish identity, acknowledging the centrality of traditional forms and ideas while also highlighting their flimsiness in the vortex of the contemporary moment.[34] William Trevor's beautifully poised *Felicia's Journey* (1994), while offering a view of Irishness that seems quite dated, is more concerned with rendering the anxieties of a middle England whose structures of living have fallen apart. In many ways, Trevor reverses all the labels and stereotypes applied to the Irish in his twist on the traditional emigration narrative. For it is the character Joe Hilditch who is mad, who lives in a twilight world of the past, suffering the onslaught of a modernity he is unable to either comprehend or deal with.

Another take on the emigration story is offered by Joseph O'Connor (1963–), who began his novelistic career with *Cowboys and Indians* (1991) and the brilliant creation of Eddie Virago. Eddie is one of the last Irish punks who, with their Mohican hairstyles and attitude, colonised the top of Grafton Street in Dublin throughout the 1980s. He is smart and knowing, and wears his irony as a shield against anything too seriously genuine that might actually have to be dealt with on an emotional level. His life is a performance of a role he imagines to be acceptable.[35] Of course, beneath this reflex defence mechanism is a rather uncertain figure: an anxious young man from a solid bourgeois background who must try to make his way in the wide world. He is representative of the 1980s generation who were caught between traditional mores and the need for fashioning new ways to think about Ireland.[36] It is an emigration story, but updated, rewriting consciously the narrative of the 1950s:

He tried to feel the way an emigrant is supposed to feel. Sentimental songs and snatches of poetry drifted like remembered smells into his consciousness and then eluded him. And though he was vaguely aware of the thousands of petulant Paddies who had crossed the same stretch of sea over the decades, and over the centuries too, he couldn't actually feel . . . Pain, loneliness, isolation, they were just words.[37]

The usual roles no longer apply, as even a new vocabulary is needed to describe this 'Ryanair' generation who live in a smaller world with a rapidly mutating idea of Ireland and Irishness. The rethinking of stereotypes happens both at home and abroad: the 'NIPPILs' (the 'new Irish professional person living in London' – educated, articulate and confident) explode the notion of the Irish 'paddy as navvy' which had so dominated the Irish emigrant story since the nineteenth century onwards. Most endearing is that despite his laconic wit and knowingness and his performative bravado, Eddie does not know everything; in other words, he is a flawed hero, a true representative of the Irish coping classes.

In many ways, it is a writer such as O'Connor who truly signals the revolution in the Irish imagination and how the Irish transform how they conceive of themselves. In a character such as Eddie Virago, we catch a glimpse of the generation that will inherit the whirlwind of the Celtic Tiger, that in very material ways live in and envisage an Ireland that is no longer perceived as marginal or see themselves as victims. One consequence of this is that the Irish past can be reimagined as something other than a narrative of disaster and nightmare. For O'Connor this eventually led to the novel *Star of the Sea* (2003), which is a narrative based round the famine and emigration. The story was continued, in a fashion, in his next novel, *Redemption Falls* (2007). Unlike other historical novels of the period, both of these works refuse to view the past from that present-centred perspective which can only lead to polemic. Rather, O'Connor attempts to write a sprawling nineteenth-century novel, and mostly succeeds. Different narratives and voices intertwine to give a near-totalised view of the events, while also acknowledging how that past comes to us through various narrative acts of writing: journalism, letters and so on. Perhaps what O'Connor learns is that the only way in which to write an epic in the contemporary moment is to actually write an epic. Rather than savagely deconstruct the codes of the traditional novel, he adheres to them, revelling in their possibility. In other words, the ironical stance of the earlier work gives way to something more profound; form and content combine to allow a complicated story to be told which remains complicated and challenging to the reader. Still, old habits do die hard and both novels close with a crafty postmodern denouement, suggesting the author retains some deliberate aloofness from the material, not allowing himself to fully succumb to the charms of the traditional novel.

Two of Deirdre Madden's (1960–) novels, *Authenticity* (2002) and *Molly Fox's Birthday* (2008), offer more measured pictures of middle-class Irish life and its various vexations. Some of her early work dealt with the North of Ireland,[38] but her talent is found not simply in her thematic concerns but in the exact quietude of her depiction of characters who are extraordinary because of their talents and their uniqueness and not because of being representative of some type or class. Her fictive world is one in which not much happens, though what does happen is delicately and often intensely believable. There are also the parallel universal concerns with the nature of art and language which, like everything else, is never forced: her characters' insights offered gently for the reader to contemplate. In both novels there are central scenes around which, perhaps, each narrative rotates, hinting at the limits of language and the reality of a human experience beyond what can be said in words. They are important moments of stillness and connection, not only with the natural world but also, significantly, with other people. The irony, of course, is that Madden must break whatever spell there might be by relating these instances of wholeness through a compromised language and the compromised form of the novel. Madden knows that to be in the world is to be in the world with other people and that what matters are the moral codes by which we interact with those others, be they family or friends. Her realm of action and interest is the private and the domestic, but working through the conflicts inherent in this sphere is necessarily a comment on the wider world of macro-politics and relations.[39]

Indeed, much writing by women of this period concerns itself with reimagining and reconfiguring the relationship between public and private experience and the notions of female/feminine power in both spheres. Mary Morrissy (1957–) in *The Pretender* (2000), dealing with a woman who pretended to be the daughter of Tsar Nicholas II, teases out the nature of identity and its improvised fictions, showing how history and the personal interact.[40] In *Mother of Pearl* (1995), Morrissy refocuses religious imagery away from the patriarchal towards feminine experience, again demonstrating how modernity demands that the individual makes use of the debris of Western culture to cobble together their own protective cultural skin.[41] Anne Enright (1962–) is also interested in refashioning traditional images of women. Her novel *The Wig My Father Wore* (1995) moves uneasily between the world of myth and television, the narrative imbued with a dream-like quality as the author intentionally attempts to avoid scrutiny. Less self-consciously working against traditional expectations is her more simplistically realistic novel *The Gathering* (2007), which won the Booker Prize for that year. Dealing with a story of a family gathering for a sibling's funeral, Enright connects with the long literary history of the wake in Irish writing, demonstrating once again how this particular ritual becomes a means for self-revelation. In the sphere of popular fiction, a writer such as Maeve Binchy (1940–) carves out her own particular niche, using the backdrop of Ireland from the 1950s to the present to deal with the social and familial problems of women devoid of the self-consciousness that a knowledge of theory and praxis brings to the work of other contemporary writers. No doubt this combination of concern and directness is one reason why her work is hugely successful. Certainly, her writing and that of others in this genre, of what has become known as 'chick lit', capture some of the energies of the traditional novel form which, in may ways, is concerned only with the immediate moment in terms of theme and also in terms of reader response.

The advent of the Celtic Tiger and its material effect on daily life within Ireland raised many questions about the ways in which the country had hitherto conceived of itself in relation to the wider world.[42] While place and location in Irish writing have always been consciously central in the way in which it has been imagined, in the globalised economic and cultural world they now become even more central. In the late 1980s and early 1990s, the political and economic global landscape altered significantly with the tearing down of the Berlin wall and the end of communist rule in Russia, the end of Apartheid in South Africa, and the active construction of a global economy that now entered into the discourse of everyday life, so that everyone might feel a part of this project – for good and for bad – and not simply the elite who have always operated on a global level. Irish politicians began to question the difference between geographic place and spiritual place, between as it was put succinctly, 'Boston or Berlin'.[43] The notion of a distinct Irish culture is not important when the forces of the marketplace begin to dominate public debate. The kind of visions figures such as Eamon de Valera and Elizabeth Bowen gave expression to in the 1940s gives way to more prosaic images of allegedly happy workers living happy lives in Hong Kong. The consequences for a cultural figuring of these issues are varied. Obviously, the age-old problem of the multiple audiences for the Irish novel remains crucially valid. Now there is the added question of 'where' Irish writing might actually come from: what place can give significance to an Irish story when everyone can live anywhere, and therefore nowhere?

Attempting to put shape on this vaguely emerging zeitgeist, Dermot Bolger argued in his 'Introduction' to *The Picador Book of Contemporary Irish Fiction* (1994) that Irish writers had moved on from the angst associated with a colonial and post-colonial relationship with Britain to a more healthy and more modern engagement with Europe and the wider world in general. In dismissing what he feels are the restrictions of tradition and a post-colonial reading of Irish culture and writing, he focuses instead on what he believes is truly positive about the contemporary Irish condition. Making reference to a short story of Colum McCann's (1965–), and quoting from another McCann story, he says:

[The story] is an evocation of the landscape and mind of Texas . . . More than ever it is clear that future editors will not just be turning to the banks of the Liffey, the Lee and the Lagan, but to McCann's 'the Thames or the Darling or the Hudson or the Loire or even the Rhine itself' to search out the new heart of Irish writing.[44]

In the same introduction, he praises other writers for their creation of an 'anonymous suburban scape' and how their stories of Dublin could be narratives from 'any modern city'.[45] The implication is clear: not only is the story of Ireland and its themes and concerns restrictive but also history and tradition taint the very location of Ireland as a source of writing. The future of Irish writing is to be discovered elsewhere. Bolger's analysis is an example of the truly provincial mind at work, as outlined by the poet Patrick Kavanagh in the 1950s: the imagination always looking to a different place for signs of life and indications of worthiness.[46] His critical narrative of escape, of the movement away into exile, is not very original or innovative in an Irish context. Indeed, he seems to suggest that emigration – even a cultural emigration, which can only ever be a form of cultural tourism doomed to deal with the shallowness of the surface – is something desirable.

Bolger's analysis is a serious misinterpretation of the contemporary moment, both in suggesting how attractive the global marketplace might be and in suggesting how untroubling such a move into that global world actually is. For instance, Colum McCann's attitude to place and space, and certainly Ireland as a place and a space, is much more critically engaged than Bolger's analysis would allow.[47] From his first novel, *Songdogs* (1995), which dealt with Ireland and Irish themes, to work such as *Dancer* (2003), *Zoli* (2006) and *Let the Great World Spin* (2009) which tell self-consciously international stories, McCann's writing traces that trajectory away from the Irish space into a wider literary universe. Importantly, not only does he make that move himself as an author but also he registers it at the level of narrative by telling the story of the repercussions of such a move by documenting the psychological trauma that it incurs. His fiction, therefore, confronts directly the conundrum of how, despite Irish space offering a bedrock of stability and continuity, the discourses that surround it tell a story of dislocation and fragmentation. In the specifically Irish context, he investigates the boundaries between Ireland and the rest of the world, dealing in a number of his works specifically with the problem of emigration and immigration. He realises how the contemporary postmodern world demands that people live in new ways. No longer do the certainties of rigid and real boundaries – national, personal or spatial – operate as they once did, as people exist imaginatively in many places simultaneously.

This Side of Brightness (1998) best exemplifies these concerns. It spans over seventy years, juxtaposing the narrative of Nathan Walker with that of his grandson Clarence – who is also known as Treefrog. Their stories are separate at the outset but merge to unite as the novel progresses. Dates are used at the head of some of the chapters, obviously charting the constant move between times and characters, back and forth. From a specifically Irish perspective, the second chapter '1916' has obvious connotations bringing to mind the Easter Rebellion and the traditional narratives of Irish history. However, McCann is consciously not telling that national story, offering an alternative history, or rather, a series of alternative histories: a labour history of those who built the subway system in New York, personal and private histories alongside public and communally shared histories. The simple point is made that different places will necessarily have different narratives and memories associated with them. Each narrative and history exists simultaneously with the others, none negating any of the others.

It is a novel about fathers and sons and the need for reconciliation between generations, between the past and the present. *This Side of Brightness* demonstrates how in the contemporary world – and in contemporary Ireland – a return to the essentials of an engagement with space is required in order that that gap between narrative and reality, between culture and physical space, can be healed. Indeed, his novel is a parable about what can occur when a person and a community are set adrift from a firm sense of place and all that home might entail. At one level, he shows his readers the terrifying aspects of a globalisation that overwhelms those on the margins. Repositioning Ireland as a central point, then, is crucial in order that a truly productive engagement with the potential of the international scene can occur and that ideas and narratives can flow in both directions, from outside in and inside out. That would be actual and affirmative globalisation, when the periphery might be able to influence the centre, while still being true to itself, to its own narratives and its own local spaces.

Éilís Ní Dhuibhne's (1954–) science fiction novel *The Bray House* (1990), set in an apocalyptic future when a nuclear explosion has put Ireland under volcanic ash, is concerned with the mechanics of how the familiar becomes exotic and strange.[48] The Bray House of the title is excavated and its contents interpreted, or misinterpreted, by Swedish archaeologists. Ní Dhuibhne teases out the power relations inherent in different uses of language and how the forms by which we attempt to know the world actually distance us from that world, making it alien and utterly strange. Varying texts and discourses – archaeology, folktale and newspaper reports – vie for attention, each offering only disconnected glimpses of this recently dead world. Various facts can be gathered and presented, the bric-à-brac of everyday life viewed as evidence, but a full picture of life in Ireland in the

1980s is always just beyond grasp. And, of course, the emotional reality of the family who lived in the Bray House can never be rendered or appreciated. It will always remain something only to be guessed at. Ní Dhuibhne creates an elaborate structure, using the conventions of the science fiction genre, to view the contemporary moment through a supposed lens of objectivity that succeeds only in making what is mundane and commonplace seem extraordinarily unfamiliar. Remarkably, then, the novel becomes a comment on the impossibility of rendering quotidian experience of life as it is lived in Ireland, as if being ordinary – being like everyone else – is not desirable and only Ireland conceived of as truly exceptional is attractive.

What exercises Ní Dhuibhne is the fear of the cliché and the stereotype and its hold on the imagination, not only of those who view Ireland from elsewhere but also on the Irish themselves. Such concerns are central to *The Dancers Dancing* (1999), a novel which meditates on the supposed city–rural divide in Irish culture, exposing the misconceptions that each place has of the other.[49] The year is 1972 and the action moves between Dublin and the Gaeltacht of Donegal. Orla Crilly's inchoate and developing perception is the focus of the novel, and is expressed and amplified brilliantly by Ní Dhuibhne in terms of the form, or forms, operating within the novel. The opening chapter of the novel, 'The Map', is highly self-conscious, raising questions about the nature of stories and storytelling. Like maps, stories are means of seeing and understanding the world: they are, in the words of the narrator, 'half true and half false'.[50] This self-consciousness is continued into the second chapter with the reader being offered a 'still-life' portrait of Orla and her friends. It is impressionistic: a mood picture, a piece of a map that must be put together to make a coherent whole. Another piece of the jigsaw puzzle is presented in the following chapter, where an opposition is established between Dublin and Tubber in the Donegal Gaeltacht: between the English and Irish languages, between work and play, between past and present. The difficulty for Orla is made clear: the map she uses at home will need readjustment in Tubber, for each place operates along its own set of codes. Or so it would first appear. For, through a series of revelations and reversals, Orla comes to understand that what was once predicated on difference, must now be reassessed as being the same.

The pivot of the novel now becomes the creation of an authentic self, complex and true, forged somewhere beyond the confines of expectation. At the summer school, Orla must negotiate between the public and private – inner and outer – spaces constantly. She wants to find a place out of which her individual voice might emerge. That place is the 'Burn'. There are five visits – with some of the other girls and on her own – to the Burn throughout the novel. Each visit is accorded a chapter and these punctuate the action of the novel, becoming the axis round which Orla's development and maturation are recorded. It is a place outside the constricting maps of either the city or the countryside: at once intimate and mysteriously unknown. In this secret world, Orla has access to aspects of herself which until to this point had been denied: the wild and forbidden become possible in the Burn. It is a place that Orla can begin to be herself – simply and uncomplicatedly (*The Dancers Dancing*, p. 73). *The Dancers Dancing* is, obviously, a *Bildungsroman*, but one that extends the possibility of the genre within a culture that has usually figured growth and development solely through sexuality. Orla comes to know how to move between life lived in public places and the inner life of the private individual. This is registered in her coming to know her body in the Burn. Yet it is suggested that sexuality is not the only means of charting that move from innocence to experience, childhood to adulthood. More significant, perhaps, is the note of uncertainty struck by the narrator at the close of the novel: she is singularly unsure as to the import of the story she has just been telling, the narrative finishing on a strange downbeat note. Rather than the expected moment of knowledge and transcendence, the narrator in the present who has been looking back at the past remains unfixed and unfinished: the story is told, but its meanings, its significance, remain endlessly open to interpretation. The project of self-creation, in other words, is necessarily ongoing.

For other writers, such as Claire Kilroy (1973–) in *Tenderwire* (2006), the move between places is simply a part of modern life to be embraced and accepted, though even in this internationalised scene Ireland is always an uncertain home, but home nonetheless. In this novel, Kilroy shows how anxiousness can revolve around the individual no matter where they might be, though all this movement between places and spaces in what appears to be sophisticated circles merely accentuates her heroine's uncertainty and her sense of loss. Kilroy's writing style is marked by confidence, as is her ability to build a plot, so that her insights into the contemporary condition are penetratingly clear. Gerard Donovan (1959–), in *Schopenhauer's Telescope* (2003), exploits the potential of the international no-place to offer something of a philosophical Socratic dialogue on the nature of warfare, among other topics. Two men begin to talk, as one digs a hole and the other watches. Moments from the past are dwelt upon: moments that underpin the cruelty and destruction that humans can inflict on one another. They role-play, they mimic, they creatively imagine the past, all in an attempt to come to some understanding about the evil that men do. At the very moment when much of the Irish novel, and the novel in general, was concerned with the postmodern pose of ironic indifference, Donovan was prepared to have something to say and not merely be content to amuse. Importantly, when history had become a utilitarian tool to justify any position one could care to imagine, a novel such as this refocused the reader onto the dilemma of how the individual responds to history. Though there is irony in that Donovan cannot ground his moral tale in any specific locale, and must keep his references vague so that his musing will take on a universal significance.

Michael Collins (1964–) also exploits the latent potential of the internationalised novel, manifesting the peculiar flourishing of genre fiction in this period. Perhaps that recognition of genre, more than the question of the place of Irish fiction, is that which signals the rapid development of the contemporary Irish novel into new realms, unburdened with traditional concerns. While his early work dealt directly with Irish themes and characters, increasingly his novels have been set in America – the vast landscape of which allows him to write different types of novel. *The Secret Life of E. Robert Pendleton* (2006) is a campus novel, while *The Keepers of Truth* (2000) and *The Resurrectionists* (2003) concentrate on how beneath the veneer of the ordinary and the mundane exists a nether world of dark deeds and hidden passions in mid-western America. A cast of stock characters fills the pages of these novels. The power of American culture to penetrate the global imagination is on view as the reader already recognises and knows the types that come and go: the local mayor, the Bible-thumping mother, the numerous middle-aged women with bad bouffant hairdos and fashion problems. In *Lost Souls* (2006), a thriller like his other American novels, Collins brilliantly deploys a cold, precise prose in his descriptions of the theatricalities and absurdities of American life. The narrative is punctuated with the sights and sounds of middlebrow television, with its game shows and sitcoms and easy answers to the complexities of modern living. As in his previous novels, Collins attempts to make a comment about the wider malaise of 1980s life, as the world moved rapidly into a new age. The genre of the murder mystery is, in a way, a lullaby for modernity: a present-day fairytale that, despite its immersion in a seedy, dark underworld, offers much-needed reassurances. For, at least, all the loose strands are satisfyingly tied up at the end and a kind of stark, uncomplicated justice is meted out with the bad getting their comeuppance and the good, while not perhaps being fully rewarded, being given the opportunity of a second chance.

The popularity of genre fiction in the present moment also manifests clearly the allure of the market. A ready-made set of codes to follow means that any writer can gain access to a niche readership, pandering to their expectations. In the hands of many contemporary writers, genre fiction is the empty canvas upon which they can play out their meticulously paced narrative twists and turns. The hugely popular work of Cecilia Aherne (1981–), Marian Keyes (1963–) and Cathy Kelly meets the desires of a 'chick lit' audience with their disposable narratives of modern love and loss. And the increasing proficiency in the thriller genre by Irish writers, for instance, suggests a means for middlebrow authors, such as John Connolly (1968–) with his series of Charlie Parker novels set in and around Portland, Maine and Declan Hughes (1964–) whose detective Ed Loy is based in Dublin, to connect with like-minded middlebrow readers beyond Ireland. This situation is compounded by the fact many younger Irish writers are the product of creative writing courses, bringing a sense of professional ease to, and aloof detachment from, their material. The style of many of these writers is one of containment and control, rather than excess. Whereas a previous generation of Irish novelists might have aspired to self-expression through art, the situation is now altered and the writerly self is subsumed into the conformities of plot and the necessities of the literary marketplace that accentuates cold and calculating conformity. Even those widely celebrated novels and novelists that apparently play with form and offer seemingly endless challenges to traditional narratives become tiresomely jaded and orthodox rather rapidly.

The underlying assumption traditionally driving the critique of space in Irish writing is that the movement is ever outwards, towards other places and other cultures. This has been upended and reversed, of course, with the experience of large-scale immigration into Celtic Tiger Ireland from the late 1990s onwards. This is connected with the changing sense of an Irish identity which confidently presents itself within the cultural global marketplace, continuing to peddle a certain type of nostalgic image and narrative that have little to do with the realities of everyday Irish life. Chris Binchy's (1970–) *Open-handed* (2008) immerses the reader in the world of the immigrant worker: there is a palpable uneasiness to their existence, their position in relation to Irish society a tenuous and unreal one. They are far too educated for the jobs they are asked to do, and the regulations by which they lived at home – class codes and moral mores – disintegrate into meaninglessness in this new place in which they live and work. But anxiety is central to the lives of the Irish characters as well, for their reality has rapidly altered too and the traditional principles by which they could negotiate relationships and work have been put under serious pressure. Doing the right thing becomes increasingly problematical because there might not be a right thing to do anymore. Marcin is Polish, a trained archaeologist; he moves between the obscurity of his digs in a nameless Dublin suburb to his job as a night porter in a big, anonymous five-star hotel. This hotel, particularly, comes to represent the dark, unpleasant reality amid the bright lights of the cityscape, a microcosm of a shiftless society. It is a nowhere, a neutral space, with people constantly coming and going, their transience a signifier of how disconnected Irish modernity actually can be.

Notes from a Coma (2005) by Mike McCormack (1965–) is a consummately up-to-date piece of writing and storytelling. All the technology and cultural debris of the contemporary moment is present: the Internet, mobile phones and the phenomenon of reality television. The story of J. J. O'Malley, adopted from a Romanian orphanage to live in Louisburgh in Mayo, who signs up for an experiment testing the effects of being deliberately sent into a deep coma, allows McCormack to ponder the nature of modern life and culture. Irish culture is benign here in its modernity; it just is as it is – as good and as bad as everywhere else. J. J's adoption forces him to create himself out of nothing, but he finds love and affection in this small town and becomes a part of the community. His real dilemma is a modernity that wrests control from the individual, where systems of economics and politics intertwine with corporate mass media which contrive to frustrate unique interventions and individual comment. The story plays with the limits of science fiction and probability, but it is the form of the novel itself that amplifies the pervading mood of dislocation.

A picture of J. J. emerges from various viewpoints and narratives, his own voice mediated through these other voices. In a formal echo of Maria Edgeworth's _Castle Rackrent_, there is also the dominating voice of the footnote offering an ongoing sociological and cultural critique of the action and of the fads and modes of contemporary Irish life. The novel opens and closes with these footnotes, propelling the main narrative or narratives into the margins. Indeed, it is the story which becomes secondary to the commentary: the experience of real life being merely one more opportunity to talk rather than be. The arch commentator declares: 'We have come to live in this deferral of ourselves, drifting away on a digital tide, a hail of ones and zeroes which sift down through the ether and resolve to a lattice of pixels on screens and printouts – our very own hauntology.'[51] J. J. finds fleeting celebrity on the Internet and on television but such fame, like so many things in the contemporary moment, is utterly disposable. After finding a distinctive voice, it has been once again pushed to the margins and the struggle of sustaining the self, Irish or otherwise, is still a work in progress. McCormack cleverly touches upon the contemporary zeitgeist of reality television and the linked upsurge in the memoir, both of which force the inner world to be lived on the outside. There is no privacy in the modern age, everything must be said, and with the private made glaringly public everything is to be laid bare to voyeuristic scrutiny. So J. J. desires to retreat into the recesses of his inner consciousness and connect with the private realm of deep dreaming. The irony is that it can only happen in the most public of arenas. McCormack offers the reader a morality tale for Irish culture in the globalised world.

There is hope, and despair, for the novel form itself in the contemporary moment. Advances in technology mean that access to the privacies of the individual are no longer confined to the novel that now must compete with other forms of communication. The difficulty is that in Ireland, as else-where, the novel must renew itself or become redundant. And yet, for Mike McCormack and others, it is still the novel form which can contain the tales of contemporary life, which can bring a semblance of shape and order to all the voices and elements of modernity, even as it is been forced into the obscurity of the white noise of technology.

John McGahern's That They May Face the Rising Sun: *saying the very last things*

At the close of *Memoir* (2005), John McGahern imagines meeting his long-dead mother on the country lanes they walked together when he was a child: 'If we could walk together through those summer lanes, with their banks of wild flowers that "cast a spell", we probably would not be able to speak, though I would want to tell her all the local news.'[1]

The tension here between the demands of accepting silence as the only possible conduit towards deep feeling and the excited desire to speak is at the heart of McGahern's aesthetic vision. It is the recognition that there is nothing to be said of a world that will go on without any heed of, or care for, the things of human utterance. And yet the fragility of the human imagination in the face of this vast indifference means that speech is never too far away. McGahern's fictive rendering of the world is thus packed with everyday bric-à-brac with the overall effect generated reminding the reader of the centrality of place and location, and of the words we use to connect with that world out there, beyond us.[2] Images of the solidity and continuity of the world abound: natural images, but also more mundane objects – clocks, tables, umbrellas – interact with the human world and human perception. The discrepancy between the realm of the consciousness 'in there' and the reality 'out there' is stressed, the human and the natural spheres colliding with differing perceptions of time. McGahern wants to stress our being a part of the world and simultaneously our being apart from it. Words, perhaps, and the act of telling might heal that wound and rupture.

McGahern's wish to tell his mother all the local news is significant. News, as something fresh, immediate and pertinent, is linked to the early novel form which aspired to the urgency of the moment and has continued to exist as the chronicler of the now. McGahern realises, too, that it is only out of the energies of the local that the universal may be fully accessed: 'Everything interesting begins with one person in one place ... No one comes out of nowhere; one room or town or locality can be made into an everywhere. The universal is the local, but with the walls taken away.'[3] This act of burrowing ever inwards actually forces the work forever outwards. This intense focus on the commonplace actuality of the everyday and the local forces his writing to transcend its time and its place and become universal.

Here, then, laid bare is John McGahern's impulse for writing, to show us, as he would show his dead mother, the very stuff of the world: its aching beauty, and the subtle tenacity of a human being-in-the-world. In the novel, *That They May Face the Rising Sun* (2002), all of his concerns – thematic as well as formal – find their most full and, perhaps, complete expression. Like W. B. Yeats in his final plays and poems, there is a conscious effort on the part of McGahern to register the fact that this is his final novel, which, despite many commentators' appraisal, in many ways stands apart from his earlier work. Only in the hindsight of the author's death can there be discerned a compelling earnestness to his writing which gives every word a peculiar power and particular point because each was written as if it were to be the last word ever to be written. Up until this point, and certainly in *Amongst Women* (1990) and the short story 'The Country Funeral', McGahern's art could be argued to follow a trajectory towards a form of redemption for his characters signalled by a transcendent moment holding out the possibility of a final reconciliation between the natural and human spheres of activity.[4]

On the surface it would seem that *That They May Face the Rising Sun* also celebrates this accommodation with nature with various underlying narratives of return within the novel giving rhythm to its progress. The novel centres on a year in the life of Joe Ruttledge and his wife Kate and their existence by a lake in County Leitrim. There is no story as such: no plot that must work itself out to conclusion. Nevertheless, while nothing much happens, everything happens: weighty import is generated from the stuff of life, the half-moments of connection and conversation, the tiniest of gestures and the subtlest of touches. In a way, it is a return to James Joyce's *Ulysses* in its nebulous open-endedness or Thomas Amory's eighteenth-century *The Life of John Buncle, Esq.* that revelled in formless digression and rambling. Each of these novels, in their own way, is enormously imbued with a joy for the density of the everyday, with the quirks and tics of unique character caught in a moment. McGahern's novel uses the unfolding movements of a single year to give a semblance of shape to the action, the pulse of the seasons finding an echo of sorts in the human world. While many might not see McGahern as overtly experimental, he actually is, but certainly not in the clumsily obvious manner of so many contemporary novelists in Ireland and elsewhere who fetishise difficulty and obscurity. He realises that the problem the novel has always experienced in the Irish context is one of the mechanics of plot, which imposes a far too predetermined, too fated and fixed purpose and design on Irish reality. McGahern undoubtedly learns from the short-story form, bringing to bear on the novel that type of technique and imagination which stresses being as opposed to doing. Thus, he reimagines the form, re-conceptualising it to the specifics of the Irish scene. In *That They May Face the Rising Sun*, he shifts his focus away from the often claustrophobic depiction of the family in his other writing outwards, managing to give voice to an entire community wherein every person – even the patently reprehensible – is permitted their position.

Certainly in the Celtic Tiger Ireland of its publication, what appears to be such a positive representation of rural Ireland as a place of possibility and celebration challenges the accepted worldview of progress. While undoubtedly this is a rendering of a world about to disappear – its slow pace of life under pressure from the quickening of modernity – McGahern's stressing, particularly, the delicate centrality of friendship offers a vision that imagines the potential of continuity beyond these characters and their particular moment.[5] Indeed, the move away from the site of family suggests as much: the future need not depend only on the notion of birth and inheritance but also on the societal codes of interaction and mutual companionship. The focus on a community is itself a reversal of the liberal humanist concentration on the individual as the measure of all things, as the centre of meaning and significance in the modern world. Though the novel revolves round Ruttledge and his wife, in truth they are just players in a wider drama along with everyone else: friends and neighbours such as Jamesie and his wife Mary, his brother Johnny who returns home after many years spent in England, John Quinn who is driven by a bestial sexuality and Patrick Ryan who never finishes building a shed for Ruttledge. And family, too, in the form of the Shah, Ruttledge's uncle, and his story of going into retirement, thicken the world rendered in the novel.

This is very much a novel about public concerns; or, rather, concerned with life lived in the public arena as opposed to the interior and private world that much modern writing concerns itself with – that, indeed, modernity concerns itself with. Characters face outwards towards other people, rather than inwards towards the self. It is a novel that turns on relationships and links between characters: the layers of multiple connections of which any society is made up. It is a novel made up of dialogue and conversation, with circling stories and anecdotes about people in the community. And even wholly disruptive figures – such as John Quinn – can be momentarily redeemed in the ordinary and everyday human ceremonies of community.

While the public realm is the place of action and interaction, McGahern is not concerned with the grand narratives of nation, politics or history, though they do exist in a shadowy form on the edge of consciousness. It is the seasons which mark the progression and developments of the work, the descriptions of the lake and the countryside through the year revealing the changing fortunes of the characters. And yet this use of the seasons suggests also a kind of timelessness: in that this year is like and will be like any other year. What is being emphasised is human time, or the limited human perception of time, and a more elemental, nature-based concept of progress. Jamesie's house is full of clocks, none of which is set to the correct time. He likes the sound of them and says: 'Who cares about time? We know the time well enough.'[6] The high modernist writers of an earlier generation desired to escape Time, to transcend its inevitable count down to mortality, but here this preoccupation is transformed into a dismissive indifference. After making this remark, Jamesie asks Ruttledge, 'Do you have any more news now before you go?' This is his currency: stories, tales and gossip, in short, 'news' – news about people and their foibles and their ways. That is what is important rather than Time, this is what marks development and progress.

This is a novel very much centred on the here and now, on the lived moment in the present. There is no real past, nor is there a sense of the future, but just an eternal present. Rather than development and progress in a linear and traditional sense, the reader is offered rhythmic recurrence. The image of the half-built shed at the close of the novel suggests that completion, or finality, is not of this world. Rather, an ongoing perpetual striving is the way of life on display. At one point Ruttledge and Kate converse:

'The greatest country in Ireland was always the world to come.'
'And all we have is the day.'
'We better make the most of it.'   (*Rising Sun*, p. 200)

Life is to be lived, and that is the greatest mystery of all. But there is death too in the novel, or one death in particular: that of Johnny the returned emigrant. The wake in Irish writing has a long history, a sign of difference and the exotic, each funeral scene subconsciously viewed as a representation of something larger than the single event: the death of a community or a nation with Ireland always dying or about to die. The scene is always presented from outside, the traveller's perspective looking in on the events. Here McGahern offers the reader a version of the wake and the funeral from within the ceremony itself. It remains mysterious, not because of ignorance but because of it being humanised and made known as the rituals surrounding the preparation for the body for burial are scrupulously detailed: they honour the dead but also make death bearable for the living. The significance of this scene has peculiar Irish resonance, but also transcends the Irish locale to inhabit the universal. It is recognition of the fragility of existence, and recognition too of the human world's efforts to comprehend death in life. It is stated that: 'The innate sacredness of each single life stood out more starkly in death than in the whole of its natural life' (*Rising Sun*, p. 273). Giving the singular body back its unique individuality in this manner is a challenge to the countless misrepresentations of the Irish person over centuries. It returns a quiet respect and dignity to the human person.

And yet there is a darker truth at work within the novel despite its obvious celebration of this community and its shared energies. After an afternoon spent with Jamesie, Ruttledge ponders his feelings:

He felt this must be happiness. As soon as the thought came to him he fought it back, blaming the whiskey. The very idea was as dangerous as presumptive speech. Happiness could not be sought or worried into being, or even fully grasped. It should be allowed its own slow pace so that it passes unnoticed if it ever comes at all. (*Rising Sun*, p. 183)

Ruttledge comes to know that the intrusion of thought or language might jeopardise this existence, dispel its magic. It would seem that he adheres to a humanistic acceptance of the human lot. But his difficulty is that he does think and he certainly speaks, as do all the characters: silence is not of this world. In a very profound way, Ruttledge, as the central consciousness within the narrative, remains set apart from the others, distant and somewhat aloof. Ruttledge does not partake in the religious customs of the community, but that eccentricity makes him only colourfully different rather than representative of an attack on communal values. His and Kate's childlessness is alluded to but never fully discussed or meditated on, but it seems clear that in a society of fecund life in the form of nature and other characters' children, their conscious decision not to have children marks them out. Throughout McGahern's fiction, sexuality is always presented as abnormal and in the figure of John Quinn in *That They May Face the Rising Sun* the reader is offered another brutal variation on this theme. In this light, Kate and Ruttledge's childlessness would seem to be a comment on that abnormality, a means of denying it and, perhaps, transcending it. Also, though it is never stated, Ruttledge as the dominant consciousness is the artist figure that might become the chronicler of this world if given half the chance. While authorial judgement is sparse, it is present – as it must be – and it is that, finally, which distances him from the world and the community he loves. Passing judgement betrays the easy existence inherent within this place, offering it up for a public consumption that it would hardly have wished for. But it is a personal tragedy only, as perhaps is Ruttledge and Kate's childlessness, for society will go on without his brooding presence contemplating it or making a work of art out of it.

It is curious that in the contemporary moment all things are deemed to be of huge significance: everything is seemingly of equal meaning. Consequently, nothing has meaning because nothing is more important than anything else. John McGahern's fiction returns us to a sense of the quiet importance of the world and our lives in that world. *That They May Face the Rising Sun's* main achievement, though, is to be discerned in its attempt to deconstruct the dominating individual consciousness, or at least acknowledge that to be in the world is to be in the world with others. His work recognises that this is the central mystery, individuals coming together and being prepared to share their lives: mystery is not to be found elsewhere, in abstract ideas of God or an afterlife, or indeed solely in the workings of nature. He realises that the real mystery is in the everyday, is in life as it is quietly lived both individually and collectively.

As a novel, *That They May Face the Rising Sun* is exemplary in its grasp of the elemental energies of the form: it is open to the knowledge that there can be no final knowledge, that there will always be something more to be said. As a novel, it could be said to be the one which the form has been moving towards, the form finally becoming a medium through which the Irish voice can be heard as it is, as it can be heard in conversation with itself and with others. To be sure, there have been other novels – especially Joyce's *Ulysses* – which have also achieved that, but McGahern's novel remains accessible to a wider audience. There are no stereotypes here, no representative types who embody national or political or historical currents, only the elusive complexities of people as they are – inconsistent and contradictory, able to hold conflicting ideas simultaneously without collapse. It is also, as it is being written, and read, continually reformatting itself and reconfiguring its own boundaries and shape, ever moving towards some final notion of what it might be, but never ultimately arriving. That has always been the story of the Irish novel, at once anxious about itself, while striving towards coherence.

Conclusion: The future of the Irish novel in the global literary marketplace

In early 2010, novelist Julian Gough, author of *Jude: Level 1* (2007), attacked his fellow Irish writers[1] for their inability or unwillingness to confront the immediate moment of Celtic and post-Celtic Tiger Ireland, making the charge they were content to wallow in the past of a pre-modern Ireland. Of course, his somewhat over-the-top and certainly tongue-in-cheek comments were intended to spur on a response, and a debate duly followed in the pages of the *Irish Times* newspaper. The merits, or not, of novels that dealt with the past and novels which dealt with the present were bandied back and forth for a number of weeks in articles and letters. The fundamental point missed, or ignored, in the debate was that it is not a novel's immediacy in terms of its content that is important but its relevancy at any given moment to its readership which marks off a novel's success or otherwise. What emerged were depressingly familiar arguments about the novel that were neither new nor fresh, but have dogged the form from its earliest appearance in Ireland. Behind the arguments about the past and the present lurked the suggestion that the form that happily flourishes elsewhere fails to flourish within an Irish context. It would seem that the Irish novel continues to be misunderstood. The discussion possessed no real historical sense of how the novel has developed in Ireland, or indeed elsewhere. This study, of course, offers such an overview of the novel's presence in Irish literature and culture, providing some sense of how the form, and its concerns and tropes, have operated in Ireland over four centuries.

If the exact beginning of the Irish novel is beset by numerous false starts, then the ending of a history of the Irish novel must also be aware that any conclusion will necessarily be arbitrary. This history of the Irish novel has traced the form's presence in Irish writing over four centuries, demonstrating clearly how writers and their work responded to ever-changing circumstances. Language, landscape and the individual have all been represented in different ways at different times, with the novel's association with the advent of modernity itself signalling how central the form should be to any understanding of Ireland's cultural history. To talk of progress and development in relation to the novel in Ireland is to miss the point about a literary form that has always 'made it up' as it went along, rewriting the rules of its own engagement with the world as it had to: startlingly new and experimental at times and reassuringly familiar at others. To see the novel as merely reflecting a gradual movement towards societal normality or maturity, to see the novel chronicling a movement away from myth and romance – the dangerous realm of illusion – towards a supposedly proper realism, is simply wrong. The novel form's inherent instability perfectly matches the obvious uncertainties and contradictions within wider cultural, political and historical life, giving often-uneasy expression to Irish anxieties. In other words, perfection – religious or secular – is not of the human world and the Irish novel form, with its lingering imperfections, inhabits and mirrors that flawed space.

At the outset of this study, it was claimed that the Irish novel has always been caught between the demands of the ordinary and the extraordinary. The act of writing the novel itself has been for Irish authors a means of registering the utter strangeness of the commonplace while simultaneously transforming the unusual into the acceptably routine. This, of course, remains the case in the contemporary moment, perhaps even more so. The reality of a global literary marketplace means that Irish culture, like all national cultures, must reimagine itself within this wider frame in order to have purchase on that worldwide consciousness. Thus, the oscillation between the competing demands of the ordinary and the extraordinary manifests itself in the recurring question of who the intended readership for Irish fiction might be. Whether it is a local or an international readership being sought will necessarily colour the nature of the stories being told, and their eventual reception. Indeed, from the perspective of the present it appears that the economic demands of the marketplace are *the* drivers of aesthetic judgement. More so than ever the Irish novel, particularly, seems to be in the grasp of vulgar fiscal forces dictating what will sell in the literary marketplace. The irony of the present moment is that access to international publishing houses has never been easier for Irish writers. Indeed, that one of the main indicators of success in contemporary Irish writing is the literary prize awarded from Britain or America[2] signals not only how the act of novel writing has entered into the realm of show business, with the emphasis on business, but also how pervasive the provincial mindset still is in Irish culture. The continuing need for approval from elsewhere remains a constant. The attraction of the international novel as witnessed, for instance, in the work of Colum McCann, Michael Collins, Claire Kilroy, Colm Toibin, Ronan Bennett and Gerard Donovan signals that the Irish writer is not only burdened with telling his or her own story but also with telling everyone else's story too. The danger is that admission into this international market might simplify the nature of the Ireland on display, steering clear of the subtleties and complexities a local reader might appreciate and expect. What might be forgotten is that while Ireland is being rendered as one-dimensional, so too is the reality of difference on a global scale. The international novel operates in the realm of accessible stereotype so that nowhere is different from anywhere and everyone is like everyone else. The rise of genre fiction in Irish writing, it could be argued, is one manifestation of this drive towards bland conformity, the rough edges of literary expression being pared down so that reader, and writer, know what to expect and get what they want. A result is that nothing seems strange anymore in a world where all things are already strange, where all things are of equal importance and where all experience is already known and shared. There seems little left for the novel to explore with the private realm now the domain of reality television and social websites on the Internet.

And yet, the novel continues to be written, and read, because it continues in its struggle, as it has always done, in its desire to be relevant. As has been argued throughout this present study, each generation of writer and critic necessarily views its own historical moment as being truly exceptional to what has gone before it. While this generation appears to operate in a totally new environment, in reality the situation with the novel in Ireland at the moment is that, in many ways, it has returned to what the novel actually was in the eighteenth and nineteenth centuries: a vulgar vehicle for throw-away stories of the immediate moment that consciously eschew the decorations and pretensions of high art.

Suffice it to say that the Irish novel has a future because it possesses a past.

Notes

NOTES FOR INTRODUCTION

1. Franco Moretti, 'On *The Novel*', in Franco Moretti (ed.), *The Novel* vol. I: *History, Geography, and Culture* (Princeton University Press, 2006), p. ix.
2. Margaret Anne Doody, *The True Story of the Novel* (New Brunswick: Rutgers University Press, 1997).
3. Franco Moretti, 'The Novel: History and Theory', *New Left Review*, 52 (July/August 2008), 124.
4. Quoted in Lawrence Howe, *Mark Twain and the Novel: The Double-cross of Authority* (Cambridge University Press, 1998), p. 1.
5. Terry Eagleton, *The English Novel: An Introduction* (Oxford: Blackwell Publishing, 2005), p. 1.
6. See Georg Lukács, *The Theory of the Novel: A Historico-philosophical Essay on the Forms of Great Epic Literature* (London: Merlin Press, 1971), p. 29.
7. For example see Ian Watts, *The Rise of the Novel: Studies in Defoe, Richardson and Fielding* (London: The Hogarth Press, 1957/1987).
8. See Frank O'Connor, *The Lonely Voice: A Study of the Short Story* (London: Macmillan, 1965), p. 17; and Sean O'Faolain, 'Fifty Years of Irish Writing', *Studies: An Irish Quarterly Review*, 51:201 (Spring, 1962), 93–105.
9. See R. F. Foster, *Luck and the Irish: A Brief History of Change, 1970–2000* (London: Penguin, 2007/2008) and the chapter entitled 'How the Short Stories Became Novels', pp. 147–183.
10. For example, see Margaret Kelleher and Philip O'Leary (eds.), *The Cambridge History of Irish Literature*, vol. I: *To 1890*; *The Cambridge History of Irish Literature*, vol. II: *1890–2000* (Cambridge University Press, 2006); and John Wilson Foster (ed.), *The Cambridge Companion to the Irish Novel* (Cambridge University Press, 2006).
11. See, for example, Franco Moretti (ed.), *The Novel*, vol. I: *History, Geography, and Culture* (Princeton University Press, 2006); and *The Novel*, vol. II: *Forms and Themes* (Princeton University Press, 2006).

NOTES FOR INTERCHAPTER 1

1. Rowland Davies, *Journal of the Very Rev. Rowland Davies, LL. D. Dean of Ross, 1689–1690*, edited with notes and appendix by Richard Caulfield (New York: AMS Press, 1968), pp. 129–130.

2. Elizabeth Bowen, *Bowen's Court*, new introduction by Thomas McCarthy (Cork: The Collins Press, 1998), p. 94.

3. Quoted in Toby Barnard, *Irish Protestant Ascents and Descents, 1641–1770* (Dublin: Four Courts, 2004), p. 145.

4. Davies, *Journal of the Very Rev. Rowland Davies*, p. 127.

5. For a very informative discussion of the novel, see Ian Campbell Ross and Anne Markey, 'From Clonmel to Peru: Barbarism and Civility in *Virtue Rewarded; or, The Irish Princess*', *Irish University Review*, 38:2 (Autumn/Winter 2008), pp. 179ff. See also 'Appendix: Miranda and the Authorship of *Virtue Rewarded*', in Anon., *Virtue Rewarded; or, The Irish Princess*, edited with introduction and notes by Ian Campbell Ross and Anne Markey (Dublin: Four Courts Press, 2010), pp. 156ff. where they suggest an author for the work.

6. Anonymous, *Virtue Rewarded; or The Irish Princess. A new Novel*, edited and introduced by Hubert McDermott (Gerrards Cross: Colin Smythe, 1992), p. 20. All future quotations will be incorporated into the main text.

7. See Roy Foster, *Oxford History of Modern Ireland* (Oxford University Press, 1992), p. 141: 'Ireland became a theatre of European war in 1689–90.'

8. Edward MacLysaght, *Irish Life in the Seventeenth Century* (Dublin: Irish Academic Press, 1939/1979).

9. See John Dunton, *Teague Land: or A Merry Ramble to the Wild Irish*, transcribed from the manuscript, edited and introduced by Andrew Carpenter (Dublin: Four Courts Press, 2003).

10. See Ian Ross and Anne Markey, 'Introduction', in Anon., *Virtue Rewarded; or, The Irish Princess*, pp. 16ff.

11. See Michael McKeon, *The Origins of the English Novel, 1600–1740* (Baltimore: Johns Hopkins University Press, 1988), pp. 5–6.

12. See James P. Carson, 'Enlightenment, Popular Culture, and Gothic Fiction', in John Richetti (ed.), *The Cambridge Companion to the Eighteenth-Century Novel* (Cambridge University Press, 1996), p. 266.

13. Fear of rapparees was very real for those in Clonmel in 1690: they attacked numerous escorts of provisions and artillery between Clonmel and Carrick in that year. See William Burke, *History of Clonmel* (Kilkenny: Roberts Brothers, 1983; 1st edn 1907), p. 111.

14. For a good discussion of this, see Andrew Carpenter, Seamus Deane and W. J. McCormack, 'Political Prose: Cromwell to O'Connell', in Seamus Deane (ed.), *The Field Day Anthology of Irish Writing*, vol. 1 (Derry: Field Day Publications, 1991), pp. 855–859.

15. Sean Connolly, 'Elite Responses to Popular Culture, 1660–1850', in James S. Donnelly and Kerby Miller (eds.), *Irish Popular Culture: 1650–1850* (Dublin: Irish Academic Press, 1998), p. 5.

NOTES FOR CHAPTER 1

1. Walter Benjamin, *Illuminations: Essays and Reflections*, edited with an Introduction by Hannah Arendt (New York: Schocken Books, 1969/1985), p. 256.

2. Davies, *Journal of the Very Rev. Rowland Davies*, p. 156.
3. W. B. Yeats, 'Introduction to The Words upon the Window-Pane', in *Explorations*, selected by Mrs W. B. Yeats (New York: Macmillan, 1962), p. 345.
4. See Joe Cleary and Clare Connolly (eds.), *The Cambridge Companion to Modern Irish Culture* (Cambridge University Press, 2005), Joe Cleary's 'Introduction: Ireland and Modernity', pp. 1–24.
5. See Catherine Skeen, 'Projecting Fictions: *Gulliver's Travels, Jack Connor*, and *John Buncle*', *Modern Philology: A Journal Devoted to Research in Medieval and Modern Literature*, 100:3 (2003), 330–359.
6. Richard Head, *The English Rogue – described in the life of Meriton Latroon a witty extravagant being a complete history of the most eminent cheats of both sexes* (London: Routledge, 1928), p. 6.
7. Head, *The English Rogue*, pp. 6–7.
8. For an interesting discussion of this novel, see George O'Brien, 'The Fictional Irishman 1665–1850', *Studies: An Irish Quarterly Review*, LXVI (Winter 1977), 319–329.
9. Doody, *The True Story of the Novel*, p. 261.
10. See Norman Vance, *Irish Literature: A Social History: Tradition, Identity and Difference* (Dublin: Four Courts Press, 1999), p. 7. See also J. C. Beckett, 'Literature in English 1691–1800' in T. W. Moody and W. E. Vaughan (eds.), *A New History of Ireland*, vol. IV: *Eighteenth Century Ireland 1691–1800* (Oxford: Clarendon Press, 1986), pp. 424–470.
11. Christopher Morash, *A History of Irish Theatre 1601–2000* (Cambridge University Press, 2003), p. 33.
12. Eagleton, *The English Novel*, p. 6.
13. Declan Kiberd, 'Irish Literature and Irish History', in Roy Foster (ed.), *Oxford History of Modern Ireland* (Oxford University Press, 1992), p. 257.
14. Louis Cullen, 'Catholics under the Penal Laws', *Eighteenth-Century Ireland/Iris an dá chultúr*, 1 (1986), 23.
15. Ian Campbell Ross, 'Prose in English, 1690–1800: From the Williamite Wars to the Act of Union', in Kelleher and O'Leary (eds.), *The Cambridge History of Irish Literature*, vol. I: *To 1890*, p. 269.
16. J. R. R. Adams, *The Printed Word and the Common Man: Popular Culture in Ulster 1700–1900* (Belfast: The Institute of Irish Studies, QUB, 1987), pp. 67–68.
17. Penelope Aubin, *The Life and Adventures of the Lady Lucy, the daughter of an Irish Lord* (London, 1726), p. 46.
18. William Congreve, 'Incognita: Or, Love and Duty Reconciled', in *An Anthology of Seventeenth-Century Fiction*, edited with an introduction and notes by Paul Salzman (Oxford University Press, 1991), p. 474.
19. See Ian Campbell Ross, Aileen Douglas and Anne Markey, 'Introduction', in Sarah Butler, *Irish Tales: or, Instructive Histories for the Happy Conduct of Life*, edited with an introduction and notes by Ian Campbell Ross, Aileen Douglas and Anne Markey (Dublin: Four Courts Press, 2010), p. 9; and Deana Rankin,

'"Shet Fourd vor Generaul Nouddificaushion": Relocating the Irish Joke, 1678–1690', *Eighteenth-Century Ireland/Iris an dá chultúr*, 16 (2001), 47–72.

20. See Joep Leerssen, *Mere Irish and Fíor-Ghael: Studies in the Idea of Irish Nationality, its Development and Literary Expression prior to the Nineteenth Century* (Cork University Press, 1996), p. 410, footnote 70. For a discussion of the identity of the author and other matters see Ian Campbell Ross, '"One of the Principle Nations in Europe": The Representation of Ireland in Sarah Butler's *Irish Tales*', *Eighteenth Century Fiction*, 7:1 (October 1994), 1–16.

21. See Christopher Morash, *A History of the Irish Theatre: 1601–2000* (Cambridge University Press, 2002), pp. 39ff.: 'How theatre uses the same material'.

22. Ross, '"One of the Principle Nations in Europe": The Representation of Ireland in Sarah Butler's *Irish Tales*', 1–16.

23. Sarah Butler, *Irish Tales: or, Instructive Histories for the Happy Conduct of Life*, p. 632.

24. *Ibid.*, p. 39.

25. *Ibid.*, p. 51.

26. Hugh MacCurtin, 'A Brief Discourse in Vindication of the Antiquity of Ireland (1717)', in Deane (ed.), *The Field Day Anthology of Irish Writing*, vol. i, p. 881.

27. Butler, *Irish Tales*, p. 39.

28. For this reading, see Siobhan Kilfeather, 'The Profession of Letters, 1700–1810', in Angela Bourke *et al.* (eds.), *The Field Day Anthology of Irish Writing*, vol. v (Cork University Press, 2002), p. 782.

29. Ross, '"One of the Principle Nations in Europe": The Representation of Ireland in Sarah Butler's *Irish Tales*', 1–16.

30. See Nicholas Canny and Anthony Pagden (eds.), *Colonial Identity in the Atlantic World: 1500–1800* (Princeton University Press, 1987).

31. Jarlath Killeen, *Gothic Ireland: Horror and the Irish Anglican Imagination in the Long Eighteenth Century* (Dublin: Four Courts Press, 2005), p. 13: 'Disruption rather than stability is a function of Irish Anglican psychology.'

32. See Benedict Anderson, *Imagined Communities: Reflections on the Origin and Spread of Nationalism* (London: Verso, 2006).

33. Jonathan Swift, *Gulliver's Travels*, edited with an introduction and notes by Paul Turner (Oxford University Press, 1998), p. 263.

34. Joseph Conrad, *Heart of Darkness*, in R. V. Cassill, *The Norton Anthology of Short Fiction* (New York: W. W. Norton and Company, 1986), p. 285.

35. Swift, *Gulliver's Travels*, p. 222.

36. Kiberd, *Irish Classics* (London: Granta Books, 2000), p. 82.

37. Eagleton, *The English Novel*, p. 45.

38. Quoted in Niall Ó Ciosáin, *Print and Popular Culture in Ireland 1750–1850* (London: Palgrave, 1997), p. 14.

39. Firdous Azim, *The Colonial Rise of the Novel* (London: Routledge, 1993), p. 122.

40. Ó Ciosáin, *Print and Popular Culture in Ireland 1750–1850*, p. 9.

41. Ross, 'Prose in English, 1690–1800', p. 259.

42. Anon., *The Adventures of Shelim O'Blunder, Esq., The Irish Beau* (London: 1751), title page.

43. See Leerssen, *Mere Irish and Fíor-Ghael: Studies in the Idea of Irish Nationality, its Development and Literary Expression prior to the Nineteenth Century*, pp. 108–110.
44. *Ibid.*, p. 17–18.
45. *Ibid.*, p. 12.
46. Ian Campbell Ross, 'An Irish Picaresque Novel: William Chaigneau's *The History of Jack Connor*', *Studies*, LXXI (1982), 270–279.
47. For this argument, see Bernard Escarbelt, 'William Chaigneau's Jack Connor: A Literary Image of the Irish Peasant', in Jacqueline Genet (ed.), *Rural Ireland, Real Ireland?* (Gerrards Cross: Colin Smythe, 1996), pp. 51–57.
48. William Chaigneau, *The History of Jack Connor* (Dublin: 1752), p. 43.
49. *Ibid.*, p. 277.
50. *Ibid.*, p. 16.
51. See Leerssen, *Mere Irish and Fíor-Ghael*, p. 408.
52. Chaigneau, *The History of Jack Connor*, p. 104.
53. See Skeen, 'Projecting Fictions', 330–359.
54. Chaigneau, *The History of Jack Connor*, vol. II, p. 351.
55. For example John Browne, 'The Benefits which arise to a Trading People from Navigable Rivers' (1729); Thomas Prior 'A list of the Absentees of Ireland' (1730); or Bishop George Berkeley *The Querist* (1753), in Deane (ed.), *Field Day Anthology of Irish Writing*, vol. I, pp. 896–907.
56. See Ian Campbell Ross, 'Thomas Amory, *John Buncle*, and the Origins of Irish Fiction', *Eire-Ireland*, XVIII:3 (1983), 71–85 (73).
57. Thomas Amory, *The Life of John Buncle, Esq.* (London: 1766), vol. I, p. vii.
58. Thomas Cogan, *John Buncle, Junior, Gentleman* (Dublin, 1776), pp. 54, 55.
59. Amory, *The Life of John Buncle, Esq.*, vol. I, pp. 1–2.
60. *Ibid.*, vol. I, pp. 288–289.
61. *Ibid.*, vol. II, pp. 178–179.
62. See Skeen, 'Projecting Fictions', 358.
63. 'Cill Chais', in *The New Oxford Book of Irish Verse*, edited with translations by Thomas Kinsella (Oxford University Press, 1989), p. 253.
64. Daniel Corkery, *The Hidden Ireland: A Study of Gaelic Munster in the Eighteenth Century* (Dublin: Gill and Macmillan, 1924/1989), p. 35.
65. See Kiberd, *Irish Classics*, pp. 1–12.
66. Seán Ó Tuama (ed.), *An Duanaire 1600–1900: Poems of the Dispossessed*, translations into English verse by Thomas Kinsella (Dublin: The Dolmen Press, 1981/1994), p. 165.
67. See Leerssen, *Mere Irish and Fíor-Ghael*, p. 194.
68. See Eagleton, *The English Novel*, pp. 79–93.
69. Barnard, *Irish Protestant Ascents and Descents, 1641–1770*, p. 130.
70. See Bourke *et al.* (eds.), *The Field Day Anthology of Irish Writing*, vol. V, p. 796.
71. Oliver Goldsmith, *The Vicar of Wakefield*, edited with an introduction by Stephen Coote (London: Penguin Books, 1766/1986), p. 49.
72. W. B. Yeats, 'The Seven Sages', in *The Collected Poems of W. B. Yeats* (London: Macmillan, 1985), p. 272.

73. David Dickson, *New Foundations: Ireland 1660–1800* (Dublin: Irish Academic Press, 1987/2000).
74. *Ibid.*, p. 104.
75. Ian Campbell Ross, 'Rewriting Irish Literary History: The Case of the Irish Novel', *Etudes Anglaises*, XXXIX:4 (October–December 1986).
76. See Bourke *et al.* (eds.), *The Field Day Anthology of Irish Writing*, vol. IV, p. 794.
77. Dorothea Du Bois, *Theodora: A Novel* (London, 1770), p. 54. See also Bourke *et al.* (eds.), *The Field Day Anthology of Irish Writing*, vol. IV, p. 796.
78. Edmund Burke, *A Philosophical Enquiry into the Origin of our Ideas of the Sublime and the Beautiful*, in Deane (ed.), *The Field Day Anthology*, vol. I, p. 803.
79. See Ross, 'Prose in English, 1690–1800', pp. 273–274.
80. See plot descriptions in Rolf Loeber and Magda Loeber, *A Guide to Irish Fiction: 1650–1900* (Dublin: Four Courts Press, 2006), pp. 1046, 15, 830.
81. See Jarlath Killeen, *Gothic Ireland*, pp. 182–190 for a fascinating discussion of this novel.
82. Regina Maria Roche, *The Children of the Abbey: A Tale* (Cork, 1798), p. 114.
83. *Ibid.*, p. 189.

NOTES FOR INTERCHAPTER 2

1. W. B. Yeats, 'Epitaph to *Responsibilities*', in *The Collected Poems of W. B. Yeats*, p. 112.
2. Seamus Deane, *Strange Country: Modernity and Nationhood in Irish Writing since 1790* (Oxford University Press, 1997), p. 39.
3. Maria Edgeworth, *Castle Rackrent: An Hibernian Tale: Taken from Facts, and from the Manners of the Irish Squires, before the year 1782*, edited with an introduction by George Watson (Oxford University Press, 1980), p. 5. Future quotations will be incorporated into the main body of the text.
4. See Kathryn Kirkpatrick, 'Putting Down the Rebellion: Notes and Glosses on Maria Edgeworth's *Castle Rackrent*', *Eire-Ireland: Journal of Irish Studies*, 30:1 (1995), 77–90.
5. See Kiberd, *Irish Classics*, pp. 249, 258.
6. Cf. Seamus Deane, *A Short History of Irish Literature* (London: Hutchinson, 1986), p. 97.
7. See Terry Eagleton, *Heathcliff and the Great Hunger: Studies in Irish Culture* (London: Verso, 1995), p. 164.
8. See Kirkpatrick, 'Putting Down the Rebellion', 88.
9. *Ibid.*, 77–90.
10. See Clíona Ó Gallchoir, *Maria Edgeworth: Women, Enlightenment and Nation* (Dublin: University College Dublin Press, 2005), pp. 60ff.
11. Ó Gallchoir makes a convincing argument for Thady's confusion and divided loyalties about the position of his son Jason being such a moment of authentic

emotion within the novel precisely because of his recognition of the complexity of his situation. See *ibid.*, pp. 67–68.

12. See Kiberd, *Irish Classics*, pp. 258–259.
13. See Kiberd, *Irish Classics*, p. 245.
14. For an overview of this, see Claire Connolly, 'Irish Romanticism, 1800–1830', in Kelleher and O'Leary (eds.), *The Cambridge History of Irish Literature*, vol. 1: *To 1890*, pp. 407–448.
15. Quoted in Kiberd, *Irish Classics*, p. 264.
16. See Joep Leerssen, *Remembrance and Imagination: Patterns in the Historical and Literary Representation of Ireland in the Nineteenth Century* (Cork University Press in association with Field Day, 1996), pp. 35–36, where he talks about the auto-exotic or erotic.

NOTES FOR CHAPTER 2

1. G. W. F. Hegel, as quoted in George Lamming, 'The Occasion for Speaking', in Bill Ashcroft *et al.* (eds.), *The Empire Writes Back: Theory and Practice in Post-colonial Literatures* (London: Routledge, 1989).
2. See Joe Cleary, *Outrageous Fortune: Capital and Culture in Modern Ireland* (Dublin: Field Day Publications, 2007), pp. 47–75.
3. See David Lloyd, *Anomalous States: Irish Writing and the Post-colonial Moment* (Dublin: The Lilliput Press, 1993), pp. 125–162.
4. Maria Edgeworth, *The Absentee* (Oxford University Press, 1988), p. 83.
5. See Melissa Fegan, '"Isn't it your own country?" The Stranger in Nineteenth-Century Irish Literature', *The Yearbook of English Studies*, 34 (2004), 31–45.
6. Leerssen, *Remembrance and Imagination*, pp. 37, 38.
7. See Mary Jean Corbett, *Allegories of Union in Irish and English Writing, 1790–1870: Politics, History, and the Family from Edgeworth to Arnold* (Cambridge University Press, 2000).
8. www.british-fiction.cf.ac.uk/titleDetails.asp?title=1806A053.
9. Sydney Owenson, *The Wild Irish Girl: A National Tale*, edited with an introduction and notes by Kathryn Kirkpatrick (Oxford University Press, 1999), p. 159.
10. See Patrick Sheeran and Nina Witoszek, *Talking to the Dead: A Study of Irish Funerary Traditions* (Amsterdam, Rodopi Press, 1998).
11. See Barry Sloan, *The Pioneers of Anglo-Irish Fiction 1800–1850* (Gerrards Cross: Colin Smythe, 1986), pp. 109ff.
12. See Katie Trumpener, *Bardic Nationalism: The Romantic Novel and the British Empire* (Princeton University Press, 1997), p. 152.
13. For a discussion of the use of dialect in nineteenth-century Irish fiction, see Deane, *Strange Country*, pp. 59ff.
14. Deane, *A Short History of Irish Literature*, p. 99.
15. See Sloan, *The Pioneers of Anglo-Irish Fiction 1800–1850*, p. 135.
16. See Siobhan Kilfeather, 'Terrific Register: The Gothicization of Atrocity in Irish Romanticism', *Boundary 2* 31:1 (2004), 56; and Miranda Burgess, 'The

National Tale and Allied Genres, 1770s–1840s', in Foster (ed.), *The Cambridge Companion to the Irish Novel*, pp. 49–50.

17. See Connolly, 'Irish Romanticism, 1800–1830', p. 415.
18. Sloan, *The Pioneers of Anglo-Irish Fiction 1800–1850*, p. 44.
19. See Deane, *A Short History of Irish Literature*, p. 100.
20. See W. J. McCormack, 'Irish Gothic and After', in Deane (ed.), *The Field Day Anthology*, vol. 11, pp. 833–834.
21. Charles Robert Maturin, *Melmoth the Wanderer*, edited with an introduction and notes by Victor Sage (London: Penguin, 2000), p. 29.
22. See Margot Gayle Backus, *The Gothic Family Romance: Heterosexuality, Child Sacrifice, and the Anglo-Irish Colonial Order* (Durham, NC: Duke University Press, 1999), pp. 113ff.
23. Bowen, *Bowen's Court*, p. 453.
24. See Doody, *The True Story of the Novel*, p. 268.
25. See Margaret Kelleher, 'Prose and Drama in English, 1830–1890: From Catholic Emancipation to the Fall of Parnell', in Kelleher and O'Leary (eds.), *The Cambridge History of Irish Literature*, vol. 1: *To 1890*, p. 452.
26. See Loeber and Loeber, *Irish Fiction*, and James H. Murphy, *Ireland: A Social, Cultural and Literary History, 1791–1891* (Dublin: Four Courts Press, 2003), pp. 161ff.
27. Deane, *A Short History of Irish Literature*, p. 105.
28. Emer Nolan, 'Banim and the Historical novel', in Jacqueline Belanger (ed.), *The Irish Novel in the Nineteenth Century: Facts and Fictions* (Dublin: Four Courts Press, 2006), pp. 80–93.
29. See www.british-fiction.cf.ac.uk/reviews/boyn26–13.html.
30. John Banim, *The Boyne Water*, introduction by Robert Lee Woolf (New York: Garland Publishing Inc., 1978), pp. 262–263.
31. See Fegan, '"Isn't it your own country?"' 31–45.
32. See John Cronin, *The Anglo-Irish Novel*: vol. 1: *The Nineteenth Century* (Belfast: Appletree Press, 1980), p. 51. Cronin argues that the psychological depth within the novel prefigures that of James Joyce's creation Stephen Dedalus.
33. See John Banim, *The Nowlans*, introduction by Kevin Casey (Belfast: Appletree Press, 1992), pp. 141ff.
34. See Sloan, *The Pioneers of Anglo-Irish Fiction 1800–1850*, p. 116.
35. Siobhan Kilfeather, 'Sex and Sensation in the Nineteenth Century Novel', in Margaret Kelleher and James Murphy (eds.), *Gender Perspectives in Nineteenth Century Ireland* (Dublin: Irish Academic Press, 1997), p. 87.
36. See Deane, *Strange Country*, pp. 58ff. for a discussion of dialect in relation to *The Collegians*.
37. Dominick Tracy, 'Idyllic Resistance in Griffin's *The Collegians*', in Belanger (ed.), *The Irish Novel in the Nineteenth Century*, p. 101.
38. Gerald Griffin, *The Collegians*, introduction by John Cronin (Belfast: Appletree Press, 1992), pp. 291ff.
39. Sloan, *The Pioneers of Anglo-Irish Fiction 1800–1850*, p. 181.

40. W. B. Yeats (ed.), *Representative Irish Tales*, foreword by Mary Helen Thuente (Gerrards Cross: Colin Smythe, 1891/1979), p. 26.

41. James M. Cahalan, *The Irish Novel: A Critical History* (Boston: Twayne Publishers, 1988), p. 61.

42. Jason King, 'Emigration and the Irish Novel', in Belanger (ed.), *The Irish Novel in the Nineteenth Century*, pp. 123–124.

43. Cf. Julian Moynahan, *Anglo-Irish: The Literary Imagination in a Hyphenated Culture* (Princeton University Press, 1995), pp. 84ff.

44. See Kelleher, 'Prose and Drama in English, 1830–1890', p. 467.

45. Quoted in *ibid.*, p. 467.

46. Gavan Duffy, 'Mr. Lever's "Irish Novels"' (1843), in Deane (ed.), *The Field Day Anthology*, vol. 1, pp. 1255ff.

47. Yeats (ed.), *Representative Irish Tales*, p. 27.

48. Moynahan, *Anglo-Irish*, p. 43.

49. William Carleton, *Traits and Stories of the Irish Peasantry*, preface by Barbara Hayley (Gerrards Cross: Colin Smythe Limited, 1990), p. ii.

50. Sloan, *The Pioneers of Anglo-Irish Fiction 1800–1850*, p. 188.

51. See Margaret Kelleher, *The Feminisation of Famine: Expressions of the Inexpressible?* (Cork University Press, 1997).

52. Figures from Murphy, *Ireland*, pp. 95ff.

53. *Ibid.*, p. 97.

54. Quoted in Melissa Fegan, *Literature and the Irish Famine 1845–1919* (Oxford: Clarendon Press, 2002), p. 119.

55. Terry Eagleton, *Heathcliff and the Great Hunger: Studies in Irish Culture*, p. 132.

56. See David A. Miller, 'The Novel and the Police', in Dorothy J. Hale (ed.), *The Novel: An Anthology of Criticism and Theory 1900–2000* (Oxford: Blackwell Publishing, 2006), pp. 541ff.

57. Anthony Trollope, *Castle Richmond* (New York: Dover Publications, 1860/1984), p. 1.

58. Fegan, *Literature and the Irish Famine 1845–1919*, p. 130.

59. William Carleton, *The Black Prophet: A Tale of Irish Famine*, introduced by Timothy Webb (Shannon: Irish University Press, 1972).

60. See Kelleher, *The Feminisation of Famine: Expressions of the Inexpressible?* p. 31.

61. *Ibid.*, pp. 33–34.

62. Carleton, *Traits and Stories of the Irish Peasantry*, p. xxiii.

63. See Kelleher, 'Prose and Drama in English, 1830–1890', p. 466.

64. See W. J. McCormack, *Sheridan Le Fanu and Victorian Ireland* (Dublin: The Lilliput Press, 1991), pp. 138–139.

65. *The Irish Times*, Monday 6 July 1863, p. 3 (www.ireland.com.remote.library. dcu.ie/newspaper/archive/1863/0706/Pg003.html#Ar00305:23C5CE26D5E02 515EC2695FF26B5EC27E5FF27C5EA29D60028A5CE2A75E02765CE2865 E0).

66. See Kersti Tarien Powell, *Irish Fiction: An Introduction* (London: Continuum Publishing Group, 2004), p. 55.

67. See Sheridan Le Fanu, *The House by the Churchyard*, introduction by Thomas Kilroy (Belfast: Appletree Press, 1992), pp. 53ff.
68. See Elizabeth Bowen, *The Mulberry Tree: Writings of Elizabeth Bowen*, selected and introduced by Hermione Lee (London: Virago Press, 1986), p. 101.
69. See Marjorie Howes, 'Misalliance and Anglo-Irish Tradition in Le Fanu's *Uncle Silas*', *Nineteenth-Century Literature*, 47:2 (September 1992), 164–186.
70. Murphy, *Ireland*, p. 84.
71. See Cronin, *The Anglo-Irish Novel*, pp. 101ff.
72. James H. Murphy, 'Catholics and Fiction during the Union, 1801–1922', in Foster (ed.), *The Cambridge Companion to the Irish Novel*, p. 104.
73. *Ibid.*, p. 104.
74. See Kelleher, 'Prose and Drama in English, 1830–1890', p. 477ff.
75. See Cahalan, *The Irish Novel: A Critical History*, pp. 76–80.
76. See Margaret Kelleher, 'Women's Fiction, 1845–1900', in Bourke *et al.* (eds.), *The Field Day Anthology of Irish Writing*, vol. v, pp. 924ff.
77. See Jill Brady Hampton, 'Ambivalent Realism: May Laffan's "Flitters, Tatters, and the Counsellor"', *New Hibernia Review*, 12:2 (Samhradh/ Summer 2008), 141.
78. Yeats (ed.), *Representative Irish Tales*, p. 321.
79. Rosa Mulholland, *Marcella Grace: An Irish Novel* (London: Kegan Paul, 1886), p. 174.
80. Murphy, *Ireland*, pp. 162–163.
81. See Kathleen Costello-Sullivan, 'Novel Traditions: Realism and Modernity in *Hurrish* and *The Real Charlotte*', in Belanger (ed.), *The Irish Novel in the Nineteenth Century*, pp. 80–93.
82. Quoted in Kelleher, 'Prose and Drama in English, 1830–1890', p. 481.
83. Cahalan, *The Irish Novel: A Critical History*, p. 82.
84. See James Murphy, '"Insouciant Rivals of Mrs Barton": Gender and Victorian Aspiration in George Moore and the Women Novelists of the *Irish Monthly*', in Margaret Kelleher and James Murphy (eds.), *Gender Perspectives in Nineteenth Century Ireland* (Dublin: Irish Academic Press, 1997) p. 227.
85. Kiberd, *Irish Classics*, p. 287.
86. Adrian Frazier, 'Irish Modernisms, 1880–1930', in Foster (ed.), *The Cambridge Companion to the Irish Novel*, p. 116.
87. See Kiberd, *Irish Classics*, pp. 287ff.
88. George Moore, *A Drama in Muslin: A Realistic Novel*, introduction by A. Norman Jeffares (Gerrards Cross: Colin Smythe, 1981), p. 204.

NOTES FOR INTERCHAPTER 3

1. Patrick Kavanagh, *A Poet's Country: Selected Prose*, edited by Antoinette Quinn (Dublin: The Lilliput Press, 2003), p. 303.
2. See Julie Anne Stevens, *The Irish Scene in Somerville and Ross* (Dublin: Irish Academic Press, 2007), pp. 49ff.

3. See Deane, *A Short History of Irish Literature*, pp. 203ff.

4. See W. J. McCormack, *Fool of the Family: A Life of J. M. Synge* (London: Weidenfeld & Nicolson, 2000).

5. See Stevens, *The Irish Scene in Somerville and Ross*, p. 49.

6. Frazier, 'Irish Modernisms, 1880–1930', p. 121.

7. Edith Somerville and Martin Ross, *The Real Charlotte* (London: Quartet Books, 1977), p. 11.

8. See Costello-Sullivan, 'Novel Traditions: Realism and Modernity in *Hurrish* and *The Real Charlotte*', pp. 150–166.

9. Ann Owens Weekes, *Irish Women Writers: An Uncharted Tradition* (Lexington: University Press of Kentucky, 1990), p. 74.

10. Moynahan, *Anglo-Irish*, p. 186.

11. Yeats, 'The Statues', in *The Collected Poems*, p. 376.

12. See Joe Cleary, 'The Nineteenth Century Irish Novel: Notes and Speculations on Literary Historiography', in Belanger (ed.), *The Irish Novel in the Nineteenth Century*, p. 216.

NOTES FOR CHAPTER 3

1. See Loeber and Loeber, *Irish Fiction*, pp. xlixff.

2. James H. Murphy, *Catholic Fiction and Social Reality in Ireland, 1873–1922* (London: Greenwood Press, 1997), p. 2.

3. See P. J. Mathews, *Revival: The Abbey Theatre, Sinn Féin, the Gaelic League and the Co-operative Movement* (Cork University Press, 2003).

4. See Douglas Hyde, 'The Necessity of De-Anglicising Ireland', in David Pierce (ed.), *Irish Writing in the Twentieth Century: A Reader* (Cork University Press, 2000).

5. See Mathews, *Revival*.

6. Walter Benjamin, 'What is Epic Theatre?', *Illuminations: Essays and Reflections*, pp. 147ff.

7. See John Wilson Foster, 'The Irish Renaissance, 1890–1940: Prose in English', in Kelleher and O'Leary (eds.), *The Cambridge History of Irish Literature*, vol. II: *1890–2000*, pp. 113ff.

8. George Orwell, 'Inside the Whale', in *Inside the Whale and Other Essays* (London: Penguin, 1967).

9. See John Wilson Foster, *Fictions of the Irish Literary Revival: A Changeling Art* (Syracuse University Press, 1987), pp. 180–181.

10. See Lyn Pykett, 'Sensation and the Fantastic in the Victorian Novel', in Deirdre David (ed.), *The Cambridge Companion to the Victorian Novel* (Cambridge University Press, 2001), pp. 192–211.

11. See Kelleher, 'Prose and Drama in English, 1830–1890', p. 482; Kelleher, 'Women's Fiction, 1845–1900', in Bourke *et al.* (eds.), *The Field Day Anthology of Irish Writing*, vol. v, pp. 924–975.

12. See Geradine Meaney, 'Decadence, Degeneration and Revolting Aesthetics: The Fiction of Emily Lawless and Katherine Cecil Thurston', *Colby Quarterly: Irish Women Novelists 1800–1940*, XXXVI:2 (June 2002), 157–175.

13. Quoted in Kelleher, 'Women's Fiction, 1845–1900', pp. 926, 929.

14. Emer Nolan, 'Postcolonial Literary Studies, Nationalism, and Feminist Critique in Contemporary Ireland', *Éire-Ireland*, 42:1&2 (Spring and Summer 2007), 336–361.

15. Adams, *The Printed Word and the Common Man*, pp. 67–68.

16. Quoted in Nolan, 'Postcolonial Literary Studies, Nationalism, and Feminist Critique in Contemporary Ireland', 348.

17. James H. Murphy, *Catholic Fiction and Social Reality in Ireland, 1873–1922* (London: Greenwood Press, 1997), p. 79.

18. See Mathews, *Revival*.

19. George A. Birmingham, 'The Literary Movement in Ireland', in Pierce (ed.), *Irish Writing in the Twentieth Century: A Reader*, p. 81.

20. See Joan Fitzpatrick Dean, 'The Riot in Westport: George A. Birmingham at Home', *New Hibernia Review*, 5:4 (2001), 9–21.

21. See Catherine Morris, 'Becoming Irish? Alice Milligan and the Revival', *Irish University Review: New Perspectives on the Irish Literary Revival* (Spring/ Summer 2003), 88.

22. See Kelleher, 'Women's Fiction, 1845–1900', p. 926.

23. See Jules Verne, *The Extraordinary Adventures of Foundling Mick* (Dublin: Royal Irish Academy, 2008).

24. For a consideration of the modernist tendencies within the Revival, see Emer Nolan, 'Modernism and the Irish Revival', in Cleary and Connolly (eds.), *The Cambridge Companion to Modern Irish Culture*, pp. 157–172.

25. See Foster, 'The Irish Renaissance, 1890–1940', 113ff. Here Wilson Foster attempts to present Irish fiction as a seamless element of British fiction in an effort to present an archipelago reading of Irish literature and culture.

26. See Franco Moretti, 'Conjectures on World Literature', *New Left Review*, 1 (January/February 2000), 54–68.

27. See Frazier, 'Irish Modernisms, 1880–1930', pp. 113–132.

28. Geradine Meaney, 'Identity and Opposition: Women's Writing, 1890–1960', in Bourke *et al.* (eds.), *The Field Day Anthology of Irish Writing*, vol. V, p. 977. See also Meaney, 'Decadence, Degeneration and Revolting Aesthetics', 157–176.

29. Nolan, 'Postcolonial Literary Studies, Nationalism, and Feminist Critique in Contemporary Ireland', 356.

30. See Declan Kiberd, 'Inventing Irelands', *The Crane Bag*, 8:1 (1984), 11–23.

31. Quoted in W. B. Yeats, *John Sherman & Dhoya*, with an afterword by Eve Patten (Dublin: The Lilliput Press, 1991), p. 96.

32. W. B. Yeats, *Autobiographies* (London: Macmillan, 1955, 1987), p. 106.

33. See Catherine Candy, *Priestly Fictions: Popular Novelists of the Early 20th Century* (Dublin: Wolfhound Press, 1995), pp. 178ff.

34. See John Cronin, *Irish Fiction: 1900–1940* (Belfast: Appletree Press, 1992), p. 24.

35. See Augustine Martin, 'Prose Fiction, 1880–1945', in Deane (ed.), *The Field Day Anthology of Irish Writing*, vol. II, p. 1040. Martin talks of the novel's 'elaborate and leisurely detail'.

36. Murphy, *Catholic Fiction and Social Reality in Ireland: 1873–1922*, p. 118.

37. Quoted in Deane (ed.), *The Field Day Anthology of Irish Writing*, vol. II, p. 1088.

38. Emer Nolan, *Catholic Emancipations: Irish Fiction from Thomas Moore to James Joyce* (Syracuse University Press, 2007), p. 129.

39. See Declan Kiberd, *Inventing Ireland: The Literature of the Modern Nation* (London: Jonathan Cape, 1995), pp. 33–50; and Jarlath Killeen, *The Faiths of Oscar Wilde: Catholicism, Folklore and Ireland* (London: Palgrave, 2005), p. 79.

40. Oscar Wilde, *The Importance of Being Earnest*, in M. H. Abrams (ed.), *The Norton Anthology of English Literature*, vol. II, 5th edn (New York: W. W. Norton and Company, 1986), p. 1682.

41. Oscar Wilde, *The Picture of Dorian Gray*, Norton Critical Edition edited by Michael Patrick Gillespie (New York: W. W. Norton and Company, 2007), p. 3.

42. Killeen, *The Faiths of Oscar Wilde*, p. 79.

43. Frazier, 'Irish Modernisms, 1880–1930', p. 122.

44. Foster, 'The Irish Renaissance, 1890–1940: Prose in English', p. 129.

45. Bram Stoker, *Dracula*, edited with an introduction and notes by Maurice Hindle (London: Penguin, 1897/1993), pp. 30–31.

46. See Nolan, *Catholic Emancipations: Irish Fiction from Thomas Moore to James Joyce*, pp. 148–149.

47. *Ibid.*, p. 148.

48. George Moore, *The Lake*, with an afterword by Richard Cave (Gerrards Cross: Colin Smythe, 1905/1921/1980), p. 1.

49. See Cleary, *Outrageous Fortune*, pp. 111–179. Here Cleary offers an insightful introduction to 'naturalism' in Irish fiction.

50. Foster, 'The Irish Renaissance, 1890–1940: Prose in English', p. 141.

51. See P. J. Mathews, 'Stirring up Disloyalty: The Boer War, the Irish Literary Theatre and the Emergence of a New Separatism', in Margaret Kelleher (ed.), *Irish University Review, Special Issue: New Perspectives on the Irish Literary Revival*, 33:1 (Spring/Summer 2003), pp. 113–114.

52. See Eamonn Hughes, '"The Fact of Me-ness": Autobiographical Writing in the Revival Period', in Kelleher (ed.), *Irish University Review, Special Issue: New Perspectives on the Irish Literary Revival*, pp. 28–45.

53. Quoted in James Joyce, *Dubliners*, edited with an introduction and notes by Terence Brown (Harmondsworth: Penguin Books, 1992), p. xv.

54. Andrew Gibson, *James Joyce*, with an introduction by Declan Kiberd (London: Reaktion Books, 2006), p. 121.

55. See Gregory Dobbins, 'Scenes of Tawdry Tribute: Modernism, Tradition, and Connolly', in P. J. Mathews (ed.), *New Voices in Irish Criticism* (Dublin: Four Courts Press, 2000), pp. 3–12.

56. James Joyce, *Ulysses*, edited with an introduction and notes by Declan Kiberd (Harmondsworth: Penguin Books, 1992), p. 42.

57. James Joyce, *A Portrait of the Artist as a Young Man*, edited with an introduction and notes by Seamus Deane (Harmondsworth: Penguin Books, 1992), p. 205.
58. Seamus Deane, 'Joyce and Nationalism', in *Celtic Revivals: Essays in Modern Irish Literature 1880–1980* (London: Faber and Faber, 1985), pp. 97, 99.
59. *Ibid.*, p. 105.
60. James Stephens, *The Charwoman's Daughter*, with an introduction by Augustine Martin (Dublin: Gill and Macmillan, 1972), p. 128.
61. *Irish Times*, 26 October 1912, p. 7.
62. James Stephens, *The Crock of Gold* (London: Macmillan, 1931), p. 51.
63. James Stephens, *The Insurrection in Dublin* (Dublin: Sceptre Books, 1965), p. 94.
64. See Diarmaid Ferriter, *The Transformaiton of Ireland 1900–2000* (London: Profile Books, 2004), p. 52.
65. See Stephen Brown, *Ireland in Fiction: A Guide to Irish Novels, Tales, Romances, and Folk-Lore* (Shannon: Irish University Press, 1969), p. 96.
66. Cormac O'Grada, 'The Jews of Ireland 1870–1930: Towards an Economic-Demographic History' (www.econ.barnard.columbia.edu/~econhist/papers/COgrada.pdf).
67. See John Wilson Foster, *Irish Novels 1890–1940: New Bearings in Culture and Fiction* (Oxford University Press, 2008), pp. 180–186 for a detailed reading of the novel.
68. Manus O'Riordan, 'Jews in Independent Ireland' in *Dublin Review of Books*, www.drb.ie/june_citizens.html.
69. Patrick MacGill, *Children of the Dead End*, introduction by Brian D. Osborne (Edinburgh: Birlinn, 2005), p. xvii.
70. See *Irish Times*, 10 April, 1914, p. 7.
71. See *Irish Times*, 3 November, 1917, p. 9.
72. See Foster, *Fictions of the Irish Literary Revival*, p. 183.
73. Cahalan, *The Irish Novel: A Critical History*, p. 124.
74. See Cleary, *Outrageous Fortune*, pp. 111–179.
75. Foster, 'The Irish Renaissance, 1890–1940: Prose in English', p. 155.
76. See Brown, *Ireland in Fiction*, pp. 101, 262.
77. Eimar O'Duffy, *The Wasted Island* (London: Macmillan, 1919/1929), p. 534.
78. Katharine Tynan, 'Recent Irish Novels', *Studies: An Irish Quarterly Review*, 9:36 (December 1920).
79. See Mervyn Wall, 'A Disenchanted Island', *Irish Times*, 19 May 1967, p. 10.
80. Eimar O'Duffy, *The Wasted Island* (London: Macmillan, 1919/1929), p. 530.
81. See Alan Titley, 'The Novel in Irish', in Foster (ed.), *The Cambridge Companion to the Irish Novel*, pp. 171–188.

NOTES FOR INTERCHAPTER 4

1. George Eliot, *Middlemarch: A Study of Provincial Life* (Oxford University Press, 1997), p. 82.
2. Quoted in *Irish Times*, Weekend Section, 16 September, 2000, p. 2.

3. See Andrew Gibson, *Joyce's Revenge: History, Politics, and Aesthetics in Ulysses* (Oxford University Press, 2005), and Gibson, *James Joyce*.

4. Joyce, *Ulysses*, p. 6.

5. Wilde, *The Picture of Dorian Gray*, p. 3.

6. Bill Ashcroft *et al.* (eds.), *The Empire Writes Back: Theory and Practice in Post-colonial Literatures* (London: Routledge, 1989).

7. Samuel Beckett, 'Dante . . . Bruno . . . Vico . . . Joyce', in Samuel Beckett and others, *Our Examination Round his Factification for Incamination of Work in Progress* (London: Faber and Faber, 1972), p. 14.

8. Richard Ellmann (ed.), *Selected Letters of James Joyce* (New York: The Viking Press, 1975), p. 271. Letter to Carlo Linati, 21 September 1920.

9. *Ibid.*, p. 77. Letter to Stanislaus Joyce, 24 September 1905. Joyce talks of his appreciation of Lermontov's novel.

10. See Edward Mendelson, 'Encyclopedic Narrative: From Dante to Pynchon', *MLN*, 91:6, *Comparative Literature* (December 1976), 1267–1275.

11. Deane, *Celtic Revivals*, p. 105.

12. Joyce, *Ulysses*, p. 267.

13. See Emer Nolan, *James Joyce and Nationalism* (London: Routledge, 1995), pp. 96ff.

14. John Nash, *James Joyce and the Act of Reception: Reading, Ireland and Modernism* (Cambridge University Press, 2006), pp. 105ff.

15. See John McGahern, 'Sierra Leone' in *The Collected Stories* (London: Faber and Faber, 1992), p. 329.

16. Homer, *The Odyssey*, translated by E. V. Rieu (London: Penguin Books, 1978), p. 184.

NOTES FOR CHAPTER 4

1. Foster, *Irish Novels 1890–1940: New Bearings in Culture and Fiction*, p. 449.

2. Seamus Deane, 'Introduction', in Edward Said *et al.*, *Nationalism, Colonialism, Literature* (Minneapolis: University of Minnesota Press, 1990), p. 13.

3. See Kiberd, *Inventing Ireland*, pp. 263ff.

4. See Terence Brown, *Ireland: A Social and Cultural History 1922–1985* (London: Fontana Press, 1985), pp. 79ff.

5. George Russell, *The Interpreters* (London: Macmillan, 1922), pp. vii–viii.

6. See Cronin, *Irish Fiction 1900–1940*, pp. 100ff.

7. See R. F. Foster, *Modern Ireland: 1600–1972* (London: Penguin Books, 1990), p. 516.

8. See Aaron Kelly, *Twentieth-Century Irish Literature: A Reader's Guide to Essential Criticism* (London: Palgrave Macmillan, 2008), pp. 33ff.

9. See Cahalan, *The Irish Novel: A Critical History*, as an example of this.

10. See Cleary, *Outrageous Fortune*, p. 140ff.

11. See Gratten Freyer, 'The Many Lives of Peadar O'Donnell', *Irish Times*, Wednesday 21 February 1973, p. 14.

12. See Brown, *Ireland: A Social and Cultural History 1922–1985*, p. 94.
13. Deane, *Celtic Revivals*, p. 32.
14. See Vera Krielkamp, *The Anglo-Irish and the Big House* (Syracuse University Press, 1998).
15. Olwen Purdue '"My Duty as an Ulster Lord of the Manor": The Big House in Northern Ireland Politics and Society 1921–1960', paper delivered at the Royal Irish Academy 'Big House in Twentieth Century Irish Writing', RIA conference, 14–15 October 2008.
16. Somerville and Ross, *The Big House of Inver* (London: Mandarin, 1991), p. 6.
17. See Krielkamp, *The Anglo-Irish and the Big House*, pp. 131ff.
18. See 'Recent Fiction', *The Irish Times*, 30 October 1925, p. 3.
19. See Maud Ellmann, *Elizabeth Bowen: The Shadow across the Page* (Edinburgh University Press, 2004).
20. Elizabeth Bowen, *To the North* (London: Penguin, 1933/1999), p. 5.
21. See Anne Owens Weekes, 'Women Novelists, 1930s–1960s', in Foster (ed.), *The Cambridge Companion to the Irish Novel*, p. 192.
22. See Eibhear Walshe and Gwenda Young (eds.), *Molly Keane: Centenary Essays* (Dublin: Four Courts Press, 2006).
23. See Foster, *Irish Novels 1890–1940: New Bearings in Culture and Fiction*, p. 466.
24. *Ibid.*, p. 466.
25. *Ibid.*, p. 472. This is also argued by Neil Corcoran, *After Yeats and Joyce: Reading Modern Irish Literature* (Oxford University Press, 1997), p. 83.
26. For more on this, see Kiberd, *Irish Classics*, pp. 556ff.
27. See Cronin, *Irish Fiction: 1900–1940*, pp. 140ff.
28. See Kiberd, *Irish Classics*, p. 562.
29. *Ibid.*, p. 572.
30. See Eibhear Walshe (ed.), *Ordinary People Dancing: Essays on Kate O'Brien* (Cork University Press, 1994).
31. See Amanda Tucker, 'A Space Between: Transitional Feminism in Kate O'Brien's *Mary Lavelle*', in *New Hibernia Review/Iris Éireannach Nua: A Quarterly Record of Irish Studies*, 12:1 (Spring 2008), 82–95.
32. Kate O'Brien, *Mary Lavelle* (London: Virago Press, 1936/1984), p. 27.
33. Eibhear Walshe, *Kate O'Brien: A Writing Life* (Dublin: Irish Academic Press, 2006), p. 66.
34. See Kiberd, *Inventing Ireland*, p. 464.
35. See Tyler Farrell, 'Austin Clarke and the Consolations of Irish Catholicism', *New Hibernia Review*, 9:4 (Winter 2005), 113–128.
36. For a discussion of the novels of Francis MacManus, see Benedict Kiely, 'Praise God for Ireland: The Novels of Francis MacManus', in *A Raid into Dark Corners and Other Essays* (Cork University Press, 1999), pp. 95–106.
37. Sean O'Faolain, *Bird Alone* (Dublin: Millington, 1936/1973), p. 186.
38. See Margaret MacCurtain, 'Recollections of Catholicism, 1906–1960', in Bourke *et al.* (eds.), *The Field Day Anthology of Irish Writing*, vol. IV, p. 570.
39. Norah Hoult, *Holy Ireland* (Dublin: Arlen House, 1935/1985), pp. 203ff.

40. See *The Irish Statesman*, 18 October 1924.

41. See Norman Vance, 'Region, realism and reaction, 1922–1972' in Foster (ed.), *The Cambridge Companion to the Irish Novel*, pp. 165–166. See also Terry Phillips, 'A Study in Grotesques: Transformations of the Human in the Writing of Liam O'Flaherty', *Gothic Studies*, 7:1 (May 2005), 41–52.

42. See Cahalan, *The Irish Novel: A Critical History*, p. 186.

43. See Kiberd, *Irish Classics*, pp. 492ff.

44. See Cahalan, *The Irish Novel: A Critical History*, p. 187.

45. For a discussion of O'Flaherty's naturalism, see Cahalan, *The Irish Novel: A Critical History*, pp. 187ff. and Cleary, *Outrageous Fortune*, pp. 144, 153ff.

46. See Fintan O'Toole, 'Rejecting the Claim that Irish Artists Ignored First World War', *Irish Times*, Weekend Section, 15 November 2008, p. 4.

47. See Liam O'Flaherty, *Mr Gilhooley* (Dublin: Wolfhound Press, 1926/1998), p. 26ff.

48. See Ernest Boyd, 'Joyce and the New Irish Writers', in Pierce (ed.), *Irish Writing in the Twentieth Century: A Reader*, p. 388.

49. Liam O'Flaherty, *The Puritan* (Dublin: Wolfhound Press, 1932/1998), p. 96.

50. See Brian Fallon, *An Age of Innocence: Irish Culture 1930–1960* (Dublin: Gill and Macmillan, 1998) for a counter-narrative to the usual reading of this period as wholly negative and backward.

51. W. B. Yeats, 'Modern Ireland: An Address to American Audience, 1932–33', in Robin Skelton and David R. Clark (eds.), *Irish Renaissance: A Gathering of Essays, Memoirs, and Letters from the Massachusetts Review* (Dublin: Dolmen, 1965), p. 24.

52. Samuel Beckett, *Murphy* (London: Picador, 1938/1973), p. 6.

53. Samuel Beckett, *Proust & 3 Dialogues with George Duthuit* (London: John Calder Limited, 1970/1965), p. 103.

54. W. B. Yeats, *The Collected Poems*, pp. 392–393.

55. Cf. Ihab Hassan, *The Dismemberment of Orpheus: Toward a Postmodern Literature* (The University of Wisconsin Press, 1971/1982), pp. 267–268.

56. Pádraigín Riggs and Norman Vance 'Irish Prose fiction' in Cleary and Connolly (eds.), *The Cambridge Companion to Modern Irish Culture*, p. 259.

57. James Joyce, *Finnegans Wake* (London: Faber and Faber, 1989), p. 628.

58. Brian O'Nolan, 'A Bash in the Tunnel', in Pierce (ed.), *Irish Writing in the Twentieth Century: A Reader*, p. 612.

59. See Deane, *A Short History of Irish Literature*, p. 186.

NOTES FOR INTERCHAPTER 5

1. Elizabeth Bowen, '*The Last September*, preface to the second U. S. edition', in *The Mulberry Tree*, p. 126.

2. Elizabeth Bowen, *The Last September* (London: Penguin, 1987), p. 60.

3. For a more detailed consideration, see Derek Hand, 'Ghosts from our Future: Elizabeth Bowen and the Unfinished Business of Living', in Eibhear Walshe (ed.), *Elizabeth Bowen: Vision and Revisions* (Dublin: Irish Academic Press, 2008).

4. See Derek Hand, 'The Anglo-Irish Big House under Pressure: Elizabeth Bowen's *The Last September* and Molly Keane's *Two Days in Aragon*', in Eibhear Walshe and Gwenda Young (eds.), *Molly Keane: Centenary Essays* (Dublin: Four Courts Press, 2006).

5. Robert Tracy, *The Unappeasable Host: Studies in Irish Identities* (Dublin: University College Dublin Press, 1998), p. 222.

6. Bowen, *The Mulberry Tree*, p. 122.

NOTES FOR CHAPTER 5

1. Elizabeth Bowen, *The Heat of the Day* (London: Penguin Books, 1949/1976), p. 80.

2. See Kiberd, *Inventing Ireland*, p. 471.

3. See Clair Wills, *That Neutral Island: A Cultural History of Ireland During the Second World War* (London: Faber and Faber, 2007); Fallon, *An Age of Innocence: Irish Culture 1930–1960*; and Nicholas Grene and Chris Morash, *Shifting Scenes: Irish Theatre-going 1955–1985* (Dublin: Carysfort Press, 2008).

4. Cleary, *Outrageous Fortune*, p. 8.

5. See O'Connor, 'The Future of Irish Literature', in Pierce (ed.), *Irish Writing in the Twentieth Century: A Reader*, p. 502: 'We have, I think, reached the end of a period.'

6. Liam O'Flaherty, *The Puritan* (Dublin: Wolfhound Press, 1932/1998), p. 38.

7. O'Connor, 'The Future of Irish Literature', p. 502.

8. *Ibid.*, p. 503.

9. Sean O'Faolain, 'Ah, Wisha! The Irish Novel', *Virginia Quarterly Review*, 17:2 (Spring 1941), 265–274.

10. See Sean O'Faolain, *The Short Story* (London: William Collins, 1948).

11. O'Connor, *The Lonely Voice: A Study of the Short Story*, p. 17.

12. See Wills, *That Neutral Island*, pp. 290ff.

13. *Ibid.*, p. 291.

14. See Fallon, *An Age of Innocence: Irish Culture 1930–1960*.

15. See Cronin, *Irish Fiction: 1900–1940*, pp. 186ff.

16. Thomas Flanagan, 'Frank O'Connor, 1903–1966', *The Kenyon Review*, 28:4 (September 1966), 452.

17. See Wills, *That Neutral Island*, p. 291.

18. See Anthony Cronin, *Dead as Doornails: A Chronicle of Life* (Dublin: Dolmen Press, 1976).

19. Seanad Éireann – Volume 27, 02 December 1942, Censorship of Publications – Motion (Resumed). www.oireachtas-debates.gov.ie.

20. Kate O'Brien, *The Land of Spices*, with a new introduction by Clare Boylan (London: Virago Press, 1941/2000), p. 157.

21. See Emma Donohue, 'Out of Order: Kate O'Brien's Lesbian Fictions', in Walshe (ed.), *Ordinary People Dancing*, pp. 36–58.

22. See Walshe, *Kate O'Brien: A Writing Life*, pp. 84ff. for a discussion of the novel.

23. *Ibid.*, p. 84.

24. Kate O'Brien, *That Lady*, with a new introduction by Desmond Hogan (London, Virago Press, 1946/1991), p. xiv.

25. For a fuller discussion see Hand, 'The Anglo-Irish Big House under Pressure', pp. 85–97.

26. Molly Keane, *Two Days in Aragon*, with a new introduction by Polly Devlin (London: Virago Press, 1985), p. 16.

27. See Rachael Sealy Lynch, '"The Fabulous Female Form": The Deadly Erotics of the Male Gaze in Mary Lavin's *The House in Clewe Street*', *Twentieth Century Literature*, 43:3 (Autumn 1997), 326.

28. Wills, *That Neutral Island*, pp. 297–298, and Clair Wills, 'Neutrality and Popular Culture', Series 1 (Spring 2008), *The Art of Popular Culture: From 'The Meeting of the Waters' to Riverdance*, Series Editor: P. J. Mathews. www.ucd.ie/scholarcast/.

29. Elizabeth Bowen, *Bowen's Court* (London: Longmans, Green & Co., 1942), pp. 339–340.

30. Eamon de Valera, 'The Undeserted Village Ireland', in Deane (ed.), *The Field Day Anthology of Irish Writing*, vol. III, p. 748.

31. Tracy, *The Unappeasable Host*, pp. 227–228.

32. Bowen, *The Mulberry Tree*, p. 216.

33. Mervyn Wall, *The Return of Fursey* (London: Pilot Press, 1948), p. 115.

34. See Robert Goode Hogan, *Mervyn Wall* (Bucknell University Press, 1972), p. 44. Hogan argues the opposite.

35. See Vance, 'Region, Realism and Reaction, 1922–1972', p. 167.

36. Kavanagh, *A Poet's Country: Selected Prose*, p. 306.

37. *Ibid.*, p. 237.

38. *Ibid.*, p. 306.

39. *Ibid.*, p. 303.

40. Patrick Kavanagh, *By Night Unstarred: An Autobiographical Novel*, edited by Peter Kavanagh (The Curragh: The Goldsmith Press, 1977).

41. Sam Hanna Bell, *December Bride* (Belfast: Blackstaff Press, 2005/1951), pp. 217, 254.

42. Vance, 'Region, Realism and Reaction, 1922–1972', p. 159.

43. Quoted in Pierce (ed.), *Irish Writing in the Twentieth Century: A Reader*, p. 649.

44. Deane, *A Short History of Irish Literature*, p. 214.

45. Conor P. O'Brien, 'Francis Stuart: Prisoner of Protest', *The Irish* Times, 5 September 1973, p. 10.

46. See Brendan McNamee, 'The Flowering Cross: Suffering, Reality, and the Christ Motif in Francis Stuart's *The Pillar of Cloud* and *Redemption*', *Christianity and Literature*, 53:1 (Autumn 2003), 41–58.

47. Francis Stuart, *The Pillar of Cloud* (Dublin: New Island Books, 1994/1948), p. 188.

48. George O'Brien, 'Contemporary Prose in English: 1940–2000', in Kelleher and O'Leary (eds.), *Cambridge History of Irish Literature*, vol. II: *1890–2000*, p. 424.

49. Walter Benjamin, *The Arcades Project*, translated by Howard Eiland and Kevin McLaughlin (Cambridge, Mass.: The Belknap Press of Harvard University Press, 2002), p. 510.

50. *Ibid.*, pp. 510ff.
51. See Richard Kearney, *Modern Movements in European Philosophy: Phenomenology, Critical Theory, Structuralsim* (Manchester University Press, 1994), p. 166.
52. Terry Eagleton, *After Theory* (New York: Basic Books, 2003), pp. 57–58.
53. See Sinead Mooney, 'Unstable Compounds: Bowen's Beckettian Affinities', *Modern Fiction Studies*, 53:2 (Summer 2007), 238–256.
54. Samuel Beckett, *Watt* (London: John Calder, 1953/1981), p. 255.
55. O'Brien, 'Contemporary Prose in English: 1940–2000', p. 424.
56. Quoted in Richard Kearney, *Transitions: Narratives in Modern Irish Culture* (Dublin: Wolfhound Press, 1988), p. 61.
57. Thomas Docherty, *Postmodernism: A Reader* (New York: Columbia University Press, 1993), p. 25.
58. Samuel Beckett, *The Beckett Trilogy: Molloy, Malone Dies, The Unnameable* (London: Picador, 1959/1979), pp. 381–382.
59. See Mooney, 'Unstable Compounds: Bowen's Beckettian Affinities', 238–256.
60. See Krielkamp, *The Anglo-Irish Novel and the Big House*, pp. 167ff.; Allen E. Austin, *Elizabeth Bowen* (New York: Twayne Publishers, 1971), pp. 75ff.; and William Heath, *Elizabeth Bowen: An Introduction to her Novels* (University of Wisconsin Press, 1961), pp. 143ff.
61. See Hand, 'Ghosts from our Future: Bowen and the Unfinished Business of Living', pp. 65–76.
62. Cf. Richard Kearney, *The Wake of the Imagination: Ideas of Creativity in Western Culture* (London: Hutchinson, 1988), p. 253.
63. See Clair Wills, ' "Half Different": The Vanishing Irish in *A World of Love*', in Eibhear Walshe (ed.), *Elizabeth Bowen* (Dublin: Irish Academic Press, 2008), p. 147.
64. Tracy, *The Unappeasable Host*, p. 255.
65. See Cleary, 'This Thing of Darkness: Conjectures on Irish Naturalism', in *Outrageous Fortune*, pp. 111–179.
66. See O'Brien, 'Contemporary Prose in English: 1940–2000', pp. 426–427.
67. See Deane, *A Short History of Irish Literature*, pp. 219–220.
68. Brian Moore, *The Lonely Passion of Judith Hearne* (London: Harper Perennial, 1955/2007), pp. 201ff.
69. See Derek Hand, 'Introduction: Benedict Kiely and the Persona of the Irish Writer', in Derek Hand and Anne Fogarty (eds.), *Irish University Review: Benedict Kiely*, 38:1 (Spring/Summer, 2008), vii–x.
70. Benedict Kiely, *Modern Irish Fiction: A Critique* (Dublin: Golden Eagle, 1950), p. vi.
71. Benedict Kiely, *The Cards of the Gambler* (Dublin: Wolfhound Press, 1995), pp. 225–226.
72. Benedict Kiely, *There was an Ancient House* (Dublin: Wolfhound Press, 1955/1998), p. 9.
73. Patrick Kavanagh, 'Yeats', in *The Complete Poems*, collected, arranged and edited by Peter Kavanagh (Newbridge: The Goldsmith Press, 1992), p. 348.

74. See John Ryan, 'Our Irish Publishers', in Pierce (ed.), *Irish Writing in the Twentieth Century: A Reader*, pp. 598–599.

75. Brendan Behan, *Borstal Boy* (London: Black Swan, 1983/1958), p. 383.

NOTES FOR INTERCHAPTER 6

1. Title is a reference to Ian MacDonald, *Revolution in the Head: The Beatles' Records and the Sixties* (London: Pimlico, 1998).

2. John Banville, *Doctor Copernicus* (London: Secker and Warburg, 1976), p. 63.

3. See Derek Hand, 'Introduction: John Banville's Quixotic Humanity', in Derek Hand (ed.), *Irish University Review: John Banville*, 36:1 (Spring/Summer 2006), viii–xii.

4. John Banville, *The Newton Letter: An Interlude* (London: Secker and Warburg, 1983), p. 50.

5. See Kersti Tarien Powell, 'The Lighted Windows: Place in John Banville's Fiction', in Hand (ed.), *Irish University Review: John Banville*, 39–51.

6. John Banville, *Eclipse* (London: Picador, 2000), p. 37.

NOTES FOR CHAPTER 6

1. Philip Larkin, 'Annus Mirabilis', in *Collected Poems*, edited with an introduction by Anthony Thwaite (London: Faber and Faber, 1988), p. 167.

2. See Foster, *Luck and the Irish*, p. 147.

3. See Ferriter, *The Transformation of Ireland: 1900–2000*, p. 555.

4. See Brown, *Ireland: A Social and Cultural History 1922–1985*, pp. 241ff.

5. Ferriter, *The Transformation of Ireland: 1900–2000*, p. 536.

6. See Augustine Martin, *Bearing Witness: Essays on Anglo-Irish Literature*, edited by Anthony Roche (Dublin: University College Dublin Press, 1996), pp. 81–99.

7. See John Wilson Foster, 'Irish Fiction 1965–1990', in Deane (ed.), *The Field Day Anthology of Irish Writing*, vol. III, p. 937.

8. See Kevin Sullivan, 'Benedict Kiely: The Making of a Novelist', in Patrick Rafroidi and Maurice Harmon (eds.), *The Irish Novel in Our Time* (Lille: Publications de l'Université de Lille III, 1975–76), p. 206.

9. Benedict Kiely, *Dogs Enjoy the Morning* (Dublin: Wolfhound Press, 1995), p. 240.

10. See Hand, 'Introduction: Benedict Kiely and the Persona of the Irish Writer', p. viii.

11. See *Irish Times*, 16 November 1974, p. 10.

12. Cahalan, *The Irish Novel: A Critical History*, p. 297.

13. See Francois Borel, ' "I am Without a Name": The Fiction of Christy Brown', in Rafroidi and Harmon (eds.), *The Irish Novel in Our Time*, pp. 287ff.

14. See Theo Dorgan and Máirín Ní Dhonnchadha (eds.), *Revising the Rising* (Derry: Field Day Publications, 1991).

15. James M. Cahalan, *Great Hatred, Little Room: The Irish Historical Novel* (Dublin: Gill and Macmillan, 1983), p. 155.
16. See Iris Murdoch, *The Red and the Green* (London: Penguin, 1965/1971), pp. 35ff.
17. Backus, *The Gothic Family Romance*, pp. 179ff.
18. See Cahalan, *Great Hatred, Little Room: The Irish Historical Novel*, p. 188.
19. See *ibid.*, p. 192.
20. See Christine St Peter, *Changing Ireland: Strategies in Contemporary Women's Fiction* (London: Macmillan Press, 2000), pp. 71–72.
21. See Deane, *A Short History of Irish Literature*, p. 211.
22. Deane, *Celtic Revivals*, p. 32.
23. See Kearney, *Transitions: Narrative in Modern Irish Culture*; also 'The Question of Tradition', *The Crane Bag*, 3:1 (1979), 58–70.
24. See Krielkamp, *The Anglo-Irish Novel and the Big House*, pp. 234ff.
25. Neil Murphy, 'Aidan Higgins', *Review of Contemporary Fiction*, 23:3 (Fall 2003), 54ff.
26. See Conor McCarthy, *Modernisation: Crisis and Culture in Ireland 1969–1992* (Dublin: Four Courts Press, 2000), pp. 80ff.
27. Vera Krielkamp, 'The Novel of the Big House', in Foster (ed.), *The Cambridge Companion to The Irish Novel*, p. 75.
28. See Ralph J. Crane, 'The Influence of Samuel Beckett on the Fiction of J. G. Farrell', *New Hibernia Review/Iris Éireannach Nua: A Quarterly Record of Irish Studies*, 9:1 (Spring 2005), 109–116.
29. See Deane, *A Short History of Irish Literature*, p. 225.
30. See O'Brien, 'Contemporary Prose in English: 1940–2000', p. 431.
31. *Ibid.*, pp. 431–432.
32. Jennifer Johnston, *How Many Miles to Babylon?* (London: Penguin, 1974/1988), p. 111.
33. See O'Brien, 'Contemporary Prose in English: 1940–2000', p. 431.
34. See Elmer Kennedy-Andrews, *Fiction and the Northern Ireland Troubles since 1969: (De-)constructing the North* (Dublin: Four Courts Press, 2003).
35. See Seamus Deane, 'Civilians and Barbarians', *Ireland's Field Day*, with an afterword by Thomas Flanagan (Notre Dame, Ind.: University of Notre Dame Press, 1983/1986), pp. 33ff.; and Richard Bourke, 'Plague Man – The Crusader in Conor Cruise O'Brien', *The Times Literary Supplement*, 13 March 2009, no. 5528, pp. 13ff.
36. For a discussion of Flanagan's novel, see Cahalan, *Great Hatred, Little Room: The Irish Historical Novel*, pp. 196–200.
37. See Deane's remark on *Castle Rackrent* in *Strange Country: Modernity and Nationhood in Irish Writing since 1790*, p. 39.
38. See Derek Hand, *John Banville: Exploring Fictions* (Dublin: The Liffey Press, 2002), pp. 23ff.
39. See Derek Hand, 'A Gothic Nightmare: John Banville's *Birchwood* and Irish History', in Patricia A. Lynch, Joachim Fischer and Brian Coates (eds.), *Back to the Present, Forward to the Past: Irish Writing and History since 1798* (Amsterdam: Rodopi Press, 2006), pp. 167ff.

40. John Banville, *Birchwood* (London: Panther Books, 1984/1973), p. 174.

41. Sean O'Faolain, 'Fifty Years of Irish Writing', in Pierce (ed.), *Irish Writing in the Twentieth Century: A Reader*, p. 741.

42. *Ibid.*, p. 744.

43. *Ibid.*, p. 746.

44. See Aibhlín McCrann (ed.), *Memories, Milestones and New Horizons: Reflections on the Regeneration of Ballymun* (Belfast: Blackstaff Press, 2008).

45. See Vance, 'Region, realism and reaction, 1922–1972', p. 168.

46. See James M. Cahalan, *Double Visions: Women and Men in Modern and Contemporary Irish Fiction* (Syracuse University Press, 1999), pp. 114ff.

47. Edna O'Brien, *James Joyce* (London: Weidenfeld and Nicolson, 1999).

48. See Arthur Marwick, *The Arts in the West since 1945* (Oxford University Press, 2002), pp. 103ff.

49. Kiberd, *Inventing Ireland*, p. 566.

50. First published as *The Lonely Girl* (1962).

51. See O'Brien, 'Contemporary Prose in English: 1940–2000', pp. 449.

52. Cahalan, *The Irish Novel: A Critical History*, p. 297.

53. See Michael Paul Gallagher, 'The Novels of John Broderick', in Rafroidi and Harmon (eds.), *The Irish Novel in Our Time*, pp. 235ff.

54. John Broderick, *The Pilgrimage* (Dublin: The Lilliput Press, 1961/2004), p. 191.

55. See Maurice Kennedy, 'Middle-Class Morality', *The Irish Times*, 28 January 1961, p. 6.

56. See Joe Cleary, 'Toward a Materialist-Formalist History of Twentieth-Century Irish Literature', *Boundary 2*, 31:1 (2004), 233–234.

57. Cleary, *Outrageous Fortune*, p. 164.

58. See O'Brien, 'Contemporary Prose in English: 1940–2000', pp. 426ff.

59. John McGahern, *Creatures of the Earth: Collected Short Stories* (London: Faber and Faber, 2006), p. 122.

60. See Grace Tighe Ledwidge, 'Death in Marriage: The Tragedy of Elizabeth Reegan in *The Barracks*', in John Brannigan (ed.), *Irish University Review*, 35:1 (Spring/Summer 2005), 90ff.

61. John McGahern, *The Barracks* (London: Faber and Faber, 2000), p. 85.

62. Cleary, *Outrageous Fortune*, pp. 164–165.

63. For a brief detailing of the bleakness of McGahern's early work, see Deane, *A Short History of Irish Literature*, pp. 221–223.

64. For a discussion of this technique, see Stanley van der Ziel, ' "All This Talk and Struggle": John McGahern's *The Dark*', in Brannigan (ed.), *Irish University Review*, 35:1 (Spring/Summer 2005), 104ff.

65. See Siobhán Holland, 'Marvellous Fathers in the Fiction of John McGahern', *The Yearbook of English Studies*, vol. 35, *Irish Writing since 1950* (2005), pp. 186–198.

66. See Eamon Maher, 'The Irish Novel in Crisis? The Example of John McGahern', in Brannigan (ed.), *Irish University Review*, 35:1 (Spring/Summer 2005), 61–62.

67. John McGahern, *The Leavetaking* (London: Faber and Faber, 1974/1984), p. 117.

NOTES FOR INTERCHAPTER 7

1. Seamus Deane, *Reading in the Dark* (London: Jonathan Cape, 1996), p. 196.
2. See Liam Harte, 'History Lessons: Postcolonialism and Seamus Deane's *Reading in the Dark*', *Irish University Review*, 30:1 (Spring/Summer, 2000), 149–162.
3. See Linden Peach, *The Contemporary Irish Novel: Critical Readings* (London: Palgrave, 2004), pp. 38ff.
4. Edna Longley quoted by Kennedy-Andrews, *Fiction and the Northern Ireland Troubles since 1969*, p. 215.
5. Elmer Kennedy-Andrews, 'The Novel and the Northern Troubles', in Foster (ed.), *The Cambridge Companion to the Irish Novel*, p. 249.

NOTES FOR CHAPTER 7

1. See, for example, McCarthy, *Modernisation, Crisis and Culture in Ireland 1969–1992*; Kearney, *Transitions: Narrative in Modern Irish Culture*; Foster, *Luck and the Irish*; Peadar Kirby, Luke Gibbons and Michael Cronin (eds.), *Reinventing Ireland: Culture, Society and the Global Economy* (London: Pluto Books, 2002); Luke Gibbons, *Transformations in Irish Culture* (Cork University Press, 1996); David Lloyd, *Ireland after History* (Cork University Press, 1999).
2. See Gerry Smyth, *The Novel and the Nation: Studies in the New Irish Fiction* (London: Pluto Press, 1997); Jennifer M. Jeffers, *The Irish Novel at the End of the Twentieth Century: Gender, Bodies, Power* (London: Palgrave, 2002); Liam Harte and Michael Parker (eds.), *Contemporary Irish Fiction: Themes, Tropes, Theories* (London: Palgrave, 2000); St Peter, *Changing Ireland: Strategies in Contemporary Women's Fiction*; Linden Peach, *The Contemporary Irish Novel: Critical Readings*.
3. For such a reading, see Foster, 'How the Short Stories Became Novels', in *Luck and the Irish*, pp. 147–183.
4. Smyth, *The Novel and the Nation*, p. 140.
5. See Kennedy-Andrews, *Fiction and the Northern Ireland Troubles since 1969*, pp. 87ff.
6. Corcoran, *After Yeats and Joyce*, p. 156.
7. Richard Haslam, ' "The Pose Arranged and Lingered Over": Visualising the "Troubles" ', in Harte and Parker (eds.), *Contemporary Irish Fiction: Themes, Tropes, Theories*, p. 202.
8. See Cahalan, *Double Visions*, p. 141.
9. See Kennedy-Andrews, *Fiction and the Northern Ireland Troubles since 1969*, pp. 102ff.
10. Smyth, *The Novel and the Nation*, p. 127.
11. See Richard Kirkland, 'Bourgeois Redemptions: the Fictions of Glenn Patterson and Robert McLiam Wilson', in Harte and Parker (eds.), *Contemporary Irish Fiction: Themes, Tropes, Theories*, pp. 213ff.
12. See Smyth, *The Novel and the Nation*, pp. 132–134.

13. See Derek Hand, 'Something Happened: Benedict's Kiely's *Nothing Happens in Carmincross* and the Breakdown of the Irish Novel', in Eibhear Walshe (ed.), *Representing the Troubles* (Dublin: Four Courts Press, 2004).

14. See Eve Patten, 'Contemporary Irish Fiction', in Foster, *The Cambridge Companion to the Irish Novel*, pp. 259ff.

15. In reference to the hugely successful and popular Hollywood movie *Forrest Gump* (1994).

16. Sebastian Barry, *The Whereabouts of Eneas McNulty* (London : Picador, 1998), p. 248.

17. For a full discussion of the politics of the novel, see Elizabeth Butler Cullingford, 'Colonial Policing: *The Steward of Christendom* and *The Whereabouts of Eneas McNulty*', *Éire-Ireland*, 39:3&4 (Fall/Winter 2004), 11–37.

18. Joseph McMinn, *The Supreme Fictions of John Banville* (Manchester University Press, 1999), p. 65.

19. John Banville, *Kepler* (London: Minerva, 1990), p. 108.

20. See Hand, *John Banville: Exploring Fictions*, pp. 106–108.

21. See Hand, 'Introduction: John Banville's Quixotic Humanity', pp. viii–xii.

22. Eibhear Walshe, 'The Vanishing Homoerotic: Colm Tóibín's Gay Fictions', *New Hibernia Review/Iris Éireannach Nua: A Quarterly Record of Irish Studies*, 10:4 (Winter 2006), 122–136.

23. See Patten, 'Contemporary Irish Fiction', pp. 261–262.

24. See Tom Herron, 'ContaminNation: Patrick McCabe's and Colm Tóibín's Pathologies of the Republic', in Harte and Parker (eds.), *Contemporary Irish Fiction: Themes, Tropes, Theories*, pp. 168ff. Also see Liam Harte, 'History, Text, and Society in Colm Tóibín's *The Heather Blazing*', *New Hibernia Review/Iris Éireannach Nua: A Quarterly Record of Irish Studies*, 6:4 (Winter 2002), 55–67.

25. Riggs and Vance, 'Irish Prose Fiction', p. 263.

26. See Cleary, *Outrageous Fortune*, pp. 215ff.

27. John McGahern, *Amongst Women* (London: Faber and Faber, 1991), p. 179.

28. See O'Brien, 'Contemporary Prose in English: 1940–2000', p. 430.

29. Ferdia MacAnna, 'The Dublin Renaissance: An Essay on Modern Dublin and Dublin Writers', *The Irish Review*, 10 (Spring 1991), 14–30.

30. *Ibid.*, p. 18.

31. See Smyth, *The Novel and the Nation*, p. 67.

32. See Benjamin, *Illuminations*, pp. 217ff.

33. See McCarthy, *Modernisation, Crisis and Culture in Ireland 1969–1992*, pp. 135–164.

34. See Smyth, *The Novel and the Nation*, pp. 146ff.

35. See George O'Brien, 'The Aesthetics of Exile', in Harte and Parker (eds.), *Contemporary Irish Fiction: Themes, Tropes, Theories*, pp. 46ff.

36. See P. J. Mathews, 'Joseph O'Connor' in Anthony Roche (ed.), *The UCD Aesthetic* (Dublin: New Island Books, 2005), pp. 256–258.

37. Joseph O'Connor, *Cowboys and Indians* (London: Sinclair-Stevenson, 1991), p. 6.

38. See Geraldine Higgins, '"A Place to Bring Anger and Grief": Deirdre Madden's Northern Irish Novels', in Bill Lazenblatt (ed.), *Writing Ulster*, no. 6: *Northern Narratives* (1999), pp. 142–161.

39. See Anne Fogarty, 'Deliberately Personal? The Politics of Identity in Contemporary Irish Women's Writing', *Nordic Irish Studies*, 1 (2002), 16.

40. See *ibid.*, pp. 10ff.

41. See Peach, *The Contemporary Irish Novel: Critical Readings*, pp. 154–168.

42. See P. J. Mathews, 'In Praise of "Hibernocentricism": Republicanism, Globalisation and Irish Culture', *The Republic*, 4 (June 2005), 7–14.

43. Mary Harney, 'Remarks by Tánaiste, Mary Harney at a Meeting of the American Bar Association in the Law Society of Ireland, Blackhall Place, Dublin on Friday 21st July 2000'. See full speech www.entemp.ie/press/2000/210700.htm.

44. Cf. Dermot Bolger, 'Introduction', in *The Picador Book of Contemporary Irish Fiction* (London: Picador, 1994), p. xxvii.

45. *Ibid.*, p. xxvi.

46. Kavanagh, *A Poet's Country: Selected Prose*, p. 237.

47. See Susan Cahill, 'Corporeal Architecture: Body and City in Colum McCann's *This Side of Brightness*', *Etudes Irlandaises*, 32:1 (Spring 2007), 43–58.

48. See Derek Hand, 'Being Ordinary: Ireland from Elsewhere: A Reading of Éilís Ní Dhuibhne's *The Bray House*', *Irish University Review*, 30:1 (Spring/Summer), 103–116.

49. See Derek Hand, 'Éilís Ní Dhuibhne', in Anthony Roche (ed.), *The UCD Aesthetic: Celebrating 150 Years of UCD Writers* (Dublin: New Island Press, 2005).

50. Éilís Ní Dhuibhne, *The Dancers Dancing* (Belfast: Blackstaff Press 1999), p. 3.

51. Mike McCormack, *Notes from a Coma* (London: Jonathan Cape, 2005), p. 111.

NOTES FOR INTERCHAPTER 8

1. John McGahern, *Memoir* (London: Faber and Faber, 2005), p. 272.

2. See Anne Goarzin, '"A Crack in the Concrete": Objects in the Works of John McGahern', *Irish University Review*, 35:1 (Spring/Summer 2005), 28–41.

3. John McGahern, 'The Local and the Universal', in John McGahern, *Love of the World: Essays*, edited by Stanley van der Ziel (London: Faber and Faber, 2009), p. 11.

4. See Cleary, *Outrageous Fortune*, p. 165.

5. For fuller discussions of various aspects of the novel, see Denis Sampson, '"Open to the World": A Reading of John McGahern's *That They May Face the Rising Sun*'; Eamon Hughes, '"All That Surrounds Our Life": Time, Sex, and Death in *That They May Face the Rising Sun*'; and Declan Kiberd, 'Fallen Nobility: The World of John McGahern', *Irish University Review*, 35:1 (Spring/Summer 2005).

6. John McGahern, *That They May Face the Rising Sun* (London: Faber and Faber, 2002), p. 99.

NOTES FOR CONCLUSION

1. See www.guardian.co.uk/books/2010/feb/11/julian-gough-irish-novlists-priestly-caste.
2. For example the Booker Prize, the American Fiction Prize, the Whitbread Award, the Impac Award and the Irish Book Award.

Bibliography

Acheson, James (ed.). *The British and Irish Novel since 1960* (London: Macmillan, 1991)

Adams, J. R. R. *The Printed Word and the Common Man: Popular Culture in Ulster 1700–1900* (Belfast: The Institute of Irish Studies, QUB, 1987)

Anderson, Benedict. *Imagined Communities: Reflections on the Origin and Spread of Nationalism* (London: Verso, 2006)

Ashcroft, Bill *et al.* (eds.). *The Empire Writes Back: Theory and Practice in Post-colonial Literatures* (London: Routledge, 1989)

Austin, Allen E. *Elizabeth Bowen* (New York: Twayne Publishers, 1971)

Azim, Firdous. *The Colonial Rise of the Novel* (London: Routledge, 1993)

Backus, Margot Gayle. *The Gothic Family Romance: Heterosexuality, Child Sacrifice, and the Anglo-Irish Colonial Order* (Durham, NC: Duke University Press, 1999)

Banville, John. *The Newton Letter: An Interlude* (London: Secker and Warburg, 1983)

Barnard, Toby. *Irish Protestant Ascents and Descents, 1641–1770* (Dublin: Four Courts, 2004)

Beckett, J. C. 'Literature in English 1691–1800', in T. W. Moody and W. E. Vaughan (eds.), *A New History of Ireland*, IV: *Eighteenth Century Ireland 1691–1800* (Oxford: Clarendon Press, 1986)

Beckett, Samuel. 'Dante ... Bruno ... Vico ... Joyce', in Samuel Beckett and others, *Our Examination Round his Factification for Incamination of Work in Progress* (London: Faber and Faber, 1972)

  Proust & 3 Dialogues with George Duthuit (London: John Calder Limited, 1970/1965)

Belanger, Jacqueline (ed.). *The Irish Novel in the Nineteenth Century: Facts and Fictions* (Dublin: Four Courts Press, 2006)

Benjamin, Walter. *Illuminations: Essays and Reflections*, edited with an Introduction by Hannah Arendt (New York: Schocken Books, 1969/1985)

  Reflections: Essays, Aphorisms, Autobiographical Writings, translated by Edmund Jephcott (New York: Schocken Books, 1978)

  The Arcades Project, translated by Howard Eiland and Kevin McLaughlin (Cambridge, Mass.: The Belknap Press of Harvard University Press, 2002)

Bhabha, Homi K. *Nation and Narration* (London: Routledge, 1990)

Birmingham, George A. 'The Literary Movement in Ireland', in David Pierce (ed.), *Irish Writing in the Twentieth Century: A Reader* (Cork University Press, 2000)

Bloom, Harold. *Where Shall Wisdom be Found?* (New York: Riverhead Books, 2004)

Borel, François. '"I am Without a Name": The Fiction of Christy Brown' in Patrick Rafroidi and Maurice Harmon (eds.), *The Irish Novel in Our Time* (Lille: Publications de l'Université de Lille III, 1975–76)

Bourke, Angela *et al.* (eds.). *The Field Day Anthology of Irish Writing*, vols. IV–V (Cork University Press, 2002)

Bourke, Richard. 'Plague Man – The Crusader in Conor Cruise O'Brien', *The Times Literary Supplement*, 13 March 2009, no. 5528

Bowen, Elizabeth. *Bowen's Court*, new introduction by Thomas McCarthy (Cork: The Collins Press, 1998; original publication, London: Longmans, Green & Co., 1942)

    The Mulberry Tree: Writings of Elizabeth Bowen selected and introduced by Hermione Lee (London: Virago Press, 1986)

Boyd, Ernest. 'Joyce and the New Irish Writers', in David Pierce (ed.), *Irish Writing in the Twentieth Century: A Reader* (Cork University Press, 2000)

Brown, Stephen. *Ireland in Fiction: A Guide to Irish Novels, Tales, Romances, and Folk-Lore* (Shannon: Irish University Press, 1969)

Brown, Terence. *Ireland: A Social and Cultural History 1922–1985* (London: Fontana Press, 1985)

    Ireland's Literature: Selected Essays (Mullingar: The Lilliput Press, 1988)

Burgess, Miranda. 'The National Tale and Allied Genres, 1770s–1840s', in John Wilson Foster (ed.), *The Cambridge Companion to the Irish Novel* (Cambridge University Press, 2006)

Burke, William. *History of Clonmel* (Kilkenny: Roberts Brothers, 1983; 1st edn 1907)

Cahalan, James M. *Double Visions: Women and Men in Modern and Contemporary Irish Fiction* (Syracuse University Press, 1999)

    Great Hatred, Little Room: The Irish Historical Novel (Dublin: Gill and Macmillan, 1983)

    The Irish Novel: A Critical History (Boston: Twayne Publishers, 1988)

Cahill, Susan. 'Corporeal Architecture: Body and City in Colum McCann's *This Side of Brightness*', *Etudes Irlandaises*, 32:1 (Spring 2007)

Candy, Catherine. *Priestly Fictions: Popular Novelists of the Early 20th Century* (Dublin: Wolfhound Press, 1995)

Canny, Nicholas and Pagden, Anthony (eds.). *Colonial Identity in the Atlantic World: 1500–1800* (Princeton University Press, 1987)

Carpenter, Andrew, Deane, Seamus and McCormack, W. J. 'Political Prose: Cromwell to O'Connell', in Seamus Deane (ed.), *The Field Day Anthology of Irish Writing*, vol. I (Derry: Field Day Publications, 1991)

Carson, James P. 'Enlightenment, Popular Culture, and Gothic Fiction', in John Richetti (ed.), *The Cambridge Companion to the Eighteenth-Century Novel* (Cambridge University Press, 1996)

Cleary, Joe. *Outrageous Fortune: Capital and Culture in Modern Ireland* (Dublin: Field Day Publications, 2007)

'The Nineteenth Century Irish Novel: Notes and Speculations on Literary Historiography', in Jacqueline Belanger (ed.), *The Irish Novel in the Nineteenth Century: Facts and Fictions* (Dublin: Four Courts Press, 2006)

'Toward a Materialist-Formalist History of Twentieth-Century Irish Literature', *Boundary 2*, 31:1 (2004)

Cleary, Joe and Connolly, Clare (eds.). *The Cambridge Companion to Modern Irish Culture* (Cambridge University Press, 2005)

Connolly, Claire. 'Irish Romanticism, 1800–1830', in Margaret Kelleher and Philip O'Leary (eds.), *The Cambridge History of Irish Literature*, vol. 1: *To 1890* (Cambridge University Press, 2006)

Connolly, Sean. 'Elite Responses to Popular Culture, 1660–1850', in James S. Donnelly and Kerby Miller (eds.), *Irish Popular Culture: 1650–1850* (Dublin: Irish Academic Press, 1998)

Corbett, Mary Jean. *Allegories of Union in Irish and English Writing, 1790–1870: Politics, History, and the Family from Edgeworth to Arnold* (Cambridge University Press, 2000)

Corcoran, Neil. *After Yeats and Joyce: Reading Modern Irish Literature* (Oxford University Press, 1997)

Corkery, Daniel. *The Hidden Ireland: A Study of Gaelic Munster in the Eighteenth Century* (Dublin: Gill and Macmillan, 1924/1989)

Costello-Sullivan, Kathleen. 'Novel Traditions: Realism and Modernity in *Hurrish* and *The Real Charlotte*', in Jacqueline Belanger (ed.), *The Irish Novel in the Nineteenth Century: Facts and Fictions* (Dublin: Four Courts Press, 2006)

Crane, Ralph J. 'The Influence of Samuel Beckett on the Fiction of J. G. Farrell', *New Hibernia Review/Iris Éireannach Nua: A Quarterly Record of Irish Studies*, 9:1 (Spring 2005)

Cronin, Anthony. *Dead as Doornails: A Chronicle of Life* (Dublin: Dolmen Press, 1976)

Cronin, John. *Irish Fiction: 1900–1940* (Belfast: Appletree Press, 1992)

The Anglo-Irish Novel, vol. 1: *The Nineteenth Century* (Belfast: Appletree Press, 1980)

Cullen, Louis. 'Catholics under the Penal Laws', *Eighteenth-Century Ireland/Iris an dá chultúr*, 1 (1986)

Cullingford, Elizabeth Butler. 'Colonial Policing: *The Steward of Christendom* and *The Whereabouts of Eneas McNulty*', *Éire-Ireland*, 39:3&4 (Fall/Winter 2004)

David, Deirdre (ed.). *The Cambridge Companion to the Victorian Novel* (Cambridge University Press, 2001)

Davies, Rowland. *Journal of the Very Rev. Rowland Davies, LL. D. Dean of Ross, 1689–1690*, edited with notes and appendix by Richard Caulfield (New York: AMS Press, 1968)

Dean, Joan Fitzpatrick. 'The Riot in Westport: George A. Birmingham at Home', *New Hibernia Review*, 5:4 (2001)

Deane, Seamus. *A Short History of Irish Literature* (London: Hutchinson, 1986)

Celtic Revivals: Essays in Modern Irish Literature 1880–1980 (London: Faber and Faber, 1985)

'Civilians and barbarians', in *Ireland's Field Day*, with an afterword by Thomas Flanagan (Notre Dame, Indiana: University of Notre Dame Press, 1983/1986)

'Introduction', in Edward Said *et al.*, *Nationalism, Colonialism, Literature* (Minneapolis: University of Minnesota Press, 1990)

Strange Country: Modernity and Nationhood in Irish Writing since 1790 (Oxford University Press, 1997)

Deane, Seamus (ed.). *The Field Day Anthology of Irish Writing*, 3 vols. (Derry: Field Day Publications, 1991)

Dermot Bolger, 'Introduction', in *The Picador Book of Contemporary Irish Fiction* (London: Picador, 1994)

de Valera, Eamon. 'The Undeserted Village Ireland', in Seamus Deane (ed.), *The Field Day Anthology of Irish Writing*, vol. III (Derry: Field Day Publications, 1991)

Dickson, David. *New Foundations: Ireland 1660–1800* (Dublin: Irish Academic Press, 1987/2000)

Dobbins, Gregory. 'Scenes of Tawdry Tribute: Modernism, Tradition, and Connolly' in P. J. Mathews (ed.), *New Voices in Irish Criticism* (Dublin: Four Courts Press, 2000)

Docherty, Thomas. *Postmodernism: A Reader* (New York: Columbia University Press, 1993)

Donohue, Emma. 'Out of Order: Kate O'Brien's Lesbian Fictions', in Eibhear Walshe (ed.), *Ordinary People Dancing* (Cork University Press, 1994)

Doody, Margaret Anne. *The True Story of the Novel* (New Brunswick: Rutgers University Press, 1997)

Dorgan, Theo and Ní Dhonnchadha, Máirín (eds.). *Revising the Rising* (Derry: Field Day Publications, 1991)

Duffy, Gavan. 'Mr. Lever's "Irish Novels"' (1843), in Seamus Deane (ed.), *The Field Day Anthology*, vol. I (Derry: Field Day Publications, 1991)

Dunton, John. *Teague Land: or A Merry Ramble to the Wild Irish*, transcribed from the manuscript, edited and introduced by Andrew Carpenter (Dublin: Four Courts Press, 2003)

Eagleton, Terry. *After Theory* (New York: Basic Books, 2003)

Heathcliff and the Great Hunger: Studies in Irish Culture (London: Verso, 1995)

The English Novel: An Introduction (Oxford: Blackwell Publishing, 2005)

Ellmann, Maud. *Elizabeth Bowen: The Shadow Across the Page* (Edinburgh: Edinburgh University Press, 2004)

Ellmann, Richard (ed.). *Selected Letters of James Joyce* (New York: The Viking Press, 1975)

Escarbelt, Bernard. 'William Chaigneau's Jack Connor: A Literary Image of the Irish Peasant', in Jacqueline Genet (ed.), *Rural Ireland, Real Ireland?* (Gerrards Cross: Colin Smythe, 1996)

Fallon, Brian. *An Age of Innocence: Irish Culture 1930–1960* (Dublin: Gill and Macmillan, 1998)

Farrell, Tyler. 'Austin Clarke and the Consolations of Irish Catholicism', *New Hibernia Review*, 9:4 (Winter 2005)

Fegan, Melissa. '"Isn't it your own country?" The Stranger in Nineteenth-Century Irish Literature', *The Yearbook of English Studies*, 34 (2004)

Literature and the Irish Famine 1845–1919 (Oxford: Clarendon Press, 2002)

Ferriter, Diarmaid. *The Transformaiton of Ireland 1900–2000* (London: Profile Books, 2004)

Flanagan, Thomas. 'Frank O'Connor, 1903–1966', *The Kenyon Review*, 28:4 (September 1966)

The Irish Novelists 1800–1850 (New York: Columbia University Press, 1959)

Fogarty, Anne. 'Deliberately Personal? The Politics of Identity in Contemporary Irish Women's Writing', *Nordic Irish Studies*, 1 (2002)

Foster, John Wilson. *Fictions of the Irish Literary Revival: A Changeling Art* (Syracuse University Press, 1987)

'Irish Fiction 1965–1990', in Seamus Deane (ed.), *The Field Day Anthology of Irish Writing*, vol. III (Derry: Field Day Publications, 1991)

Irish Novels 1890–1940: New Bearings in Culture and Fiction (Oxford University Press, 2008)

'The Irish Renaissance, 1890–1940: Prose in English', in Margaret Kelleher and Philip O'Leary (eds.), *The Cambridge History of Irish Literature*, vol. II: *1890–2000* (Cambridge University Press, 2006)

Foster, John Wilson (ed.). *The Cambridge Companion to the Irish Novel* (Cambridge University Press, 2006)

Foster, R. F. *Luck and the Irish: A Brief History of Change, 1970–2000* (London: Penguin, 2007/2008)

Modern Ireland: 1600–1972 (London: Penguin Books, 1990)

Oxford History of Modern Ireland (Oxford University Press, 1992)

Frazier, Adrian. 'Irish Modernisms, 1880–1930', in John Wilson Foster (ed.), *The Cambridge Companion to the Irish Novel* (Cambridge University Press, 2006)

Gallagher, Michael Paul. 'The Novels of John Broderick', in Patrick Rafroidi and Maurice Harmon (eds.), *The Irish Novel in Our Time* (Lille: Publications de l'Université de Lille III, 1975–76)

Genet, Jacqueline (ed.). *The Big House in Ireland: Reality, and Representation* (Dingle: Brandon, 1991)

Gibbons, Luke. *Edmund Burke and Ireland: Aesthetics, Politics, and the Colonial Sublime* (Cambridge University Press, 2003)

Transformations in Irish Culture (Cork University Press, 1996)

Gibson, Andrew. *James Joyce*, with an introduction by Declan Kiberd (London: Reaktion Books, 2006)

Joyce's Revenge: History, Politics, and Aesthetics in Ulysses (Oxford University Press, 2005)

Goarzin, Anne. '"A Crack in the Concrete": Objects in the Works of John McGahern', *Irish University Review*, 35:1 (Spring/Summer 2005)

Grene, Nicholas and Morash, Christopher. *Shifting Scenes: Irish Theatre-going 1955–1985* (Dublin: Carysfort Press, 2008)

Hampton, Jill Brady. 'Ambivalent Realism: May Laffan's "Flitters, Tatters, and the Counsellor"', *New Hibernia Review*, 12:2 (Samhradh/Summer, 2008)

Hand, Derek. 'A Gothic Nightmare: John Banville's Birchwood and Irish History', in Patricia A. Lynch, Joachim Fischer and Brian Coates (eds.), *Back to the Present, Forward to the Past: Irish Writing and History since 1798* (Amsterdam: Rodopi Press, 2006)

'Being Ordinary: Ireland from Elsewhere: A Reading of Éilís Ní Dhuibhne's *The Bray House*', *Irish University Review*, 30:1 (Spring/Summer, 2000)

'Éilís Ní Dhuibhne', in Anthony Roche (ed.), *The UCD Aesthetic: Celebrating 150 Years of UCD Writers* (Dublin: New Island Press, 2005)

'Ghosts from our Future: Elizabeth Bowen and the Unfinished Business of Living', in Eibhear Walshe (ed.), *Elizabeth Bowen: Vision and Revisions* (Dublin: Irish Academic Press, 2008)

John Banville: Exploring Fictions (Dublin: The Liffey Press, 2002)

'Something Happened: Benedict's Kiely's Nothing Happens in Carmincross and the Breakdown of the Irish Novel', in Eibhear Walshe (ed.), *Representing the Troubles* (Dublin: Four Courts Press, 2004)

'The Anglo-Irish Big House under Pressure: Elizabeth Bowen's *The Last September* and Molly Keane's *Two Days in Aragon*', in Eibhear Walshe and Gwenda Young (eds.), *Molly Keane: Centenary Essays* (Dublin: Four Courts Press, 2006)

Hand, Derek (ed.). *Irish University Review: John Banville*, 36:1 (Spring/Summer 2006)

Hand, Derek and Fogarty, Anne (eds.). *Irish University Review: Benedict Kiely*, 38:1 (Spring/Summer, 2008)

Harte, Liam. 'History Lessons: Postcolonialism and Seamus Deane's *Reading in the Dark*', *Irish University Review*, 30:1 (Spring/Summer, 2000)

'History, Text, and Society in Colm Tóibín's *The Heather Blazing*', *New Hibernia Review/Iris Éireannach Nua: A Quarterly Record of Irish Studies*, 6:4 (Winter 2002)

Harte, Liam and Parker, Michael (eds.). *Contemporary Irish Fiction: Themes, Tropes, Theories* (London: Palgrave, 2000)

Haslam, Richard. '"The Pose Arranged and Lingered Over": Visualising the "Troubles"', in Liam Harte and Michael Parker (eds.), *Contemporary Irish Fiction: Themes, Tropes, Theories* (London: Palgrave, 2000)

Hassan, Ihab. *The Dismemberment of Orpheus: Toward a Postmodern Literature* (The University of Wisconsin Press, 1971/1982)

Heaney, Seamus. *Preoccupations: Selected Prose 1968–1978* (London: Faber and Faber, 1980)

Heath, William. *Elizabeth Bowen: An Introduction to her Novels* (University of Wisconsin Press, 1961)

Herron, Tom. 'ContaminNation: Patrick McCabe's and Colm Tóibín's Pathologies of the Republic', in Liam Harte and Michael Parker (eds.),

Contemporary Irish Fiction: Themes, Tropes, Theories (London: Palgrave, 2000)

Higgins, Geraldine. '"A Place to Bring Anger and Grief": Deirdre Madden's Northern Irish Novels', in Bill Lazenblatt (ed.), *Writing Ulster*, no. 6: *Northern Narratives* (1999)

Hogan, Robert Goode. *Mervyn Wall* (Bucknell University Press, 1972)

Holland, Siobhán. 'Marvellous Fathers in the Fiction of John McGahern', *The Yearbook of English Studies*, 35: *Irish Writing since 1950* (2005)

Hopper, Keith. *Flann O'Brien: A Portrait of the Artist as a Young Post-Modernist* (Cork University Press, 2009)

Howe, Lawrence. *Mark Twain and the Novel: The Double-cross of Authority* (Cambridge University Press, 1998)

Howes, Marjorie. 'Misalliance and Anglo-Irish Tradition in Le Fanu's Uncle Silas', *Nineteenth-Century Literature*, 47:2 (September, 1992)

Hughes, Eamonn. '"The Fact of Me-ness": Autobiographical Writing in the Revival Period', in Margaret Kelleher (ed.), *Irish University Review: Special Issue, New Perspectives on the Irish Literary Revival*, 33:1 (Spring/Summer 2003)

Hyde, Douglas. 'The Necessity of De-Anglicising Ireland', in David Pierce (ed.), *Irish Writing in the Twentieth Century: A Reader* (Cork University Press, 2000)

Jackson, Rosemary. *Fantasy: The Literature of Subversion* (London: Routledge, 1981)

Jeffers, Jennifer M. *The Irish Novel at the End of the Twentieth Century: Gender, Bodies, Power* (London: Palgrave, 2002)

Kavanagh, Patrick. *A Poet's Country: Selected Prose*, edited by Antoinette Quinn (Dublin: The Lilliput Press, 2003)

'Yeats', in *The Complete Poems*, collected, arranged and edited by Peter Kavanagh (Newbridge: The Goldsmith Press, 1992)

Kearney, Richard. *Modern Movements in European Philosophy: Phenomenology, Critical Theory, Structuralism* (Manchester University Press, 1994)

On Stories (New York : Routledge, 2002)

'The Question of Tradition', *The Crane Bag*, 3:1 (1979)

The Wake of the Imagination: Ideas of Creativity in Western Culture (London: Hutchinson, 1988)

Transitions: Narratives in Modern Irish Culture (Dublin: Wolfhound Press, 1988)

Kelleher, Margaret. 'Prose and Drama in English, 1830–1890: from Catholic Emancipation to the Fall of Parnell', in Margaret Kelleher and Philip O'Leary (eds.), *The Cambridge History of Irish Literature*, vol. 1: *To 1890* (Cambridge University Press, 2006)

The Feminisation of Famine: Expressions of the Inexpressible? (Cork University Press, 1997)

'Women's Fiction, 1845–1900', in Angela Bourke *et al.* (eds.), *The Field Day Anthology of Irish Writing*, vol. v: *Irish Women's Writing and Traditions* (Cork University Press, 2002)

Kelleher, Margaret and Murphy, James (eds.). *Gender Perspectives in Nineteenth Century Ireland* (Dublin: Irish Academic Press, 1997)

Kelleher, Margaret and O'Leary, Philip (eds.). *The Cambridge History of Irish Literature*, 2 vols. (Cambridge University Press, 2006)

Kelly, Aaron. *Twentieth-Century Irish Literature: A Reader's Guide to Essential Criticism* (London: Palgrave Macmillan, 2008)

Kennedy-Andrews, Elmer. *Fiction and the Northern Ireland Troubles since 1969: (De-)constructing the North* (Dublin: Four Courts Press, 2003)

'The Novel and the Northern Troubles', in John Wilson Foster (ed.), *The Cambridge Companion to the Irish Novel* (Cambridge University Press, 2006)

Kiberd, Declan. *Inventing Ireland: The Literature of the Modern Nation* (London: Jonathan Cape, 1995)

'Inventing Irelands', *The Crane Bag*, 8:1 (1984)

Irish Classics (London: Granta Books, 2000)

'Irish Literature and Irish History', in Roy Foster (ed.), *Oxford History of Modern Ireland* (Oxford University Press, 19??), p. 257

The Irish Writer and the World (Cambridge University Press, 2005)

Ulysses and Us (London: Faber and Faber, 2009)

Kiely, Benedict. *A Raid into Dark Corners and Other Essays* (Cork University Press, 1999)

Modern Irish Fiction: A Critique (Dublin: Golden Eagle, 1950)

Kilfeather, Siobhan. 'Sex and Sensation in the Nineteenth Century Novel', in Margaret Kelleher and James Murphy (eds.), *Gender Perspectives in Nineteenth Century Ireland* (Dublin: Irish Academic Press, 1997)

'Terrific Register: The Gothicization of Atrocity in Irish Romanticism', *Boundary 2*, 31:1 (2004)

'The Profession of Letters, 1700–1810', in Angela Bourke *et al.* (eds.), *The Field Day Anthology of Irish Writing*, vol. v (Cork University Press, 2002)

Killeen, Jarlath. *Gothic Ireland: Horror and the Irish Anglican Imagination in the Long Eighteenth Century* (Dublin: Four Courts Press, 2005)

The Faiths of Oscar Wilde: Catholicism, Folklore and Ireland (London: Palgrave, 2005)

King, Jason. 'Emigration and the Irish Novel' in Jacqueline Belanger (ed.), *The Irish Novel in the Nineteenth Century: Facts and Fictions* (Dublin: Four Courts Press, 2006)

Kirby, Peadar, Gibbons, Luke and Cronin, Michael (eds.). *Reinventing Ireland: Culture, Society and the Global Economy* (London: Pluto Books, 2002)

Kirkland, Richard. 'Bourgeois Redemptions: The Fictions of Glenn Patterson and Robert McLiam Wilson' in Liam Harte and Michael Parker (eds.), *Contemporary Irish Fiction: Themes, Tropes, Theories* (London: Palgrave, 2000)

Kirkpatrick, Kathryn. *Border Crossings: Irish Women Writers and National Identities* (Tuscaloosa: University of Alabama Press, 2000)

'Putting Down the Rebellion: Notes and Glosses on Maria Edgeworth's *Castle Rackrent*', *Eire-Ireland: Journal of Irish Studies*, 30:1 (1995)

Krielkamp, Vera. *The Anglo-Irish and the Big House* (Syracuse University Press, 1998)

'The Novel of the Big House', in John Wilson Foster (ed.), *The Cambridge Companion to The Irish Novel* (Cambridge University Press, 2006)

Lamming, George. 'The Occasion for Speaking', in Bill Ashcroft *et al.* (eds.), *The Empire Writes Back: Theory and Practice in Post-colonial Literatures* (London: Routledge, 1989)

Larkin, Philip. 'Annus Mirabilis', in *Collected Poems*, edited with an introduction by Anthony Thwaite (London: Faber and Faber, 1988)

Ledwidge, Grace Tighe. 'Death in Marriage: The Tragedy of Elizabeth Reegan in *The Barracks*', in John Brannigan (ed.), *Irish University Review*, 35:1 (Spring/ Summer 2005)

Leerssen, Joep. *Mere Irish and Fíor-Ghael: Studies in the Idea of Irish Nationality, its Development and Literary Expression prior to the Nineteenth Century* (Cork University Press, 1986/1996)

Remembrance and Imagination: Patterns in the Historical and Literary Representation of Ireland in the Nineteenth Century (Cork University Press in association with Field Day, 1996)

Lloyd, David. *Anomalous States: Irish Writing and the Post-colonial Moment* (Dublin: The Lilliput Press, 1993)

Ireland after History (Cork University Press, 1999)

Loeber, Rolf and Loeber, Magda. *A Guide to Irish Fiction: 1650–1900* (Dublin: Four Courts Press, 2006)

Lukács, Georg. *The Historical Novel*, translated by Hannah and Stanley Mitchell (London: Merlin Press, 1989)

The Theory of the Novel: A Historico-philosophical Essay on the Forms of Great Epic Literature, translated from the German by Anna Bostock (London: Merlin Press, 1971)

Lynch, Rachael Sealy. '"The Fabulous Female Form": The Deadly Erotics of the Male Gaze in Mary Lavin's *The House in Clewe Street*', *Twentieth Century Literature*, 43:3 (Autumn 1997)

MacAnna, Ferdia. 'The Dublin Renaissance: An Essay on Modern Dublin and Dublin Writers', *The Irish Review*, 10 (Spring 1991)

MacCurtain, Margaret. 'Recollections of Catholicism, 1906–1960', in Angela Bourke *et al.* (eds.), *The Field Day Anthology of Irish Writing*, vol. IV (Cork University Press, 2002)

MacDonald, Ian. *Revolution in the Head: The Beatles' Records and the Sixties* (London: Pimlico, 1998)

MacLysaght, Edward. *Irish Life in the Seventeenth Century* (Dublin: Irish Academic Press, 1939/1979)

Maher, Eamon. 'The Irish Novel in Crisis? The Example of John McGahern', in John Brannigan (ed.), *Irish University Review*, 35:1 (Spring/Summer 2005)

Martin, Augustine. *Bearing Witness: Essays on Anglo-Irish Literature*, edited by Anthony Roche (Dublin: University College Dublin Press, 1996)

'Prose Fiction, 1880–1945', in Seamus Deane (ed.), *The Field Day Anthology of Irish Writing* (Derry: Field Day Publications, 1991)

Martin, Augustine (ed.). *The Genius of Irish Prose* (Dublin: The Mercier Press, 1985)

Marwick, Arthur. *The Arts in the West since 1945* (Oxford University Press, 2002)

Mathews, P. J. 'In Praise of "Hibernocentricism": Republicanism, Globalisation and Irish Culture', *The Republic*, 4 (June 2005)

'Joseph O'Connor', in Anthony Roche (ed.), *The UCD Aesthetic* (Dublin: New Island Books, 2005)

Revival: The Abbey Theatre, Sinn Féin, the Gaelic League and the Co-operative Movement (Cork University Press, 2003)

'Stirring up Disloyalty: The Boer War, the Irish Literary Theatre and the Emergence of a New Separatism', in Margaret Kelleher (ed.), *Irish University Review: Special Issue, New Perspectives on the Irish Literary Revival*, 33:1 (Spring/Summer 2003)

McCarthy, Conor. *Modernisation: Crisis and Culture in Ireland 1969–1992* (Dublin: Four Courts Press, 2000)

McCormack, W. J. *Ascendancy and Tradition in Anglo-Irish Literary History from 1789–1939* (Oxford: Clarendon Press, 1985)

Dissolute Characters: Irish Literary History through Balzac, Sheridan Le Fanu, Yeats and Bowen (Manchester University Press, 1993)

Fool of the Family: A Life of J. M. Synge (London: Weidenfeld & Nicolson, 2000)

From Burke to Beckett: Ascendancy, Tradition and Betrayal in Literary History (Cork University Press, 1994).

'Irish Gothic and After', in Seamus Deane (ed.), *The Field Day Anthology* (Derry: Field Day Publications, 1991)

Sheridan Le Fanu and Victorian Ireland (Dublin: The Lilliput Press, 1991)

McCrann, Aibhlín (ed.). *Memories, Milestones and New Horizons: Reflections on the Regeneration of Ballymun* (Belfast: Blackstaff Press, 2008)

McGahern, John. *Love of the World: Essays*, edited by Stanley van der Ziel (London: Faber and Faber, 2009)

McHale, Brian. *Postmodernist Fiction* (New York and London: Methuen, 1987)

McKeon, Michael. *The Origins of the English Novel, 1600–1740* (Baltimore: Johns Hopkins University Press, 1988)

McMinn, Joseph. *The Supreme Fictions of John Banville* (Manchester University Press, 1999)

McNamee, Brendan. 'The Flowering Cross: Suffering, Reality, and the Christ Motif in Francis Stuart's *The Pillar of Cloud* and *Redemption*', *Christianity and Literature*, 53:1 (Autumn 2003)

Meaney, Geradine. 'Decadence, Degeneration and Revolting Aesthetics: The Fiction of Emily Lawless and Katherine Cecil Thurston', *Colby Quarterly: Irish Women Novelists 1800–1940*, XXXVI:2 (June 2002)

'Identity and Opposition: Women's Writing, 1890–1960', in Angela Bourke *et al.* (eds.), *The Field Day Anthology of Irish Writing*, vol. V: *Irish Women's Writing and Traditions* (Cork University Press, 2002)

Mendelson, Edward. 'Encyclopedic Narrative: from Dante to Pynchon', *MLN*, 91:6, *Comparative Literature* (December 1976)

Mercier, Vivian. *The Irish Comic Tradition* (Oxford University Press, 1969)

Miller, David A. 'The Novel and the Police', in Dorothy J. Hale (ed.), *The Novel: An Anthology of Criticism and Theory 1900–2000* (Oxford: Blackwell Publishing, 2006)

Mooney, Sinead. 'Unstable Compounds: Bowen's Beckettian Affinities', *Modern Fiction Studies*, 53:2 (Summer 2007)

Morash, Christopher. *A History of Irish Theatre 1601–2000* (Cambridge University Press, 2002)

Moretti, Franco. 'Conjectures on World Literature', *New Left Review*, 1 (January/February 2000)

   'On the Novel' in Franco Moretti (ed.), *The Novel*, vol. 1: *History, Geography, and Culture* (Princeton University Press, 2006)

   'The Novel: History and Theory', *New Left Review*, 52 (July/August 2008)

Moretti, Franco (ed.). *The Novel*, vol. 1: *History, Geography, and Culture* (Princeton University Press, 2006)

   The Novel, vol. 11: *Forms and Themes* (Princeton University Press, 2006)

Morris, Catherine. 'Becoming Irish? Alice Milligan and the Revival', *Irish University Review: New Perspectives on the Irish Literary Revival* (Spring/Summer 2003)

Moynahan, Julian. *Anglo-Irish: The Literary Imagination in a Hyphenated Culture* (Princeton University Press, 1995)

Murphy, James H. 'Catholics and Fiction during the Union, 1801–1922', in John Wilson Foster (ed.), *The Cambridge Companion to the Irish Novel* (Cambridge University Press, 2006)

   Catholic Fiction and Social Reality in Ireland, 1873–1922 (London: Greenwood Press, 1997)

   '"Insouciant Rivals of Mrs Barton": Gender and Victorian Aspiration in George Moore and the Women Novelists of the *Irish Monthly*', in Margaret Kelleher and James Murphy (eds.), *Gender Perspectives in Nineteenth Century Ireland* (Dublin: Irish Academic Press, 1997)

   Ireland: A Social, Cultural and Literary History, 1791–1891 (Dublin: Four Courts Press, 2003)

Murphy, Neil. *Irish Fiction and Postmodern Doubt: An Analysis of the Epistemological Crisis in Modern Irish Fiction* (New York: Edwin Mellen Press, 2004)

   'Aidan Higgins', *Review of Contemporary Fiction*, 23:3 (Fall 2003)

Nash, John. *James Joyce and the Act of Reception: Reading, Ireland and Modernism* (Cambridge University Press, 2006)

Nolan, Emer. 'Banim and the Historical Novel', in Jacqueline Belanger (ed.), *The Irish Novel in the Nineteenth Century: Facts and Fictions* (Dublin: Four Courts Press, 2006)

   Catholic Emancipations: Irish Fiction from Thomas Moore to James Joyce (Syracuse University Press, 2007)

   James Joyce and Nationalism (London: Routledge, 1995)

   'Modernism and the Irish Revival', in Joe Cleary and Claire Connolly (eds.), *The Cambridge Companion to Modern Irish Culture* (Cambridge University Press, 2005)

'Postcolonial Literary Studies, Nationalism, and Feminist Critique in Contemporary Ireland', *Éire-Ireland*, 42:1&2 (Spring and Summer 2007)

Ó Ciosáin, Niall. *Print and Popular Culture in Ireland 1750–1850* (London: Palgrave, 1997)

Ó Gallchoir, Clíona. *Maria Edgeworth: Women, Enlightenment and Nation* (University College Dublin Press, 2005)

Ó Tuama, Seán (ed.). *An Duanaire 1600–1900: Poems of the Dispossessed*, translations into English verse by Thomas Kinsella (Dublin: The Dolmen Press, 1981/1994)

O'Brien, Edna. *James Joyce* (London: Weidenfeld and Nicolson, 1999)

O'Brien, George. 'Contemporary Prose in English: 1940–2000', in Margaret Kelleher and Philip O'Leary (eds.), *Cambridge History of Irish Literature*, vol. II: *1890–2000* (Cambridge University Press, 2006)

'The Aesthetics of Exile', in Liam Harte and Michael Parker (eds.), *Contemporary Irish Fiction: Themes, Tropes, Theories* (London: Palgrave, 2000)

'The Fictional Irishman 1665–1850', *Studies: An Irish Quarterly Review*, LXVI (Winter 1977)

O'Connor, Frank. 'The Future of Irish Literature', in David Pierce (ed.), *Irish Writing in the Twentieth Century: A Reader* (Cork University Press, 2000)

The Lonely Voice: A Study of the Short Story (London: Macmillan, 1965)

O'Faolain, Sean. 'Ah, Wisha! The Irish Novel', *Virginia Quarterly Review*, 17:2 (Spring 1941)

'Fifty Years of Irish Writing', in David Pierce (ed.), *Irish Writing in the Twentieth Century: A Reader* (Cork University Press, 2000)

'Fifty Years of Irish Writing', *Studies: An Irish Quarterly Review*, 51:201 (Spring 1962)

The Short Story (London: William Collins, 1948)

O'Grada, Cormac. 'The Jews of Ireland 1870–1930: Towards an Economic-Demographic History' www.econ.barnard.columbia.edu/~econhist/papers/COgrada.pdf

O'Nolan, Brian. 'A Bash in the Tunnel', in David Pierce (ed.), *Irish Writing in the Twentieth Century: A Reader* (Cork University Press, 2000)

O'Riordan, Manus. 'Jews in Independent Ireland', in *Dublin Review of Books*, www.drb.ie/june_citizens.html

Orwell, George. 'Inside the Whale' in *Inside the Whale and Other Essays* (London: Penguin, 1967)

Parrinder, Patrick. *Nation and Novel: The English Novel from its Origins to the Present Day* (Oxford University Press, 2006)

Patten, Eve. 'Contemporary Irish Fiction', in John Wilson Foster, *The Cambridge Companion to the Irish Novel* (Cambridge University Press, 2006)

Peach, Linden. *The Contemporary Irish Novel: Critical Readings* (London: Palgrave, 2004)

Phillips, Terry. 'A Study in Grotesques: Transformations of the Human in the Writing of Liam O'Flaherty', *Gothic Studies*, 7:1 (May 2005)

Pierce, David (ed.), *Irish Writing in the Twentieth Century: A Reader* (Cork University Press, 2000)

Powell, Kersti Tarien. *Irish Fiction: An Introduction* (London: Continuum Publishing Group, 2004)

'The Lighted Windows: Place in John Banville's Fiction', in Derek Hand (ed.), *Irish University Review: John Banville*, 36:1 (Spring/Summer 2006)

Pykett, Lyn. 'Sensation and the Fantastic in the Victorian Novel', in Deirdre David (ed.), *The Cambridge Companion to the Victorian Novel* (Cambridge University Press, 2001)

Rafroidi, Patrick and Harmon, Maurice (eds.). *The Irish Novel in Our Time* (Lille: Publications de l'Université de Lille III, 1975–76)

Rankin, Deana. '"Shet Foord vor Generaul Nouddificaushion": Relocating the Irish Joke, 1678–1690', *Eighteenth-Century Ireland / Iris an dá chultúr*, 16 (2001)

Riggs, Pádraigín and Vance, Norman. 'Irish Prose Fiction', in Joe Cleary and Claire Connolly (eds.), *The Cambridge Companion to Modern Irish Culture* (Cambridge University Press, 2005)

Roche, Anthony (ed.). *The UCD Aesthetic* (Dublin: New Island Books, 2005)

Ross, Ian Campbell. 'An Irish Picaresque Novel: William Chaigneau's *The History of Jack Connor*', *Studies*, LXXI (1982)

'Fiction to 1800', in Seamus Deane (ed.), *The Field Day Anthology of Irish Writing*, vol. 1 (Derry: Field Day Publications, 1991)

'"One of the Principle Nations in Europe": The Representation of Ireland in Sarah Butler's *Irish Tales*', *Eighteenth Century Fiction*, 7:1 (October 1994)

'Prose in English, 1690–1800: From the Williamite Wars to the Act of Union', in Margaret Kelleher and Philip O'Leary (eds.), *The Cambridge History of Irish Literature*, vol. 1: *To 1890* (Cambridge University Press, 2006)

'Rewriting Irish Literary History: The Case of the Irish Novel', *Etudes Anglaises*, XXXIX:4 (October–December 1986)

'Thomas Amory, *John Buncle*, and the Origins of Irish Fiction', *Eire-Ireland*, XVIII:3 (1983)

Ross, Ian Campbell and Markey, Anne. 'From Clonmel to Peru: Barbarism and Civility in *Vertue Rewarded; or, The Irish Princess*', *Irish University Review*, 38:2 (Autumn/Winter 2008)

Ryan, John. 'Our Irish Publishers', in David Pierce (ed.), *Irish Writing in the Twentieth Century: A Reader* (Cork University Press, 2000)

Ryan, Ray. *Ireland and Scotland: Literature and Culture, State and Nation, 1966–2000* (Oxford University Press, 2002)

Ryan, Ray (ed.). *Writing the Irish Republic: Literature, Culture, Politics 1949–1999* (London: Macmillan, 2000)

Sheeran, Patrick and Witoszek, Nina. *Talking to the Dead: A Study of Irish Funerary Traditions* (Amsterdam: Rodopi Press, 1998)

Skeen, Catherine. 'Projecting Fictions: *Gulliver's Travels*, *Jack Connor*, and *John Buncle*', *Modern Philology: A Journal Devoted to Research in Medieval and Modern Literature*, 100:3 (2003)

Sloan, Barry. *The Pioneers of Anglo-Irish Fiction 1800–1850* (Gerrards Cross: Colin Smythe, 1986)

Smyth, Gerry. *The Novel and the Nation: Studies in the New Irish Fiction* (London: Pluto Press, 1997)

St Peter, Christine. *Changing Ireland: Strategies in Contemporary Women's Fiction* (London: Macmillan Press, 2000)

Stevens, Julie Anne. *The Irish Scene in Somerville and Ross* (Dublin: Irish Academic Press, 2007)

Sullivan, Kevin. 'Benedict Kiely: The Making of a Novelist', in Patrick Rafroidi and Maurice Harmon (eds.), *The Irish Novel in Our Time* (Lille: Publications de l'Université de Lille III, 1975–76)

Taafe, Carol. *Ireland Through the Looking Glass: Flann O'Brien, Myles na gCopaleen and Irish Cultural Debate* (Cork University Press, 2008)

Titley, Alan. 'The Novel in Irish', in John Wilson Foster (ed.), *The Cambridge Companion to the Irish Novel* (Cambridge University Press, 2006)

Tracy, Dominick. 'Idyllic Resistance in Griffin's The Collegians', in Jacqueline Belanger (ed.), *The Irish Novel in the Nineteenth Century: Facts and Fictions* (Dublin: Four Courts Press, 2006)

Tracy, Robert. *The Unappeasable Host: Studies in Irish Identities* (University College Dublin Press, 1998)

Trumpener, Katie. *Bardic Nationalism: The Romantic Novel and the British Empire* (Princeton University Press, 1997)

Tucker, Amanda. 'A Space Between: Transitional Feminism in Kate O'Brien's *Mary Lavelle*', *New Hibernia Review/Iris Éireannach Nua: A Quarterly Record of Irish Studies*, 12:1 (Spring 2008)

Tynan, Katharine. 'Recent Irish Novels', *Studies: An Irish Quarterly Review*, 9:36 (December 1920)

Van der Ziel, Stanley. '"All This Talk and Struggle": John McGahern's *The Dark*', in John Brannigan (ed.), *Irish University Review*, 35:1 (Spring/Summer 2005)

Vance, Norman. *Irish Literature: A Social History: Tradition, Identity and Difference* (Dublin: Four Courts Press, 1999)

'Region, Realism and Reaction, 1922–1972', in John Wilson Foster (ed.), *The Cambridge Companion to the Irish Novel* (Cambridge University Press, 2006)

Walshe, Eibhear. *Kate O'Brien: A Writing Life* (Dublin: Irish Academic Press, 2006)

'The Vanishing Homoerotic: Colm Tóibín's Gay Fictions', *New Hibernia Review/Iris Éireannach Nua: A Quarterly Record of Irish Studies*, 10:4 (Winter 2006)

Walshe, Eibhear (ed.). *Ordinary People Dancing: Essays on Kate O'Brien* (Cork University Press, 1994)

Walshe, Eibhear and Young, Gwenda (eds.). *Molly Keane: Centenary Essays* (Dublin: Four Courts Press, 2006)

Watts, Ian. *The Rise of the Novel: Studies in Defoe, Richardson and Fielding* (London: The Hogarth Press, 1957/1987)

Weekes, Ann Owens. *Irish Women Writers: An Uncharted Tradition* (Lexington: University Press of Kentucky, 1990)

'Women Novelists, 1930s–1960s', in John Wilson Foster, *The Cambridge Companion to the Irish Novel* (Cambridge University Press, 2006)

Wills, Clair. '"Half Different": The Vanishing Irish in *A World of Love*', in Eibhear Walshe (ed.), *Elizabeth Bowen* (Dublin: Irish Academic Press, 2008),

'Neutrality and Popular Culture', The Art of Popular Culture: From 'The Meeting of the Waters' to *Riverdance*, Series 1 (Spring 2008), Series Editor: P. J. Mathews, www.ucd.ie/scholarcast/

That Neutral Island: A Cultural History of Ireland During the Second World War (London: Faber and Faber, 2007)

Yeats, W. B. 'Introduction to The Words upon the Window-Pane', in *Explorations*, selected by Mrs W. B. Yeats (New York: Macmillan, 1962)

'Modern Ireland: An Address to American Audience, 1932–33', in Robin Skelton and David R. Clark (eds.), *Irish Renaissance: A Gathering of Essays, Memoirs, and Letters from the Massachusetts Review* (Dublin: Dolmen, 1965)

The Collected Poems of W. B. Yeats (London: Macmillan, 1985)

Yeats, W. B. (ed.), *Representative Irish Tales*, foreword by Mary Helen Thuente (Gerrards Cross: Colin Smythe, 1891/1979)

Index